The
Greatest
Baseball Stories
Ever Told

The
Greatest
Baseball Stories
Ever Told

**EDITED AND WITH AN INTRODUCTION BY
JEFF SILVERMAN**

THE LYONS PRESS
Guilford, Connecticut
An imprint of The Globe Pequot Press

The Globe Pequot Press, P.O. Box 480, Guilford, CT 06437.

The Lyons Press is an imprint of The Globe Pequot Press.

Printed in the United States of America

10 9 8 7 6 5 4 3 2

ISBN 1-58574-364-X

Design by Compset, Inc.

The Library of Congress Cataloging-in-Publication Data is available on file.

For Abby . . .

my favorite second baseman, on and off the field

Acknowledgments

Tips of the cap go to Nick Lyons, Tony Lyons, and Bill Wolfsthal for their backing; Mark Weinstein, for making the hard work look easy; and Abby Van Pelt, for the way she inspires me each and every day.

Contents

Introduction

I came of age in my relationship to the National Pastime at a moment my father deemed the most tragic in the game's history: the year the Giants and Dodgers manifested their destinies. This baseball diaspora might have been swell if you hung your cap in San Francisco or Los Angeles, but my father, rooted in New York from the day of his birth to his last breath eighty-eight years later, came unglued. This was betrayal. He was a Giants fan. At seven, I was naturally one, too.

At eight, I was still a Giants fan, but from a distance that grew more distant every day; out of sight, out of mind. In the evenings, my father tried his best to find his exiles on the radio. While he fiddled with the static of his past, I'd slip off into the present, my allegiance shifting, to the living room, where I could watch the Yankees almost every night on our new black-and-white TV. The radio was my father's generation; television was mine. It didn't matter to me that he hated the Yankees. They were here. They were now.

And they were mine.

In my father's heart, he understood that, and if he never fully made peace with it, he did his fatherly best to accommodate the shift. In August of 1958, he went so far as to enter the very belly of the beast—Yankee Stadium—to take me to my first Major League game. Hand in hand, we walked up the ramps to the mezzanine level. Arriving at our section, he told me to wait in the tunnel's shadow, and proceeded a few steps into the sunlight before instructing me to come ahead. Years later, I asked why he did that. He said he'd just wanted to see my face when I first saw the field. He knew something enormous would be happening.

He knew I'd be crossing a threshold. He knew that until that moment, my image of the game was a child's image—small and gray, confined to the dimensions of our television. Now, it was about to grow—quite literally. The dimensions were colossal. They shimmered with color. He knew this wasn't just his game anymore, it was officially mine, too, and no TV set in any living room in the universe could contain what I was experiencing. I wanted to hold on to that feeling. I wanted that feeling to last.

In the decades since, I've realized that feeling had nothing to do with Yankees, Giants, or any particular team at all. It was the exuberance at the heart of the game itself I was sensing, and it's an exuberance that manages to renew itself within me whenever I step through the right literary tunnel and find a terrific piece of baseball writing in the sunlight on the other end. Fact or fiction, reportage or essay, light or heavy, old or new, it doesn't matter. The game's best stories all offer their own threshold moments. They give the game color. They make it feel big.

Of course, they also explain and analyze, reveal and entertain. They explore our heroes and scrutinize our goats, contemplate our myths and inspect the truth behind them. They give us the score. But on the most visceral level, it goes back to that initial moment of exuberance for me. If a great baseball story has even a hint of it, it makes the game feel new again. Without it, it doesn't matter what other marvelous trait it exhibits. It might dazzle us, but it won't touch us. A great story must do both.

In one way or another, every spot in the order of THE GREATEST BASEBALL STORIES EVER TOLD succeeds in the spirit of that charge to touch and to dazzle—at least for me. Did I bat 1.000 in my choices? I hope so, but if no one won more games than Cy Young, no one lost more either. Back to the hitting metaphor: I just happily took my cuts.

Which brings me to the title of this collection. It's a hanging curve if ever there was one, and we all know what can happen to a hanging curve. So let me just step up and say this with no equivocation whatsoever: Some of the stories that follow are on everybody's list of "Greatest Baseball Stories Ever Told," and each is certainly on somebody's.

Full of color, bigger than life, they are Hall of Famers, every one of them.

Jeff Silverman
summer, 2001

Who's on First?

ABBOTT & COSTELLO

Who's up first?
    "Who's on First?"
    Who wrote it?
    "Who's on First?"
    Yeah.
    "Who?"
    That's what I'm asking.
    "I don't know."
    Third base . . .

Peel the comic genius from this most famous of all comedy baseball routines, and the question's not "Who's on First?" but who first pitched it. Like so much of what took root in the oral traditions of vaudeville, "Who's on First?" evolved over time. While other teams performed it, it's now impossible to hear voices other than Bud Abbott's and Lou Costello's playing pepper with its patter. For full effect, it begs to be heard—sorry, THE GREATEST BASEBALL STORIES EVER TOLD doesn't come with a CD—but, even when it enters through the eyes instead of the ears, it's amazingly funny.

Abbott and Costello regularly tinkered with the piece, particularly the opening, which they'd adjust to fit the demands of their audience. The version presented here aired in the mid-1940s on a baseball-themed episode of Abbott and Costello's radio show built around the Yankees. It begins with Lou called up to the club's roster with Bud coming along as coach to keep him in line.

Abbott: Well, Costello, I'm going to New York with you. The Yankees' manager, Bucky Harris, gave me a job as coach for as long as you're on the team.

Costello: Look, Abbott, if you're the coach, you must know all the players.

Abbott: I certainly do.

Costello: Well, you know I've never met the guys. So you'll have to tell me their names, and then I'll know who's playing on the team.

Abbott: Oh, I'll tell you their names, but, you know, it seems to me they give these ball players now-a-days very peculiar names.

Costello: You mean funny names?

Abbott: Strange names, pet names . . . like Dizzy Dean . . .

Costello: His brother Daffy . . .

Abbott: Daffy Dean . . .

Costello: And their French cousin.

Abbott: French?

Costello: Goofé.

Abbott: Goofé. Dean. Well, let's see, we have on the bags, Who's on first, What's on second, I Don't Know is on third . . .

Costello: That's what I want to find out.

Abbott: I say Who's on first, What's on second, I Don't Know's on third.

Costello: Are you the manager?

Abbott: Yes.

Costello: You gonna be the coach too?

Abbott: Yes.

Costello: And you don't know the fellows' names.

Abbott: Well, I should.

Costello: Well then who's on first?

Abbott: Yes.

Costello: I mean the fellow's name.

Abbott: Who.

Costello: The guy on first.

Abbott: Who.

Costello: The first baseman.

Abbott: Who.

Costello: The guy playing . . .

Abbott: Who is on first!

Costello: I'm asking you who's on first.

Abbott: That's the man's name.

Costello: That's who's name?

Abbott: Yes.

Costello: Well go ahead and tell me.

Abbott: That's it.

Costello: That's who?

Abbott: Yes.

PAUSE.

Costello: Look, you gotta first baseman?

Abbott: Certainly.

Costello: Who's playing first?

Abbott: That's right.

Costello: When you pay off the first baseman every month, who gets the money?

Abbott: Every dollar of it.

Costello: All I'm trying to find out is the fellow's name on first base.

Abbott: Who.

Costello: The guy that gets . . .

Abbott: That's it.

Costello: Who gets the money . . .

Abbott: He does, every dollar of it. Sometimes his wife comes down and collects it.

Costello: Who's wife?

Abbott: Yes.

PAUSE.

Abbott: What's wrong with that?

Costello: All I wanna know is when you sign up the first baseman, how does he sign his name?

Abbott: Who.

Costello: The guy.

Abbott: Who.

Costello: How does he sign . . .

Abbott: That's how he signs it.

Costello: Who?

Abbott: Yes.

PAUSE.

Costello: All I'm trying to find out is what's the guy's name on first base.

Abbott: No. What is on second base.

Costello: I'm not asking you who's on second.

Abbott: Who's on first.

Costello: One base at a time!

Abbott: Well, don't change the players around.

Costello: I'm not changing nobody!

Abbott: Take it easy, buddy.

Costello: I'm only asking you, who's the guy on first base?

Abbott: That's right.

Costello: Okay.

Abbott: All right.

PAUSE.

Costello: What's the guy's name on first base?

Abbott: No. What is on second.

Costello: I'm not asking you who's on second.

Abbott: Who's on first.

Costello: I don't know.

Abbott: He's on third, we're not talking about him.

Costello: Now how did I get on third base?

Abbott: Why, you mentioned his name.

Costello: If I mentioned the third basemen's name, who did I say is playing third?

Abbott: No. Who's playing first.

Costello: What's on first base?

Abbott: What's on second.

Costello: I don't know.

Abbott: He's on third.

Costello: There I go, back on third again!

PAUSE.

Costello: Would you just stay on third base and don't go off it.

Abbott: All right, what do you want to know?

Costello: Now who's playing third base?

Abbott: Why do you insist on putting Who on third base?

Costello: What am I putting on third.

Abbott: No. What is on second.

Costello: You don't want who on second?

Abbott: Who is on first.

Costello: I don't know.

Together: Third base!

PAUSE.

Costello: Look, you gotta outfield?

Abbott: Sure.

Costello: The leftfielder's name?

Abbott: Why.

Costello: I just thought I'd ask you.

Abbott: Well, I just thought I'd tell ya.

Costello: Then tell me who's playing leftfield.

Abbott: Who's playing first.

Costello: I'm not . . . stay out of the infield!!! I want to know what's the guy's name in left field?

Abbott: No, What is on second.

Costello: I'm not asking you who's on second.

Abbott: Who's on first!

Costello: I don't know.

Together: Third base!

PAUSE.

Costello: The leftfielder's name?

Abbott: Why.

Costello: Because!

Abbott: Oh, he's centerfield.

PAUSE.

Costello: Look, you gotta pitcher on this team?

Abbott: Sure.

Costello: The pitcher's name?

Abbott: Tomorrow.

Costello: You don't want to tell me today?

Abbott: I'm telling you now.

Costello: Then go ahead.

Abbott: Tomorrow!

Costello: What time?

Abbott: What time what?

Costello: What time tomorrow are you gonna tell me who's pitching?

Abbott: Now listen. Who is not pitching.

Costello: I'll break your arm if you say who's on first!!! I want to know what's the pitcher's name?

Abbott: What's on second.

Costello: I don't know.
Together: Third base!
PAUSE.
Costello: Gotta catcher?
Abbott: Certainly.
Costello: The catcher's name?
Abbott: Today.
Costello: Today, and tomorrow's pitching.
Abbott: Now you've got it.
Costello: All we got is a couple of days on the team.
PAUSE.
Costello: You know I'm a catcher too.
Abbott: So they tell me.
Costello: I get behind the plate to do some fancy catching, Tomorrow's pitching on my team and a heavy hitter gets up. Now the heavy hitter bunts the ball. When he bunts the ball, me, being a good catcher, I'm gonna throw the guy out at first. So I pick up the ball and throw it to who?
Abbott: Now that's the first thing you've said right.
Costello: I don't even know what I'm talking about!
PAUSE.
Abbott: That's all you have to do.
Costello: Is to throw the ball to first base.
Abbott: Yes!
Costello: Now who's got it?
Abbott: Naturally.
PAUSE.
Costello: Look, if I throw the ball to first base, somebody's gotta get it. Now who has it?
Abbott: Naturally.
Costello: Who?
Abbott: Naturally.
Costello: Naturally?
Abbott: Naturally.
Costello: So I pick up the ball and I throw it to Naturally.
Abbott: No you don't. You throw the ball to Who.
Costello: Naturally.
Abbott: That's different.
Costello: That's what I said.
Abbott: You're not saying it . . .

Costello: I throw the ball to Naturally.

Abbott: You throw it to Who.

Costello: Naturally.

Abbott: That's it.

Costello: That's what I said!

Abbott: You ask me.

Costello: I throw the ball to who?

Abbott: Naturally.

Costello: Now you ask me.

Abbott: You throw the ball to Who?

Costello: Naturally.

Abbott: That's it.

Costello: Same as you! Same as YOU!!! I throw the ball to who. Who- ever it is drops the ball and the guy runs to second. Who picks up the ball and throws it to What. What throws it to I Don't Know. I Don't Know throws it back to Tomorrow, triple play. Another guy gets up and hits a long fly ball to Because. Why? I don't know! He's on third and I don't give a darn!

Abbott: What?

Costello: I said, "I don't give a darn!"

Abbott: Oh, that's our shortstop.

Wait Till Next Year

DORIS KEARNS GOODWIN

There are two overriding reasons to head out to the ball park. One is to watch the game. The other is to *see* it. There's a difference. You can't tell that difference without a scorecard.

If baseball weaves a tangled web—and it does—keeping score can set us free. A completed scorecard brings order out of chaos. It decodes the mysteries, predicts inevitabilities, narrows possibilities, and reveals the invisible plain as day. Crises and their resolutions begin to make themselves apparent. Wherever we're sitting, the game is literally in our laps.

Historian Doris Kearns Goodwin learned that lesson as a child growing up on Long Island, and she relates it in this excerpt from her memoir *Wait Till Next Year*. Knowing how to keep score would certainly turn into an advantage when it came time for her to make sense of LBJ, Franklin and Eleanor Roosevelt, and the entire Kennedy and Fitzgerald clans.

When I was six, my father gave me a bright-red scorebook that opened my heart to the game of baseball. After dinner on long summer nights, he would sit beside me in our small enclosed porch to hear my account of that day's Brooklyn Dodger game. Night after night he taught me the odd collection of symbols, numbers, and letters that enable a baseball lover to record every action of the game. Our score sheets had blank boxes in which we could draw our own slanted lines in the form of a diamond as we followed players around the bases. Wherever the baserunner's progress stopped, the line stopped. He instructed me to fill in the unused boxes at the end of each inning with an elaborate checkerboard design which made it absolutely clear who had been the last to bat and who would lead off the next inning. By the time I had mastered the art of scorekeeping, a lasting bond had been forged among my father, baseball, and me.

All through the summer of 1949, my first summer as a fan, I spent my afternoons sitting cross-legged before the squat Philco radio which stood as a permanent fixture on our porch in Rockville Centre, on the South Shore of Long Island, New York. With my scorebook spread before me, I attended Dodger games through the courtly voice of Dodger announcer Red Barber. As he announced the lineup, I carefully printed each player's name in a column on the left side of my sheet. Then, using the standard system my father had taught me, which assigned a number to each position in the field, starting with a "1" for the pitcher and ending with a "9" for the right fielder, I recorded every play. I found it difficult at times to sit still. As the Dodgers came to bat, I would walk around the room, talking to the players as if they were standing in front of me. At critical junctures, I tried to make a bargain, whispering and cajoling while Pee Wee Reese or Duke Snider stepped into the batter's box: "Please, please, get a hit. If you get a hit now, I'll make my bed every day for a week." Sometimes, when the score was close and the opposing team at bat with men on base, I was too agitated to listen. Asking my mother to keep notes, I left the house for a walk around the block, hoping that when I returned the enemy threat would be over, and once again we'd be up at bat. Mostly, however, I stayed at my post, diligently recording each inning so that, when my father returned from his job as bank examiner for the State of New York, I could recreate for him the game he had missed.

When my father came home from the city, he would change from his three-piece suit into long pants and a short-sleeved sport shirt, and come downstairs for the ritual Manhattan cocktail with my mother. Then my parents would summon me for dinner from my play on the street outside our house. All through dinner I had to restrain myself from telling him about the day's game, waiting for the special time to come when we would sit together on the couch, my scorebook on my lap.

"Well, did anything interesting happen today?" he would begin. And even before the daily question was completed I had eagerly launched into my narrative of every play, and almost every pitch, of that afternoon's contest. It never crossed my mind to wonder if, at the close of a day's work, he might find my lengthy account the least bit tedious. For there was mastery as well as pleasure in our nightly ritual. Through my knowledge, I commanded my father's undivided attention, the sign of his love. It would instill in me an early awareness of the power of narrative, which would introduce a lifetime of story-telling, fueled by the naive confidence that others would find me as entertaining as my father did.

Michael Francis Aloysius Kearns, my father, was a short man who appeared much larger on account of his erect bearing, broad chest, and thick neck. He had a ruddy Irish complexion, and his green eyes flashed with humor and vitality. When he smiled his entire face was transformed, radiating enthusiasm and friendliness. He called me "Bubbles," a pet name he had chosen, he told me, because I seemed to enjoy so many things. Anxious to confirm his description, I refused to let my enthusiasm wane, even when I grew tired or grumpy. Thus excitement about things became a habit, a part of my personality, and the expectation that I should enjoy new experiences often engendered the enjoyment itself.

These nightly recountings of the Dodgers' progress provided my first lessons in the narrative art. From the scorebook, with its tight squares of neatly arranged symbols, I could unfold the tale of an entire game and tell a story that seemed to last almost as long as the game itself. At last, I was unable to resist the temptation to skip ahead to an important play in later innings. At times, I grew so excited about a Dodger victory that I blurted out the final score before I had hardly begun. But as I became more experienced in my storytelling, I learned to build a dramatic story with a beginning, middle, and end. Slowly, I learned that if I could recount the game, one batter at a time, inning by inning, without divulging the outcome, I could keep the suspense and my father's interest alive until the very last pitch. Sometimes I pretended that I was the great Red Barber himself, allowing my voice to swell when reporting a home run, quieting to a whisper when the action grew tense, injecting tidbits about the players into my reports. At critical moments, I would jump from the couch to illustrate a ball that turned foul at the last moment or a dropped fly that was scored as an error.

"How many hits did Roy Campanella get?" my dad would ask. Tracing my finger across the horizontal line that represented Campanella's at bats that day, I would count. "One, two, three. Three hits, a single, a double, and another single." "How many strikeouts for Don Newcombe?" It was easy. I would count the Ks. "One, two . . . eight. He had eight strikeouts." Then he'd ask me more subtle questions about different plays—whether a strikeout was called or swinging, whether the double play was around the horn, whether the single that won the game was hit to left or right. If I had scored carefully, using the elaborate system he had taught me, I would know the answers. My father pointed to the second inning, where Jackie Robinson had hit a single and then stolen second. There was excitement in his voice. "See, it's all here. While Robinson was dancing off second, he rattled the pitcher so badly that the next two guys walked to load the bases. That's the impact Robinson makes, game after game. Isn't he something?" His smile at such moments inspired me to take my responsibility seriously.

Sometimes, a particular play would trigger in my father a memory of a similar situation in a game when he was young, and he would tell me stories about the Dodgers when he was a boy growing up in Brooklyn. His vivid tales featured strange heroes such as Casey Stengel, Zack Wheat, and Jimmy Johnston. Though it was hard at first to imagine that the Casey Stengel I knew, the manager of the Yankees, with his colorful language and hilarious antics, was the same man as the Dodger outfielder who hit an inside-the-park home run at the first game ever played at Ebbets Field, my father so skillfully stitched together the past and the present that I felt as if I were living in different time zones. If I closed my eyes, I imagined I was at Ebbets Field in the 1920s for that celebrated game when Dodger right fielder Babe Herman hit a double with the bases loaded, and through a series of mishaps on the base paths, three Dodgers ended up at third base at the same time. And I was sitting by my father's side, five years before I was born, when the lights were turned on for the first time at Ebbets Field, the crowd gasping and then cheering as the summer night was transformed into startling day.

When I had finished describing the game, it was time to go to bed, unless I could convince my father to tally each player's batting average, reconfiguring his statistics to reflect the developments of that day's game. If Reese went 3 for 5 and had started the day at .303, my father showed me, by adding and multiplying all the numbers in his head, that his average would rise to .305. If Snider went 0 for 4 and started the day at .301, then his average would dip four points below the .300 mark. If Carl Erskine had let in three runs in seven innings, then my father would multiply three times nine, divide that by the number of innings pitched, and magically tell me whether Erskine's earned-run average had improved or worsened. It was this facility with numbers that had made it possible for my father to pass the civil-service test and become a bank examiner despite leaving school after the eighth grade. And this job had carried him from a Brooklyn tenement to a house with a lawn on Southard Avenue in Rockville Centre.

All through that summer, my father kept from me the knowledge that running box scores appeared in the daily newspapers. He never mentioned that these abbreviated histories had been a staple feature of the sports pages since the nineteenth century and were generally the first thing he and his fellow commuters turned to when they opened the *Daily News* and the *Herald Tribune* in the morning. I believed that, if I did not recount the games he had missed, my father would never have been able to follow our Dodgers the proper way, day by day, play by play, inning by inning. In other words, without me, his love of baseball would be forever unfulfilled.

I had the luck to fall in love with baseball at the start of an era of pure delight for New York fans. In each of the nine seasons from 1949 to 1957—spanning much of my childhood—we would watch one of the three New York teams—the Dodgers, the Giants, or the Yankees—compete in the World Series. In this golden era, the Yankees won five consecutive World Series, the Giants won two pennants and one championship and five pennants, while losing two additional pennants in the last inning of the last game of the season.

In those days before players were free agents, the starting lineups remained basically intact for years. Fans gave their loyalty to a team, knowing the players they loved would hold the same positions and, year after year, exhibit the same endearing quirks and irritating habits. And what a storied lineup my Dodgers had in the postwar seasons: Roy Campanella started behind the plate, Gil Hodges at first, Jackie Robinson at second, Pee Wee Reese at short, Billy Cox at third, Gene Hermanski in left, Duke Snider in center, and Carl Furillo in right. Half of that lineup—Reese, Robinson, Campanella, and Snider—would eventually be elected to the Hall of Fame; Gil Hodges and Carl Furillo would likely have been enshrined in Cooperstown had they played in any other decade or for any other club. Never would there be a better time to be a Dodger fan.

The Web of the Game

ROGER ANGELL

Roger Angell is like a crafty pitcher. When he's in his groove, he's untouchable. And in those rare moments of writing about baseball for *The New Yorker* when he's not been in top form—he is, after all, his own hardest act to follow—he still dazzles with his deftness.

Pitching forms the heart of this 1981 gem of a piece on a gem of a game; baseball's very timelessness forms its soul. In it, Angell is caught—strong-armed might be more appropriate—between baseball's past and baseball's future. As spun by Angell, it's a blissful place to be.

An afternoon in mid-May, and we are waiting for the game to begin. We are in shadow, and the sunlit field before us is a thick, springy green—an old diamond, beautifully kept up. The grass continues beyond the low chain-link fence that encloses the outfield, extending itself on the right-field side into a rougher, featureless sward that terminates in a low line of distant trees, still showing a pale, early-summer green. We are almost in the country. Our seats are in the seventh row of the grandstand, on the home side of the diamond, about halfway between third base and home plate. The seats themselves are more comforting to spirit than to body, being a surviving variant example of the pure late–Doric Polo Grounds mode: the backs made of a continuous running row of wood slats, divided off by pairs of narrow cast-iron arms, within which are slatted let-down seats, grown arthritic with rust and countless layers of gray paint. The rows are stacked so closely upon each other (one discovers) that a happening on the field of sufficient interest to warrant a rise or half-rise to one's feet is often made more memorable by a sharp crack to the kneecaps delivered by the backs of the seats just forward; in time, one finds that a dandruff of gray paint flakes from the same source has fallen on one's lap and scorecard. None of this matters, for this view and these stands and this park—it is Yale Field, in New Haven—are renowned for their felicity. The grandstand is a low, penumbrous steel-post shed that holds the infield in a pleasant horseshoe-curved embrace. The back wall of the grandstand, behind the uppermost row of seats, is broken by an arcade of open arches, admitting a soft back light that silhouettes the upper audience and also discloses an overhead bonework of struts and beams supporting the roof—the pigeonland of all the ballparks of our youth. The game we are waiting for—Yale vs. St. John's University—is a considerable event, for it is part of the National Collegiate Athletic Association's northeast regional tournament, the winner of which will qualify for a berth at the national collegiate championships in Omaha in June, the World Series of college baseball. Another pair of teams, Maine and Central Michigan—the Black Bears and the Chippe-was—have just finished their game here, the first of a doubleheader. Maine won it, 10–2, but the ultimate winner will not be picked here for three more days, when the four teams will have completed a difficult double-elimination tournament. Good, hard competition, but the stands at Yale Field are half empty today. Call them half full, because everyone on hand—some twenty-five hundred fans—must know something about the quality of the teams here, or at least enough to qualify either as a partisan or as an expert, which would explain the hum of talk and expectation that runs through the grandstand even while the Yale team, in pinstriped home whites, is still taking infield practice.

I am seated in a little sector of senior New Haven men—Townies rather than Old Elis. One of them a couple of rows in front of me says, "They used to fill this place in the old days, before there was all the baseball on TV."

His neighbor, a small man in a tweed cap, says, "The biggest crowd I ever saw in here—the biggest ever, I bet—was for a high-school game. Shelton and Naugatuck, about twenty years ago."

An old gent with a cane, seated just to my left, says, "They filled it up that day the Yankees came here, with Ruth and Gehrig and the rest of them. An exhibition game."

A fan just beyond the old gentleman—a good-looking man in his sixties, with an open, friendly face, a large smile, and a thick stand of gray hair—leans toward my neighbor and says, "When *was* that game, Joe? 1930? 1932?"

"Oh, I can't remember," the old man says. "Somewhere in there. My youngest son was mascot for the Yankees that day, so I could figure it out, I suppose." He is not much interested. His eyes are on the field. "Say, look at these fellows throw!" he says. "Did you see that outfielder peg in the ball?"

"That was the day Babe Ruth said this was about the best-looking ballpark he'd ever ever seen," the man beyond says. "You remember that."

"I can remember long before this park was built," the old man says. "It was already the Yale ballfield when I got here, but they put in these stands later—Who is this shortstop? He's a hefty-looking bird."

"How many Yale games do you think you've seen, Joe?" the smiling man asks.

"Oh, I couldn't begin to count them. But I haven't seen a Yale team play in—I don't know how long. Not for years. These fellows today, they play in the Cape Cod League in the summers. They let the freshmen play here now, too. They recruit them more, I suppose. They're athletes—you can see that."

The Yale team finishes its warmup ritual, and St. John's—light-gray uniforms with scarlet cap bills and scarlet socks—replaces it on the field.

"St. John's has always had a good club," the old man tells me. "Even back when my sons were playing ball, it was a good ball team. But not as good as this one. Oh, my! Did you see this catcher throw down to second? Did you see that! I bet you in all the years I was here I didn't have twenty fellows who could throw."

"Your sons played here?" I asked him. "For Yale?"

"My son Joe was captain in '41," he says. "He was a pitcher. He pitched against my son Steve here one day. Steve was pitching for Colgate, and my other son, Bob—my youngest—was on the same Colgate team. A good little left-handed first baseman."

I am about to ask how that game turned out, but the old man has taken out a small gold pocket watch, with a hunting case, which he snaps open. Three-fourteen. "Can't they get this *started?*" he says impatiently.

I say something admiring about the watch, and he hands it to me carefully. "I've had that watch for sixty-eight years," he says. "I always carried it in my vest pocket, back when we wore vests."

The little watch has a considerable heft to it: a weight of authority. I turn it over and find an inscription on the back. It is in script and a bit worn, but I can still make it out:

PRESENTED TO JOE WOOD
BY HIS FRIEND A. E. SMITH
IN APPRECIATION OF HIS SPLENDID
PITCHING WHICH BROUGHT THE
WORLD'S CHAMPIONSHIP
TO BOSTON IN 1912.

"Who was A. E. Smith, Mr. Wood?" I ask.

"He was a manufacturer."

I know the rest. Joe Wood, the old gentleman on my left, was the baseball coach at Yale for twenty years—from 1923 to 1942. Before that, he was a sometime outfielder for the Cleveland Indians, who batted .366 in 1921. Before *that,* he was a celebrated right-handed pitcher for the Boston Red Sox—Smokey Joe Wood, who won thirty-four games for the Bosox in 1912, when he finished up with a record of 34–5, pitching ten shutouts and sixteen consecutive victories along the way. In the World Series that fall—one of the two or three finest ever played—he won three of the four games he pitched, including the famous finale: the game of Hooper's catch and Snodgrass's muff and Tris Speaker's killing tenth-inning single. Next to Walter Johnson, Smokey Joe Wood was the most famous fastballer of his era. Still is, no doubt, in the minds of the few surviving fans who saw him at his best. He is ninety-one years old.

None of this, I should explain—neither my presence at the game nor my companions in the stands—was an accident. I had been a fervent admirer of Smokey Joe Wood ever since I read his account of his baseball beginnings and his subsequent career in Lawrence Ritter's *The Glory of Their Times,* a cherished, classic volume of oral history of the early days of the pastime. Mr. Wood was in his seventies when that book was published, in 1966, and I was startled and pleased a few weeks ago when I ran across an article by Joan Whaley, in *Baseball Digest,* which informed me that he was still hale and still talking baseball in stimulating fashion. He was living with a married daughter in New Haven, and my first impulse was to jump in my car and drive up to press a call. But something held me back; it did not seem quite right to present myself uninvited at his door, even as a pilgrim. Then Ron Darling and Frank Viola gave me my chance. Darling, who was a junior at Yale this past year, is the best pitcher ever to take the mound for the Blue. He is better than Johnny Broaca, who went on to pitch for the Yankees and the Indians for five seasons in the mid-nineteen-thirties; he is better than Frank Quinn, who compiled a 1.57 career earned-run average at Yale in 1946, '47, and '48. (He is also a better all-around ballplayer than George Bush, who played first base and captained the

Elis in 1948, and then somehow drifted off into politics instead of baseball.) Darling, a right-handed fastball thrower, won eleven games and lost two as a sophomore, with an earned-run average of 1.31, and this year he was 0–3 and 2.42, with eighty-nine strikeouts in his ninety-three innings of work—the finest college pitcher in the Northeast, according to major-league scouts, with the possible exception of Frank Viola, a junior left-handed curveball ace at St. John's, who was undefeated this year, 9–0, and had a neat earned-run average of 1.00. St. John's, a Catholic university in Queens, is almost a baseball power-house—not quite in the same class, perhaps, as such perennial national champi-ons or challengers as Arizona, Arizona State, Texas, and Southern California, whose teams play Sun Belt schedules of close to sixty games, but good enough to have gone as the Northeast's representative to the national tournament in Omaha in 1980, where Viola defeated the eventual winner, Arizona, in the first round. St. John's, by the way, does not recruit high-school stars from faraway states, as do most of these rival college powers; all but one player on this year's thirty-three-man Redmen squad grew up and went to school in New York City or in nearby suburbs. This 1981 St. John's team ran off an awesome 31–2 record, capturing the Eastern College Metro (Greater New York, that is) elim-ination, while Yale, winning its last nine games in a row, concluded its regular season with a record of 24–12–1, which was good enough to win its first East-ern Intercollegiate League championship since 1956. (That tie in Yale's record was a game against the University of Central Florida, played during the Elis' spring-training tour in March, and was called because of darkness after seven innings, with the score tied at 21–21. Darling did not pitch that day.) The two teams, along with Central Michigan (Mid-America Conference) and Maine (New England Conference), qualified for the tournament at New Haven, and the luck of the draw pitted Yale (and Darling) against St. John's (and Viola) in the second game of the opening doubleheader. Perfect. Darling, by the way, had indicated that he might be willing to turn professional this summer if he were to be picked in an early round of the annual amateur draft conducted by the major leagues in mid-June, and Viola had been talked about as a potential big-leaguer ever since his freshman year, so their matchup suddenly became an obligatory reunion for every front-rank baseball scout east of the Ohio River. (About fifty of them turned up, with their speed-guns and clipboards, and their glowing reports of the game, I learned later, altered the draft priorities of sev-eral clubs.)

Perfect, but who would get in touch with Mr. Wood and persuade him to come out to Yale Field with me for the game? Why, Dick Lee would—Dick Lee, *of course.* Richard C. Lee (he was the smiling man sitting just beyond

Smokey Joe in our row) is a former Democratic mayor of New Haven, an extremely popular (eight consecutive terms, sixteen years in office), innovative officeholder who, among other things, presided over the widely admired urban renewal of his city during the nineteen-sixties and, before that, thought up and pushed through the first Operation Head Start program (for minority-group preschoolers) in the country. Dick Lee knows everybody in New Haven, including Smokey Joe Wood and several friends of mine there, one of whom provided me with his telephone number. I called Lee at his office (he is assistant to the chairman of the Union Trust Company, in New Haven) and proposed our party. "Wonderful!" he cried at once. "You have come to the right man. I'll bring Joe. Count on me!" Even over the telephone, I could see him smiling.

Dick Lee did not play baseball for Yale, but the nature of his partisanship became clear in the very early moments of the Yale-St. John's game. "Yay!" he shouted in a stentorian baritone as Ron Darling set down three St. John's batters in order in the first. "Yah, Ron *baby!*" he boomed out as Darling dismissed three more batters in the second, fanning the last two. "Now *c'mon,* Yale! Let's get something started, gang! Yay!" Lee had told me that he pitched for some lesser-known New Haven teams—the Dixwell Community House sandlot team and the Jewish Home for Children nine (the Utopians), among others—while he was growing up in the ivyless New Hallville neighborhood. Some years later, having passed up college altogether, he went to work for Yale as its public-relations officer. By the time he became mayor, in 1953, the university was his own—another precinct to be worried about and looked after. A born politician, he appears to draw on some inner deep-water reservoir of concern that enables him to preside effortlessly and affectionately over each encounter of his day; he was the host at our game, and at intervals he primed Joe Wood with questions about his baseball past, which he seemed to know almost by heart.

"Yes, that's right, I did play for the Bloomer Girls a few games," Mr. Wood said in response to one such cue. "I was about sixteen, and I was pitching for our town team in Ness City, Kansas. The Bloomer Girls were a barnstorming team, but they used to pick up a few young local fellows on the sly to play along with them if they needed to fill out their lineup. I was one of those. I never wore a wig, though—I wouldn't have done that. I guess I looked young enough to pass for a girl anyway. Bill Stern, the old radio broadcaster, must have used that story about forty times, but he always got it wrong about the wig."

There was a yell around us, and an instantly ensuing groan, as Yale's big freshman catcher, Tony Paterno, leading off the bottom of the second, lined sharply to the St. John's shortstop, who made a fine play on the ball. Joe Wood peered intently out at the field through his thickish horn-rimmed spectacles. He shook his head a little. "You know, I can't hardly follow the damned ball now," he said. "It's better for me if I'm someplace where I can get up high behind the plate. I was up to Fenway Park for two games last year, and they let me sit in the press box there at that beautiful park. I could see it all from there. The grounds keeper has got that field just like a living room."

I asked him if he still rooted for the Red Sox.

"Oh, yes," he said. "All my life. A couple of years ago, when they had that big lead in the middle of the summer, they asked me if I'd come up and throw out the first ball at one of their World Series games or playoff games. But then they dropped out of it, of course. Now it looks like it'll never happen."

He spoke in a quiet, almost measured tone, but there was no tinge of disappointment or self-pity in it. It was the voice of age. He was wearing a blue windbreaker over a buttoned-up plaid shirt, made formal with a small dark-red bow tie. There was a brown straw hat on his bald head. The years had imparted a delicate thinness to the skin on his cheeks and neck, but his face had a determined look to it, with a strong chin and a broad, unsmiling mouth. Watching him, I recalled one of the pictures in *The Glory of Their Times*—a team photograph taken in 1906, in which he is sitting cross-legged down in front of a row of men in baggy baseball pants and lace-up, collared baseball shirts with "NESS CITY" across the front in block letters. The men are standing in attitudes of cheerful assurance, with their arms folded, and their mushy little baseball gloves are hanging from their belts. Joe Wood, the smallest player in the picture, is wearing a dark warmup shirt, with the sleeves rolled halfway up his forearms, and his striped baseball cap is pushed back a little, revealing a part in the middle of his hair. There is an intent, unsmiling look on his boyish face—the same grave demeanor you can spot in a subsequent photograph, taken in 1912, in which he is standing beside his Red Sox manager, Jake Stahl, and wearing a heavy woollen three-button suit, a stiff collar, a narrow necktie with a stickpin, and a stylish black porkpie hat pulled low over his handsome, famous face: Smokey Joe Wood at twenty-two. (The moniker, by the way, was given him by Paul Shannon, a sportswriter for the Boston *Post;* before that, he was sometimes called Ozone Wood—"ozone" for the air cleaved by the hapless batters who faced him.) The young man in the photographs and the old man beside me at the ballpark had the same broad, sloping shoulders, but there was nothing burly or physically imposing about him then or now.

"What kind of a pitcher were you, Mr. Wood?" I asked him.

"I had a curve and a fastball," he said. "That's all. I didn't even have brains enough to slow up on the batters. The fastball had a hop on it. You had to be *fast* to have that happen to the ball."

I said that I vividly recalled Sandy Koufax's fastball, which sometimes seemed to jump so violently as it crossed the plate that his catcher had to shoot up his mitt to intercept it.

"Mine didn't go up that far. Just enough for them to miss it." He half turned to me as he said this, and gave me a little glance and an infinitesimal smile. A twinkle. "I don't know where my speed came from," he went on. "I wasn't any bigger or stronger-looking then than I am now. I always could throw hard, and once I saw I was able to get batters out, I figured I was crazy enough to play ball for a living. My father was a criminal lawyer in Kansas, and before that out in Ouray, Colorado, where I first played ball, and my brother went to law school and got a degree, but I didn't even graduate from high school. I ate and slept baseball all my life."

★   ★   ★   ★   ★

The flow of recollection from Joe Wood was perhaps not as smooth and rivery as I have suggested here. For one thing, he spoke slowly and with care—not unlike the way he walked to the grandstand at Yale Field from the parking lot beyond left field, making his way along the grass firmly enough but looking where he was going, too, and helping himself a bit with his cane. Nothing infirm about him, but nothing hurrying or sprightly, either. For another, the game was well in progress by now, and its principals and sudden events kept interrupting our colloquy. Ron Darling, a poised, impressive figure on the mound, alternated his popping fastballs with just enough down-breaking sliders and an occasional curveball to keep the St. John's batters unhappy. Everything was thrown with heat—his strikeout pitch is a Seaver-high fastball, but his slider, which slides at the last possible instant, is an even deadlier weapon— but without any signs of strain or anxiety. He threw over the top, smoothly driving his front (left) shoulder at the batter in picture-book style, and by the third or fourth inning he had imposed his will and his pace on the game. He was rolling. He is a dark-haired, olive-skinned young man (he lives in Millbury, Massachusetts, near Worcester, but he was born in Hawaii; his mother is Chinese-Hawaiian by birth) with long, powerful legs, but his pitcherlike proportions tend to conceal, rather than emphasize, his six feet two inches and his hundred and ninety-five pounds. He also swings the bat well enough (.331 this year) to play right field for Yale when he isn't pitching; in our game he was the designated hitter as well as the pitcher for the Elis.

"That's a nice build for a pitcher, isn't it?" Joe Wood murmured during the St. John's fifth. Almost as he spoke, Darling executed a twisting dive to his right to snaffle a hard-hit grounder up the middle by Brian Miller, the St. John's shortstop, and threw him out at first. ("Hey-*hey!*" Dick Lee cried. "Yah, Ronnie!") "*And* he's an athlete out there," Wood added. "The scouts like that, you know. Oh, this fellow's a lot better than Broaca ever was."

Frank Viola, for his part, was as imperturbable as Darling on the mound, if not quite as awesome. A lanky, sharp-shouldered lefty, he threw an assortment of speeds and spins, mostly sinkers and down-darting sliders, that had the Yale batters swinging from their shoe tops and, for the most part, hammering the ball into the dirt. He had the stuff and poise of a veteran relief pitcher, and the St. John's infield—especially Brian Miller and a stubby, ebullient second baseman named Steve Scafa—performed behind him with the swift, almost haughty confidence that imparts an elegance and calm and sense of ease to baseball at its best. It was a scoreless game after five, and a beauty.

"What was the score of that game you beat Walter Johnson in, in your big year?" Dick Lee asked our guest between innings.

We all knew the answer, I think. In September of 1912, Walter Johnson came to Fenway Park (it was brand-new that year) with the Senators and pitched against young Joe Wood, who then had a string of thirteen consecutive victories to his credit. That summer, Johnson had established a league record of sixteen straight wins, so the matchup was not merely an overflow, sellout affair but perhaps the most anticipated, most discussed non-championship game in the American League up to that time.

"We won it, 1–0," Joe Wood said quietly, "but it wasn't his fault I beat him that day. If he'd had the team behind him that I did, he'd have set every kind of record in baseball. You have to remember that Walter Johnson played for a second-division team almost all through his career. All those years, and he had to work from the bottom every time he pitched."

"Were you faster than he was?" I asked.

"Oh, I don't think there was ever anybody faster than Walter," he murmured.

"But Johnson said just the opposite!" Dick Lee cried. "He said no one was faster than *you.*"

"He was just that kind of fellow, to say something like that," Wood said. "That was just like the man. Walter Johnson was a great big sort of a pitcher, with hands that came clear down to his knees. Why, the way he threw the ball, the only reason anybody ever got even a foul off him was because everybody in the league knew he'd never come inside to a batter. Walter Johnson was a prince of men—a gentleman first, last, and always."

It came to me that this was the first time I had ever heard anybody use the phrase "a prince of men" in a non-satiric fashion. In any case, the Johnson-Wood argument did not really need settling, then or now. Smokey Joe went on to tie Johnson with sixteen straight victories that season—an American League record, subsequently tied by Lefty Grove and Schoolboy Rowe. (Over in the National League that year, Rube Marquard won *nineteen* straight for the Giants—a single-season mark first set by Tim Keefe of the Giants in 1888 and untouched as yet by anyone else.) Johnson and Wood pretty well divided up the A.L. mound honors that summer, when Johnson won thirty-two games and lost twelve, posting the best earned-run average (1.39) and the most strike-outs (three hundred and three), while Wood won the most games and estab-lished the best winning percentage with his 34–5 mark (not including his three World Series wins, of course).

These last figures are firmly emplaced in the baseball crannies of my mind, and in the minds of most students of the game, because, it turned out, they represent the autumn of Joe Wood's pitching career as well as its first full flowering. Early in the spring of 1913, he was injured in a fielding play, and he was never near to being the same pitcher again. One of the game's sad specula-tions over the years has been what Joe Wood's status in the pantheon of great pitchers would be if he had remained sound. I did not need any reminder of his accident, but I had been given one just the same when Dick Lee intro-duced me to him, shortly before the game. We had stopped to pick up Mr. Wood at his small, red-shuttered white house on Marvel Road, and when he came down the concrete path to join us I got out of Lee's Cadillac to shake the hand that once shook the baseball world.

"Mr. Wood," I said, "this is a great honor."

"Ow—*ow!*" he cried, cringing before me and attempting to extricate his paw.

"Oh, oh . . . I'm *terribly* sorry," I said, appalled. "Is it—is this because of your fall off the roof?" Three years ago, at the age of eighty-eight, he had fallen off a ladder while investigating a leak, and had cracked several ribs.

"Hell, no!" he said indignantly. "This is the arm I threw out in 1913!"

I felt awful. I had touched history—and almost brought it to his knees.

Now, at the game, he told me how it all happened. "I can't remember now if it was on the road or at Fenway Park," he said. "Anyway, it was against Detroit. There was a swinging bunt down the line, and I went to field it and slipped on the wet grass and went down and landed on my hand. I broke it right here." He pointed to a spot just below his wrist, on the back of his freck-led, slightly gnarled right hand. "It's what they call a subperiosteal fracture.

They put it in a cast, and I had to sit out awhile. Well, this was in 1913, right after we'd won the championship, and every team was out to get us, of course. So as soon as the cast came off, the manager would come up to me every now and then and want to know how soon I was going to get back to pitching. Well, maybe I got back to it too soon and maybe I didn't, but the arm never felt right again. The shoulder went bad. I still went on pitching, but the fastball had lost that hop. I never threw a day after that when I wasn't in pain. Most of the time, I'd pitch and then it would hurt so bad that I wasn't able to raise my hand again for days afterward. So I was about a halftime pitcher after that. You have to understand that in those days if you didn't work you didn't get paid. Now they lay out as long as they need to and get a shot of that cortisone. But we had to play, ready or not. I was a married man, just starting a family, and in order to get my check I had to be in there. So I pitched."

He pitched less, but not much less well. In 1915, he was 15–5 for the Red Sox, with an earned-run average of 1.49, which was the best in the league. But the pain was so persistent that he sat out the entire 1916 season, on his farm, near Shohola, Pennsylvania, hoping that the rest would restore his arm. It did not. He pitched in eight more games after that—all of them for the Cleveland Indians, to whom he was sold in 1917—but he never won again.

"Did you become a different kind of pitcher after you hurt your arm?" I asked. "More off-speed stuff, I mean?"

"No, I still pitched the fastball."

"But all that pain—"

"I tried not to think about that." He gave me the same small smile and bright glance. "I just loved to be out there," he said. "It was as simple as that."

★   ★   ★   ★   ★

Our afternoon slid by in a distraction of baseball and memory, and I almost felt myself at some dreamlike doubleheader involving the then and the now—the semi-anonymous strong young men waging their close, marvellous game on the sunlit green field before us while bygone players and heroes of baseball history—long gone now, most of them—replayed their vivid, famous innings for me in the words and recollections of my companion. Yale kept putting men aboard against Viola and failing to move them along; Rich Diana, the husky center fielder (he is also an All-Ivy League halfback), whacked a long double to left but then died on second—the sixth stranded Eli base runner in five innings. Darling appeared to be struggling a little, walking two successive batters in the sixth, but he saved himself with a whirling pickoff to second base—a timed play brilliantly completed by his shortstop, Bob Brooke—and then struck out St. John's big first baseman, Karl Komyathy, for the last out. St. John's had yet to manage a hit against him.

In the home half of the sixth, Yale put its leadoff batter aboard with a single but could not bunt him along. Joe Wood was distressed. "I could teach these fellows to bunt in one minute," he said. "Nobody can't hardly bunt any-more. You've got to get your weight more forward than he did, so you're not reaching for the ball. And he should have his right hand higher up on the bat."

The inning ended, and we reversed directions once again. "Ty Cobb was the greatest bat-handler you ever saw," Wood said. "He used to go out to the ballpark early in the morning with a pitcher and work on hitting the ball to all fields, over and over. He batted that strange way, with his fists apart, you know, but he could have hit just as well no matter how he held it. He just knew what to do with a bat in hand. And baserunning—why, I saw him get on base and steal second, steal third, and then steal home. *The* best. A lot of fellows in my time shortened up on the bat when they had to—that's what the St. John's boys should try against this good pitcher. Next to Cobb, Shoeless Joe Jackson was the best left-handed hitter I ever saw, and he was always down at the end of the bat until there were two strikes on him. Then he'd shorten up a little, to give himself a better chance."

Dick Lee said, "That's what you've been telling Charlie Polka, isn't it, Joe?"

"Yes, sir, and it's helped him," Wood said. "He's tried it, and now he knows that all you have to do is make contact and the ball will fly a long way."

Both men saw my look of bewilderment, and they laughed together.

"Charlie Polka is a Little League player," Dick Lee explained. "He's about eleven years old."

"He lives right across the street from me," Wood said. "He plays for the 500 Blake team—that's named for a restaurant here in town. I've got him shortened up on the bat, and now he's a hitter. Charlie Polka is a natural."

"Is that how you batted?" I asked.

"Not at first," he said. "But after I went over to Cleveland in 1917 to join my old roommate, Tris Speaker, I started to play the outfield, and I began to take up on the bat, because I knew I'd have to hit a little better if I was going to make the team. I never was any wonder at the plate, but I was good enough to last six more years, playing with Spoke."

Tris Speaker (Wood had called him by his old nickname, Spoke) was the Joe DiMaggio or Willie Mays of the first two decades of this century—the nonpareil center fielder of his day. "He had a beautiful left-handed arm," Joe Wood said. "He always played very shallow in center—you could do that in those days, because of the dead ball. I saw him make a lot of plays to second base from there—pick up what looked like a clean single and fire the ball to second in time to force the base runner coming down from first. Or he could throw the ball behind a runner and pick him off that way. And just as fine a man as he was a ballplayer. He was a Southern gentleman—well, he was from Hubbard, Texas. Back in the early days, when we were living together on the beach at Winthrop during the season, out beyond Revere, Spoke would sometimes cook up a mess of fried chicken in the evening. He'd cook, and then I'd do the dishes."

Listening to this, I sensed the web of baseball about me. Tris Speaker had driven in the tying run in the tenth inning of the last game of the 1912 World Series, at Fenway Park, after Fred Merkle and Chief Meyers, of the Giants, had let his easy foul pop fall untouched between them. A moment or two later, Joe Wood had won his third game of the Series and the Red Sox were champions. My father saw that game—he was at Harvard Law School at the time, and got a ticket somehow—and he told me about it many times. He was terrifically excited to be there, but I think my mother must have relished the famous victory even more. She grew up in Boston and was a true Red Sox fan, even though young women didn't go to many games then. My father grew up in Cleveland, so he was an Indians rooter, of course. In 1915, my parents got married and went to live in Cleveland, where my father began to practice law. Tris Speaker was traded to the Indians in 1916—a terrible shock to Red Sox fans—and Joe Wood came out of his brief retirement to join him on the club a year later. My parents' first child, my older sister, was born in Cleveland late in 1916, and the next year my father went off to Europe—off to the war. My mother once told me that in the summer afternoons of 1917 she would often push a baby carriage past League Park, the Indians' home field, out on Linwood Avenue, which was a block or two away from my parents' house. Sometimes there was a game going on, and if she heard a roar of pleasure from the fans inside she would tell herself that probably Tris Speaker had just done something special. She was lonely in Cleveland, she told me, and it made her feel good to know that Tris Speaker was there in the same town with her. "Tris Speaker and I were traded to Cleveland in the same year," she said.

A yell and an explosion of cheering brought me back to Yale Field. We were in the top of the seventh, and the Yale second baseman and captain, Gerry

Harrington, had just leaped high to snatch down a burning line drive—the force of it almost knocked him over backward in midair. Then he flipped the ball to second to double off a St. John's base runner and end the inning. "These fellows came to *play!*" Dick Lee said.

Most no-hitters produce at least one such heaven-sent gift somewhere along the line, and I began to believe that Ron Darling, who was still untouched on the mound, might be pitching the game of his young life. I turned to ask Mr. Wood how many no-hitters he recalled—he had seen Mathewson and Marquard and Babe Ruth (Ruth, the pitcher, that is) and Coveleski and the rest of them, after all—but he seemed transfixed by something on the field. "Look at *that!*" he said, in a harsh, disbelieving way. "This Yale coach has his own coaches out there on the lines, by God! They're professionals—not just players, the way I always had it when I was here. The coach has his own coaches . . . I never knew that."

"Did you have special coaches when you were coming up with the Red Sox?" I said, hoping to change his mood. "A pitching coach, I mean, or a batting coach??"

He didn't catch the question, and I repeated it.

"No, no," he said, a little impatiently. "We talked about the other players and the pitchers among ourselves in those days. We players. We didn't need anybody to help us."

He was staring straight ahead at the field. I thought he looked a bit chilly. It was well past five o'clock now, and a skim of clouds had covered the sun.

Dick Lee stole a glance at him, too. "Hey, Joe, doesn't this Darling remind you a little of Carl Hubbell on the mound?" he said in a cheerful, distracting sort of voice. "The way he picks up his front leg, I mean. You remember how Hubbell would go way up on the stretch and then drop his hands down by his ankles before he threw the ball?"

"Hubbell?" Joe Wood said. He shook his head, making an effort. "Well, to me this pitcher's a little like that fellow Eckersley," he said slowly. "The way he moves forward there."

He was right. Ron Darling had exactly the same float and glide that the Red Sox' Dennis Eckersley conveys when he is pitching well.

"How do today's players compare with the men you played with, Mr. Wood?" I asked.

"I'd rather not answer that question," he said. He had taken out his watch again. He studied it and then tucked it away carefully, and then he glanced over at me, perhaps wondering if he had been impolite. "That Pete Rose plays hard," he added. "Him and a few more. I don't *like* Pete Rose, exactly, but he looks like he plays the game the way we did. He'd play for the fun of it if he had to."

He resumed his study of the field, and now and then I saw him stare again at the heavyset Yale third-base coach on our side of the diamond. Scoreless games make for a long day at the ballpark, and Joe Wood's day had probably been longer than ours. More than once, I had seen him struggle to his feet to catch some exciting play or moment on the field, only to have it end before he was quite up. Then he would sit down again, leaning on his cane while he lowered himself. I had more questions for Mr. Wood, but now I tried to put them out of my mind. Earlier in the afternoon, he had re-marked that several old Yale players had dropped in at his house before the game to say hello and to talk about the old days. "People come by and see me all the time," he had said. "People I don't even know, from as far away as Colorado. Why, I had a fellow come in all the way from Canada the other day, who just wanted to talk about the old days. They all want that, some-how. It's gone on too long."

It had gone on for him, I realized, for as long as most lifetimes. He had played ball for fourteen years, all told, and people had been asking him to talk about it for nearly sixty years. For him, the last juice and sweetness must have been squeezed out of these ancient games years ago, but he was still expected to respond to our amateur expertise, our insatiable vicarious-ness. Old men are patronized in much the same fashion as athletes; because we take pride in them, we expect their intimacy in return. I had intruded after all.

★　　★　　★　　★　　★

We were in the eighth now . . . and then in the ninth. Still no score, and each new batter, each pitch was greeted with clappings and deepening cries of encouragement and anxiety from the stands and the players alike. The close-packed rows hummed with ceaseless, nervous sounds of conversation and speculation—and impatience for the dénouement, and a fear of it, too. All around me in our section I could see the same look of resignation and bore-dom and pleasure that now showed on my own face, I knew—the look of longtime fans who understand that one can never leave a very long close game, no matter how much inconvenience and exasperation it imposes on us. The difficulty of baseball is imperious.

"Yay! Yay!" Dick Lee cried when Yale left fielder Joe Dufek led off the eighth with a single. "Now come *on,* you guy! I gotta get home for dinner."

But the next Yale batter bunted into a force play at second, and the chance was gone. "Well, all right—for *breakfast!*" Lee said, slumping back in his seat.

The two pitchers held us—each as intent and calm and purposeful as the other. Ron Darling, never deviating from the purity of his stylish body-lean and leg-crook and his riding, down-thrusting delivery, poured fastballs through the diminishing daylight. He looked as fast as ever now, or faster, and in both the ninth and the tenth he dismissed the side in order and with four more strikeouts. Viola was dominant in his own fashion, also setting down the Yale hitters one, two, three in the ninth and tenth, with a handful of pitches. His rhythm—the constant variety of speeds and location on his pitches—had the enemy batters leaning and swaying with his motion, and, as antistrophe, was almost as exciting to watch as Darling's flair and flame. With two out in the top of the eleventh, a St. John's batter nudged a soft little roller up the first-base line—such an easy, waiting, schoolboy sort of chance that the Yale first base-man, O'Connor, allowed the ball to carom off his mitt: a miserable little butchery, except that the second baseman, seeing his pitcher sprinting for the bag, now snatched up the ball and flipped it toward him almost despairingly. Darling took the toss while diving full-length at the bag and, rolling in the dirt, beat the runner by a hair.

"Oh, my!" said Joe Wood. "Oh, my, oh, my!"

Then in the bottom of the inning Yale suddenly loaded the bases—a hit, a walk, another walk (Viola was just missing the corners now)—and we all came to our feet, yelling and pleading. The tilted stands and the low roof deepened the cheers and sent them rolling across the field. There were two out, and the Yale batter, Dan Costello, swung at the first pitch and bounced it gently to short, for a force that ended the rally. Somehow, I think, we knew that we had seen Yale's last chance.

"I would have taken that pitch," I said, entering the out in my score-card. "To keep the pressure on him."

"I don't know," Joe Wood said at once. "He's just walked two. You might get the cripple on the first pitch and then see nothing but hooks. Hit away."

He was back in the game.

Steve Scafa, leading off the twelfth, got a little piece of Darling's first pitch on the handle of his bat, and the ball looped softly over the shortstop's head and into left: a hit. The loudspeakers told us that Ron Darling's eleven innings of no-hit pitching had set a new N.C.A.A. tournament record. Everyone at Yale Field stood up—the St. John's players, too, coming off their bench and out onto the field—and applauded Darling's masterpiece. We were scarcely seated again before Scafa stole second as the Yale catcher, Paterno, bobbled the pitch. Scafa, who is blurrily quick, had stolen thirty-five bases during the season. Now he stole third as well. With one out and runners at the corners (the other St. John's man had reached first on an error), Darling ran the count to three and two and fanned the next batter—his fifteenth strikeout of the game. Two out. Darling sighed and stared in, and then stepped off the mound while the St. John's coach put in a pinch-runner at first—who took off for second on the very next pitch. Paterno fired the ball quickly this time, and Darling, staggering off the mound with his follow-through, did not cut it off. Scafa came ten feet down the third-base line and stopped there, while the pinch-runner suddenly jammed on the brakes, stranding himself between first and second: a play, clearly—an inserted crisis. The Yale second baseman glanced twice at Scafa, freezing him, and then made a little run at the hung-up base runner to his left and threw to first. With that, Scafa instantly broke for the plate. Lured by the vision of the third out just a few feet away from him on the base path, the Yale first baseman hesitated, fractionally and fatally, before he spun and threw home, where Scafa slid past the tag and came up, leaping and clapping, into the arms of his teammates. That was the game. Darling struck out his last man, but a new St. John's pitcher, a right-handed fireballer named Eric Stampfl, walked on and blew the Elis away in their half.

"Well, that's a shame," Joe Wood said, getting up for the last time. It was close to six-thirty, but he looked fine now. "If that man scores before the third out, it counts, you know," he said. "That's why it worked. I never saw a better-played game anyplace—college or big-league. That's a swell ballgame."

★   ★   ★   ★   ★

Several things happened afterward. Neither Yale nor St. John's qualified for the college World Series, it turned out; the University of Maine defeated St. John's in the final game of the playoffs at New Haven (neither Viola nor Darling was sufficiently recovered from his ordeal to pitch again) and made the trip to Omaha, where it, too, was eliminated. Arizona State won the national title. On June 9th, Ron Darling was selected by the Texas Rangers at the major-league amateur-player draft in New York. He was the ninth player in the country to be chosen. Frank Viola, the thirty-seventh pick, went to the Minnesota Twins. (The Seattle Mariners, who had the first pick this year, had been ready to take Darling, which would have made him the coveted No. 1 selection in the draft, but the club backed off at the last moment because of Darling's considerable salary demands. As it was, he signed with the Rangers for a hundred-thousand-dollar bonus.) On June 12th, the major-league players unanimously struck the twenty-six big-league teams. The strike has brought major-league ball to a halt, and no one can predict when play will resume. Because of this sudden silence, the St. John's-Yale struggle has become the best and most vivid game of the year for me, so far. It may stay that way even after the strike ends. "I think that game will always be on my mind," Ron Darling said after it was over. I feel the same way. I think I will remember it all my life. So will Joe Wood. Somebody will probably tell Ron Darling that Smoke Joe Wood was at the game that afternoon and saw him pitch eleven scoreless no-hit innings against St. John's and someday—perhaps years from now, when he, too, may possibly be a celebrated major-league strikeout artist—it may occur to him that his heartbreaking 0–1 loss in May 1981 and Walter Johnson's 0–1 loss at Fenway Park in September 1912 are now woven together into the fabric of baseball. Pitch by pitch, inning by inning, Ron Darling had made that happen. He stitched us together.

Alibi Ike

RING LARDNER

Batting fourth . . .

The cleanup position. The spot reserved for the heaviest hitter.

In this lineup that goes to Ring Lardner (1885–1933) and his treasure, "Alibi Ike." It says so right here.

Lardner's career began in sports and spread into fiction, regularly blending the two with hilarious results. His work could be as biting as it was funny, and while he often wrote about seemingly simple characters, the work itself was beautifully crafted, flowing with a complex undertow.

While a sportswriter at the *Chicago Tribune,* Lardner began stitching together a series of stories in letter form about a hayseed rookie named Jack Keefe. When the *Tribune* deemed Lardner's slangy use of language inappropriate for its readership, Lardner sold the stories to the *Saturday Evening Post.* They were a smash from the get-go. Between their publication in the Post and their collection as *You Know Me, Al,* Lardner created another baseball character, one with an excuse for everything. Lardner sold him to the *Post,* as well, and on July 31, 1915, the *Saturday Evening Post* introduced "Alibi Ike," Lardner's most enduring creation, without no extenuation whatsoever.

1

His right name was Frank X. Farrell, and I guess the X stood for "Excuse me." Because he never pulled a play, good or bad, on or off the field, without apologizin' for it.

"Alibi Ike" was the name Carey wished on him the first day he reported down south. O' course we all cut out the "Alibi" part of it right away for the fear he would overhear it and bust somebody. But we called him "Ike" right to his face and the rest of it was understood by everybody on the club except Ike himself.

He ast me one time, he says:

"What do you all call me Ike for? I ain't no Yid."

"Carey give you the name," I says. "It's his nickname for everybody he takes a likin' to."

"He mustn't have only a few friends then," says Ike. "I never heard him say 'Ike' to nobody else."

But I was goin' to tell you about Carey namin' him. We'd been workin' out two weeks and the pitchers was showin' somethin' when this bird joined us. His first day out he stood up there so good and took such a reef at the old pill that he had everyone lookin'. Then him and Carey was together in left field, catchin' fungoes, and it was after we was through for the day that Carey told me about him.

"What do you think of Alibi Ike?" ast Carey.

"Who's that?" I says.

"This here Farrell in the outfield," says Carey.

"He looks like he could hit," I says.

"Yes," says Carey, "but he can't hit near as good as he can apologize."

Then Carey went on to tell me what Ike had been pullin' out there. He'd dropped the first fly ball that was hit to him and told Carey his glove wasn't broke in good yet, and Carey says the glove could easy of been Kid Gleason's gran'father. He made a whale of a catch out o' the next one and Carey says "Nice work!" or somethin' like that, but Ike says he could of caught the ball with his back turned only he slipped when he started after it and, besides that, the air currents fooled him.

"I thought you done well to get to the ball," says Carey.

"I ought to been settin' under it," says Ike.

"What did you hit last year?" Carey ast him.

"I had malaria most o' the season," says Ike. "I wound up with .356."

"Where would I have to go to get malaria?" says Carey, but Ike didn't wise up.

I and Carey and him set at the same table together for supper. It took him half an hour longer'n us to eat because he had to excuse himself every time he lifted his fork.

"Doctor told me I needed starch," he'd say, and then toss a shovelful o' potatoes into him. Or, "They ain't much meat on one o' these chops," he'd tell us, and grab another one. Or he'd say: "Nothin' like onions for a cold," and then he'd dip into the perfumery.

"Better try that apple sauce," says Carey. "It'll help your malaria."

"Whose malaria?" says Ike. He'd forgot already why he didn't only hit .356 last year.

I and Carey begin to lead him on.

"Whereabouts did you say your home was?" I ast him.

"I live with my folks," he says. "We live in Kansas City—not right down in the business part—outside a ways."

"How's that come?" says Carey. "I should think you'd get rooms in the post office."

But Ike was too busy curin' his cold to get that one.

"Are you married?" I ast him.

"No," he says. "I never run round much with girls, except to shows onct in a wile and parties and dances and roller skatin'."

"Never take 'em to the prize fights, eh?" says Carey.

"We don't have no real good bouts," says Ike. "Just bush stuff. And I never figured a boxin' match was a place for the ladies."

Well, after supper he pulled a cigar out and lit it. I was just goin' to ask him what he done it for, but he beat me to it.

"Kind o' rests a man to smoke after a good work-out," he says. "Kind o' settles a man's supper, too."

"Looks like a pretty good cigar," says Carey.

"Yes," says Ike. "A friend o' mine give it to me—a fella in Kansas City that runs a billiard room."

"Do you play billiards?" I ast him.

"I used to play a fair game," he says. "I'm all out o' practice now—can't hardly make a shot."

We coaxed him into a four-handed battle, him and Carey against Jack Mack and I. Say, he couldn't play billiards as good as Willie Hoppe; not quite. But to hear him tell it, he didn't make a good shot all evenin'. I'd leave him an awful-lookin' layout and he'd gather 'em up in one try and then run a couple o' hundred, and between every carom he'd say he'd put too much stuff on the ball, or the English didn't take, or the table wasn't true, or his stick was crooked, or somethin'. And all the time he had the balls actin' like they was Dutch soldiers and him Kaiser William. We started out to play fifty points, but we had to make it a thousand so as I and Jack and Carey could try the table.

The four of us set round the lobby a wile after we was through playin', and when it got along toward bedtime Carey whispered to me and says:

"Ike'd like to go to bed, but he can't think up no excuse."

Carey hadn't hardly finished whisperin' when Ike got up and pulled it:

"Well, good night, boys," he says. "I ain't sleepy, but I got some gravel in my shoes and it's killin' my feet."

We knowed he hadn't never left the hotel since we'd came in from the grounds and changed our clo'es. So Carey says:

"I should think they'd take them gravel pits out o' the billiard room."

But Ike was already on his way to the elevator, limpin'.

"He's got the world beat," says Carey to Jack and I. "I've knew lots o' guys that had an alibi for every mistake they made; I've heard pitchers say that the ball slipped when somebody cracked one off'n 'em; I've heard infielders complain of a sore arm after heavin' one into the stand, and I've saw outfielders tooken sick with a dizzy spell when they've misjudged a fly ball. But this baby can't even go to bed without apologizin', and I bet he excuses himself to the razor when he gets ready to shave."

"And at that," says Jack, "he's goin' to make us a good man."

"Yes," says Carey, "unless rheumatism keeps his battin' average down to .400."

Well, sir, Ike kept whalin' away at the ball all through the trip till everybody knowed he'd won a job. Cap had him in there regular the last few exhibition games and told the newspaper boys a week before the season opened that he was goin' to start him in Kane's place.

"You're there, kid," says Carey to Ike, the night Cap made the 'nnouncement. "They ain't many boys that wins a big league berth their third year out."

"I'd of been up here a year ago," says Ike, "only I was bent over all season with lumbago."

2

It rained down in Cincinnati one day and somebody organized a little game o' cards. They was shy two men to make six and ast I and Carey to play.

"I'm with you if you get Ike and make it seven-handed," says Carey.

So they got a hold of Ike and we went up to Smitty's room.

"I pretty near forgot how many you deal," says Ike. "It's been a long wile since I played."

I and Carey give each other the wink, and sure enough, he was just as ig'orant about poker as billiards. About the second hand, the pot was opened two or three ahead of him, and they was three in when it come his turn. It cost a buck, and he throwed in two.

"It's raised, boys," somebody says.

"Gosh, that's right, I did raise it," says Ike.

"Take out a buck if you didn't mean to tilt her," says Carey.

"No," says Ike, "I'll leave it go."

Well, it was raised back at him and then he made another mistake and raised again. They was only three left in when the draw come. Smitty'd opened with a pair o' kings and he didn't help 'em. Ike stood pat. The guy that'd raised him back was flushin' and he didn't fill. So Smitty checked and Ike bet and didn't get no call. He tossed his hand away, but I grabbed it and give it a look. He had king, queen, jack and two tens. Alibi Ike he must have seen me peekin', for he leaned over and whispered to me.

"I overlooked my hand," he says. "I thought all the wile it was a straight."

"Yes," I says, "that's why you raised twice by mistake."

They was another pot that he come into with tens and fours. It was tilted a couple o' times and two o' the strong fellas drawed ahead of Ike. They each drawed one. So Ike throwed away his little pair and come out with four tens. And they was four treys against him. Carey'd looked at Ike's discards and then he says:

"This lucky bum busted two pair."

"No, no, I didn't," says Ike.

"Yes, yes, you did," says Carey, and showed us the two fours.

"What do you know about that?" says Ike. "I'd of swore one was a five spot."

Well, we hadn't had no pay day yet, and after a wile everybody except Ike was goin' shy. I could see him gettin' restless and I was wonderin' how he'd make the get-away. He tried two or three times. "I got to buy some collars before supper," he says.

"No hurry," says Smitty. "The stores here keeps open all night in April."

After a minute he opened up again.

"My uncle out in Nebraska ain't expected to live," he says. "I ought to send a telegram."

"Would that save him?" says Carey.

"No, it sure wouldn't," says Ike, "but I ought to leave my old man know where I'm at."

"When did you hear about your uncle?" says Carey.

"Just this mornin'," says Ike.

"Who told you?" ast Carey.

"I got a wire from my old man," says Ike.

"Well," says Carey, "your old man knows you're still here yet this afternoon if you was here this mornin'. Trains leavin' Cincinnati in the middle o' the day don't carry no ball clubs."

"Yes," says Ike, "that's true. But he don't know where I'm goin' to be next week."

"Ain't he got no schedule?" ast Carey.

"I sent him one openin' day," says Ike. "But it takes mail a long time to get to Idaho."

"I thought your old man lived in Kansas City," says Carey.

"He does when he's home," says Ike.

"But now," says Carey, "I s'pose he's went to Idaho so as he can be near your sick uncle in Nebraska."

"He's visitin' my other uncle in Idaho."

"Then how does he keep posted about your sick uncle?" ast Carey.

"He don't," says Ike. "He don't even know my other uncle's sick. That's why I ought to wire and tell him."

"Good night!" says Carey.

"What town in Idaho is your old man at?" I says.

Ike thought it over.

"No town at all," he says. "But he's near a town."

"Near what town?" I says.

"Yuma," says Ike.

Well, by this time he'd lost two or three pots and he was desperate. We was playin' just as fast as we could, because we seen we couldn't hold him much longer. But he was tryin' so hard to frame an escape that he couldn't pay no attention to the cards, and it looked like we'd get his whole pile away from him if we could make him stick.

The telephone saved him. The minute it begun to ring, five of us jumped for it. But Ike was there first.

"Yes," he says, answerin' it. "This is him. I'll come right down."

And he slammed up the receiver and beat it out o' the door without even sayin' good-bye.

"Smitty'd ought to locked the door," says Carey.

"What did he win?" ast Carey.

We figured it up—sixty-odd bucks.

"And the next time we ask him to play," says Carey, "his fingers will be so stiff he can't hold the cards."

Well, we set round a wile talkin' it over, and pretty soon the telephone rung again. Smitty answered it. It was a friend of his'n from Hamilton and he wanted to know why Smitty didn't hurry down. He was the one that had called before and Ike had told him he was Smitty.

"Ike'd ought to split with Smitty's friend," says Carey.

"No," I says, "He'll need all he won. It costs money to buy collars and to send telegrams from Cincinnati to your old man in Texas and keep him posted on the health o' your uncle in Cedar Rapids, D.C."

3

And you ought to heard him out there on that field! They wasn't a day when he didn't pull six or seven, and it didn't make no difference whether he was goin' good or bad. If he popped up in the pinch he should of made a base hit and the reason he didn't was so-and-so. And if he cracked one for three bases he ought to had a home run, only the ball wasn't lively, or the wind brought it back, or he tripped on a lump o' dirt, roundin' first base.

They was one afternoon in New York when he beat all records. Big Marquard was workin' against us and he was good.

In the first innin' Ike hit one clear over that right field stand, but it was a few feet foul. Then he got another foul and then the count come to two and two. Then Rube slipped one acrost on him and he was called out.

"What do you know about that!" he says afterward on the bench. "I lost count. I thought it was three and one, and I took a strike."

"You took a strike all right," says Carey. "Even the umps knowed it was a strike."

"Yes," says Ike, "but you can bet I wouldn't of took it if I'd knew it was the third one. The score board had it wrong."

"That score board ain't for you to look at," says Cap. "It's for you to hit that old pill against."

"Well, says Ike, "I could of hit that one over the score board if I'd knew it was the third."

"Was it a good ball?" I says.

"Well, no, it wasn't," says Ike. "It was inside."

"How far inside?" says Carey.

"Oh, two or three inches or half a foot," says Ike.

"I guess you wouldn't of threatened the score board with it then," says Cap.

"I'd of pulled it down the right foul line if I hadn't thought he'd call it a ball," says Ike.

Well, in New York's part o' the innin' Doyle cracked one and Ike run back a mile and a half and caught it with one hand. We was all sayin' what a whale of a play it was, but he had to apologize just the same as for gettin' struck out.

"That stand's so high," he says, "that a man don't never see a ball till it's right on top o' you."

"Didn't you see that one?" ast Cap.

"Not at first," says Ike; "not till it raised up above the roof o' the stand."

"Then why did you start back as soon as the ball was hit?" says Cap.

"I knowed by the sound that he'd got a good hold of it," says Ike.

"Yes," says Cap, "but how'd you know what direction to run in?"

"Doyle usually hits 'em that way, the way I run," says Ike.

"Why don't you play blindfolded?" says Carey.

"Might as well, with that big high stand to bother a man," says Ike. "If I could of saw the ball all the time I'd of got it in my hip pocket."

Along in the fifth we was one run to the bad and Ike got on with one out. On the first ball throwed to Smitty, Ike went down. The ball was outside and Meyers throwed Ike out by ten feet.

You could see Ike's lips movin' all the way to the bench and when he got there he had his piece learned.

"Why didn't he swing?" he says.

"Why didn't you wait for his sign?" says Cap.

"He give me his sign," says Ike.

"What is his sign with you?" says Cap.

"Pickin' up some dirt with his right hand," says Ike.

"Well, I didn't see him do it," Cap says.

"He done it all right," says Ike.

Well, Smitty went out and they wasn't no more argument till they come in for the next innin'. Then Cap opened it up.

"You fellas better get your signs straight," he says.

"Do you mean me?" says Smitty.

"Yes," Cap says. "What's your sign with Ike?"

"Slidin' my left hand up to the end o' the bat and back," says Smitty.

"Do you hear that, Ike?" ast Cap.

"What of it?" says Ike.

"You says his sign was pickin' up dirt and he says it's slidin' his hand. Which is right?"

"I'm right," says Smitty. "But if you're arguin' about him goin' last innin', I didn't give him no sign."

"You pulled your cap down with your right hand, didn't you?" ast Ike.

"Well, s'pose I did," says Smitty. "That don't mean nothin'. I never told you to take that for a sign, did I?"

"I thought maybe you meant to tell me and forgot," says Ike.

They couldn't none of us answer that and they wouldn't of been no more said if Ike had of shut up. But wile we was settin' there Carey got on with two out and stole second clean.

"There!" says Ike. "That's what I was tryin' to do and I'd of got away with it if Smitty's swang and bothered the Indian."

"Oh!" says Smitty. "You was tryin' to steal then, was you? I thought you claimed I give you the hit and run."

"I didn't claim no such a thing," says Ike. "I thought maybe you might of gave me a sign, but I was goin' anyway because I thought I had a good start."

Cap prob'ly would of hit him with a bat, only just about that time Doyle booted one on Hayes and Carey come acrost with the run that tied.

Well, we go into the ninth finally, one and one, and Marquard walks McDonald with nobody out.

"Lay it down," says Cap to Ike.

And Ike goes up there with orders to bunt and cracks the first ball into that right-field stand! It was fair this time, and we're two ahead, but I didn't think about that at the time. I was too busy watchin' Cap's face. First he turned pale and then he got red as fire and then he got blue and purple, and finally he just laid back and busted out laughin'. So we wasn't afraid to laugh ourself when we seen him doin' it, and when Ike come in everybody on the bench was in hysterics.

But instead o' takin' advantage, Ike had to try and excuse himself. His play was to shut up and he didn't know how to make it.

"Well," he says, "if I hadn't hit quite so quick at that one I bet it'd of cleared the center-field fence."

Cap stopped laughin'.

"It'll cost you plain fifty," he says.

"What for?" says Ike.

"When I say 'bunt' I mean 'bunt,' " says Cap.

"You didn't say 'bunt,' " says Ike.

"I says 'Lay it down,' " says Cap. "If that don't mean 'bunt,' what does it mean?"

" 'Lay it down' means 'bunt' all right," says Ike, "but I understood you to say 'Lay on it.' "

"All right," says Cap, "and the little misunderstandin' will cost you fifty."

Ike didn't say nothin' for a few minutes. Then he had another bright idear.

"I was just kiddin' about misunderstandin' you," he says. "I knowed you wanted me to bunt."

"Well, then, why didn't you bunt?" ast Cap.

"I was goin' to on the next ball," says Ike. "But I thought if I took a good wallop I'd have 'em all fooled. So I walloped at the first one to fool 'em, and I didn't have no intention o' hittin' it."

"You tried to miss it, did you?" says Cap.

"Yes," says Ike.

"How'd you happen to hit it?" ast Cap.

"Well," Ike says, "I was lookin' for him to throw me a fast one and I was goin' to swing under it. But he come with a hook and I met it right square where I was swingin' to go under the fast one."

"Great!" says Cap. "Boys," he says, "Ike's learned how to hit Marquard's curve. Pretend a fast one's comin' and then try to miss it. It's a good thing to know and Ike'd ought to be willin' to pay for the lesson. So I'm goin' to make it a hundred instead o' fifty."

The game wound up 3 to 1. The fine didn't go, because Ike hit like a wild man all through that trip and we made pretty near a clean-up. The night we went to Philly I got him cornered in the car and I says to him:

"Forget them alibis for a wile and tell me somethin'. What'd you do that for, swing that time against Marquard when you was told to bunt?"

"I'll tell you," he says. "That ball he throwed me looked just like the one I struck out on in the first innin' and I wanted to show Cap what I could of done to that other one if I'd knew it was the third strike."

"But," I says, "the one you struck out on in the first innin' was a fast ball."

"So was the one I cracked in the ninth," says Ike.

4

You've saw Cap's wife, o' course. Well, her sister's about twict as good-lookin' as her, and that's goin' some.

Cap took his missus down to St. Louis the second trip and the other one come down from St. Joe to visit her. Her name is Dolly, and some doll is right.

Well, Cap was goin' to take the two sisters to a show and he wanted a beau for Dolly. He left it to her and she picked Ike. He'd hit three on the nose that afternoon—off'n Sallee, too.

They fell for each other that first evenin'. Cap told us how it come off. She begin flatterin' Ike for the star game he'd played and o' course he begin excusin' himself for not doin' better. So she thought he was modest and it went strong with her. And she believed everything he said and that made her solid with him—that and her make-up. They was together every mornin' and evenin' for the five days we was there. In the afternoons Ike played the grandest ball you ever see, hittin' and runnin' the bases like a fool and catchin' everything that stayed in the park.

I told Cap, I says: "You'd ought to keep the doll with us and he'd make Cobb's figures look sick."

But Dolly had to go back to St. Joe and we come home for a long serious.

Well, for the next three weeks Ike had a letter to read every day and he'd set in the clubhouse readin' it till mornin' practice was half over. Cap didn't say nothin' to him, because he was goin' so good. But I and Carey wasted a lot of our time tryin' to get him to own up who the letters was from. Fine chanct!

"What are you readin'?" Carey'd say. "A bill?"

"No," Ike'd say, "not exactly a bill. It's a letter from a fella I used to go to school with."

"High school or college?" I'd ask him.

"College," he'd say.

Then he'd stall a wile and then he'd say:

"I didn't go to the college myself, but my friend went there."

"How did it happen you didn't go?" Carey'd ask him.

"Well," he'd say, "they wasn't no colleges near where I lived."

"Didn't you live in Kansas City?" I'd say to him.

One time he'd say he did and another time he didn't. One time he says he lived in Michigan.

"Where at?" says Carey.

"Near Detroit," he says.

"Well," I says, "Detroit's near Ann Arbor and that's where they got the university."

"Yes," says Ike, "they got it there now, but they didn't have it there then."

"I come pretty near goin' to Syracuse," I says, "only they wasn't no railroads runnin' through there in them days."

"Where'd this friend o' yours go to college?" says Carey.

"I forget now," says Ike.

"Was it Carlisle?" ast Carey.

"No," says Ike. "His folks wasn't very well off."

"That's what barred me from Smith," I says.

"I was goin' to tackle Cornell's," says Carey, "but the doctor told me I'd have hay fever if I didn't stay up North."

"Your friend writes long letters," I says.

"Yes," says Ike; "he's tellin' me about a ballplayer."

"Where does he play?" ast Carey.

"Down in the Texas League—Fort Wayne," says Ike.

"It looks like a girl's writin'," Carey says.

"A girl wrote it," says Ike. "That's my friend's sister, writin' for him."

"Didn't they teach writin' at this here college where he went?" says Carey.

"Sure," Ike says, "they taught writin', but he got his hand cut off in a railroad wreck."

"How long ago?" I says.

"Right after he got out o' college," says Ike.

"Well," I says, "I should think he'd of learned to write with his left hand by this time."

"It's his left hand that was cut off," says Ike; "and he was left-handed."

"You get a letter every day," says Carey. "They're all the same writin'. Is he tellin' you about a different ball player every time he writes?"

"No," Ike says. "It's the same ball player. He just tells me what he does every day."

"From the size o' the letters, they don't play nothin' but doubleheaders down there," says Carey.

We figured that Ike spent most of his evenin's answerin' the letters from his "friend's sister," so we kept tryin' to date him up for shows and parties to see how he'd duck out of 'em. He was bugs over spaghetti, so we told him one day that they was goin' to be a big feed of it over to Joe's that night and he was invited.

"How long'll it last?" he says.

"Well," we says, "we're goin' right over there after the game and stay till they close up."

"I can't go," he says, "unless they leave me come home at eight bells."

"Nothin' doin'," says Carey. "Joe'd get sore."

"I can't go then," says Ike.

"Why not?" I ast him.

"Well," he says, "my landlady locks up the house at eight and I left my key home."

"You can come and stay with me," says Carey.

"No," he says, "I can't sleep in a strange bed."

"How do you get along when we're on the road?" says I.

"I don't never sleep the first night anywheres," he says. "After that I'm all right."

"You'll have time to chase home and get your key right after the game," I told him.

"The key ain't home," says Ike. "I lent it to one o' the other fellas and he's went out o' town and took it with him."

"Couldn't you borry another key off'n the landlady?" Carey ast him.

"No," he says, "that's the only one they is."

Well, the day before we started East again, Ike come into the club-house all smiles.

"Your birthday?" I ast him.

"No," he says.

"What do you feel so good about?" I says.

"Got a letter from my old man," he says. "My uncle's goin' to get well."

"Is that the one in Nebraska?" says I.

"Not right in Nebraska," says Ike. "Near there."

But afterwards we got the right dope from Cap. Dolly'd blew in from Missouri and was goin' to make the trip with her sister.

5

Well, I want to alibi Carey and I for what come off in Boston. If we'd of had any idear what we was doin', we'd never did it. They wasn't nobody outside o' maybe Ike and the dame that felt worse over it than I and Carey.

The first two days we didn't see nothin' of Ike and her except out to the park. The rest o' the time they was sight-seein' over to Cambridge and down to Revere and out to Brook-a-line and all the other places where the rubes go.

But when we come into the beanery after the third game Cap's wife called us over.

"If you want to see somethin' pretty," she says, "look at the third finger on Sis's left hand."

Well, o' course we knowed before we looked that it wasn't goin' to be no hangnail. Nobody was su'prised when Dolly blew into the dinin' room with it—a rock that Ike'd bought off'n Diamond Joe the first trip to New York City. Only o' course it'd been set into a lady's-size ring instead o' the automobile tire he'd been wearin'.

Cap and his missus and Ike and Dolly ett supper together, only Ike didn't eat nothin', but just set there blushin' and spillin' things on the table-cloth. I heard him excusin' himself for not havin' no appetite. He says he couldn't never eat when he was clost to the ocean. He'd forgot about them sixty-five oysters he destroyed the first night o' the trip before.

He was goin' to take her to a show, so after supper he went upstairs to change his collar. She had to doll up, too, and o 'course Ike was through long before her.

If you remember the hotel in Boston, they's a little parlor where the piano's at and then they's another little parlor openin' off o' that. Well, when Ike come down Smitty was playin' a few chords and I and Carey was harmonizin'. We seen Ike go up to the desk to leave his key and we called him in. He tried to duck away, but we wouldn't stand for it.

We ast him what he was all duded up for and he says he was goin' to the theayter.

"Goin' alone?" says Carey.

"No," he says, "a friend o' mine's goin' with me."

"What do you say if we go along?" says Carey.

"I ain't only got two tickets," he says.

"Well," says Carey, "we can go down there with you and buy our own seats; maybe we can all go together."

"No," says Ike. "They ain't no more seats. They're all sold out."

"We can buy some off'n the scalpers," says Carey.

"I wouldn't if I was you," says Ike. "They say the show's rotten."

"What are you goin' for, then?" I ast.

"I didn't hear about it bein' rotten till I got the tickets," he says.

"Well," I says, "if you don't want to go I'll buy the tickets from you."

"No," says Ike, "I wouldn't want to cheat you. I'm stung and I'll just have to stand for it."

"What are you goin' to do with the girl, leave her here at the hotel?"

"What girl?" says Ike.

"The girl you ett supper with," I says.

"Oh," he says, "we just happened to go into the dinin' room together, that's all. Cap wanted I should set down with 'em."

"I noticed," says Carey, "that she happened to be wearin' that rock you bought off'n Diamond Joe."

"Yes," says Ike. "I lent it to her for a wile."

"Did you lend her the new ring that goes with it?" I says.

"She had that already," says Ike. "She lost the set out of it."

"I wouldn't trust no strange girl with a rock o'mine," says Carey.

"Oh, I guess she's all right," Ike says. "Besides, I was tired o' the stone. When a girl asks you for somethin', what are you goin' to do?"

He started out toward the desk, but we flagged him.

"Wait a minute!" Carey says. "I got a bet with Sam here, and it's up to you to settle it."

"Well," says Ike, "make it snappy. My friend'll be here any minute."

"I bet," says Carey, "that you and that girl was engaged to be married."

"Nothin to it," says Ike.

"Now look here," says Carey, "this is goin' to cost me real money if I lose. Cut out the alibi stuff and give it to us straight. Cap's wife just as good as told us you was roped."

Ike blushed like a kid.

"Well, boys," he says, "I may as well own up. You win, Carey."

"Yatta boy!" says Carey. "Congratulations!"

"You got a swell girl, Ike," I says.

"She's a peach," says Smitty.

"Well, I guess she's OK," says Ike. "I don't know much about girls."

"Didn't you never run round with 'em?" I says.

"Oh, yes, plenty of 'em," says Ike. "But I never seen none I'd fall for."

"That is, till you seen this one," says Carey.

"Well," says Ike, "this one's OK, but I wasn't thinkin' about gettin' married for a wile."

"Who done the askin'—her?" says Carey.

"O, no," says Ike, "but sometimes a man don't know what he's gettin' into. Take a good-lookin' girl, and a man gen'ally almost always does about what she wants him to."

"They couldn't no girl lasso me unless I wanted to be lassoed," says Smitty.

"Oh, I don't know," says Ike. "When a fella gets to feelin' sorry for one of 'em it's all off."

Well, we left him go after shakin' hands all round. But he didn't take Dolly to no show that night. Some time while we was talkin' she'd come into that other parlor and she'd stood there and heard us. I don't know how much she heard. But it was enough. Dolly and Cap's missus took the midnight train for New York. And from there Cap's wife sent her on her way back to Missouri.

She'd left the ring and a note for Ike with the clerk. But we didn't ask Ike if the note was from his friend in Fort Wayne, Texas.

6

When we'd came to Boston Ike was hittin' plain .397. When we got back home he'd fell off to pretty near nothin'. He hadn't drove one out o' the infield in any o' them other Eastern parks, and he didn't even give no excuse for it.

To show you how bad he was, he struck out three times in Brooklyn one day and never opened his trap when Cap ast him what was the matter. Before, if he'd whiffed oncet in a game he'd of wrote a book tellin' why.

Well, we dropped from first place to fifth in four weeks and we was still goin' down. I and Carey was about the only ones in the club that spoke to each other, and all as we did was remind ourself o' what a boner we'd pulled.

"It's goin' to beat us out o' the big money," says Carey.

"Yes," I says. "I don't want to knock my own ball club, but it looks like a one-man team, and when that one man's dauber's down we couldn't trim our whiskers."

"We ought to knew better," says Carey.

"Yes," I says, "but why should a man pull an alibi for bein' engaged to such a bearcat as she was?"

"He shouldn't," says Carey. "But I and you knowed he would or we'd never started talkin' to him about it. He wasn't no more ashamed o' the girl than I am of a regular base hit. But he just can't come clean on no subjec'."

Cap had the whole story, and I and Carey was as pop'lar with him as an umpire.

"What do you want me to do, Cap?" Carey'd say to him before goin' up to hit.

"Use your own judgment," Cap'd tell him. "We want to lose another game."

But finally, one night in Pittsburgh, Cap had a letter from his missus and he come to us with it.

"You fellas," he says, "is the ones that put us on the bum, and if you're sorry I think theys a chancet for you to make good. The old lady's out to St. Joe and she's been tryin' her hardest to fix things up. She's explained that Ike don't mean nothin' with his talk; I've wrote and explained that to Dolly, too. But the old lady says that Dolly says that she can't believe it. But Dolly's still stuck on this baby, and she's pinin' away just the same as Ike. And the old lady says she thinks if you two fellas would write to the girl and explain how you was always kiddin' with Ike and leadin' him on, and how the ball club was all shot to pieces since Ike quit hittin', and how he acted like he was goin' to kill himself, and this and that, she'd fall for it and maybe soften down. Dolly, the old lady says, would believe you before she'd believe I and the old lady, because she thinks it's her we're sorry for, and not him."

Well, I and Carey was only too glad to try and see what we could do. But it wasn't no snap. We wrote about eight letters before we got one that looked good. Then we give it to the stenographer and had it wrote out on a typewriter and both of us signed it.

It was Carey's idear that made the letter good. He stuck in somethin' about the world's serious money that our wives wasn't goin' to spend unless she took pity on a "boy who was so shy and modest that he was afraid to come right out and say that he had asked such a beautiful and handsome girl to become his bride."

That's prob'ly what got her, or maybe she couldn't of held out much longer anyway. It was four days after we sent the letter that Cap heard from his missus again. We was in Cincinnati.

"We've won," he says to us. "The old lady says that Dolly says she'll give him another chance. But the old lady says it won't do no good for Ike to write a letter. He'll have to go out there."

"Send him tonight," says Carey.

"I'll pay half his fare," I says.

"I'll pay the other half," says Carey.

"No," says Cap, "the club'll pay his expenses. I'll send him scoutin'."

"Are you goin' to send him tonight?"

"Sure," says Cap. "But I'm goin' to break the news to him right now. It's time we win a ball game."

So in the clubhouse, just before the game, Cap told him. And I certainly felt sorry for Rube Benton and Red Ames that afternoon! I and Carey was standin' in front o' the hotel that night when Ike come out with his suitcase.

"Sent home?" I says to him.

"No," he says, "I'm goin' scoutin'."

"Where to?" I says. "Fort Wayne?"

"No, not exactly," he says.

"Well," says Carey, "have a good time."

"I ain't lookin' for no good time," says Ike. "I says I was goin' scoutin'."

"Well, then," says Carey, "I hope you see somebody you like."

·"And you better have a drink before you go," I says.

"Well," says Ike, "they claim it helps a cold."

Ty Cobb's Wild Ten-Month Fight to Live

AL STUMP

In 1960, Ty Cobb designated Al Stump (1916–1995) to be the ghost of his memoirs. For the next year, Stump held on for dear life as the ornery, ailing Cobb regularly exploded. Stump finished the book—*My Life in Baseball: The True Record*—just before Cobb's death. It was a whitewash from cover to cover. Cobb had wrangled final approval over everything, and Cobb, being Cobb, invoked it spikes high.

Stump had the last word, though. Twice.

Not long after Cobb's death, *True* magazine published Stump's spellbinding saga of life with the Georgia Peach. Then, in 1994, he set the rest of the True Record straight with the publication of *Cobb,* one of the best sports biographies ever written. In that same year, Ron Shelton, who's featured elsewhere in these pages, adapted *Ty Cobb's Wild Ten-Month Fight to Live* into the movie *Cobb,* with Tommy Lee Jones in the title role, and Robert Wuhl as Al Stump. You can catch a glimpse of the real Stump in a cinema verite cameo sitting at the bar.

During his long career, Stump's byline appeared regularly in *Esquire, Colliers, Sports Illustrated, Sport* and the *Saturday Evening Post,* and he wrote four books. In the 1970s, he covered the Charles Manson murder trial for my old paper, *The Los Angeles Herald Examiner,* where his wife, Jo Mosher, was the travel editor during my own adventures as a Hollywood columnist some years later.

Ever since sundown in the Sierra range, Nevada intermountain radio had been crackling warnings: "Route 50 now highly dangerous. Motorists stay off. Repeat: AVOID ROUTE 50."

By 1:00 A.M. the twenty-one-mile, steep-pitched passage from Lake Tahoe's sixty-eight-hundred-foot altitude into Carson City, a snaky grade most of the way, was snow-struck, ice-sheeted, thick with rock slides, and declared unfit for all transport vehicles by the State Highway Patrol.

It was right down Ty Cobb's alley. Anything that smacked of the apparently impossible brought an unholy gleam to his eye. The gleam had been there in 1959 when a series of lawyers advised Cobb that he stood no chance in court against the Sovereign State of California in a dispute over income taxes, whereupon he bellowed defiance and sued the state for sixty thousand dollars plus damages. It had been there more recently when doctors warned that liquor would kill him. From a pint of whiskey per day he upped his consumption to a quart and more.

Sticking out his grizzled chin, he had told me, "I think we'll take a little run into town tonight."

A blizzard rattled the windows of Cobb's luxurious hunting lodge on the eastern crest of Lake Tahoe, but to forbid him anything—even at the age of seventy-three—was to tell an ancient tiger not to snarl. Cobb was both the greatest of all ballplayers and a multimillionaire whose monthly income from stock dividends, rents, and interest ran to twelve thousand dollars. And he was a man contemptuous of any law other than his own.

"We'll drive in," he announced, "and shoot some craps, see a show, and say hello to Joe DiMaggio—he's in Reno at the Riverside Hotel."

I looked at him and felt a chill. Cobb, sitting there haggard and unshaven in his pajamas and a fuzzy old green bathrobe at one o'clock in the morning, wasn't fooling.

"Let's not," I said. "You shouldn't be anywhere but in bed."

"Don't argue with me!" he barked. "There are fee-simple sons of bitches all over the country who've tried it and wished they hadn't." He glared at me, flaring the whites of his eyes the way he'd done for twenty-four years at quaking pitchers, basemen, umpires, fans, and sportswriters.

"If you and I are going to get along," he went on ominously, "*don't increase my tension.*"

It was the winter of 1960. We were alone in his isolated, ten-room lakeside lodge—bearskin floor rugs, mounted game trophies on walls—with a lot of work to do. We'd arrived six days earlier, loaded with a large smoked ham, a twenty-pound turkey, a case of scotch, and another of champagne, for the purpose of collaborating on Ty's autobiography, a book that he'd refused to write for more than thirty years but had suddenly decided to publish before he died. In almost a week's time we hadn't accomplished thirty minutes' worth of work.

The reason: Cobb didn't need a high-risk auto trip into Reno, but immediate hospitalization, and through the emergency-room entrance. He was desperately ill, and had been so even before we left California.

We had traveled 250 miles to Tahoe in Cobb's black Imperial limousine, carrying with us a virtual drugstore of medicines. These included digoxin (for his leaky heart), Darvon (for his aching back), Tace (for a recently operated-upon malignancy of the pelvic area), Fleet's Compound (for his impacted bowels), Librium (for his "tension"—that is, his violent rages), codeine (for his pain), and an insulin needle-and-syringe kit (for his diabetes), among a dozen other panaceas that he'd substituted for ongoing medical care. Cobb hated doctors. "When they meet an undertaker on the street," he said, "the boys wink at each other."

His sense of balance was precarious. He tottered about the lodge, moving from place to place by grasping the furniture. On a public street, he couldn't navigate twenty feet without clutching my shoulder, leaning most of his 208 pounds upon me and shuffling along with a spraddle-legged gait. His bowels wouldn't work, a near-total stoppage that brought groans of agony from Cobb when he sought relief. He was feverish. There was no one at the Tahoe hideaway but the two of us to treat his critical condition.

Everything that hurts had caught up with his six-foot, one-inch body at once, and he plied himself with pink, green, orange, yellow, and purple pills—often guessing at the amounts, since labels had peeled off some of the bottles. But he wouldn't hear of hospitalizing himself.

"The hacksaw artists have taken fifty thousand dollars from me," he said, "and they'll get no more." He spoke of a "quack" who'd treated him a few years earlier. "The joker got funny and said he found urine in my whiskey. I fired him."

His diabetes required a precise food-insulin balance. Cobb's needle wouldn't work. He misplaced the directions for his daily insulin dosage and his hands shook uncontrollably when he went to plunge the needle into his abdominal wall. He spilled more of the stuff than he injected.

He'd been warned by experts, from Johns Hopkins to California's Scripps Clinic, that liquor was deadly for him. Tyrus snorted and began each day with several gin and orange juices, then switched to "buzzers" of Old Rarity scotch, which held him until the night hours when sleep was impossible, and he tossed down cognac, champagne, or "Cobb cocktails"—Southern Comfort stirred into hot water and honey.

A careful diet was essential. Cobb wouldn't eat. The lodge was without a cook or other help—in the previous six months, he had fired two cooks, a male nurse, and a handyman in fits of anger—and any food I prepared for him he nibbled at, then pushed away. As of the night of the blizzard, the failing, splenetic old monarch of baseball hadn't touched solid food in three days, existing almost solely on quarts of booze and mixers.

My reluctance to prepare the car for the Reno trip burned him up. He beat his fists on the arms of his easy chair. "I'll go alone!" he threatened.

I was certain he'd try. The storm had worsened, but once Cobb set his mind on an idea, nothing could alter it. Beyond that, I'd already found that to oppose or annoy him was to risk a fierce explosion. An event of a week earlier had proved that point. It was then that I discovered he carried a loaded Luger wherever he went, looking for opportunities to use it.

En route to Lake Tahoe, we'd stopped overnight at a motel near Hangtown, California. During the night a party of drunks made a loud commotion in the parking lot. In my room adjacent to Cobb's I heard him cursing and then his voice, booming out the window.

"Get out of here, you——heads!"

The drunks replied in kind. Groping his way to the door, Cobb fired three shots into the dark that resounded like cannon claps. Screams and yells followed. Reaching my door, I saw the drunks climbing one another's backs in their rush to flee. The frightened motel manager, and others, arrived. Before anyone could think of calling the police, the manager was cut down by the most caustic tongue ever heard in a baseball clubhouse.

"What kind of pesthouse is this!" roared Cobb. "Who gave you a license, you mugwump? Get the hell out of here and see that I'm not disturbed! I'm a sick man and I want it quiet!"

"B-b-beg your pardon, Mr. Cobb," the manager said feebly. He apparently felt so honored to have as a customer the national game's most exalted figure that no cops were called. When we drove away the next morning, a crowd gathered and stood gawking with expressions of disbelief.

Down the highway, with me driving, Cobb checked the Luger and reloaded its nine-shell clip. "Two of those shots were in the air," he remarked. "The third kicked up gravel. I've got permits for this gun from governors of three states. I'm honorary deputy sheriff of California and a Texas Ranger. So we won't be getting any complaints."

He saw nothing strange in his behavior. Ty Cobb's rest had been disturbed; therefore, he had every right to shoot up the neighborhood.

At about that moment I began to develop a nervous twitch, which grew worse in about the time it takes to say Grover Cleveland Alexander of the Philadelphia Phillies. I'd heard reports of Cobb's weird and violent ways without giving them much credence. Until early 1960 my own experience with the legendary Georgia Peach had been slight, amounting mainly to meetings in Scottsdale, Arizona, and New York to discuss book-writing arrangements and to sign the contract.

Locker-room stories of Ty's eccentricities, wild temper, wars with his own teammates, egotism, and miserliness sounded like the usual scandal-mongering you get in sports. I'd heard that Cobb had flattened a heckler in San Francisco's Domino Club with one punch; that he had been sued by Elbie Felts, an ex–Coast League player, after assaulting him; that he booby-trapped his main home, a Spanish-mission villa at Atherton, California, with high-voltage wires; that he'd walloped his ex-wives; that he'd been jailed in Placerville, California, at the age of sixty-eight for speeding, abusing a traffic cop, and then inviting the judge to return to law school at his, Cobb's, expense.

I passed these things off. The one and only Ty Cobb wished to write his memoirs, and I felt distinctly honored to be named his collaborator. As the poet Cowper reflected, "The innocents are gay." I was eager to start. Then a few weeks before the book work began, I was taken aside and tipped off by an in-law of Cobb's and by one of Cobb's former teammates on the Detroit Tigers that I hadn't heard the half of it. "Back out of this book deal," they urged. "You'll never finish it and you might get hurt."

They went on: "Nobody can live with Ty. Nobody ever has. That includes two wives who left him, butlers, housekeepers, chauffeurs, nurses, and a few mistresses. He drove off all his friends long ago. Max Fleischmann, the yeast-cake heir, was a pal of Ty's until the night a house guest of Fleischmann's made a remark about Cobb spiking other players when he ran bases. The man only asked if it was true. Cobb knocked the guy into a fishpond and never spoke to him again. Another time, a member of Cobb's family crossed him—a woman, mind you. He broke her nose with a ball bat.

"Do you know about the butcher? Ty didn't like some fish he bought. In the fight, he broke up the butcher shop. Had to settle fifteen hundred dollars on the butcher out of court after going to jail. He had a gun in his possession at the time."

"But I'm dealing with him strictly on business," I said.

"So was the butcher," replied my informants.

"In baseball," the ex-teammate said, "a few of us who really knew him well realized that he was wrong in the head—unbalanced. He played like a demon and had everybody hating him because he *was* a demon. That's how he set all those records that nobody has come close to since 1928. It's why he was always in a brawl, on the field, in the clubhouse, behind the stands, in the stands, on the street. The public's never known it, but Cobb's always been off the beam where other people are concerned. Sure, he made millions in the stock market—but that's only cold dollars. He carried a gun wherever he went in the big league and scared hell out of us. He's mean, tricky, and dangerous. Look out he doesn't blow up some night and clip you with a bottle. He specializes in throwing bottles.

"Now that he's sick he's worse than ever. And you've signed up to stay with him for months. The time will come when you'll want to write in his book about the scandals and wild brannigans he was in—and he'll chop you down. Don't be a sucker."

Taken aback, but still skeptical, I launched the job. My first task was to drive Cobb to his Lake Tahoe retreat, where, he declared, we could work uninterrupted.

Everything went wrong from the start. The Hangtown gunplay incident was an eye-opener. Next came a series of events, among them Cobb's determination to set forth in a blizzard to Reno, which were too strange to explain away. Everything had to suit his pleasure, or else he threw a tantrum. He prowled about the lodge at night with the Luger in hand, suspecting trespassers (there had once been a break-in at the place). I slept with one eye open, ready to move fast if necessary.

Well past midnight that evening, full of pain and ninety-proof, he took out the Luger, letting it casually rest between his knees. I had continued to object to a Reno excursion in such weather.

He looked at me with tight fury and said, biting out the words, "In 1912—and you can write this down—I killed a man in Detroit. He and two other hoodlums jumped me on the street early one morning with a knife. I was carrying something that came in handy in my early days—a Belgian-made pistol with a heavy raised sight at the barrel end.

"Well, the damned gun wouldn't fire and they cut me up the back."

Making notes as fast as he talked, I asked, "Where in the back?"

"WELL, DAMMIT ALL TO HELL, IF YOU DON'T BELIEVE ME, COME AND LOOK!" Cobb flared, jerking up his shirt. When I protested that I believed him implicitly but only wanted a story detail, he picked up a half-full whiskey glass and smashed it against the brick fireplace. So I gingerly took a look. A faint whitish scar ran about six inches up his lower left back.

"Satisfied?" jeered Cobb.

He described how, after a battle, the men fled before his fists.

"What with you wounded and the odds three to one," I said, "that must have been a relief."

"Relief? Do you think they could pull that on *me?* I WENT AFTER THEM!"

Anyone else would have felt lucky to be out of it, but Cobb had chased one of the mugs into a dead-end alley. "I used that gun sight to rip and slash and tear him for about ten minutes until he had no face left," related Ty with relish. "Left him there, not breathing, in his own rotten blood."

"What was the situation—where were you going when it happened?"

"To catch a train to a ball game."

"You saw a doctor instead?"

"I DID NOTHING OF THE SORT, DAMMIT. I PLAYED THE NEXT DAY AND GOT THREE BASE HITS."

Records I later inspected bore out every word of it: on August 3, 1912, in a blood-soaked, makeshift bandage, Ty Cobb hit 2 doubles and a triple for Detroit, and only then was treated for the painful knife slash. He was that kind of ballplayer, through a record 3,033 games. No other pro athlete burned with Cobb's flame. Boze Bulger, a great old-time baseball critic, said, "He was possessed by the Furies."

Finishing his tale, Cobb looked me straight in the eye.

"*You are driving me into Reno tonight,*" he said softly. The Luger in his hand was dangling floorward.

Even before I opened my mouth, Cobb knew he'd won. He had an extra sense about the emotions he produced in others—in this case, fear. As far as I could see (lacking expert diagnosis and as a layman understands the symptoms), he wasn't merely erratic and trigger tempered, but suffering from megalomania, or acute self-worship, delusions of persecution, and more than a touch of dipsomania.

Although I'm not proud of it, he scared hell out of me most of the time I was around him.

And now Cobb gave me the first smile of our association. "To get along with me," he repeated softly, "*don't increase my tension.*"

Before describing the Reno expedition, I would like to say, in this frank view of a mighty man, that the most spectacular, enigmatic, and troubled of all American sport figures had his good side, which he tried his best to conceal. During the final ten months of his life I was his constant companion. Eventually I put him to bed, prepared his insulin, picked him up when he fell down, warded off irate taxi drivers, bill collectors, bartenders, waiters, clerks, and private citizens whom Cobb was inclined to punch, cooked what food he could digest, drew his bath, got drunk with him, and knelt with him in prayer on black nights when he knew death was near. I ducked a few bottles he threw, too.

I think, because he forced upon me a confession of his most private thoughts, along with details of his life, that I know the answer to the central, overriding secret of his life. Was Ty Cob psychotic throughout his baseball career? The answer is yes.

Kids, dogs, and sick people flocked to him and he returned their instinctive liking. Money was his idol, but from his approximate $12 million fortune he assigned large sums to create the Cobb Educational Fund, which financed hundreds of needy youngsters through college. He built and endowed a first-class hospital for the poor of his backwater hometown, Royston, Georgia. When Ty's spinster sister, Florence, was crippled, he tenderly cared for her until her last days. The widow of a one-time American League batting champion would have lived in want but for Ty's steady financial support. A Hall of Fame catcher, beaned by a pitched ball and enfeebled, came under Cobb's wing for years. Regularly he mailed dozens of anonymous checks to indigent old ballplayers (relayed by a third party)—a rare act among retired tycoons in other lines of business.

If you believe such acts didn't come hard for Cobb, table the thought. He was the world's champion pinchpenny.

Some 150 fan letters reached him monthly, requesting his autograph. Many letters enclosed return-mail stamps. Cobb used the stamps for his own outgoing mail. The fan letters he burned. "Saves on firewood," he muttered.

In December of 1960, Ty hired a one-armed "gentleman's gentleman" named E. Anthony Brown. Although steadily criticized, poor Brownie worked hard as cook and butler. But when he mixed up a grocery order one day, he was fired, given a check for the week's pay—forty-five dollars—and sent packing.

Came the middle of that night and Cobb awakened me.

"We're driving into town *right now*," he stated, "to stop payment on Brownie's check. The bastard talked back to me when I discharged him. He'll get no more of my money."

All remonstrations were futile. There was no phone, so we had to drive from Cobb's Tahoe lodge into Carson City, where he woke up the president of the First National Bank of Nevada and arranged for a stop-pay on a piddling check. The president tried to conceal his irritation; Cobb was a big depositor in his bank.

"Yes, sir, Ty," he said. "I'll take care of it first thing in the morning."

"You goddamn well better," snorted Cobb. And then we drove through the 3:00 A.M. darkness back to the lake.

But this jaunt was a light workout compared to the treacherous Reno trip he now directed we make.

Two cars were available at the lodge. Cobb's 1956 Imperial had no tire chains; the other buggy was equipped for snow driving.

"We'll need both cars for this operation," he ordered. "One car might break down. I'll drive mine, you take the one with chains. You go first. I'll follow your chain marks."

For Cobb to tackle precipitous Route 50 was unthinkable. The Tahoe road, with its two-hundred-foot drop-offs, had killed a record eighty motorists. Along with his illness, drunkenness, and no chains, he had weak eyes and was without a driver's license. California had turned him down at his last test; he hadn't bothered to apply in Nevada.

Urging him to ride with me was a waste of breath, however.

A howling wind hit my Buick a solid blow as we shoved off. Sleet stuck to the windshield faster than the wipers could clear it. For the first three miles, snowplows had been active, and at fifteen miles per hour, in second gear, I managed to hold the road. But then came Spooner's Summit, 6,900 feet high, and beyond it a steep descent of nine miles. Behind me, headlamps blinking, Cobb honked his horn, demanding more speed. Chainless, he wasn't getting traction. *The hell with him,* I thought. Slowing to low gear, fighting to hold a roadbed I couldn't see even with my head stuck out the window, I skidded along. No other traffic was on the road that night as we did our crazy tandem around icy curves, at times brushing the guardrails. Cobb was blaring his horn steadily now.

And then here came Cobb.

Tiring of my creeping pace, he gunned the Imperial around me in one big skid. I caught a glimpse of an angry face under a big Stetson hat and a waving fist. He was doing a good thirty miles per hour when he'd gained twenty-five yards on me, fishtailing right and left, but straightening as he slid out of sight in the thick sleet.

I let him go. Suicide wasn't in my contract.

The next six miles was a matter of feeling the way and praying. Near a curve I saw taillights to the left. Pulling up, I found Ty's car swung sideways and buried, nose down, in a snowbank, the hind wheels two feet in the air. Twenty yards away was a sheer drop-off into a canyon.

"You hurt?" I asked.

"Bumped my——head," he muttered. He lit a cigar and gave four-letter regards to the highway department for not illuminating the "danger" spot. His forehead was bruised and he'd broken his glasses.

In my car, we groped our way down-mountain, a nightmare ride, with Cobb alternately taking in scotch from a thermos jug and telling me to step on it. At 4:00 A.M. in Carson City, an all-night garageman used a broom to clean the car of snow and agreed to pick up the Imperial—"when the road's passable."

"It's passable," said Ty. "I just opened it."

With dawn breaking, we reached Reno. All I wanted was a bed, and all Cobb wanted was a craps table.

He was rolling now, pretending he wasn't ill; with the scotch bracing him, Ty was able to walk into the Riverside Hotel casino with a hand on my shoulder and without staggering as obviously as usual. Everybody present wanted to meet him. Starlets from a film unit on location in Reno flocked around, and comedian Joe E. Lewis had the band play *"Sweet Georgia Brown"*— Ty's favorite tune.

"Hope your dice are still honest," he told Riverside co-owner Bill Miller. "Last time I was here I won twelve thousand dollars in three hours."

"How I remember, Ty," said Miller. "How I remember."

A scientific craps player who'd won and lost his hefty sums in Nevada in the past, Cobb bet hundred-dollar chips, his eyes alert, not missing a play around the board. He soon decided that the table was cold and we moved to another casino, then a third. At the last stop, Cobb's legs grew shaky. Holding himself up by leaning on the table edge with his forearms, he dropped three hundred dollars, then had a hot streak in which he won eight hundred. His voice was a croak as he told the other players, "Watch 'em and weep."

But then suddenly his voice came back. When the stickman raked the dice his way, Cobb loudly said, "You touched the dice with your hand."

"No, sir," said the stickman. "I did not."

"I don't lie!" snarled Cobb.

"I don't lie, either," insisted the stickman.

"Nobody touches my dice!" Cobb, swaying on his feet, eyes blazing, worked his way around the table toward the croupier. It was a weird tableau. In his crumpled Stetson and expensive camel's-hair coat, stained and charred with cigarette burns, a three-day beard grizzling his face, the fuming old giant of baseball towered over the dapper gambler.

"You fouled the dice, I saw you," growled Cobb, and then he swung.

The blow missed as the stickman dodged, but, cursing and almost falling, Cobb seized the wooden rake and smashed it across the table. I jumped in and caught him under the arms as he sagged.

And then, as quickly as possible, we were put out into the street by two large uniformed guards. "Sorry, Mr. Cobb," they said unhappily, "but we can't have this."

A crowd had gathered, and as we started down the street, Cobb swearing and stumbling, clinging to me, I couldn't have felt more conspicuous if I'd been strung naked from the neon arch across Virginia Street, Reno's main drag. At the corner, Ty was struck by an attack of breathlessness. "Get to stop," he gasped. Feeling him going limp on me, I turned his big body against a lamppost, braced my legs, and with an underarm grip held him there until he caught his breath. He panted and gasped for air.

His face gray, he murmured, "Reach into my left-hand coat pocket." Thinking he wanted his bottle of heart pills, I did. But instead I pulled out a six-inch-thick wad of currency, secured by a rubber band. "Couple of thousand there," he said weakly. "Don't let it out of sight."

At the nearest motel, where I hired a single room with two twin beds, he collapsed on the bed in his coat and hat and slept. After finding myself some breakfast, I turned in.

Hours later I heard him stirring. "What's this place?" he muttered.

I told him the name of the motel—TraveLodge.

"Where's the bankroll?"

"In your coat. You're wearing it."

Then he was quiet.

After a night's sleep, Cobb felt well enough to resume his gambling. In the next few days, he won more than three thousand dollars at the tables, and then we went sightseeing in historic Virginia City. There, as in all places, he stopped traffic. And had the usual altercation. This one was at the Bucket of Blood, where Cobb accused the bartender of serving watered scotch. The bartender denied it. Crash! Another drink went flying.

Back at the lodge a week later, looking like the wrath of John Barleycorn and having refused medical aid in Reno, he began to suffer new and excruciating pains in his hips and lower back. But between groans he forced himself to work an hour a day on his autobiography. He told inside baseball stories, never published:

"Frank Navin, who owned the Detroit club for years, faked his turnstile count to cheat the visiting team and Uncle Sam. So did Big Bill Devery and Frank Farrell, who owned the New York Highlanders—later called the Yankees.

"Walter Johnson, 'the Big Train,' tried to kill himself when his wife died.

"Grover Cleveland Alexander wasn't drunk out there on the mound, the way people thought. He was an epileptic. Old Pete would fall down with a seizure between innings, then go back and pitch another shutout.

"John McGraw hated me because I tweaked his nose in broad daylight in the lobby of the Oriental Hotel, in Dallas, after earlier beating the hell out of his second baseman, Buck Herzog, upstairs in my room."

But before we were well started, Cobb suddenly announced we'd go riding in his twenty-three-foot Chris-Craft speedboat, tied up in a boathouse below the lodge. When I went down to warm it up, I found the boat on the bottom of Lake Tahoe, sunk in fifteen feet of water.

My host broke all records for blowing his stack when he heard the news. He saw in this a sinister plot: "I told you I've got enemies all around here! It's sabotage as sure as I'm alive!"

A sheriff's investigation turned up no clues. Cobb sat up for three nights with his Luger. "I'll salivate the first dirty skunk who steps foot around here after dark."

(Parenthetically, Cobb had a vocabulary all his own. To "salivate" something meant to destroy it. Anything easy was "softy boiled," to outsmart someone was to "slip him the oskafagus," and all doctors were "truss-fixers." People who displeased him—and this included a high percentage of those he met—were "fee-simple sons of bitches," "mugwumps," "lead-heads," or, if female, "lousy slits.")

Lake Tahoe friends of Cobb's had stopped visiting him long before, but one morning an attractive blonde of about fifty came calling. She was an old chum—in a romantic way, I was given to understand, in bygone years—but Ty greeted her coldly. "Lost my sexual powers when I was sixty-nine," he said when she was out of the room. "What the hell use to me is a woman?"

The lady had brought along a three-section electric vibrator bed, which she claimed would relieve Ty's back pains. We helped him mount it. He took a twenty-minute treatment. Attempting to dismount, he lost his balance and fell backward. The contraption jackknifed and Cobb was pinned, yelling and swearing, under a pile of machinery.

After we freed him and helped him to a chair, he told the lady—in the choicest gutter language—where she could put the bed. She left, sobbing.

"That's no way to talk to an old friend, Ty," I said. "She was trying to do you a favor."

"And you're a hell of a poor guest around here, too!" he thundered. "You can leave any old time!" He quickly grabbed a bottle and heaved it in my direction.

"Thought you could throw straighter than that!" I yelled back. Fed up with him, I started to pack my bags.

Before I'd finished, Cobb broke out a bottle of vintage malt scotch, said I was "damned sensitive," half-apologized, and the matter was forgotten— for now.

While working one morning on an outside observation deck, I heard a thud inside. On his bedroom floor, sprawled on his back, lay the Georgia Peach. He was unconscious, his eyes rolled back, breathing shallowly. I thought he was dying.

There was no telephone. "Eavesdroppers on the line," Cobb had told me; "I had it cut off." I ran down the road to a neighboring home and phoned a Carson City doctor, who promised to come immediately.

Back at the lodge, Ty remained stiff and stark on the floor, little bubbles escaping his lips. His face was bluish white. With much straining, I lifted him halfway to the bed, and by shifting holds finally rolled him onto it and covered him with a blanket. Twenty minutes passed. No doctor.

Ten minutes later, I was at the front door, watching for the doctor's car, when I heard a sound. There stood Ty, swaying on his fee. "You want to do some work on the book?" he said.

His recovery didn't seem possible. "But you were out cold a minute ago," I said.

"Just a dizzy spell. Have 'em all the time. Must have hit my head on the bedpost when I fell."

The doctor, arriving, found Cobb's blood pressure standing at a grim 210/90 on the gauge. His temperature was 101 degrees and, from gross neglect of his diabetes, he was in a state of insulin shock, often fatal if not quickly treated. "I'll have to hospitalize you, Mr. Cobb," said the doctor.

Weaving his way to a chair, Cobb coldly waved him away. "Just send me your bill," he grunted. "I'm going home."

"Home" was the multimillionaire's main residence at Atherton, California, on the San Francisco Peninsula, 250 miles away, and it was there he headed later that night.

With some hot soup and insulin in him, Cobb had recovered with the same unbelievable speed he's shown in baseball. In his heyday, trainers often sewed up deep spike cuts in his knees, shins, and thighs, on a clubhouse bench, without anesthetic, and he didn't lose an inning. Famed sportswriter Grantland Rice, one 1920 day in New York, sat beside a bedridden, feverish Cobb, whose thighs, from sliding, were a mass of raw flesh. Rice urged him not to play. Sixteen hours later, Cobb beat the Yankees with five hits in six times at bat, plus two steals.

On the ride to Atherton, he yelled insults at several motorists who moved too slowly to suit him. Reaching home, Ty said he felt ready for another drink.

My latest surprise was Cobb's eleven-room, two-story, richly landscaped Spanish-California villa at 48 Spencer Lane, an exclusive neighborhood. You could have held a ball game on the grounds. But the rich mansion had no lights, no heat, no hot water. It was in blackout.

"I'm suing the Pacific Gas and Electric Company," he explained, "for overcharging me on the service. Those rinky-dinks tacked an extra sixteen dollars on my bill. Bunch of crooks. When I wouldn't pay, they cut off my utilities. Okay—I'll see them in court."

For months previously, Ty Cobb had lived in an all but totally dark house. The only illumination was candlelight. The only cooking facility was a portable Coleman camper's stove. Bathing was impossible, unless you could take it cold. The electric stove, refrigerator, deep freeze, radio, and television, of course, didn't work. Cobb had vowed to "hold the fort" until his case against PG&E was settled. Simultaneously, he had filed a sixty-thousand-dollar suit in San Francisco Superior Court against the State of California to recover state income taxes already collected—on the argument that he wasn't a permanent resident of California, but of Nevada, Georgia, Arizona, and other waypoints. State's attorneys claimed he spent at least six months per year in Atherton, and thus had no case. "I'm gone so much from here," Cobb claimed, "that I'll win hands down." All legal opinion, I later learned, held just the opposite view, but Cobb ignored the lawyers' advice.

Next morning, I arranged with Ty's gardener, Hank, to turn on the lawn sprinklers. In the outdoor sunshine, a cold-water shower was easier to take. From then on, the backyard became my regular washroom.

The problem of lighting a desk, enabling us to work on the book, was solved by stringing two hundred feet of cord, plugged into an outlet of a neighboring house, through hedges and flower gardens and into the window of Cobb's study, where a single naked bulb hung over the chandelier provided illumination. The flickering shadows cast by the single light made the vast old house seem haunted. No "ghost" writer ever had more ironical surroundings.

At various points around the premises, Ty showed me where he'd once installed high-voltage wires to stop trespassers. "Curiosity seekers?" I asked. "Hell, no," he said. "Detectives broke in here looking for evidence against me in a divorce suit. After a couple of them got burned, they stopped coming."

To reach our bedrooms, my host and I groped our way down long, black corridors. Twice he fell in the dark, and finally he collapsed completely. He was so ill that he was forced to check in to Stanford Hospital in nearby Palo Alto. Here another shock was in store.

One of the physicians treating Ty, a Dr. E. R. Brown, said, "Do you mean to say that this man has traveled seven hundred miles in the last month without medical care?"

"Doctor," I said, "I've hauled him in and out of saloons, motels, gambling joints, steambaths, and snowbanks. There's no holding him."

"It's a miracle he's alive. He has most of the major ailments I know about."

Dr. Brown didn't reveal Ty's main ailment to me. Cobb himself broke the news one night from his hospital bed. "It's cancer," he said bluntly. "About a year ago I had most of my prostate gland removed when they found it was malignant. Now it's spread up into the back bones. These pill-peddlers here won't admit it, but I haven't got a chance." Cobb made me swear I'd never divulge his secret before he died. "If it gets in the papers, the sob sisters will have a field day. I don't want sympathy from anybody."

At Stanford, where he absorbed seven massive doses of cobalt radiation, the ultimate cancer treatment, he didn't act like a man on his last legs. Even before his strength returned, he was in the usual form. "They won't let me have a drink" he said indignantly. "I want you to get me a bottle of sixteen-year-old. Smuggle it in your tape-recorder case."

I tried, telling myself that no man with terminal cancer deserves to be dried out, but sharp-eyed nurses and orderlies were watching. They searched Ty's closet, found the bottle, and over his hollers of protest appropriated it.

"We'll have to slip them the oskafagus," said Ty.

Thereafter, a drink of scotch and water sat in plain view in his room, on his bedside table, under the very noses of his physicians—and nobody suspected a thing. The whiskey was in an ordinary water glass, and in the liquid reposed Ty's false teeth. Nobody thought to frisk the dental fluid.

There were no dull moments while Cobb was at Stanford, one of the largest and highest-rated medical centers in the United States. He was critical of everything. He told one specialist that he was not even qualified to be an intern, and advised the hospital dietitian—loudly—that she and the kitchen workers were in a conspiracy to poison him with their "foul" dishes. To a nurse he snapped, "If Florence Nightingale knew about you, she'd spin in her grave."

Between blasts he did manage to buckle down to work on the book, dictating long into the night into a microphone suspended over his bed. Slowly the stormy details of his professional life came out. He spoke often of having "forgiven" his many baseball enemies, and then lashed out at them with such passionate phrases that it was clear he'd done no such thing. High on his hate list were John McGraw of the Giants; New York sportswriters; Hub Leonard, a pitcher who in 1926 accused Cobb and Tris Speaker of fixing a Detroit-Cleveland game, which led to Cobb's retirement as Tiger manager; American League president Ban Johnson; one-time Detroit owner Frank Navin; former baseball commissioner Kenesaw Mountain Landis; and all those who intimated that Cobb ever used his spikes on another player without having been attacked first.

After a night when he slipped out of the hospital, against all orders, and drove with me to a San Francisco Giants–Cincinnati Reds game at Candlestick Park, thirty miles away, Stanford Hospital decided it couldn't keep Tyrus R. Cobb, and he was discharged. For his extensive treatment, his bill ran to more than twelve hundred dollars.

"That's a nice racket you boys have here," he told the discharging doctors. "You clip the customers, charge them for the use of everything from bedpans to the steam heat."

"Good-bye, Mr. Cobb," snapped the medical men.

Soon after this Ty caught a plane to Georgia and I went along. "I want to see some of the old places again before I die," he declared.

It now was Christmas Eve of 1960 and I'd been with him for a lot of months and completed only four chapters. The project had begun to look hopeless. In Royston, his birthplace, a town of twenty-five hundred, Cobb wanted to head for the local cemetery. I drove him there and helped him climb a windswept hill through the growing dusk. Light snow fell. Faintly, Yule chimes could be heard.

Amongst the many headstones, Ty looked for the plot he'd reserved for himself while in California; he couldn't find it. His temper began to boil: "Dammit, I ordered the biggest mausoleum in the graveyard! I know it's around here somewhere." On the next hill, we found it: a large marble walk-in-size structure with COBB engraved over the entrance.

"You want to pray with me?" he said gruffly. We knelt and tears came to his eyes.

Within the tomb, he pointed to crypts occupied by the bodies of his father, Professor William Herschel Cobb, his mother, Amanda Chitwood Cobb, and his sister, Florence, whom he'd had disinterred and placed there. "My father," he said reverently, "was the greatest man I ever knew. He was a scholar, state senator, editor, and philosopher—a saintly man. I worshiped him. So did all the people around here. He was the only man who ever made me do his bidding."

Rising painfully, Ty braced himself against the marble crypt that soon would hold his body. There was an eerie silence in the tomb. He said deliberately, "My father had his head blown off with a shotgun when I was eighteen years old—*by a member of my own family.* I didn't get over that. I've never gotten over it."

We went back down the hill to the car. I asked no questions that day. Later, from family sources and old Georgian friends of the diamond idol, I learned details of the killing. News of it reached Ty in Augusta, where he was playing minor-league ball, on August 9, 1905. A few days later he was told that he'd been purchased by the Detroit Tigers and was to report immediately. "In my grief," Cobb later said, "going up didn't matter much . . . it felt like the end of me."

Came March of 1961 and I remained stuck to the Georgia Peach like court plaster. He'd decided we were born pals, meant for each other, that we'd complete a baseball book that would beat everything ever published. He had astonished doctors by rallying from the spreading cancer, and between bouts of transmitting his life and times to a tape recorder, he was raising more whoopee than he had at Lake Tahoe and Reno.

Spring-training time for the big leagues had arrived, and we were ensconced in a deluxe suite at the Ramada Inn at Scottsdale, Arizona, close by the practice parks of the Red Sox, Indians, Giants, and Cubs. Here, each year, Cobb held court. He didn't go to see anybody. Ford Frick, Joe Cronin, Ted Williams, and other diamond notables came to him. While explaining to sportswriters why modern stars couldn't compare to the Wagners, Lajoies, Speakers, Jacksons, Johnsons, Mathewsons, and Planks of his day, Ty did other things.

For one, he commissioned a well-known Arizona artist to paint him in oils. He was emaciated, having dropped from 208 pounds to 176. The preliminary sketches showed up his sagging cheeks and thin neck. "I wouldn't let you kalsomine my toilet," ripped out Ty as he fired the artist.

But he was anything but eccentric when analyzing the Dow-Jones averages and playing the stock market. Twice a week he phoned experts around the country, determined good buys, and bought in blocks of five hundred to fifteen hundred shares. He made money consistently, even when bedridden, with a mind that read behind the fluctuations of a dozen different issues. "The State of Georgia," Ty remarked, "will realize about one million dollars from inheritance taxes when I'm dead. But there isn't a man alive who knows what I'm worth." According to the *Sporting News,* there was evidence upon Cobb's death that his worth approximated $12 million. Whatever the true figure, he did not confide the precise amount to me—or, most probably, to anyone except the attorneys who drafted his last will and testament. And Cobb fought off making his will until the last moment.

His fortune began accumulating in 1909, when he bought cotton futures and United (later General) Motors stock and did well in copper-mining investments. As of 1961 he was also "Mr. Coca-Cola," holding more than twenty thousand shares of that stock, valued at eighty-five dollars per share. Wherever he traveled, he carried with him, stuffed into an old brown leather bag, more than $1 million in stock certificates and negotiable government bonds. The bag was never locked up. Cobb assumed nobody would dare rob him. He tossed the bag into any handy corner of a room, inviting theft. Finally, in Scottsdale, it turned up missing.

Playing Sherlock, he narrowed the suspects to a room maid and a man he'd hired to cook meals. When questioned, the maid broke into tears and the cook quit—fired, said Cobb. Hours later, I discovered the bag under a pile of dirty laundry.

Major-league owners and league officials hated to see Cobb coming, for he thought their product was putrid and said so, incessantly. "Today they hit for ridiculous averages, can't bunt, can't steal, can't hit-and-run, can't place-hit to the opposite field, and you can't call them ballplayers." He told sportswriters, "I blame Ford Frick, Joe Cronin, Bill Harridge, Horace Stoneham, Dan Topping, and others for trading in crazy style and wrecking baseball's traditional league lines. These days, any tax-dodging mugwump with a bankroll can buy a franchise, field some semipros, and get away with it. Where's our integrity? Where's *baseball?*"

No one could quiet Cobb. Who else had a record lifetime batting average of .367, made 4,191 hits, scored 2,244 runs, won 12 batting titles, stole 892 bases, repeatedly beat whole teams by his own efforts alone? Who was first into the Hall of Fame? Not Babe Ruth—but Cobb, by a landslide vote. And whose records still mostly stood, more than thirty years later? Say it again—*thirty years.*

By early April, he could barely make it up the ramp of the Scottsdale stadium, even with my help. He had to stop, gulping for breath, because of his failing ticker. But he kept coming to games, loving the indelible sounds of a ballpark. His courage was tremendous. "Always be ready to catch me if I start to fall," he said. "I'd hate to go down in front of the fans."

People of all ages were overcome with emotion upon meeting him; no sports celebrity I've known produced such an effect upon the public. At a 1959 stop in Las Vegas, Clark Gable himself had stood in a line to shake the gnarly Cobb hand.

We went to buy a cane. At a surgical supply house, Cobb inspected a dozen twenty-five-dollar malacca sticks, then bought the cheapest white-ash cane they had—four dollars. "I'm a plain man," he informed the clerk, the ten-thousand-dollar diamond ring on his finger glittering.

But pride kept the old tiger from ever using the cane, any more than he'd wear the six-hundred-dollar hearing aid built into the bow of his glasses other than away from the crowd.

One day a Mexican taxi driver aggravated Cobb with his driving. Throwing the fare on the ground, Cobb waited until the cabbie had bent to retrieve it, then tried to punt him like a football.

"What's your sideline," he inquired, "selling opium?"

It was all I could do to keep the driver from swinging at him. Later, a lawyer called on Cobb, threatening a damage suit. "Get in line, there's five hundred ahead of you," said Tyrus, waving him away.

Every day was a new adventure. He was fighting back against the pain that engulfed him—cobalt treatments no longer helped—and anywhere we went I could count on trouble. He threw a salt shaker at a Phoenix waiter, narrowly missing. One of his most treasured friendships—with Ted Williams, peerless batsman of the 1930s to 1950s—came to an end.

From the early 1940s, Williams had sat at Ty Cobb's feet. They met often, and exchanged long letters on the science of batting. At Scottsdale one day, Williams dropped by Ty's rooms. He hugged Ty, fondly rumpled his hair, and accepted a drink. Presently the two men fell into an argument over which players should make up the all-time, all-star team. Williams declared, "I want DiMaggio and Hornsby over anybody you can mention."

Cobb's face grew dark. "Don't give me that! Hornsby couldn't go back for a pop fly and he lacked smartness. DiMaggio couldn't hit with Tris Speaker or Joe Jackson."

"The hell you say!" came back Williams jauntily. "Hornsby out-hit *you* a couple of years."

Almost leaping from his chair, Cobb shook a fist. He'd been given the insult supreme—for Cobb always resented, and finally hated, Rogers Hornsby.

Not until Cobb was in his sixteenth season did the ten-years-younger Hornsby top him in the batting averages. "Get——away from me!" choked Cobb. "Don't come back!"

Williams left with a quizzical expression, not sure how much Cobb meant it. The old man meant it all the way. He never invited Williams back, or talked to him, or spoke his name again. "I cross him off," he told me.

We left Arizona shortly thereafter for my home in Santa Barbara, California. Now failing fast, Ty had accepted an invitation to be my guest. Two doctors inspected him at the beach house by the Pacific and gave their opinions: he had a few months of life left, no more. The cancer had invaded the tissue and bones of his skull. His pain was unrelenting—requiring steady sedation—yet with teeth bared, sweat streaking his face, he fought off medical science. "They'll never get me on their f— hypnotics," he swore. "I'll never die an addict . . . an idiot . . ."

He shouted, "Where's anybody who cares about me? Where are they? The world's lousy . . . no good."

One night later, on May 1, the Georgian sat propped up in bed, overlooking a starlit ocean. He had a habit, each night, of rolling up his trousers and placing them under his pillow—an early-century ballplayer's trick, dating from the time when Ty slept in strange places and might be robbed. I knew that his ever-present Luger was tucked into that pants roll.

I'd never seen him so sunk in despair. At last the fire was going out. "Do we die a little at a time, or all at once?" he wondered aloud. "I think Max had the right idea."

The reference was to his one-time friend, multimillionaire Max Fleischmann, who'd cheated lingering death by cancer some years earlier by putting a bullet through his brain. Ty spoke of Babe Ruth and Rogers Hornsby, other carcinoma victims. "If Babe had been told what he had in time, he could've got it over with."

Cobb was well read in poetry. One night he quoted a passage he'd always liked by Don Marquis: "There I stood at the gate of God, drunk but unafraid."

Had I left Ty alone that night, I believe he would have pulled the trigger. His three living children—two sons were dead—had withdrawn from him. In the wide world that had sung his fame, he had not one intimate friend remaining.

But we talked, and prayed, until dawn, and slight sleep came. In the morning, aided by friends, we put him into a car and drove him home, to the big, gloomy house up north in Atherton. Ty spoke only twice during the six-hour drive.

"Have you got enough to finish the book?" he asked.

"More than enough."

"Give 'em the word then. I had to fight all my life to survive. They all were against me . . . tried every dirty trick to cut me down. But I beat the bastards and left them in the ditch. Make sure the book says that . . ."

I was leaving him now, permanently, and had to ask one question I'd never put to him before.

"Why did you fight so hard in baseball, Ty?"

He'd never looked fiercer than then, when he answered. "I did it for my father, who was an exalted man. They killed him when he was still young. They blew his head off the same week I became a major-leaguer. He never got to see me play. Not one game, not an inning. But I knew he was watching me . . . and I never let him down. *Never.*"

You can make what you want of that. Keep in mind that Casey Stengel said, later: "I never saw anyone like Cobb. No one even close to him as the greatest ballplayer. Ruth was sensational. Cobb went beyond that. When he wiggled those wild eyes at a pitcher, you knew you were looking at the one bird no one could beat. It was like he was superhuman."

To me it seems that the violent death of a dominating father whom a sensitive, highly talented boy loved and feared deeply, engendered, through some strangely supreme desire to vindicate that "saintly" father, the most violent, successful, thoroughly maladjusted personality ever to pass across American sports. The shock ticked the eighteen-year-old's mind, making him capable of incredible feats.

Off the field and on, he remained at war with the world. To reinforce the pattern, he was viciously hazed by Detroit Tiger veterans when he was a rookie. He was bullied, ostracized, and beaten up—in one instance, a 210-pound catcher named Charlie Schmidt broke the 165-pound Ty Cobb's nose and closed both of his eyes. It was persecution, immediately heaped upon one of the deepest desolations a young man can experience.

There can be no doubt about it: Ty Cobb was a badly disturbed personality. It is not hard to understand why he spent his entire adult life in deep conflict. Nor why a member of his family, in the winter of 1960, told me, "I've spent a lot of time terrified of him . . . and I think he was psychotic from the time he left Georgia to play in the big league."

I believe that he was far more than the fiercest of all competitors. He was a vindicator, a man who believed that "father was watching" and who could not put that father's terrible death out of his mind. The memory of it menaced his sanity.

The fact that he recognized and feared mental illness is revealed in a tape recording he made, in which he describes his own view of himself: "I was like a steel spring with a growing and dangerous flaw in it. If it is wound too tight or has the slightest weak point, the spring will fly apart and then it is done for . . ."

The last time I saw him, he was sitting in his armchair in the Atherton mansion. The place was still without lights or heat. I shook his hand in farewell—a degree of closeness had developed between us, if short of friendship—and he held it a moment longer.

"What about it? Do you think they'll remember me?" He tried to say it as if it weren't important.

"They'll always remember you," I replied.

On July 8, I received in the mail a photograph of Ty's mausoleum on the hillside in the Royston cemetery with the words scribbled on the back: "Any time now." Nine days later, at age seventy-four, he died in an Atlanta hospital. Before going, he opened the brown bag, piled $1 million in negotiable securities beside his bed, and placed the Luger atop them.

From all of major-league baseball, three men, and three men only, attended his funeral.

So ended the battle. "He was the greatest and most amazing ballplayer I ever saw," attested Hall of Famer George Sisler, himself a candidate for best-ever honors. "There will never be another like him, he was a genius," said baseball sage Connie Mack in his old age. To Babe Ruth he was "the hardest to beat SOB of them all." So ended the struggle of the most feared, castigated, and acclaimed figure ever to plant his spikes in a batter's box. It was final innings on a personal tragedy. Ty Cobb had himself entombed in a chamber directly across from that of his father, Professor William Herschel Cobb, in dusty little Roystontown where it had all begun.

Hub Fans Bid Kid Adieu

JOHN UPDIKE

Neither John Updike nor his classic account of Ted Williams's final game needs any introduction, but there *is* a story behind the tale.

Updike almost missed the game.

He'd been married for seven years at the time, and was, he's explained, "falling in love away from marriage." On the appointed day, he took a taxi to her place on Beacon Hill, but she wasn't home. He went out to Fenway. "And my virtue was rewarded."

As is ours whenever we read—or re-read—this extraordinary *New Yorker* essay. Still, one overwhelmingly existential question remains: Had she *not* been out, and Updike *not* been on hand to witness it, would Williams still have hit that storybook home run in the final at-bat of his marvelous career?

Fenway Park, in Boston, is a lyric little bandbox of a ball park. Everything is painted green and seems in curiously sharp focus, like the inside of an old-fashioned peeping-type Easter egg. It was built in 1912 and rebuilt in 1934, and offers, as do most Boston artifacts, a compromise between Man's Euclidean determinations and Nature's beguiling irregularities. Its right field is one of the deepest in the American League, while its left field is the shortest; the high left-field wall, three hundred and fifteen feet from home plate along the foul line, virtually thrusts its surface at right-handed hitters. On the afternoon of Wednesday, September 28, as I took a seat behind third base, a uniformed groundkeeper was treading the top of this wall, picking batting-practice home runs out of the screen, like a mushroom gatherer seen in Wordsworthian perspective on the verge of a cliff. The day was overcast, chill, and uninspirational. The Boston team was the worst in twenty-seven seasons. A jangling medley of incompetent youth and aging competence, the Red Sox were finishing in seventh place only because the Kansas City Athletics had locked them out of the cellar. They were scheduled to play the Baltimore Orioles, a much nimbler blend of May and December, who had been dumped from pennant contention a week before by the insatiable Yankees. I, and 10,453 others, had shown up primarily because this was the Red Sox's last home game of the season, and therefore the last time in all eternity that their regular left fielder, known to the headlines as TED, KID, SPLINTER, THUMPER, TW, and, most cloyingly, MISTER WONDERFUL, would play in Boston. "WHAT WILL WE DO WITHOUT TED? HUB FANS ASK" ran the headline on a newspaper being read by a bulb-nosed cigar smoker a few rows away. Williams's retirement had been announced, doubted (he had been threatening retirement for years), confirmed by Tom Yawkey, the Red Sox owner, and at last widely accepted as the sad but probable truth. He was forty-two and had redeemed his abysmal season of 1959 with a—considering his advanced age—fine one. He had been giving away his gloves and bats and had grudgingly consented to a sentimental ceremony today. This was not necessarily his last game; the Red Sox were scheduled to travel to New York and wind up the season with three games there.

I arrived early. The Orioles were hitting fungos on the field. The day before, they had spitefully smothered the Red Sox, 17–4, and neither their faces nor their drab gray visiting-team uniforms seemed very gracious. I wondered who had invited them to the party. Between our heads and the lowering clouds a frenzied organ was thundering through, with an appositeness perhaps accidental, "You *maaaade* me love you, I didn't wanna do it, I didn't wanna do it . . ."

The affair between Boston and Ted Williams has been no mere summer romance; it has been a marriage, composed of spats, mutual disappointments, and, toward the end, a mellowing hoard of shared memories. It falls into three stages, which may be termed Youth, Maturity, and Age; or Thesis, Antithesis, and Synthesis; or Jason, Achilles, and Nestor.

First, there was the by now legendary epoch when the young bridegroom came out of the West, announced "All I want out of life is that when I walk down the street folks will say 'There goes the greatest hitter who ever lived.' " The dowagers of local journalism attempted to give elementary deportment lessons to this child who spake as a god, and to their horror were themselves rebuked. Thus began the long exchange of backbiting, hat-flipping, booing, and spitting that has distinguished Williams's public relations. The spitting incidents of 1957 and 1958 and the similar dockside courtesies that Williams has now and then extended to the grandstand should be judged against this background: The left-field stands at Fenway for twenty years have held a large number of customers who have bought their way in primarily for the privilege of showering abuse on Williams. Greatness necessarily attracts debunkers but in Williams's case the hostility has been systematic and unappeasable. His basic offense against the fans has been to wish that they weren't there. Seeking a perfectionist's vacuum, he has quixotically desired to sever the game from the ground of paid spectatorship and publicity that supports it. Hence his refusal to tip his cap to the crowd or turn the other cheek to newsmen. It has been a costly theory—it has probably cost him, among other evidences of goodwill, two Most Valuable Player awards, which are voted by reporters—but he has held to it from his rookie year on. While his critics, oral and literary, remained beyond the reach of his discipline, the opposing pitchers were accessible, and he spanked them to the tune of .406 in 1941. He slumped to .356 in 1942 and went off to war.

In 1946, Williams returned from three years as a marine pilot to the second of his baseball avatars, that of Achilles, the hero of incomparable prowess and beauty who nevertheless was to be found sulking in his tent while the Trojans (mostly Yankees) fought through to the ships. Yawkey, a timber and mining maharajah, had surrounded his central jewel with many gems of slightly lesser water, such as Bobby Doerr, Dom DiMaggio, Rudy York, Birdie Tebbetts, and Johnny Pesky. Throughout the late forties, the Red Sox were the best paper team in baseball, yet they had little three-dimensional to show for it, and if this was a tragedy, Williams was Hamlet. A succinct review of the indictment—and a fair sample of appreciative sports-page prose—appeared the very day of Williams's valedictory, in a column by Huck Finnegan in the *Boston American* (no sentimentalist, Huck):

Williams's career, in contrast [to Babe Ruth's], has been a series of failures except for his averages. He flopped in the only World Series he ever played in (1946) when he batted only .200. He flopped in the playoff game with Cleveland in 1948. He flopped in the final game of the 1949 season with the pennant hinging on the outcome (Yanks 5, Sox 3). He flopped in 1950 when he returned to the lineup after a two-month absence and ruined the morale of a club that seemed pennant-bound under Steve O'Neill. It has always been Williams's records first, the team second, and the Sox non-winning record is proof enough of that.

There are answers to all this, of course. The fatal weakness of the great Sox slugging teams was not-quite-good-enough pitching rather than Williams's failure to hit a home run every time he came to bat. Again, Williams's depressing effect on his teammates has never been proved. Despite ample coaching to the contrary, most insisted that they *liked* him. He has been generous with advice to any player who asked for it. In an increasingly combative baseball atmosphere, he continued to duck beanballs docilely. With umpires he was gracious to a fault. This courtesy itself annoyed his critics, whom there was no pleasing. And against the ten crucial games (the seven World Series games with the St. Louis Cardinals, the 1948 play-off with the Cleveland Indians, and the two-game series with the Yankees at the end of the 1949 season, winning either one of which would have given the Red Sox the pennant) that make up the Achilles' heel of Williams's record, a mass of statistics can be set showing that day in and day out he was no slouch in the clutch. The correspondence columns of the Boston papers now and then suffer a sharp flurry of arithmetic on this score; indeed, for Williams to have distributed all his hits so they did nobody else any good would constitute a feat of placement unparalleled in the annals of selfishness.

Whatever residue of truth remains of the Finnegan charge those of us who love Williams must transmute as best we can, in our own personal crucibles. My personal memories of Williams begin when I was a boy in Pennsylvania, with two last-place teams in Philadelphia to keep me company. For me, "W'ms, if" was a figment of the box scores who always seemed to be going 3-for-5. He radiated, from afar, the hard blue glow of high purpose. I remember listening over the radio to the All-Star Game of 1946, in which Williams hit two singles and two home runs, the second one off a Rip Sewell "blooper" pitch; it was like hitting a balloon out of the park. I remember watching one of his home runs from the bleachers of Shibe Park; it went over the first baseman's head and rose meticulously along a straight line and was still rising when it cleared the fence. The trajectory seemed qualitatively different from anything anyone else might hit. For me, Williams is the classic ballplayer of the game on a hot August weekday, before a small crowd, when the only thing at stake is the tissue-thin difference between a thing done well and a thing done ill. Baseball is a game of the long season, of relentless and gradual averaging-out. Irrelevance—since the reference point of most individual games is remote and statistical—always threatens its interest, which can be maintained not by the occasional heroics that sportswriters feed upon but by players who always *care;* who care, that is to say, about themselves and their art. Insofar as the clutch hitter is not a sportswriter's myth, he is a vulgarity, like a writer who writes only for money. It may be that, compared to managers' dreams such as Joe DiMaggio and the always helpful Stan Musial, Williams is an icy star. But of all team sports, baseball, with its graceful intermittences of action, its immense and tranquil field sparsely settled with poised men in white, its dispassionate mathematics, seems to me, best suited to accommodate, and be ornamented by, a loner. It is an essentially lonely game. No other player visible to my generation has concentrated within himself so much of the sport's poignance, has so assiduously refined his natural skills, has so constantly brought to the plate that intensity of competence that crowds the throat with joy.

By the time I went to college, near Boston, the lesser stars Yawkey had assembled around Williams had faded, and his craftsmanship, his rigorous pride, had become itself a kind of heroism. This brittle and temperamental player developed an unexpected quality of persistence. He was always coming back—back from Korea, back from a broken collarbone, a shattered elbow, a bruised heel, back from drastic bouts of flu and ptomaine poisoning. Hardly a season went by without some enfeebling mishap, yet he always came back, and always looked like himself. The delicate mechanism of timing and power seemed locked, shockproof, in some case outside his body. In addition to injuries, there were a heavily publicized divorce, and the usual storms with the press, and the Williams Shift—the maneuver, custom-built by Lou Boudreau, of the Cleveland Indians, whereby three infielders were concentrated on the right side of the infield, where a left-handed pull hitter like Williams generally hits the ball. Williams could easily have learned to punch singles through the vacancy on his left and fattened his average hugely. This was what Ty Cobb, the Einstein of average, told him to do. But the game had changed since Cobb; Williams believed that his value to the club and to the game was as a slugger, so he went on pulling the ball, trying to blast it through three men, and paid the price of perhaps fifteen points of lifetime average. Like Ruth before him, he bought the occasional home run at the cost of many directed singles—a calculated sacrifice certainly not, in the case of a hitter as average-minded as Williams, entirely selfish.

After a prime so harassed and hobbled, Williams was granted by the relenting fates a golden twilight. He became at the end of his career perhaps the best *old* hitter of the century. The dividing line came between the 1956 and the 1957 seasons. In September of the first year, he and Mickey Mantle were contending for the batting championship. Both were hitting around .350, and there was no one else near them. The season ended with a three-game series between the

Yankees and the Sox, and living in New York then, I went up to the Stadium. Williams was slightly shy of the four hundred at-bats needed to qualify; the fear was expressed that the Yankee pitchers would walk him to protect Mantle. Instead, they pitched to him—a wise decision. He looked terrible at the plate, tired and discouraged and unconvincing. He never looked very good to me in the Stadium. (Last week, in *Life,* Williams, a sportswriter himself now, wrote gloomily of the Stadium, "There's the bigness of it. There are those high stands and all those people smoking—and, of course, the shadows. . . . It takes at least one series to get accustomed to the Stadium and even then you're not sure.") The final outcome in 1956 was Mantle .353, Williams .345.

The next year, I moved from New York to New England, and it made all the difference. For in September of 1957, in the same situation, the story was reversed. Mantle finally hit .365; it was the best season of his career. But Williams, though sick and old, had run away from him. A bout of flu had laid him low in September. He emerged from his cave in the Hotel Somerset haggard but irresistible; he hit four successive pinch-hit home runs. "I feel terrible," he confessed, "but every time I take a swing at the ball it goes out of the park." He ended the season with thirty-eight home runs and an average of .388, the highest in either league since his own .406, and, coming from a decrepit man of thirty-nine, an even more supernal figure. With eight or so of the "leg hits" that a younger man would have beaten out, it would have been .400. And the next year, Williams, who in 1949 and 1953 had lost batting championships by decimal whiskers to George Kell and Mickey Vernon, sneaked in behind his teammate Pete Runnels and filched his sixth title, a bargain at .328.

In 1959, it seemed all over. The dinosaur thrashed around in the .200 swamp for the first half of the season, and was even benched ("rested," Manager Mike Higgins tactfully said). Old foes like the late Bill Cunningham began to offer batting tips. Cunningham thought Williams was jiggling his elbows; in truth, Williams's neck was so stiff he could hardly turn his head to look at the pitcher. When he swung, it looked like a Calder mobile with one thread cut; it reminded you that since 1953 Williams's shoulders had been wired together. A solicitous pall settled over the sports pages. In the two decades since Williams had come to Boston, his status had imperceptibly shifted from that of a naughty prodigy to that of a municipal monument. As his shadow in the record books lengthened, the Red Sox teams around him declined, and the entire American League seemed to be losing life and color to the National. The inconsistency of the new superstars—Mantle, Colavito, and Kaline—served to make Williams appear all the more singular. And off the field, his private philanthropy—in particular his zealous chairmanship of the

Jimmy Fund, a charity for children with cancer—gave him a civic presence somewhat like that of Richard Cardinal Cushing. In religion, Williams appears to be a humanist, and a selective one at that, but he and the cardinal, when their good works intersect and they appear in the public eye together, make a handsome and heartening pair.

Humiliated by his 1959 season, Williams determined, once more, to come back. I, as a specimen Williams partisan, was both glad and fearful. All baseball fans believe in miracles; the question is, how *many* do you believe in? He looked like a ghost in spring training. Manager Jurges warned us ahead of time that if Williams didn't come through he would be benched, just like anybody else. As it turned out, it was Jurges who was benched. Williams entered the 1960 season needing eight home runs to have a lifetime total of 500; after one time at bat in Washington, he needed seven. For a stretch, he was hitting a home run every second game that he played. He passed Lou Gehrig's lifetime total, then the number 500, then Mel Ott's total, and finished with 521, thirteen behind Jimmy Foxx, who alone stands between Williams and Babe Ruth's unapproachable 714. The summer was a statistician's picnic. His two-thousandth walk came and went, his eighteen-hundredth run batted in, his sixteenth All-Star Game. At one point, he hit a home run off a pitcher, Don Lee, off whose father, Thornton Lee, he had hit a home run a generation before. The only comparable season for a forty-two-year-old man was Ty Cobb's in 1928. Cobb batted .323 and hit one homer. Williams batted .316 but hit twenty-nine homers.

In sum, though generally conceded to be the greatest hitter of his era, he did not establish himself as "the greatest hitter who ever lived." Cobb, for average, and Ruth, for power, remain supreme. Cobb, Rogers, Hornsby, Joe Jackson, and Lefty O'Doul, among players since 1900, have higher lifetime averages than Williams's .344. Unlike Foxx, Gehrig, Hack Wilson, Hank Greenberg, and Ralph Kiner, Williams never came close to matching Babe Ruth's season home-run total of sixty. In the list of major league batting records, not one is held by Williams. He is second in walks drawn, third in home runs, fifth in lifetime averages, sixth in runs batted in, eighth in runs scored and in total bases, fourteenth in doubles, and thirtieth in hits. But if we allow him merely average seasons for the four-plus seasons he lost to two wars, and add another season for the months he lost to injuries, we get a man who in all the power totals would be second, and not a very distant second, to Ruth. And if we further allow that these years would have been not merely average but prime years, if we allow for all the months when Williams was playing in sub-par condition, if we permit his early and later years in baseball to be some sort of index of what the middle years could have been, if we give him a right-field fence that is not, like Fenway's, one of the most distant in the league, and if—the least excusable "if"—we imagine him condescending to outsmart the Williams Shift, we can defensibly assemble, like a colossus induced from the sizable fragments that do remain, a statistical figure not incommensurate with his grandiose ambition. From the statistics that are on the books, a good case can be made that in the *combination* of power and average Williams is first; nobody else ranks so high in both categories. Finally, there is the witness of the eyes; men whose memories go back to Shoeless Joe Jackson—another unlucky natural—rank him and Williams together as the best-looking hitters they have seen. It was for our last look that ten thousand of us had come.

Two girls, one of them with pert buckteeth and eyes as black as vest buttons, the other with white skin and flesh-colored hair, like an underdeveloped photograph of a redhead, came and sat on my right. On my other side was one of those frowning, chestless young-old men who can frequently be seen, often wearing sailor hats, attending ball games alone. He did not once open his program but instead tapped it, rolled up, on his knee as he gave the game his disconsolate attention. A young lady, with freckles and a depressed, dainty nose that by an optical illusion seemed to thrust her lips forward for a kiss, sauntered down into the box seats and with striking aplomb took a seat right behind the roof of the Oriole dugout. She wore a blue coat with a Northeastern University emblem sewed to it. The girls beside me took it into their heads that this was Williams's daughter. She looked too old to me, and why would she be sitting behind the visitors' dugout. On the other hand, from the way she sat there, staring at the sky and French-inhaling, she clearly was *some*body. Other fans came and eclipsed her from view. The crowd looked less like a weekday ball park crowd than like the folks you might find in Yellowstone National Park, or emerging from automobiles at the top of scenic Mount Mansfield. There were a lot of competitively well-dressed couples of tourist age, and not a few babes in arms. A row of five seats in front of me was abruptly filled with a woman and four children, the youngest of them two years old, if that. Someday, presumably, he could tell his grandchildren that he saw Williams play. Along with these tots and second-honeymooners, there were Harvard freshmen, giving off that peculiar nervous glow created when a quantity of insouciance is saturated with insecurity; thick-necked army officers with brass on their shoulders and lead in their voices; pepperings of priests; perfumed bouquets of Roxbury Fabian fans; shiny salesmen from Albany and Fall River; and those gray, hoarse men—taxidrivers, slaughterers, and bartenders—who will continue to click through the turnstiles long after everyone else has deserted to television and tramporamas. Behind me, two young male voices blossomed, cracking a joke about God's five proofs that Thomas Aquinas exists—typical Boston College levity.

The batting cage was trundled away. The Orioles fluttered to the sidelines. Diagonally across the field, by the Red Sox dugout, a cluster of men in overcoats were festering like maggots. I could see a splinter of white uniform, and Williams's head, held at a self-deprecating and evasive tilt. Williams's conversational stance is that of a six-foot-three-inch man under a six-foot ceiling. He moved away to the patter of flash bulbs, and began playing catch with a young Negro outfielder named Willie Tasby. His arm, never very powerful, had grown lax with the years, and his throwing motion was a kind of muscular drawl. To catch the ball, he flicked his glove hand onto his left shoulder (he batted left but threw right, as every schoolboy ought to know) and let the ball plop into it comically. This catch session with Tasby was the only time all afternoon I saw him grin.

A tight little flock of human sparrows who, from the lambient and pampered pink of their faces, could only have been Boston politicians moved toward the plate. The loudspeakers mammothly coughed as someone huffed on the microphone. The ceremonies began. Curt Gowdy, the Red Sox radio and television announcer, who sounds like everybody's brother-in-law, delivered a brief sermon, taking the two words "pride" and "champion" as his text. It began, "Twenty-one years ago, a skinny kid from San Diego, California . . ." and ended, "I don't think we'll ever see another like him." Robert Tibolt, chairman of the board of the Greater Boston Chamber of Commerce, presented Williams with a big Paul Revere silver bowl. Harry Carlson, a member of the sports committee of the Boston Chamber, gave him a plaque, whose inscription he did not read in its entirety, out of deference to Williams's distaste for this sort of fuss. Mayor Collins presented the Jimmy Fund with a thousand-dollar check.

Then the occasion himself stooped to the microphone, and his voice sounded, after the others, very Californian; it seemed to be coming, excellently amplified, from a great distance, adolescently young and as smooth as a butternut. His thanks for the gifts had not died from our ears before he glided, as if helplessly, into "In spite of all the terrible things that have been said about me by the maestros of the keyboard up there . . ." He glanced up at the press rows suspended above home plate. (All the Boston reporters, incidentally, reported the phrase as "knights of the keyboard," but I heard it as "maestros" and prefer it that way.) The crowd tittered, appalled. A frightful vision flashed upon me, of the press gallery pelting Williams with erasers, of Williams clambering up the foul screen to slug journalists, of a riot, of Mayor Collins being crushed. ". . . And they *were* terrible things," Williams insisted, with level melancholy, into the mike. "I'd like to forget them, but I can't." He paused, swallowing his memories, and went on. "I want to say that my years in Boston have been the greatest thing in my life." The crowd, like an immense sail going limp in a change of wind, sighed with relief. Taking all the parts himself, Williams then acted out a vivacious little morality drama in which an imaginary tempter came to him at the beginning of his career and said, "Ted, you can play anywhere you like." Leaping nimbly into the role of his younger self (who in biographical actuality had yearned to be a Yankee), Williams gallantly chose Boston over all the other cities, and told us that Tom Yawkey was the greatest owner in baseball and we were the greatest fans. We applauded ourselves heartily. The umpire came out and dusted the plate. The voice of doom announced over the loudspeakers that after Williams's retirement his uniform number, 9, would be permanently retired—the first time the Red Sox had so honored a player. We cheered. The national anthem was played. We cheered. The game began.

Williams was third in the batting order, so he came up in the bottom of the first inning, and Steve Barber, a young pitcher who was not yet born when Williams began playing for the Red Sox, offered him four pitches, at all of which he disdained to swing, since none of them were within the strike zone. This demonstrated simultaneously that Williams's eyes were razor-sharp and that Barber's control wasn't. Shortly, the bases were full, with Williams on second. "Oh, I hope he gets held up at third! That would be wonderful," the girl beside me moaned, and, sure enough, the man at bat walked and Williams was delivered into our foreground. He struck the pose of Donatello's David, the third-base bag being Goliath's head. Fiddling with his cap, swapping small talk with the Oriole third baseman (who seemed delighted to have him drop in), swinging his arms with a sort of prancing nervousness, he looked fine—flexible, hard, and not unbecomingly substantial through the middle. The long neck, the small head, the knickers whose cuffs were worn down near his ankles—all these points, often observed by caricaturists, were visible in the flesh.

One of the collegiate voices behind me said, "He looks old, doesn't he, old; big deep wrinkles in his face . . ."

"Yeah," the other voice said, "but he looks like an old hawk, doesn't he?"

With each pitch, Williams danced down the baseline, waving his arms and stirring dust, ponderous but menacing, like an attacking goose. It occurred to about a dozen humorists at once to shout "Steal home! Go, go!" Williams's speed afoot was never legendary. Lou Clinton, a young Sox outfielder, hit a fairly deep fly to center field. Williams tagged up and ran home. As he slid across the plate, the ball, thrown with unusual heft by Jackie Brandt, the Oriole center fielder, hit him on the back.

"Boy, he was really loafing, wasn't he?" one of the boys behind me said.

"It's cold," the other explained. "He doesn't play well when it's cold. He likes heat. He's a hedonist."

The run that Williams scored was the second and last of the inning. Gus Triandos, of the Orioles, quickly evened the score by plunking a home run over the handy left-field wall. Williams, who had had this wall at his back for twenty years, played the ball flawlessly. He didn't budge. He just stood there, in the center of the little patch of grass that his patient footsteps had worn brown, and, limp with lack of interest, watched the ball pass overhead. It was not a very interesting game. Mike Higgins, the Red Sox manager, with nothing to lose, had restricted his major league players to the left-field line— along with Williams, Frank Malzone, a first-rate third baseman, played the game—and had peopled the rest of the terrain with unpredictable youngsters fresh, or not so fresh, off the farms. Other than Williams's recurrent appearances at the plate, the *maladresse* of the Sox infield was the sole focus of suspense; the second baseman turned every grounder into a juggling act, while the shortstop did a breathtaking impersonation of an open window. With this sort of assistance, the Orioles wheedled their way into a 4–2 lead. They had early replaced Barber with another young pitcher, Jack Fisher. Fortunately (as it turned out), Fisher is no cutie; he is willing to burn the ball through the strike zone, and inning after inning this tactic punctured Higgins's string of test balloons.

Whenever Williams appeared at the Plate—pounding the dirt from his cleats, gouging a pit in the batter's box with his left foot, wringing resin out of the bat handle with his vehement grip, switching the stick at the pitcher with an electric ferocity—it was like having a familiar Leonardo appear in a shuffle of *Saturday Evening Post* covers. This man, you realized—and here, perhaps, was the difference, greater than the difference in gifts—really intended to hit the ball. In the third inning, he hoisted a high fly to deep center. In the fifth, we thought he had it; he smacked the ball hard and high into the heart of his power zone, but the deep right field in Fenway and the heavy air and a casual east wind defeated him. The ball died. Al Pilarcik leaned his back against the big "380" painted on the right-field wall and caught it. On another day, in another park, it would have been gone. (After the game, Williams said, "I didn't think I could hit one any harder than that. The conditions weren't good.")

The afternoon grew so glowering that in the sixth inning the arc lights were turned on—always a wan sight in the daytime, like the burning head-lights of a funeral procession. Aided by the gloom, Fisher was slicing through the Sox rookies, and Williams did not come to bat in the seventh. He was sec-ond up in the eighth. This was almost certainly his last time to come to the plate in Fenway Park, and instead of merely cheering, as we had at his three previous appearances, we stood, all of us—stood and applauded. Have you ever heard applause in a ball park? Just applause—no calling, no whistling, just an ocean of handclaps, minute after minute, burst after burst, crowding and run-ning together in continuous succession like the pushes of surf at the edge of the sand. It was a somber and considered tumult. There was not a boo in it. It seemed to renew itself out of a shifting set of memories as the kid, the marine, the veteran of feuds and failures and injuries, the friend of children, and the enduring old pro evolved down the bright tunnel of twenty-one summers to-ward this moment. At last, the umpire signaled for Fisher to pitch; with the other players, he had been frozen in position. Only Williams had moved during the ovation, switching his bat impatiently, ignoring everything except his cher-ished task. Fisher wound up, and the applause sank into a hush.

Understand that we were a crowd of rational people. We knew that a home run cannot be produced at will; the right pitch must be perfectly met and luck must ride with the ball. Three innings before, we had seen a brave ef-fort fail. The air was soggy; the season was exhausted. Nevertheless, there will always lurk, around a corner in a pocket of our knowledge of the odds, an in-defensible hope, and this was one of the times, which you now and then find in sports, when a density of expectation hangs in the air and plucks an event out of the future.

Fisher, after his unsettling wait, was wide with the first pitch. He put the second one over, and Williams swung mightily and missed. The crowd grunted, seeing that classic swing, so long and smooth and quick, exposed, naked in its failure. Fisher threw the third time, Williams swung again, and there it was. The ball climbed on a diagonal line into the vast volume of air over center field. From my angle, behind third base, the ball seemed less an ob-ject in flight than the tip of a towering, motionless construct, like the Eiffel Tower or the Tappan Zee Bridge. It was in the books while it was still in the sky. Brandt ran back to the deepest corner of the outfield grass; the ball de-scended beyond his reach and struck in the crotch where the bullpen met the wall, bounced chunkily, and, as far as I could see, vanished.

Like a feather caught in a vortex, Williams ran around the square of bases at the center of our beseeching screaming. He ran as he always ran out home runs—hurriedly, unsmiling, head down, as if our praise were a storm of rain to get out of. He didn't tip his cap. Though we thumped, wept, and chanted "We want Ted" for minutes after he hid in the dugout, he did not come back. Our noise for some seconds passed beyond excitement into a kind of immense open anguish, a wailing, a cry to be saved. But immortality is non-transferable. The papers said that the other players, and even the umpires on the field, begged him to come out and acknowledge us in some way, but he never had and did not now. Gods do not answer letters.

Every true story has an anticlimax. The men on the field refused to disappear, as would have seemed decent, in the smoke of Williams's miracle. Fisher continued to pitch, and escaped further harm. At the end of the inning, Higgins sent Williams out to his left-field position, then instantly replaced him with Carrol Hardy, so we had a long last look at Williams as he ran out there and then back, his uniform jogging, his eyes steadfast on the ground. It was nice, and we were grateful, but it left a funny taste.

One of the scholasticists behind me said, "Let's go. We've seen everything. I don't want to spoil it." This seemed a sound aesthetic decision. Williams's last word had been so exquisitely chosen, such a perfect fusion of expectation, intention, and execution, that already it felt a little unreal in my head, and I wanted to get out before the castle collapsed. But the game, though played by clumsy midgets under the feeble glow of the arc lights, began to tug at my attention, and I loitered in the runway until it was over. Williams's homer had, quite incidentally, made the score 4–3. In the bottom of the ninth inning, with one out, Marlin Coughtry, the second-base juggler, singled. Vic Wertz, pinch-hitting, doubled off the left-field wall, Coughtry advancing to third. Pumpsie Green walked, to load the bases. Willie Tasby hit a double-play ball to the third baseman, but in making the pivot throw Billy Klaus, an ex-Red Sox infielder, reverted to form and threw the ball past the first baseman and into the Red Sox dugout. The Sox won, 5–4. On the car radio as I drove home I heard that Williams had decided not to accompany the team to New York. So he knew how to do even that, the hardest thing. Quit.

Casey at the Congress

Stengel. Congress. Testimony.

Is there a more incongruous triple play?

You could look it up . . .

For the record, Casey delivered his oral hieroglyphics to a 1958 Senate subcommittee looking into the continued exemption of professional sports from antitrust laws. The venue hardly matters; whatever the issues, the Ol' Perfessor had his way of clarifying them.

SENATOR KEFAUVER: Mr. Stengel, you are the manager of the New York Yankees. Will you give us very briefly your background and your views about this legislation?

MR. STENGEL: Well, I started in professional ball in 1910. I have been in professional ball, I would say, for forty-eight years. I have been employed by numerous ball clubs in the majors and in the minor leagues.

I started in the minor leagues with Kansas City. I played as low as Class D ball, which was at Shelbyville, Kentucky, and also Class C ball and Class A ball, and I have advanced in baseball as a ballplayer.

I had many years that I was not so successful as a ballplayer, as it is a game of skill. And then I was no doubt discharged by baseball in which I had to go back to the minor leagues as a manager, and after being in the minor leagues as a manager, I became a major-league manager in several cities and was discharged, we call it discharged because there was no question I had to leave.

And I returned to the minor leagues at Milwaukee, Kansas City and Oakland, California, and then returned to the major leagues.

In the last ten years, naturally, in major-league baseball with the New York Yankees; the New York Yankees have had tremendous success, and while I am not a ballplayer who does the work, I have no doubt worked for a ball club that is very capable in the office.

I have been up and down the ladder. I know there are some things in baseball thirty-five to fifty years ago that are better now than they were in those days. In those days, my goodness, you could not transfer a ball club in the minor leagues, Class D, Class C ball, Class A ball.

How could you transfer a ball club when you did not have a highway? How could you transfer a ball club when the railroad then would take you to a town, you got off and then you had to wait and sit up five hours to go to another ball club?

How could you run baseball then without night ball?

You had to have night ball to improve the proceeds, to pay larger salaries, and I went to work, the first year I received $135 a month.

I thought that was amazing. I had to put away enough money to go to dental college. I found out it was not better in dentistry. I stayed in baseball. Any other question you would like to ask me?

SENATOR KEFAUVER: Mr. Stengel, are you prepared to answer particularly why baseball wants this bill passed?

MR. STENGEL: Well, I would have to say at the present time, I think that baseball has advanced in this respect for the player help. That is an amazing statement for me to make, because you can retire with an annuity at fifty and what organization in America allows you to retire at fifty and receive money?

I want to further state that I am not a ballplayer, that is, put into that pension fund committee. At my age, and I have been in baseball, well, I will say I am possibly the oldest man who is working in baseball. I would say that when they start an annuity for the ballplayers to better their conditions, it should have been done, and I think it has been done.

I think it should be the way they have done it, which is a very good thing.

The reason they possibly did not take the managers in at that time was because radio and television or the income to ball clubs was not large enough that you could have put in a pension plan.

Now I am not a member of the pension plan. You have young men here who are, who represent the ball clubs.

They represent the players and since I am not a member and don't receive pension from a fund which you think, my goodness, he ought to be declared in that, too, but I would say that is a great thing for the ballplayers.

That is one thing I will say for the ballplayers, they have an advanced pension fund. I should think it was gained by radio and television or you could not have enough money to pay anything of that type.

Now the second thing about baseball that I think is very interesting to the public or to all of us that it is the owner's own fault if he does not improve his club, along with the officials in the ball club and the players.

Now what causes that?

If I am going to go on the road and we are a traveling ball club and you know the cost of transportation now—we travel sometimes with three Pullman coaches, the New York Yankees and remember I am just a salaried man, and do not own stock in the New York Yankees. I found out that in traveling with the New York Yankees on the road and all, that it is the best, and we have broken records in Washington this year, we have broken them in every city but New York and we have lost two clubs that have gone out of the city of New York.

Of course, we have had some bad weather, I would say that they are mad at us in Chicago, we fill the parks.

They have come out to see good material. I will say they are mad at us in Kansas City, but we broke their attendance record.

Now on the road we only get possibly 27 cents. I am not positive of these figures, as I am not an official.

If you go back fifteen years or so if I owned stock in the club, I would give them to you.

SENATOR KEFAUVER: Mr. Stengel, I am not sure that I made my question clear.

MR. STENGEL: Yes, sir. Well, that is all right. I am not sure I am going to answer yours perfectly, either.

SENATOR O'MAHONEY: How many minor leagues were there in baseball when you began?

MR. STENGEL: Well, there were not so many at that time because of this fact: Anybody to go into baseball at that time with the educational schools that we had were small, while you were probably thoroughly educated at school, you had to be—we only had small cities that you could put a team in and they would go defunct.

Why, I remember the first year I was at Kankakee, Illinois, and a bank offered me $550 if I would let them have a little notice. I left there and took a uniform because they owed me two weeks' pay. But I either had to quit but I did not have enough money to go dental college so I had to go with the manager down to Kentucky.

What happened there was if you got by July, that was the big date. You did not play night ball and you did not play Sundays in half of the cities on account of a Sunday observance, so in those days when things were tough, and all of it was, I mean to say, why they just closed up July 4 and there you were sitting there in the depot.

You could go to work someplace else, but that was it.

So I got out of Kankakee, Illinois, and I just go there for the visit now.

SENATOR CARROLL: The question Senator Kefauver asked you was what, in your honest opinion, with your forty-eight years of experience, is the need for this legislation in view of the fact that baseball has not been subject to antitrust laws?

MR. STENGEL: No.

SENATOR LANGER: Mr. Chairman, my final question. This is the Antimonopoly Committee that is sitting here.

MR. STENGEL: Yes, sir.

SENATOR LANGER: I want to know whether you intend to keep on monopolizing the world's championship in New York City.

MR. STENGEL: Well, I will tell you. I got a little concern yesterday in the first three innings when I saw the three players I had gotten rid of, and I said when I lost nine what am I going to do and when I had a couple of my players I thought so great of that did not do so good up to the sixth inning I was more confused but I finally had to go and call on a young man in Baltimore that we don't own and the Yankees don't own him, and he is doing pretty good, and I would actually have to tell you that I think we are more the Greta Garbo type now from success.

We are being hated, I mean, from the ownership and all, we are being hated. Every sport that gets too great or one individual—but if we made 27 cents and it pays to have a winner at home, why would not you have a good winner in your own park if you were an owner?

That is the result of baseball. An owner gets most of the money at home and it is up to him and his staff to do better or they ought to be discharged.

SENATOR KEFAUVER: Thank you very much, Mr. Stengel. We appreciate your presence here. Mr. Mickey Mantle, will you come around? . . . Mr. Mantle, do you have any observations with reference to the applicability of the antitrust laws to baseball?

MR. MANTLE: My views are just about the same as Casey's.

Going to the Moon

BILL BARICH

Russians play hockey, basketball, volleyball and chess. They put the shot and hurl the javelin. They box. They wrestle. They whip us in the biathlon.

But they don't play baseball.

Except they do. Kind of.

Bill Barich's evocative works include the books *Laughing in the Hills, Traveling Light,* and *Crazy for Rivers.* In the late 1980s, he caught, in the pages of *The New Yorker,* the personalities and misadventures of the Moscow Red Devils as they barnstormed through the San Francisco Bay Area.

Whenever the Moscow Red Devils go barnstorming through a foreign country, they bring along twenty baseball players, a manager, a couple of coaches, and an equipment wrangler named Arkady, who has a bristly crewcut and often dresses in jeans and a leather flight jacket bearing an insignia patch from the fire department of West Babylon, New York. In some ways, Arkady is as important to the team as German Gulbitt, its crack pitcher, because he is in charge of selling the souvenirs that provide the Red Devils with some extra cash to supplement their monthly salary of roughly two hundred and fifty rubles.

Before each game, Arkady grabs a prominent spot in the grandstand and spreads out his wares, which include lacquered boxes, nesting dolls, cheap bracelets, Red Army hats, Rasputin caps of fake fur, Red Devils baseball cards, and a variety of Soviet watches that do everything from registering blood pressure to gauging barometric pressure. There is a set price for every item, of course, but it is set in Arkady's head and can be adjusted, depending on demand. On the March afternoon when I first met him, while the Red Devils were playing an exhibition game at Diablo Valley College, east of San Francisco, he was bargaining with a woman over the price of a nesting doll in the shape of Mikhail Gorbachev.

"Expensive in Russia," he said. "You can pay twenty-five dollars?"

"Well, I don't know," the woman replied, sounding as if she were worried about buying a Communist knickknack.

Arkady lifted Gorby and broke him apart to reveal a smaller doll inside. "Look, Brezhnev." Arkady smiled. Inside Brezhnev was Nikita Khrushchev. Inside Khrushchev was Joseph Stalin. And inside Stalin was a very tiny Vladimi Lenin.

"How about twenty dollars?"

"Sure," Arkady agreed, tossing in a hammer-and-sickle pin.

The Red Devils were making a whirlwind tow-week tour of some junior colleges and high schools in the Bay Area, and Diablo Valley was their third stop. I had looked them up after reading a little piece about them in a San Francisco newspaper. It told how a customs inspector at the Moscow airport had interrogated Andrei Tzelikovsky, their right fielder, about the strange wooden object he was carrying—a baseball bat. Tzelikovsky explained that it was for playing an American sport. "I'm going to play baseball in United States," he added, to which the inspector, still eying the bat, inquired, "Tell me, how far are you supposed to throw it?" After that, Tzelikovsky and the other ballplayers passed successfully through security, survived an arduous flight, and were now boarded at a Marriott Hotel in San Ramon, an East Bay suburb, where their rooms, outfitted with cable TV, executive-style desks, and miniature bottles of shampoo, were more opulent than anything in Moscow.

For a while after arriving, the Red Devils had suffered from jet lag, which was complicated by the newness of everything they saw in San Ramon—clean, sparkling buildings everywhere, all of them untouched by the perils of time—and although they claimed to be over their symptoms, they were still having some trouble on the ballfield. They had dropped their first two exhibition games by wide margins, and the scoreboard at Diablo Valley showed that they were behind by twenty-one runs in the top of the seventh inning.

That was to be expected, perhaps, since the Red Devils, for all their enthusiasm, are probably not much better than a top-notch high-school team in the United States. But at the same time, it was a far cry from their performance at home the previous season, when they'd won all but two of their twenty-eight games and had defeated their arch-rivals, the Red Army club, to take the baseball championship of the U.S.S.R.

Baseball is such a new sport in the Soviet Union that discrepancies are bound to occur. The Russians love gymnastics, they wax poetic over soccer, but to date most of them have not been tempted to pick up a mitt or put on a pair of spikes. Until the era of *glasnost,* in fact, you could have driven from Ashkhabad to Zyryanka without ever bumping into anybody playing catch. Only when the International Olympic Committee voted to make baseball part of the Olympic Games did the Soviet authorities decide to sponsor teams. The Red Devils began their efforts the following spring with a modest advertisement in a Moscow sporting gazette, which invited interested athletes, gifted or merely courageous, to attend a training camp at a local university.

Andrei Tzelikovsky was among the first to report. He is the team's best speaker of English, so he was acting as its spokesman on the California tour. (Most Red Devils have acquired only one complete English sentence, which is "Would you like to buy this?") Tall, fair-haired, and broad-shouldered, with an innocent, boyish face, Tzelikovsky looks younger than he is—twenty-two—even though he carries himself with an astonishing seriousness of purpose. This was his fourth trip to the States, and he was starting to learn the media ropes. When we were introduced, I tested his grasp of the vernacular by commenting that he was "getting a lot of ink," and he just blinked, nodded resolutely, and said, "Ya, ya, I know." He has a profound sense of the game's traditions and its lore, which has led him to adopt, in homage, a bad habit: he chews tobacco (Red Man) mixed with shredded bubble gum, spitting so stylishly that his all-time favorite player, Shoeless Joe Jackson, would be proud.

Tzelikovsky has a knack for telling a story, and he once explained to me how he developed his unusual affection for baseball. He said that at the age of six he was admitted to a Red Army volleyball academy in Moscow, where talented children are groomed for stardom. But four years later his father accepted a post with the Soviet trade mission in Montreal, and the family moved. By chance, the Tzelikovskys rented an apartment right across from the Montreal Expos' stadium, and almost immediately little Andrei grew curious about all the noise and excitement over there, pleading with his parents to take him to a game until his father broke down and bought some tickets. Bored, Tzelikovsky *père* went back to the apartment after the second inning, but his son remained seated, watching in wide-eyed wonder until the last out. The experience turned him into a rabid Expos fan, and he followed them on TV, collecting baseball books and magazines and even a few instructional videos, which he watched again and again on his VCR.

When the Tzelikovskys returned to Moscow, Andrei reentered the volleyball academy, but his heart wasn't in it anymore. (Every time he says the words *Red Army,* he makes a face, as if he'd just been served a plate of month-old cabbage.) He no longer dreamed of being famous for spiking shots over a net; instead, he wanted to be a baseball player. There were no diamonds anywhere in the city, though, so he practiced at a neighborhood park every Sunday, using a stick and a tennis ball to give his friends batting instruction. He did not touch a real bat in Russia until he went out for the Olympic team.

His memories of the training camp are still vivid, in fact. The scene was chaotic, he says, at least in the early days, with dozens of fit-looking, well-intentioned Soviet men gripping baseballs and pegging them to one another, often missing their intended target by more than a yard. Still, out of the chaos a number of promising athletes emerged, and they formed the nucleus of the Red Devils: four tennis players, an Olympic medalist in handball, Tzelikovsky himself, and three former javelin throwers, who gave up factory jobs to become pitchers.

"It was difficult at first," Tzelikovsky told me, tugging at the bill of his red cap, which had the letters CCCP stitched in gold across its crown. "Our equipment was not very good. We just had some old stuff that Cuban players had left behind. Our own players didn't know the rules. Sometimes, if they hit the ball they ran to third base instead of to first. And our Soviet umpires didn't know the rules, either. They made them up for their own pleasure. How could we argue with them? The first game we ever played, we lost 48–0, to a visiting team from Nicaragua. We needed coaching very badly. One afternoon on the metro, I was riding home from a game in my uniform, and an American, a student, came up to me. He had pitched for Colgate University—do you know about Colgate?—so I asked him to come out and teach us about curveballs." Tzelikovsky paused to shrug. "In this way," he said, "we began to improve."

When the Red Devils were still down by twenty-one runs in the middle of the seventh inning, the various coaches, umpires, factotums, and functionaries in attendance at Diablo Valley reached a wise and probably merciful decision, relying on some English and some sign language, to call the game. There was a little daylight left, so the Soviet players took advantage of it by retreating to the batting cages and laboring at their hitting until dusk, pointing up how disciplined and hardworking they are. If you're a Red Devil, you don't want to miss a practice session unless you have a good excuse. Alexei Pavlinchuk, the team's manager, a Sverdlovsk native with penetrating eyes, runs a tight ship and doles out fines with abandon. Anyone caught drinking without permission loses half his salary for the month. Smoking without permission is also frowned on, and costs the perpetrator a fourth of his salary. If you curse, you pay ten rubles for the first offense and double that for the second. There is no appeal.

While the Red Devils were taking their cuts, I sat in the stands with Tim Hickerson, who was responsible for bringing the Soviet team to California. A former minor leaguer in the Chicago Cubs system, Hickerson is an intelligent, soft-spoken man in his mid-thirties who loves baseball as much as Andrei Tzelikovsky does. As the proprietor of a fledgling travel agency in San Francisco, he arranges vacations abroad for American amateurs who want to play against foreign teams in their natural habitat, and does the same sort of thing for foreign teams that want to come to the United States. The Red Devils were involved in such an exchange program. Hickerson had sent a team from Monte Vista High School, in Danville, near San Ramon, on a ten-day trip to Moscow, and now a boosters' group from Monte Vista was reciprocating by hosting the Soviets, providing them with complimentary lodging and meals along with their airfare.

The Red Devils' next game was in Stockton, at Delta Junior College, and when Hickerson offered me a ride to the ballpark I accepted. He picked me up at the Marriott in a beat-up Chevy Nova, cream-colored, whose odometer had rolled over at least once. The car made odd sounds. It did not inspire confidence. But Hickerson, who sometimes drives a cab to stay afloat, appeared to be in control of the vehicle. Although he isn't in playing condition anymore, he still has an athlete's reflexes. He was an All-Conference center fielder during his university days, at Berkeley—Jackie Jensen recruited him—but he's built more like a catcher, thick through the chest and stubby in the legs. I mentioned this to him, and he said that he used to be taller, but he'd fallen off a roof while working as a roofer eleven years ago and had shrunk a little.

As an exercise, I once scribbled out a list of all the jobs Hickerson has held. It read like an author's bio from the he-man epoch of American literature, when no dust jacket was complete without a catalog of unpredictable employment. In addition to being a roofer, he'd been a logger, an usher at a theater, a reporter for the *People's Daily World,* a baseball manager in the Italian major leagues, the stage manager for a travelling French magician, and a batting coach in Managua. Then, too, you had to take his aspirations into account. He had wanted to act, to direct films, and also to be a writer in the way of Hemingway or Henry Miller, all to no avail.

We had spectacular weather for our trip to Stockton. The night before, an Alaskan storm had blown through California, leaving the green hills of the

East Bay dusted with snow. Creeks that had been dead dry a month ago were running high and muddy, spilling over rocks and flowing down past black oaks and pepper trees. There was a sweet fragrance in the air, and I found myself thinking about Andrei Tzelikovsky, who would already be at the ballpark, dressed in his uniform and eager for action.

Hickerson was daydreaming about baseball, too. It's his central obsession, and he said that if his travel business clicks he hopes to coach or play in Japan or Australia, or maybe in Cuba—anywhere, really, that he can get a game. He has already played in Moscow, having gone there with a team of over-the-hill baseball lovers, among them an attorney, a doctor, and a psychologist. For the privilege of engaging the Red Devils on their home turf, the American wannabes paid Hickerson about three thousand dollars apiece. Hickerson had been to the Soviet Union before, so he informed his charges that they were in for culture shock, not a Club Med holiday. They should expect sterile rooms, flimsy towels, rough toilet paper, and lots of cheese, sausage, caviar, and heavy brown bread.

If Hickerson has any regrets about his devotion to baseball, they focus on his failure to make the big leagues. After leaving Berkeley, he played with the Bradenton Cubs in the Florida rookie league and did well enough to be asked to the Cubs' instructional-league camp that fall. When he hit .349 in a forty-game season, he was sure that he'd be offered a AAA contract. Instead, the Cubs sent him a contract similar to the one he'd had in the rookie league. He accepted the contract very reluctantly, and when he went to Arizona for spring training, he had some run-ins with the Cubs front office and was dropped from the squad. He figured that on the basis of his hitting another team would want him, but he was turned down everywhere. He handled the dismissal poorly and became a little lost and purposeless until, through the intercession of a baseball pal from Berkeley, he landed a manager's job in San Giovanni in Persiceto, Italy.

Hickerson had never heard of San Giovanni in Persiceto, but he learned that it was a city of about twenty thousand, not far from Bologna. He lived in one room at the Hotel Leone and earned about five hundred dollars a month for directing a team of semi-pros, who played their games on weekends. Of necessity he became fluent in Italian. He loved Italian food, women, and wine, and made many friends. In the off-season, when there wasn't any baseball, he sometimes stayed in San Giovanni anyway and supported himself by giving English lessons.

In all, he managed five different Italian clubs over the next few years. The players he dealt with could be peculiarly challenging in their demands.

Hickerson once had an American transplant who wouldn't practice unless he could get bacon and eggs at a trattoria every morning. He had an outfielder who tried to catch fly balls by holding his mitt stationary in front of his face. He had a pitcher who declined to issue intentional walks, because they reflected badly on his masculinity.

"After my first season at San Giovanni, I went back to California for a couple of years and then took a job in Castenaso," he told me, flipping on his directional signal as we approached Stockton. "I got fired for arguing with the team's owner. I thought that was it for Italy, so I went home again, but then I changed my mind and came back for one more try. Nobody hired me, though, and by the summer I was sitting around in San Giovanni with a bottle of whiskey and a plane ticket to the United States. But on the day I was going to leave I got a message that the *presidente* of the Sant'Arcangelo di Romagna club was coming to see me. He pulled up in a huge Peugeot sedan. He was a big, fat guy, maybe three hundred pounds, whose passion was collecting stamps. He asked me to take over Sant'Arcangelo for the second half of the season, and gave me a car, an apartment, and even a washing machine.

"I had a great success and turned the team from losers into winners. We were based near Rimini, and we used to drink Chianti and swim in the Adriatic to celebrate our victories. The Florence Lions, one of Italy's top teams, hired me away from Sant'Arcangelo, but they expected a miracle from me, and when I didn't deliver it they fired me. After that, the only club that wanted me was Godo. Do you know Godo?" I said that I didn't, and Hickerson said, "Godo is in the second division."

The two oldest players on the Red Devils, Leonid Korneyev and German Gulbitt—thirty-four and thirty-six, respectively—are pitchers, although Korneyev, who carries a big bat, doubles as a first baseman. By virtue of their maturity, they seemed to be enjoying the tour more than the younger players, not taking things quite so seriously. At the Marriott one night, Gulbitt approached me dressed in an incredible suit with inch-wide gray and white stripes and tried to sell me a Soviet watch. When I said, *"Nyet,"* politely and with a grin, Gulbitt reacted merrily, as if we were just messing around, and gave me a gentle little pat on the back before continuing to work his way through the potential customers in the hotel lobby.

Korneyev happened to be on the mound at Delta Junior College when Hickerson and I arrived. Heavyset and powerful-looking, he throws hard for a Red Devil, and the Mustangs of Delta were having difficulty timing his pitches. To the amazement of practically everyone, the score was tied at 3–all in the bottom of the third inning. The ballpark at the college was really very pretty and well maintained, and that might have contributed to the Red Devils' improving their game. There were dugouts and new bleachers, the grass had recently been cut, and an outfield wall (a row of tall bushes behind a chain-link fence) bound all the elements together in a sweet symmetry. A decent crowd had turned out, too, more than a hundred people, and everyone would laugh good-naturedly when, say, Alexander Krupenchenkov came to bat and a student announcer on the P.A. system tried to wrap his tongue around the unfamiliar syllables.

Stockton has always had a reputation as a conservative city, so it surprised me when the fans applauded the Soviet players for making a nice catch or stealing a base, but Hickerson told me he'd observed this phenomenon every time he'd seen the Red Devils compete in the United States. Apparently, Americans were touched by their earnestness and wanted them to know they were appreciated. As we sat watching the game, another thing that Hickerson had said resonated in my mind—that because the Red Devils had learned their baseball as adults, their movements on the field seemed slightly unnatural. For instance, although they threw with marvelous accuracy, there was usually a noticeable hitch, or a slight pause, *before* the throw, which indicated that a thought had preceded the action. The smooth, silky quality of intuition that sends a shortstop gliding toward the hole in advance of a ball's being hit there was missing from their play.

The Red Devils were also lacking in infield chatter. A kind of loose-limbed, high-spirited jive runs through an American team when it's humming, but the Soviets were not yet comfortable enough on a baseball diamond to relax. Sometimes they were as studiously correct as pupils at a dancing school, concentrating so hard on their steps that they scarcely heard the melody. The word "fun" was not a constant in their vocabulary. But, on the other hand, they were still in the early stages of their evolution, and had only just reached the point where they were starting to invent some baseball slang. They called the diamond, in Russian, "the square." A pop fly was a "candle." If a player made a sharp, precise throw, someone might say, "Sergei, that was a real bayonet!" The area where the infield dirt gives way to the crescent-shaped outfield grass was known as "the moon," and this allowed the Red Devils to indulge a lyrical impulse by saying, when Tzelikovsky trotted to his position, "Andrei has gone to the moon."

Like most forcibly retired baseball managers, Hickerson has trouble attending a game without voicing his opinions. At Stockton, he kept second-guessing Pavlinchuk. Doubtless Hickerson would have liked to don a Red

Devils uniform and assume the managerial helm. Although his Russian was limited to a few phrases, he knew some of the Soviet players by name and had conversed with them both here and abroad, often through an interpreter. If a ballplayer asked him for some batting tips, he was glad to oblige.

Unfortunately for the Red Devils, the tide began to turn in the fifth inning. They stayed in contention, tying the score again at 5–all, but the Mustangs had the home-field advantage, and they chipped away at the Soviet pitchers and went on to win by four runs. This was the closest the Red Devils had ever come to a victory in California, but they still didn't look very happy. They weren't fond of losing to Americans. They had a diplomatic attitude about it, though, and immediately embarked on their postgame ritual, emptying their duffelbags and displaying the goods that they'd brought along to barter.

The Mustangs stepped tentatively forward and fingered the clothing, as they might at a flea market. Yevgeny Puchkov (.444 average last year) had a deal going with one Mustang, who wanted to trade an old mitt for something Russian. Along with generating some slang, the Red Devils are acquiring nicknames, the Puchkov, who has a brooding countenance, is known as Mubarak, because he resembles the Egyptian President. Infielder Ilya Bogatirev picked up the moniker Home Boy on the team's last American swing, while Alexander Vidyaev, a second baseman, must toil under the weight of a Russian diminutive—Malenky (Little One)—which, though it's endearing, he hates.

"You got any of those funky fur hats?" the Mustang asked. "That's what I really want to trade you for."

Puchkov examined the mitt on offer, which was streaked and pitted and begrimed and had turned a skunky shade of blackish brown. "No hats," he said, before reaching into his bag and pulling out a tank top that showed a cartoonish Gorby and several apparatchiks astride Harley-Davidson motorcycles. The legend beneath the illustration, done in heavy-metal style, read "Kremlin Crew." Gorby had the middle finger of one hand extended.

The tank top made the Mustang giggle. "No way I want that," he protested. "I want one of them fur hats."

"No hats," Puchov informed him again, shaking his head wearily, as if the Mustang had overlooked a tremendous bargain.

Every dedicated ballplayer keeps a mental record of how he's doing, and when fans asked Andrei Tzelikovsky for a rundown of his stats after the Delta Junior College game, he said, "I am three for nine at the plate. I have made no fielding errors." That was a satisfactory performance, he felt, although not exactly thrilling. Tzelikovsky wished that he had the uncanny grace of his batting hero, Ted Williams, whose book *The Science of Hitting* he'd read more than twenty times. Once, while we were hanging out, I brought up a famous story about Williams' eyesight, which was supposed to be so sharp that he could see, in minute particulars, his bat making contact with the ball.

"Ya, ya, I know," Tzelikovsky said. He told me that he hoped Pavlinchuk might let him pitch an inning or two before the tour was over. He had pitched in Moscow, he said, and a radar gun had clocked his fastball at seventy-eight miles per hour.

On his free afternoons, Tzelikovsky had been joining his teammates on field trips coordinated by the Red Devils' hosts in San Ramon. The players went to Chinatown in San Francisco, and they were bused to various suburban malls and invited to do some browsing. This put them in a bit of a fix, since they had only a little ready cash, but they learned to bypass Macy's and Nordstrom and head for discount stores like Kmart, where, at rock-bottom prices, they bought fanny packs, Walkman knock-offs, and cheap sets of carving knives.

When there were no special activities planned, Tzelikovsky liked to stay in his room at the hotel. He relished the spaciousness and the privacy, and watched ballgames and movies on TV. As his executive-style desk, he wrote postcards to his friends and family. An only child, he still lived with his mother and father, even though they were disappointed in him for dropping volleyball (and the safety of a career in the Red Army) for the iffiness of Soviet baseball. Out of his salary, he contributed fifty rubles a month toward household expenses. The Tzelikovskys were feeling a financial pinch these days, like most other Russians, he said. The shelves in Moscow's food stores were frequently empty, and the lines of customers were long.

As an antidote to all this, Tzelikovsky made it a point to treat himself to lunch every afternoon at the McDonald's in Red Square—it was his only luxury. In his scrupulous way, he'd been comparing the McDonald's cuisine in the Bay Area with the franchised food at home. The burgers tasted the same, he submitted, but in the milkshakes he detected subtle differences.

He enjoyed telling me about the famous baseball players he'd met, too. In Baltimore once, he had spent time with Mark McGwire and picked up some pointers, while in Moscow fate had led him to an encounter with Sadaharu Oh, Japan's greatest slugger and a figure of near-mythological proportions. Tzelikovsky watched Oh give a batting demonstration and then—better yet—had an opportunity to speak with him and get some Zen-like advice.

"Baseball is cooperation, not competition," Oh instructed him. "A pitcher is your friend, not your enemy. He is sending you a gift, and it is your responsibility as a batter to send it right back to him, toward the bleachers."

One night at the end of the Red Devils' tour, Tzelikovsky had to go to San Francisco for a radio interview, and we decided to ride in together with Tim Hickerson as our chauffeur. Waiting in the hotel lobby for the guest of honor to finish his shower, Hickerson looked ill at ease in the presence of so much marble and glitter. In his current economic state, an Italian meal at a North Beach restaurant amounted to a splurge, he confessed. But Hickerson felt no ambivalence about starting a new business at a time in life when some of his contemporaries were already looking forward to retiring. "I like travelling," he said happily. "I like Russians. I like being in uniform and chewing tobacco. I like bullshitting. Hey, I get to be a little boy again!"

When Tzelikovsky swept into the lobby, clean and neat in his best clothes, we piled into the Nova and took off for the city. Tzelikovsky showed no signs of nervousness. He assured us that he'd been on the radio before, and once he was in front of a microphone at KSFO-AM, he proved to be in his element, nimbly fielding questions from callers.

"Hiya, Andrei. I was just wondering, you admire any American players?"

"Ya. Here are three—Lenny Dykstra, Bob Welch, and Mark McGwire. I met Mark McGwire in Baltimore. I have a letter he wrote to me in Moscow."

"Is he a good guy?"

"Ya."

"Andrei, how do you keep up with baseball when you're over there in Russia?"

"It's difficult. I listen to Voice of America for the scores."

"Yo, Andrei. It's cool you're here in California, man. What do you think about Rickey Henderson? He's making, like—what?—three million dollars?"

"Rickey is worth it."

"You really think that?"

"Rickey is worth every penny."

After the interview, Tzelikovsky wanted to peek into the Hard Rock Cafe. (One T-shirt that the Red Devils were selling had the restaurant's emblem on it, with the words "Hard Rock" in Cyrillic.) While Hickerson idled at the curb, I led Tzelikovsky through the door and into a dining room decked out with electric guitars, Elvis photos, gold records, and other rock-and-roll memorabilia. The place must have appeared unimaginably bright and wealthy to Tzelikovsky, but he didn't seem to be impressed, and said as we left that he had always thought it was a *private* club. Then we parked at a McDonald's and bought him a dinner of a Big Mac, fries, some kind of pie-like thing, and a chocolate milkshake, all to go.

And then we were on the freeway again, returning to San Ramon. It was a moonless night, and we drove through a landscape of farms, ranches, and weedy fields mixed in with new suburbs and industrial parks. On the radio, Tzelikovsky had been careful not to say anything critical of the United States, so I asked him to tell me, in all honesty, if there was anything about the country that he didn't like. He meditated for a minute and said, "The people here live very far from one another." He said it soberly. After that, we changed the subject to baseball, and Tzelikovsky spoke of his eagerness for the U.S.S.R. season to begin. The Soviet first division was going to expand to ten teams, so the Red Devils would play fifty-four games, not just twenty-eight. There were supposed to be teams in Kiev, Vladivostok, Odessa, and Tbilisi. At the mention of Tbilisi, Hickerson got excited and said, "Tbilisi? I'd love to play in Georgia!"

In the morning, the Red Devils had a game with the Monte Vista High School team. The weather did them a favor this time, turning cool and blustery and reminding them of Moscow. Tzelikovsky was in a batting cage practicing his swing when I got there, and after he finished we talked by the dugout. He proudly showed me his most recent American purchase—a plaque with Mark McGwire's picture on it, which he had bartered for at a sporting-goods store. But he soon became gloomy and serious again, and told me that he hadn't yet bought any gifts for his parents, because he had no money left. It occurred to me that it might not be a bad thing to own a nesting doll, so we haggled over the one Andrei had in his duffelbag and settled on a price of twenty dollars. When I gave him the bill, he folded it in quarters, stuck it in a pocket, shook hands with me, and said, in his grave manner, "Thank you very much." He tapped the dirt from his spikes after that, adjusted his cap, and ran briskly toward the outfield, going to the moon.

The Birth of Joe Hardy

DOUGLASS WALLOP

Somewhere inside all of us, there's a Major Leaguer aching to break free. You know how the fantasy goes. The dramatic home run. The sensational catch. The champagne in the clubhouse. The toast of the town. But, of course, a fantasy is just that: a fantasy. Reality intrudes, and the reverie's discarded like an old pine-tar rag in the existential on-deck circle. Unless you happened to be Douglass Wallop (1920–1984). He gave his form. Of course, he was hooked on impossible dreams. He rooted for the Washington Senators.

In 1954, Wallop updated the Faust legend with a baseball spin in his enormously popular novel, *The Year the Yankees Lost the Pennant*. The book sold more than 2 million copies, spawned the Broadway musical *Damn Yankees,* then was pretty much forgotten. Which is too bad. The book is terrific.

It opens with a tired, middle-aged real-estate salesman named Joe Boyd making a pact with the devil (Mr. Applegate, a Yankee fan, no less) that will turn him into the superstar his beloved Senators need to lead them to the promised land. In the selection that follows, we witness Boyd's thrilling transformation into Joe Hardy, Washington wonder boy.

It turns out that real fantasy beneath *The Year the Yankees Lost the Pennant* had nothing to do with the Faust legend, Lucifer on earth, or even the possibility of a Joe Hardy. The real fantasy was promoting the illusion that the Senators could actually capture another flag. They hadn't won a pennant since 1933, and—to give the devil and expansion their due—never would.

The original Senators moved to Minnesota after the 1960 season. The motley crew installed to replace them in time to muff the first ball JFK would throw out in 1961 would also abandon Washington—to become the Texas Rangers. Interestingly, a former Texas Ranger owner, George W. Bush, has since established his own franchise in Washington.

History will determine the equitability of that trade.

B riggs Stadium," Joe said as he got into the taxi and then, waving briefly to Applegate, sat back expectantly.

They had shopped until one o'clock and lunched at the hotel. It was now about three.

"Just get in the cab and relax," had been Applegate's final instruction. "By the time you get to the ball park you'll be the new guy."

The new guy, they agreed, should have a different name, and their choice had been Joe Hardy because, as Applegate pointed out, it sounded rather athletic.

But it was still Joe Boyd who sat in the taxi. This was evident from the mirror which Joe, sitting on the edge of the seat, watched intently: Still Joe Boyd's gray hair and mild blue eyes, although not Joe Boyd's clothes. In the mirror, beneath the creased and grizzled chin and slack folds of throat showed now the collar of a white oxford button-down shirt and the knot of a black and yellow tie of regimental stripes, neither of which items Joe Boyd had ever worn but about which Applegate was insistent. Joe looked again at the rest of the outfit Applegate had assembled so finically—the gray flannel slacks and the shetland jacket, a soft tan in shade. The slacks were tight in the waist and seat, and the jacket too large in the shoulders, but Applegate said these matters would be taken care of as soon as he became the new guy.

The blocks were passing rapidly and Joe, his eye on the mirror again, asked, "How much farther now?"

"Just a few blocks more," the driver said.

Joe's brow furrowed. He lit a cigarette, dragged on it twice and flipped it out the window. "Okay, Applegate, okay, how about it?" he muttered, thinking again that a taxi was a ridiculous place to pick for the transformation, if indeed there was to be a transformation. At the same time he was struck by the thought that it was brash of him to talk to Applegate so disrespectfully. Yet, already, he seemed to have lost his awe of Applegate. To have spent the past few hours with him, to have watched his picayune attention to detail, to have listened to his endlessly detailed instructions, was to lose awe. For long minutes at a time he had caught himself thinking that this companion in shopping and later in luncheon was indeed nothing more than a man named Applegate.

The cab was cutting over to the curb lane and pulling to a stop.

The mirror still showed the face of Joe Boyd, and it was with irritation that Joe reached into his pocket for a bill. Still watching the mirror, he handed it to the driver over the seat.

It must have happened when he switched his glance to count the change the driver was dropping into his palm, for with the dropping of the last dime he saw a concerned expression pass over the driver's face. The quarter Joe returned as a tip was unnoticed.

He looked quickly at the mirror and then, grinning, got out and slammed the door. "Good luck, driver," he said in a vibrating voice and then headed for the ball-park entrance, carrying in his mind's eye the image of a young face, of close-cropped hair, blond as his had been blond in youth, of a face grown ruddy and flesh become firm and of eyes clear and snapping.

There had been a time, some years before, when he had taken his vacation with a guy in the office; his two weeks had fallen squarely athwart an antique show for which Bess had been committed months in advance to act as hostess-guide. Setting off on a poker and fishing trip, he had felt guilt and elation, and it was this combination, only with much more of each, that he felt now as he asked the way to the visiting team's dressing room and was directed along a concrete runway beneath the grandstand.

The teams were meeting in a twi-night doubleheader, starting at six o'clock.

Joe tried the door. It was locked and, dropping his equipment bag, he waited. Ten minutes passed. Assuring himself that no one was in sight, he jogged a distance down the runway, then broke into a sprint. Grinning, he returned to the doorway and did a few deep knee bends.

At four o'clock some of the players began to arrive, and in another few minutes Joe spied Mr. Benny van Buren, the Washington team's manager, hurrying along the runway, wearing a harassed look and, perhaps because of it, instantly recognizable from his pictures. Mr. van Buren was a man of a weathered, rather florid countenance, with sandy, tufted eyebrows. He had reached the door and his hand was on the knob before Joe spoke his name.

"I beg your pardon, Mr. van Buren, my name is Joe Hardy," Joe said, holding out his hand which, after a second's hesitation, Mr. van Buren shook without enthusiasm.

"What can I do for you, son?" he said.

"I'd like a tryout," Joe said, indicating the equipment bag at Mr. van Buren's feet. "I've got all my stuff right here."

Mr. van Buren looked from valise to Joe with eyes crinkled at the corners from many long nights of squinting at pop flies against light towers. They were the eyes of a man who has known great suffering, and Joe felt a wave of sympathy. In his playing days, Mr. van Buren had been a hell-for-leather third baseman, the best the team had ever had. Managing a seventh-place team these five years must have been gall.

"If I could just hit a couple while the team's taking batting practice," Joe went on as Mr. van Buren still hesitated. "That's all the time I'd need. Okay?"

"Where've you been playing, fella?" Mr. van Buren asked.

"Oh, here and there," Joe said, quickly adding, "I wouldn't take up more than a minute or two."

"Where is here and there?" Mr. van Buren persisted.

"Well, to be honest, it was mostly sandlot ball, but I can hit a ball quite a distance, I think."

"You think?"

"Well, I'm pretty sure."

At this point a swarthy individual with a dour expression approached.

"Hiya, Rocky, how's the wing?" Mr. van Buren asked.

The newcomer shook his head ruefully. "Wing's okay, Ben," he said, "but I've got a terrific headache. I don't think I'd better pitch tonight."

Mr. van Buren frowned. "Headache from what?" he asked.

"Well, it was so hot and I didn't feel like going out, so I was sitting up in the hotel room, watching TV most of the day, and it gave me a buster of a headache."

Again Mr. van Buren frowned, and Joe felt his own brow crease in sympathy with the manager. This must be Rocky Pratt, the guy everybody said had so much potential but who never delivered. With an attitude like this it was small wonder.

"I've tried aspirin," the indisposed pitcher went on, "but it didn't help."

Mr. van Buren looked up with an expression blended of disdain and hopelessness. "Okay," he said curtly, "suppose you pitch batting practice. Maybe it'll help your head." He turned to Joe. "Okay, kid, there's your man. Go out and let's see what you can do."

The pitcher shrugged and entered the dressing room. As Joe bent to pick up the bag, he was clapped on the shoulder, and Mr. van Buren was smiling. "That," he said, "in case you don't know it, son, was Mr. Rocky Pratt, and there's something very tragic about the case of Mr. Pratt. For five years he's been wanting us to trade him to the Yankees. Only—" and Mr. van Buren chuckled—"the Yankees don't want him."

Joe dressed uneasily, his back to the room, his face to the recesses of an empty locker, worried for a while that Applegate, with his already apparent fondness for bum jokes, might pull a switch on him, and he would be exposed before this group of stalwarts as a fifty-year-old real-estate salesman.

As a safeguard, he put on the baseball cap Applegate had provided, pulling its long peak low over his eyes and then listening, with growing surprise and some disappointment, to the conversation going on about the room. Without ever really thinking about it, he had always assumed that the men of a seventh-place team would be cast down in gloom. He had pictured them with clenched fists and teeth and narrowed eyes, somewhat the way he felt he himself looked as he listened to a baseball broadcast.

But around him there were only relatively happy sounds. A couple of guys were discussing TV programs they had known and two others their children. Somebody told a joke. Rocky Pratt was being addressed in a low voice by someone who laughed every few seconds. "Nuts," Pratt interpolated. Then the low voice and the laugh, and from Pratt: "Yeah? Oh, yeah? Nuts."

And now and then the sound of spiked shoes on concrete as one after another of the players finished dressing and headed for the field.

Joe shook his head, puzzled. The thrill would be less in bailing out a team bland in defeat. And then he remembered Mr. van Buren and felt better. Mr. van Buren was a man who cared.

Hanging on the inside of the locker door was a small mirror and, bending down, Joe took a look at the lean face beneath the peak of the cap. He liked what he saw, then thought again of Bess as she must have appeared when she read his note; he looked longer and still liked what he saw. It's only for a little while, he told himself, and I can go back if I like. That's the good part of it.

It was a glaringly hot afternoon, or should have been, Joe thought, as he walked out onto the field; and then he halted in his tracks, a smile spreading slowly over his face. It should have been apparent immediately, but not until now had he grasped it. Since the second he stepped from the taxi, he had felt neither heat nor humidity. Applegate was a man of many facets.

Still smiling, he looked around the park. Except for a few refreshment butchers, the stands were empty. A couple of guys were in the outfield shagging flies and a few others were fooling around the infield. The rest were still in the dressing room. Rocky Pratt was already on the hill, loosening up and pausing now and then to press the heel of his hand to his temple and shake his head vigorously.

Joe walked over to the dugout, picked up a bat and immediately put it down again, remembering all he had read about ball players and their favorite bats. A player was sitting in a corner of the dugout, clipping his nails. "Take one of those on the end," he said, not looking up.

"Thanks," Joe said, selected one, and headed for the plate.

The batting cage had been wheeled up and Pratt was firing them in hard. Joe watched, suddenly uneasy. Applegate now was far away, and although this might be a young man's body it was still Joe Boyd inside. Joe Boyd inside was at the moment very queasy. And there was still Joe Boyd's memory—the memory, for instance, of how Joe Boyd in his youth had been a terrible sucker for a roundhouse curve.

The ball came toward the plate like a bullet and hit the catcher's mitt with the report of a cannon.

Affecting nonchalance, Joe gazed toward the outfield, noticing on the scoreboard that the Yankees were leading the Indians six to one in the fifth.

That helped. Gripping the bat, he took a couple of practice swings and was surprised at the co-ordination in his muscles and at the way his stomach stretched tight as he pivoted.

"Okay," Pratt said.

Many hours before, Joe had decided that he would swing left-handed, and it was as a left-handed batter that he stepped now to the plate.

Pratt's first pitch zipped in under his wrists, and he stood with rooted spikes, not offering. Again the ball came in and once more he stood frozen. The catcher made a sound of impatience.

"There's nothing to it," Applegate had said. "All you gotta do is swing. I'll take care of the rest."

On the next pitch he swung. The ball soared on a line into deepest center field.

"Nice poke, kid," the catcher muttered.

"But after you get the feel of one or two, you're on your own," Applegate had said. "Oh, I may decide to amuse myself occasionally but don't get the idea you're going to be any robot. You'll be on your own."

The next one he hit into the same spot.

"Nice poke again, boy."

Something was bubbling up inside Joe, making him want to laugh, but he set his jaw, dug in his spikes.

"See what you can do with this one," Pratt called. He delivered, and then turned to watch the ball sail into deep right center.

"Hey," Joe heard a voice shouting, "somebody better go in and get Benny out here. Hold it a minute, Rocky."

Pratt stood on the mound, bouncing the ball in his glove. Joe waggled the bat, not so much as wanting to disturb the position of his feet for fear of breaking the spell.

When Mr. van Buren appeared he called, "Bear down this time, Rocky," and took a stand near the first-base coach's box.

Other activity ceased. Additional players hurried from the dressing room, and while all watched, Joe Hardy swung four times more; three were modest-length home runs, and the fourth went clear over the upper right-field stands, quite a poke in Detroit.

At this point, Mr. van Buren called a halt. "Okay, kid," he said in a restrained voice; but his grip on Joe's biceps as he steered him toward the dugout was anything but calm. At the same time he started shouting hoarsely, "Kent! Where's Kent? . . . Well, go find him, quick!"

Kent Kenyon, Joe learned in a few minutes, was the club's road secretary, the only official traveling with the team who was authorized to sign new players to a contract.

★　　★　　★　　★　　★

The next morning Joe tried to buy a Washington paper first at the hotel, but he had to walk three blocks before he found a place that sold one. It was the same paper which Bess, perhaps even at this moment, was spreading beside her plate at breakfast. But certainly not to its sports page, Joe knew. More likely to the obituary page.

It was to the sports page that he opened it immediately, and his eye ran straight off to the right-hand column. He read:

"Detroit, July 22—Two pinch-hit home runs off the bat of a 21-year-old ex-sandlotter carried the Nats to a double win over the Tigers tonight, for their first twin victory of the season. The scores were 6 to 3 and 5 to 4.

"Young Joe Hardy, signed to a Washington contract less than an hour before the curtain-raiser of the twi-night affair, produced the Frank Merriwell pokes each time in the ninth inning, driving across four runs in all."

Joe skimmed two paragraphs and came to:

"Young Hardy, about whom little is known save that he never before had played organized ball, was sent up to the plate in the first game with the score tied 3 and 3 in the ninth and two men on base. He hit a 2 and 0 pitch into the stands to give his mates the ball game.

"In the nightcap the score was again tied, this time at four apiece, when Joe was called from the dugout to swing for Bill Gregson. He responded with another home run in almost the same spot as the first.

"The double win halted, at least temporarily, the Nats' nosedive toward seventh place and moved them to within three games of the fifth-place Tigers.

"Manager Benny van Buren, highly elated over young Hardy's feats, said the young man would be in the starting lineup for tomorrow's finale with the Tigers, after which the team moves on to Chicago. Oddly enough, young Hardy says he's not particular about what position he plays. Van Buren said he has right field in mind for the redoubtable neophyte."

"Well I'll be damned, how do you like that?" Joe asked himself jubilantly. With springs in his legs, he began walking swiftly back to the hotel, constructing an imaginary telephone conversation.

"Bess," he would say, "did you see about me in the paper this morning?"

Or he would call the office and say, "Hey, did any of you guys happen to read about a certain party named Joe Hardy in this morning's paper?" And then, his voice swelling, "Well, that's me. Joe Boyd. I'm in Detroit. We'll be home to play the Yankees the end of the week and I want to see you guys out there."

Or he would clip the story and send it to Ruth and her husband in Oklahoma with a bombshell P.S.

But as he neared the hotel, his pace dragged. He could, of course, do none of these things.

In the lobby, he dropped into a chair and read again, less jubilantly, of his exploits the evening before. When he reached the phrase "redoubtable neophyte," the thrill was the same and yet . . .

Folding the paper, he went into breakfast. Something was missing. It was like being on a television program in a strange city, with no friends to watch. He was the star performer, but he was performing in a void, with nobody from his past life to applaud, unless it was a man named Applegate.

A Scotchman, a Phantom,
and a Shiny Blue Jacket

WILLIE MORRIS

Willie Morris (1934–1999) understood place. Journalist, novelist, memoirist, and, at 33, the youngest editor of *Harper's,* the nation's oldest magazine, he had an enormous sense of the Mississippi he was born in and would return to. In books like *Last of the Southern Girls, My Dog Skip, Good Old Boy,* and *North Towards Home,* Mississippi was as much a character as it was a setting. This chapter from the latter, an exquisite reminiscence, treats baseball as both a character and a place, as well.

Like Mark Twain and his comrades growing up a century before in another village on the other side of the Mississippi, my friends and I had but one sustaining ambition in the 1940s. Theirs in Hannibal was to be steamboat men, ours in Yazoo was to be major-league baseball players. In the summers, we thought and talked of little else. We memorized batting averages, fielding averages, slugging averages, we knew the roster of the Cardinals and the Red Sox better than their own managers must have known them, and to hear the broadcasts from all the big-city ballparks with their memorable names—the Polo Grounds, Wrigley Field, Fenway Park, the Yankee Stadium—was to set our imagination churning for the glory and riches those faraway places would one day bring us. One of our friends went to St. Louis on his vacation to see the Cards, and when he returned with the autographs of Stan Musial, Red Schoendienst, Country Slaughter, Marty Marion,

Joe Garagiola, and a dozen others, we could hardly keep down our envy. I hated that boy for a month, and secretly wished him dead, not only because he took on new airs but because I wanted those scraps of paper with their magic characters. I wished also that my own family were wealthy enough to take me to a big-league town for two weeks, but a bigger place even than St. Louis: Chicago, maybe, with not one but two teams, or best of all to New York, with three. I had bought a baseball cap in Jackson, a real one from the Brooklyn Dodgers, and a Jackie Robinson Louisville Slugger, and one day when I could not even locate any of the others for catch or for baseball talk, I sat on a curb on Grand Avenue with the most dreadful feelings of being caught forever by time—trapped there always in my scrawny and helpless condition. *I'm ready, I'm ready,* I kept thinking to myself, but that remote future when I would wear a cap like that and be a hero for a grandstand full of people seemed so far away I knew it would never come. I must have been the most dejected-looking child you ever saw, sitting hunched up on the curb and dreaming of glory in the mythical cities of the North. I felt worse when a carload of high school boys halted right in front of where I sat, and they started reciting what they always did when they saw me alone and daydreaming: *Wee Willie Winkie walks through the town, upstairs and downstairs in his nightgown.* Then one of them said, "Winkie, you *gettin'* much?" "You bastards!" I shouted, and they drove off laughing like wild men.

Almost every afternoon when the heat was not unbearable my father and I would go out to the old baseball field behind the armory to hit flies. I would stand far out in center field, and he would station himself with a fungo at home plate, hitting me one high fly, or Texas Leaguer, or line drive after another, sometimes for an hour or more without stopping. My dog would get out there in the outfield with me, and retrieve the inconsequential dribblers or the ones that went too far. I was light and speedy, and could make the most fantastic catches, turning completely around and forgetting the ball sometimes to head for the spot where it would descend, or tumbling head-on for a diving catch. The smell of that new-cut grass was the finest of all smells, and I could run forever and never get tired. It was a dreamy, suspended state, those late afternoons, thinking of nothing but outfield flies as the world drifted lazily by on Jackson Avenue. I learned to judge what a ball would do by instinct, heading the way it went as if I owned it, and I knew in my heart I could make the big time. Then, after all that exertion, my father would shout, "I'm whupped!" and we would quit for the day.

When I was twelve I became a part-time sportswriter for the *Yazoo Herald,* whose courtly proprietors allowed me unusual independence. I wrote up an occasional high school or Legion game in a florid prose, filled with phrases like "two-ply blow" and "circuit-ringer." My mentor was the sports editor of the *Memphis Commercial Appeal,* whose name was Walter Stewart, a man who could invest the most humdrum athletic contest with the elements of Shakespearean tragedy. I learned whole paragraphs of his by heart, and used some of his expressions for my reports on games between Yazoo and Satartia, or the other teams. The summer when I was twelve, having never seen a baseball game higher than the Jackson Senators of Class B, my father finally relented and took me to Memphis to see the Chicks, who were Double A. It was the farthest I had ever been from home, and the largest city I had ever seen; I walked around in a state of joyousness, admiring the crowds and the big park high above the River and, best of all, the grand old lobby of the Chisca Hotel.

Staying with us at the Chisca were the Nashville Vols, who were there for a big series with the Chicks. I stayed close to the lobby to get a glimpse of them; when I discovered they spent all day, up until the very moment they left for the ballpark, playing the pinball machine, I stationed myself there too. Their names were Tookie Gilbert, Smokey Burgess, Chuck Workman, and Bobo Holloman, the latter being the one who got as far as the St. Louis Browns, pitched a no-hitter in his first major-league game, and failed to win another before being shipped down forever to obscurity; one afternoon my father and I ran into them outside the hotel on the way to the game and gave them a ride in our taxi. I could have been fit for tying, especially when Smokey Burgess tousled my hair and asked me if I batted right or left, but when I listened to them as they grumbled about having to get out to the ballpark so early, and complained about the season having two more damned months to go and about how ramshackle their team bus was, I was too disillusioned even to tell my friends when I got home.

Because back home, even among the adults, baseball was all-meaning; it was the link with the outside. A place known around town simply as The Store, down near the train depot, was the principal center of this ferment. The Store had sawdust on the floor and long shreds of flypaper hanging from the ceiling. Its most familiar staples were Rexall supplies, oysters on the half-shell, legal beer, and illegal whiskey, the latter served up, Mississippi bootlegger style, by the bottle from a hidden shelf and costing not merely the price of the whiskey but the investment in gas required to go to Louisiana to fetch it. There was a long counter in the back. On one side of it, the white workingmen congregated after hours every afternoon to compare the day's scores and talk batting averages, and on the other side, also talking baseball, were the Negroes, juxtaposed in a face-to-face arrangement with the whites. The scores were chalked up on a blackboard hanging on a red and purple wall, and the conversations were carried on in fast, galloping shouts from one end of the room to the other. An intelligent white boy of twelve was even permitted, in that atmosphere of heady freedom before anyone knew the name of Justice Warren or had heard much of the United States Supreme Court, a quasi-public position favoring the Dodgers, who had Jackie Robinson, Roy Campanella, and Don Newcombe—not to mention, so it was rumored, God knows how many Chinese and mulattoes being groomed in the minor leagues. I remember my father turned to some friends at The Store one day and observed, "Well, you can say what you want to about that nigger Robinson, but he's got *guts*," and to a man the others nodded, a little reluctantly, but in agreement nonetheless. And one of them said he had read somewhere that Pee Wee Reese, a white Southern boy, was the best friend Robinson had on the team, which proved they had chosen the right one to watch after him.

There were two firehouses in town, and on hot afternoons the firemen at both establishments sat outdoors in their shirtsleeves, with the baseball broadcast turned up as loud as it would go. On his day off work my father, who had left Cities Service and was now a bookkeeper for the wholesale grocery, usually started with Firehouse No. 1 for the first few innings and then hit No. 2 before ending up at The Store for the postgame conversations.

I decided not to try out for the American League Junior Baseball team that summer. Legion baseball was an important thing for country boys in those parts, but I was too young and skinny, and I had heard that the coach, a dirt farmer known as Gentleman Joe, made his protégés lie flat in the infield while he walked on their stomachs; he also forced them to take three-mile runs through the streets of town, talked them into going to church, and persuaded them to give up Coca-Colas. A couple of summers later, when I did go out for the team, I found out that Gentleman Joe did in fact insist on these soul-strengthening rituals; because of them, we won the Mississippi State Championship and the merchants in town took up a collection and sent us all the way to St. Louis to see the Cards play the Phillies. My main concern that earlier summer, however, lay in the more academic aspects of the game. I knew more about baseball, its technology and its ethos, than all the firemen and Store experts put together. Having read most of its literature, I could give a sizable lecture on the infield-fly rule alone, which only a thin minority of the townspeople knew existed. Gentleman Joe was held in some esteem for his strategical sense, yet he was the only man I ever knew who could call for a sacrifice bunt with two men out and not have a bad conscience about it. I remember one dismaying moment that came to me while I was watching a country semi-pro game. The home team had runners on first and third with one out, when the batter hit a ground ball to the first baseman, who stepped on first then threw to second. The shortstop, covering second, stepped on the base but made no attempt to tag the runner. The man on third had crossed the plate, of course, but the umpire, who was not very familiar with the subtleties of the rules, signaled a double play. Sitting in the grandstand, I knew that it was not a double play at all and that the run had scored, but when I went down, out of my Christian duty, to tell the manager of the local team that he had just been done out of a run, he told me I was crazy. This was the kind of brainpower I was up against.

That summer the local radio station, the one where we broadcast our Methodist programs, started a baseball quiz program. A razor blade company offered free blades and the station chipped in a dollar, all of which went to the first listener to telephone with the right answer to the day's baseball question. If there was no winner, the next day's pot would go up a dollar. At the end of the month they had to close down the program because I was winning all the money. It got so easy, in fact, that I stopped phoning in the answers some afternoons so that the pot could build up and make my winnings more spectacular. I netted about twenty-five dollars and a ten-year supply of double-edged, smooth-contact razor blades before they gave up. One day, when the jackpot was a mere two dollars, the announcer tried to confuse me. "Babe Ruth," he said, "hit sixty home runs in 1927 to set the major-league record. What man had the next-highest total?" I telephoned and said, "George Herman Ruth. He hit fifty-nine in another season." My adversary, who had developed an acute dislike of me, said that was not the correct answer. He said it should have been *Babe* Ruth. This incident angered me, and I won for the next four days, just for the hell of it.

On Sunday afternoons, we sometimes drove out of town and along hot, dusty roads to baseball fields that were little more than parched red clearings, the outfield sloping out of the woods and ending in some tortuous gully full of yellowed paper, old socks, and vintage cow shit. One of the backwoods teams had a fastball pitcher named Eckert, who didn't have any teeth, and a fifty-year-old left-handed catcher named Smith. Since there were no catcher's mitts made for left-handers, Smith had to wear a mitt on his throwing hand. In his simian posture he would catch the ball and toss it lightly into the air and then whip his mitt off and catch the ball in his bare left hand before throwing it back. It was a wonderfully lazy way to spend those Sunday afternoons—my father and my friends and I sitting in the grass behind the chicken-wire backstop with eight or ten dozen farmers, watching the wrong-handed catcher go through his contorted gyrations, and listening at the same time to our portable radio, which brought us the rising inflections of a baseball announcer called the Old Scotchman. The sounds of the two games, our own and the one being broadcast from Brooklyn or Chicago, merged and rolled across the bumpy outfield and the gully into the woods; it was a combination that seemed perfectly natural to everyone there.

I can see the town now on some hot, still weekday afternoon in mid-summer: ten thousand souls and nothing doing. Even the red water truck was a diversion, coming slowly up Grand Avenue with its sprinklers on full force, the water making sizzling steam-clouds on the pavement while half-naked Negro children followed the truck up the street and played in the torrent until they got soaking wet. Over on Broadway, where the old men sat drowsily in straw chairs on the pavement near the Bon-Ton Café, whittling to make the time pass, you could laze around on the sidewalks—barefoot, if your feet were tough enough to stand the scalding concrete—watching the big cars with out-of-state plates whip by, the driver hardly knowing and certainly not caring what place this was. Way up that fantastic hill, Broadway seemed to end in a seething mist—little heat mirages that shimmered off the asphalt; on the main street itself there would be only a handful of cars parked here and there, and the merchants and the lawyers sat in the shade under their broad awnings, talking slowly, aimlessly, in the cryptic summer way. The one o'clock whistle at the sawmill would send out its loud bellow, reverberating up the streets to the bend in the Yazoo River, hardly making a ripple in the heavy somnolence.

But by two o'clock almost every radio in town was tuned in to the Old Scotchman. His rhetoric dominated the place. It hovered in the branches of the trees, bounced off the hills, and came out of the darkened stores; the merchants and the old men cocked their ears to him, and even from the big cars that sped by, their tires making lapping sounds in the softened highway, you could hear his voice, being carried past you out into the delta.

The Old Scotchman's real name was Gordon McLendon, and he described the big-league games for the Liberty Broadcasting System, which had outlets mainly in the South and the Southwest. He had a deep, rich voice, and I think he was the best rhetorician, outside of Bilbo and Nye Bevan, I have ever heard. Under his handling a baseball game took on a life of its own. As in the prose of the *Commercial Appeal*'s Walter Stewart, his games were rare and remarkable entities; casual pop flies had the flow of history behind them, double plays resembled the stark clashes of old armies, and home runs deserved acknowledgment on earthen urns. Later, when I came across Thomas Wolfe, I felt I had heard him before, from Shibe Park, Crosley Field, or the Yankee Stadium.

One afternoon I was sitting around my house listening to the Old Scotchman, admiring the vivacity of a man who said he was a contemporary of Connie Mack. (I learned later that he was twenty-nine.) That day he was doing the Dodgers and the Giants from the Polo Grounds. The game, as I recall, was in the fourth inning, and the Giants were ahead by about 4 to 1. It was a boring game, however, and I began experimenting with my father's shortwave radio, an impressive mechanism a couple of feet wide, which had an aerial that almost touched the ceiling and the name of every major city in the world on its dial. It was by far the best radio I had ever seen; there was not another one like it in town. I switched the dial to shortwave and began picking up African drum music, French jazz, Australian weather reports, and a lecture from the British Broadcasting Company on the people who wrote poems for Queen Elizabeth. Then a curious thing happened. I came across a baseball game—the Giants and the Dodgers, from the Polo Grounds. After a couple of minutes I discovered that the game was in the eighth inning. I turned back to the local station, but here the Giants and Dodgers were still in the fourth. I turned again to the shortwave broadcast and listened to the last inning, a humdrum affair that ended with Carl Furillo popping out to shortstop, Gil Hodges grounding out second to first, and Roy Campanella lining out to center. Then I went back to the Old Scotchman and listened to the rest of the game. In the top of the ninth, an hour or so later, a ghostly thing occurred; to my astonishment and titillation, the game ended with Furillo popping out to short, Hodges grounding out second to first, and Campanella lining out to center.

I kept this unusual discovery to myself, and the next day, an hour before the Old Scotchman began his play-by-play of the second game of the series, I dialed the shortwave frequency, and, sure enough, they were doing the Giants and the Dodgers again. I learned that I was listening to the Armed Forces Radio Service, which broadcast games played in New York. As the game progressed I began jotting down notes on the action. When the first four innings were over I turned to the local station just in time to get the Old Scotchman for the first batter. The Old Scotchman's account of the game matched the shortwave's almost perfectly. The Scotchman's, in fact, struck me as being considerably more poetic than the one I had heard first. But I did not doubt him, since I could hear the roar of the crowd, the crack of the bat, and the Scotchman's precise description of foul balls that fell into the crowd, the gestures of the base coaches, and the expression on the face of a small boy who was eating a lemon popsicle in a box seat behind first base. I decided that the broadcast was being delayed somewhere along the line, maybe because we were so far from New York.

That was my first thought, but after a close comparison of the two broadcasts for the rest of the game, I sensed that something more sinister was taking place. For one thing, the Old Scotchman's description of the count on a batter, though it jibed 90 percent of the time, did not always match. For another, the Scotchman's crowd, compared with the other, kept up an ungodly noise. When Robinson stole second on shortwave, he did it without drawing a throw and without sliding, while for Mississippians the feat was performed in a cloud of angry, petulant dust. A foul ball that went over the grandstand and out of the park for shortwave listeners in Alaska, France, and the Argentine produced for the firemen, bootleggers, farmers, and myself a primitive scramble that ended with a feeble old lady catching the ball on the first bounce to the roar of an assembly that would have outnumbered Grant's at Old Cold Harbor. But the most revealing development came after the Scotchman's game was over. After the usual summaries, he mentioned that the game had been "recreated." I had never taken notice of that particular word before, because I lost interest once a game was over. I went to the dictionary, and under "recreate" I found, "To invest with fresh vigor and strength; to refresh, invigorate (nature, strength, a person or thing)." The Old Scotchman most assuredly invested a game with fresh vigor and strength, but this told me nothing. My deepest suspicions were confirmed, however, when I found the second definition of the word—"To create anew."

So there it was. I was happy to have fathomed the mystery, as perhaps no one else in the whole town had done. The Old Scotchman, for all his wondrous expressions, was not only several innings behind every game he described but was no doubt sitting in some air-conditioned studio in the hinterland, where he got the happenings of the game by news ticker; sound effects accounted for the crack of the bat and the crowd noises. Instead of being disappointed in the Scotchman, I was all the more pleased by his genius, for he made pristine facts more actual than actuality, a valuable lesson when the day finally came that I started reading literature. I must add, however, that this appreciation did not obscure the realization that I had at my disposal a weapon of unimaginable dimensions.

Next day I was at the shortwave again, but I learned with much disappointment that the game being broadcast on shortwave was not the one the Scotchman had chosen to describe. I tried every afternoon after that and discovered that I would have to wait until the Old Scotchman decided to do a game out of New York before I could match his game with the one described live on shortwave. Sometimes, I learned later, these coincidences did not occur for days; during an important Dodger or Yankee series, however, his game and that of the Armed Forces Radio Service often coincided for two or three days running. I was happy, therefore, to find, on an afternoon a few days later, that both the shortwave and the Scotchman were carrying the Yankees and the Indians.

I settled myself at the shortwave with notebook and pencil and took down every pitch. This I did for four full innings, and then I turned back to the town station, where the Old Scotchman was just beginning the first inning. I checked the first batter to make sure the accounts jibed. Then, armed with my notebook, I ran down the street to the corner grocery, a minor outpost of baseball intellection, presided over by my young Negro friend Bozo, a knowledgeable student of the game, the same one who kept my dog in bologna. I found Bozo behind the meat counter, with the Scotchman's account going full blast. I arrived at the interim between the top and bottom of the first inning.

"Who's pitchin' for the Yankees, Bozo?" I asked.

"They're pitchin' Allie Reynolds," Bozo said. "Old Scotchman says Reynolds really got the stuff today. He just set 'em down one, two, three."

The Scotchman, meanwhile, was describing the way the pennants were flapping in the breeze. Phil Rizzuto, he reported, was stepping to the plate.

"Bo," I said, trying to sound cut and dried, "you know what I think? I think Rizzuto's gonna take a couple of fast called strikes, then foul one down the left-field line, and then line out straight to Boudreau at short."

"Yeah?" Bozo said. He scratched his head and leaned lazily across the counter.

I went up front to buy something and then came back. The count worked to nothing and two on Rizzuto—a couple of fast called strikes and a foul down the left side. "This one," I said to Bozo, "he lines straight to Boudreau at short."

The Old Scotchman, pausing dramatically between words as was his custom, said, "Here's the pitch on its way—There's a hard line drive! But Lou Boudreau's there at shortstop and he's got it. Phil hit that one on the nose, but Boudreau was right there."

Bozo looked over at me, his eyes bigger than they were. "How'd you know that?" he asked.

Ignoring this query, I made my second prediction. "Bozo," I said, "Tommy Henrich's gonna hit the first pitch up against the right-field wall and slide in with a double."

"How come you think so?"

"Because I can predict anything that's gonna happen in baseball in the next ten years," I said. "I can tell you anything."

The Old Scotchman was describing Henrich at the plate. "Here comes the first pitch. Henrich swings, there's a hard smash into right field! . . . This one may be out of here! It's going, going—*No!* It's off the wall in right center. Henrich's rounding first, on his way to second. Here's the relay from Doby . . . Henrich slides in safely with a double!" The Yankee crowd sent up an awesome roar in the background.

"Say, how'd you know that?" Bozo asked. "How'd you know he was gonna wind up at second?"

"I just can tell. I got extra-vision," I said. On the radio, far in the background, the public-address system announced Yogi Berra. "Like Berra right now. You know what? He's gonna hit a one-one pitch down the right-field line—"

"How come you know?" Bozo said. He was getting mad.

"Just a second," I said. "I'm gettin' static." I stood dead still, put my hands up against my temples and opened my eyes wide. "Now it's comin' through clear. Yeah, Yogi's gonna hit a one-one pitch down the right-field line, and it's gonna be fair by about three or four feet—I can't say exactly—and Henrich's gonna score from second, but the throw is gonna get Yogi at second by a mile."

This time Bozo was silent, listening to the Scotchman, who described the ball and the strike, then said: "Henrich takes the lead off second. Benton looks over, stretches, delivers. Yogi swings." (There was the bat crack.) "There's a line drive down the right side! It's barely inside the foul line. It may go for extra bases! Henrich's rounding third and coming in with a run. Berra's moving toward second. Here comes the throw! . . . And they *get* him! They get Yogi easily on the slide at second!"

Before Bozo could say anything else, I reached in my pocket for my notes. "I've just written down here what I think's gonna happen in the first four innings," I said. "Like DiMag. See, he's gonna pop up to Mickey Vernon at first on a one-nothing pitch in just a minute. But don't you worry. He's gonna hit a 380-foot homer in the fourth with nobody on base on a full count. You just follow these notes and you'll see I can predict anything that's gonna happen in the next ten years." I handed him the paper, turned around, and left the store just as DiMaggio, on a one-nothing pitch, popped up to Vernon at first.

Then I went back home and took more notes from the shortwave. The Yanks clobbered the Indians in the late innings and won easily. On the local station, however, the Old Scotchman was in the top of the fifth inning. At this juncture I went to the telephone and called Firehouse No. 1.

"Hello," a voice answered. It was the fire chief.

"Hello, Chief, can you tell me the score?" I said. Calling the firehouse for baseball information was a common practice.

"The Yanks are ahead, 5–2."

"This is the Phantom you're talkin' with," I said.

"Who?"

"The Phantom. Listen carefully, Chief. Reynolds is gonna open this next inning with a pop-up to Doby. Then Rizutto will single to left on a one-one count. Henrich's gonna force him at second on a two-and-one pitch but make it to first. Berra's gonna double to right on a nothing-and-one pitch, and Henrich's goin' to third. DiMaggio's gonna foul a couple off and then double down the left-field line, and both Henrich and Yogi are gonna score. Brown's gonna pop out to third to end the inning."

"Aw, go to hell," the chief said, and hung up.

This was precisely what happened, of course. I phoned No. 1 again after the inning.

"Hello."

"Hi. This is the Phantom again."

"Say, how'd you know that?"

"Stick with me," I said ominously, "and I'll feed you predictions. I can predict anything that's gonna happen anywhere in the next ten years." After a pause I added, "Beware of fire real soon," for good measure, and hung up.

I left my house and hurried back to the corner grocery. When I got there, the entire meat counter was surrounded by friends of Bozo's, about a dozen of them. They were gathered around my notes, talking passionately and shouting. Bozo saw me standing by the bread counter. "There he is! That's the one!" he declared. His colleagues turned and stared at me in undisguised awe. They parted respectfully as I strolled over to the meat counter and ordered a dime's worth of bologna for my dog.

A couple of questions were directed at me from the group, but I replied, "I'm sorry for what happened in the fourth. I predicted DiMag was gonna hit a full-count pitch for that homer. It came out he hit it on two-and-two. There was too much static in the air between here and New York."

"Too much *static?*" one of them asked.

"Yeah. Sometimes the static confuses my extra-vision. But I'll be back tomorrow if everything's okay, and I'll try not to make any more big mistakes."

"Big mistakes!" one of them shouted, and the crowd laughed admiringly, parting once more as I turned and left the store. I wouldn't have been at all surprised if they had tried to touch the hem of my shirt.

That day was only the beginning of my brief season of triumph. A schoolmate of mine offered me five dollars, for instance, to tell him how I had known that Johnny Mize was going to hit a two-run homer to break up one particularly close game for the Giants. One afternoon, on the basis of a lopsided first four innings, I had an older friend sneak into The Store and place a bet, which netted me $14.50. I felt so bad about it I tithed $1.45 in church the following Sunday. At Bozo's grocery store I was a full-scale oracle. To the firemen I remained the Phantom, and firefighting reached a peak of efficiency that month, simply because the firemen knew what was going to happen in the late innings and did not need to tarry when an alarm came.

One afternoon my father was at home listening to the Old Scotchman with a couple of out-of-town salesmen from Greenwood. They were sitting in the front room, and I had already managed to get the first three or four innings of the Cardinals and the Giants on paper before they arrived. The Old Scotchman was in the top of the first when I walked in and said hello. The men were talking business and listening to the game at the same time.

"I'm gonna make a prediction," I said. They stopped talking and looked at me. "I predict Musial's gonna take a ball and a strike and then hit a double to right field, scoring Schoendienst from second, but Marty Marion's gonna get tagged out at the plate."

"You're mighty smart," one of the men said. He suddenly sat up straight when the Old Scotchman reported, "Here's the windup and the pitch coming in . . . Musial *swings!*" (Bat crack, crowd roar.) "He drives one into right field! This one's going up against the boards! . . . Schoendienst rounds third. He's coming on in to score! Marion dashes around third, legs churning. His cap falls off, but here he *comes!* Here's the toss to the plate. He's nabbed at home. He is *out* at the plate! Musial holds at second with a run-producing double."

Before I could parry the inevitable questions, my father caught me by the elbow and hustled me into a back room. "How'd you know that?" he asked.

"I was just guessin'," I said. "It was nothin' but luck."

He stopped for a moment, and then a new expression showed on his face. "Have *you* been callin' the firehouse?" he asked.

"Yeah, I guess a few times."

"Now, you tell me how you found out about all that. I mean it."

When I told him about the shortwave, I was afraid he might be mad, but on the contrary he laughed uproariously. "Do you remember these next few innings?" he asked.

"I got it all written down," I said, and reached in my pocket for the notes. He took the notes and told me to go away. From the yard, a few minutes later, I heard him predicting the next inning to the salesmen.

A couple of days later, I phoned No. 1 again. "This is the Phantom," I said. "With two out, Branca's gonna hit Stinky Stanky with a fastball, and then Alvin Dark's gonna send him home with a triple."

"Yeah, we know it," the fireman said in a bored voice. "We're listenin' to a shortwave too. You think you're somethin', don't you? You're Ray Morris's boy."

I knew everything was up. The next day, as a sort of final gesture, I took some more notes to the corner grocery in the third or fourth inning. Some of the old crowd was there, but the atmosphere was grim. They looked at me coldly. "Oh, man," Bozo said, "*we* know the Old Scotchman ain't at that game. He's four or five innings behind. He's makin' all that stuff up." The others grumbled and turned away. I slipped quietly out the door.

My period as a seer was over, but I went on listening to the shortwave broadcasts out of New York a few days more. Then, a little to my surprise, I went back to the Old Scotchman, and in time I found that the firemen, the bootleggers, and the few dirt farmers who had shortwave sets all did the same. From then on, accurate, up-to-the-minute baseball news was in disrepute there. I believe we all went back to the Scotchman not merely out of loyalty but because, in our great isolation, he touched our need for a great and unmitigated eloquence.

Joe's American Legion Junior team actually amounted to an all-star squad from all the country towns surrounding ours; it was easier to make the high school team first. On Tuesday and Friday afternoons we would ride in our red and black bus through the heavy green woods to the small crossroads towns to play the locals. The crowds would sometimes be in a foul frame of mind, especially if the farmers had got hold of the corn gourd early in the day. Since we were the "city boys," with our pictures in the *Yazoo Herald* every now and again, we were particularly ripe for all that boondocks venom. The farmers would stand around the field shouting obscenities at the "slickers," sometimes loosening up their lungs with a vicious organized whoop that sounded like a cross between a rebel yell and a redneck preacher exorcizing the Devil and all his family. more often than not, to compound the injury, we got beat. Yet far from being gracious in victory, those sons of dirt farmers rubbed our noses in our own catastrophes, taunting us with threats to whip us all over again in the outfield pasture, while their elders stood around in a group as our coach chased us into the bus and shouted, "You ain't such hot stuff, slickers!" or "Go on back to town now, boys, and get your *photos* took some more." One afternoon when I ruined the no-hitter the best pitcher in the country had going (he later made Double-A), with a broken-bat fluke into right field in the eighth inning, I thought those farmers might slice me in pieces and feed me to the boll weevils. "You proud of that little skinny hit?" one of them shouted at me, standing with his nose next to mine, and his companion picked up the broken bat that had done the evil deed and splintered it apart against a tree trunk. When we beat the same team two or three weeks later on our home field, I ran into their shortstop and catcher, two tough hardnoses, on Main Street the following Saturday. They sidled right up to me and waited there glowering, breathing in my face and not saying a word for a while. We stood nostril-to-nostril until one of them said, "You think you're somethin' don't you, bastid? Beat us at home with your crooked umpires. Next time you come see us we'll whup you 'til the shit turns green." And they did.

The next summer, when I made the Legion team, I finally came under the tutelage of Gentleman Joe, a hard taskmaster of the old school despite his unfamiliarity with "stragety," as he called it. Gentleman Joe would always have us pray before a game, and sometimes between innings when he going got rough. He was a big one for church, and began to remind me more and more of my old fourth-grade teacher. But his pep talks, back behind the shabby old grandstand of our playing field, drew on such pent-up emotions, being so full of Scriptures and things of God's earth, that I suspected we were being enlisted, not to play baseball, but to fight in the Army of the Lord.

That was the team which won the Mississippi championship, beating almost everybody without much trouble. Before the final game for the championship in Greenwood, with four thousand people waiting in the stands, Gentleman Joe delivered the best speech of all. "*Gentlemen,*" he said, using that staple designation which earned him his nickname, "I'm just a simple farmer. Fifteen acres is all I got, and two mules, a cow, and a lot of mouths to feed." He paused between his words, and his eyes watered over. "I've neglected my little crop because of this team, and the weevils gave me trouble last year, and they're doin' it again now. I ain't had enough rain, and I don't plan to get much more. The corn looks so brown, if it got another shade browner it'd flake right off. But almost every afternoon you'd find me in my pickup on the way to town to teach you gentlemen the game of baseball. You're fine Christian gentlemen who don't come no finer. But I saw you gettin' a little lazy yestiddy, showin' off some to all them cute little delta girls in the bleachers. We didn't come way up here to show off, we come up here to *win!*" Then, his pale blue eyes flashing fire, half whispering and half shouting, he said: "Gentlemen, I want us to pray, and then . . . I want you to go out there on that field and win this Miss'ippi championship! You'll be proud of it for the rest of your lives. You'll remember it when you're ole men. You'll think about it when you're dyin' and your teeth are all gone. You'll be able to tell your grandchildren about this day. Go out there, gentlemen, and *win this ball game for your coach!*" After we prayed, and headed for that field like a pack of wild animals, the third baseman and I shouted in unison, and we meant it: "Boys, let's get out and win for our *coach!*" That fall they gave us shiny blue jackets, with "Miss. State Champions" written on the back; I was so happy with that jacket I almost wore it out. And when my old dog Skip died of a heart attack trying to outflank a flea that had plagued him since the Roosevelt Administration, looking at me with his sad black eyes and expiring in a sigh as old as death, that is what I wrapped him in before I took him in my arms and put him in the ground.

Two or three years later, when we were past the age for Legion competition, I had my last confrontation with baseball. The owner of the tire store organized a semi-pro team, made up of college and high school players from around the state. There was a popular tire that year called the "Screaming Eagle," and thus we were the Yazoo "Screaming Eagles," the pride of the delta. Out of a roster of fourteen, one made it to the major leagues, one to a Triple-A league, and two to Double-A. That team won the Deep South championship, and at the national tournament in Wichita beat the U.S. Navy and ended up close to the top.

The state league we played in, making twenty-five or thirty dollars apiece a game, was composed of both delta and hill-country towns, and we played to big Saturday night crowds who had heard about the Screaming Eagles, under lights so faulty that it was difficult to see a ball coming at you in the outfield. Insects bigger than fifty-cent pieces caromed off the bulbs and zoomed around us in our isolated stations in the field, and the ground was full of holes, ruts, and countless other hazards. Playing center field one night in one of the hill towns, I went back to examine a sloping red mound of earth that served as the outfield fence; I discovered a strand of barbed wire eight or ten feet long, an old garbage can full of broken beer bottles, and a narrow hole, partially covered with Johnson grass, that looked as if it might be the home for the local rattlers. The most indigenous field of all was near a little delta town called Silver City. It was built right on a cotton field and was owned by the two young heirs to the plantation on which it sat, one of whom later made it all the way to the New York Yankees. The grandstand would seat close to two thousand people, but the lights were so bad you had to exert all your finer perceptions to discriminate between the bugs and the balls; this took genius, and tested one's natural instincts. It was here, in the state finals, that a sinking line drive came toward me in right field, with the bases loaded and two out in the first inning; I lost track of that ball the moment it came out of the infield. A second later I felt a sharp blow on my kneecap, and then I saw the ball bouncing thirty feet away over by the bleachers. "*Get* it boy! Stomp on it! Piss on it!" the enemy bleacher section shouted gleefully, and by the time I could retrieve it three runs had scored. Between innings our pitcher, who soon would be pitching in the major leagues for the Pittsburgh Pirates, looked at me wordlessly, but with a vicious and despairing contempt. Right then, with the world before me, I promised myself that if I ever made it to those mythical cities of the North, the ones I had dreamed about in my Brooklyn cap, it would have to be with a different set of credentials.

On Jackie Robinson

RED BARBER

Jackie Robinson said, "A life is not important except in the impact it has on other lives." His life was enormously important on a grand scale. But impact is also important one on one.

I was eleven when I met him. My mother had taken me out of school for my monthly orthodontist's appointment. I never liked those mornings of poking and prodding, but lunch in Manhattan at the premier dining establishment of my choice—as long as my choice was Schraaft's, Prexy's, the Automat, or Chock Full o' Nuts—beat the school cafeteria on Long Island every time. I always opted for the Automat. Except this once. I decided it was time to try Chock Full o' Nuts.

I didn't need to see a menu; my culinary tastes were defined then by hamburger. But something told me that I needed to see the man who was eating alone a few booths away. I recognized him immediately. He had one of the most recognizable faces in the world.

Though Robinson's career had ended by the time the game had sunk its hooks into me, I knew him. I knew pretty much everything an eleven-year-old needed to know about him. I knew he was the first. I knew he was good. I knew he was important.

And I knew this chance might not come again. I needed to get his autograph.

I approached him nervously. My mother had told me that he was some kind of Chock Full o' Nuts executive, as good a reason as any for him to be eating there, and I imagined he was probably the one who taste-tested the coffee, which, I figured, must be a very important job. Before I could excuse myself, he lowered his cup and locked his eyes on mine as he probably had on thousands of star-struck boys before me. His face was friendly, his eyes, unwavering, were soft and approachable. His shoulders slumped slightly with the kind of weight that doesn't show up on a scale. I introduced myself, apologized

127

for interrupting, and asked if he might sign an autograph for me. He smiled, and, in return, engaged me. He asked me where I was from, whether I played ball, what position I played, and who my favorite team was. Then he scribbled his "Jackie Robinson" on a napkin, and extended his hand. I thanked him. I wanted to scream.

A few minutes later, he stopped at our booth on his way out. He introduced himself to my mother, then asked if I might not prefer an autographed photo to a flimsy paper napkin. My answer required no words. He wrote down my address. We shook on it.

When he left, my mother, being my mother, pricked the balloon. "Don't expect anything," she cautioned. "He was just being polite."

Three days later, an envelope arrived addressed to me with the Chock Full o' Nuts logo in the corner. Inside was a photo of Jackie Robinson in his Brooklyn uniform with a personal greeting scrawled across the heart of his strike zone.

Jackie Robinson had come through. He may have crossed a powerful public line to become a hero, but, in the elementary act of keeping his word, he helped establish for me the no less powerful, though more personal, line that defines a human being.

His impact on Red Barber was a good deal more public and a good deal more compelling. His very presence forced Barber to take stock of who he was and what he believed in. A child of the Deep South with all that then implied, Barber (1908–1992) came north in the 1930s to begin a career in sports broadcasting that would deservedly enshrine him in Cooperstown. He was the Dodgers' announcer when Branch Rickey decided it was time to obliterate the game's color line. Barber, as he recalls in this episode from his 1968 autobiography *Rhubarb in the Catbird Seat,* was the first person outside of Rickey's family to be let in on Rickey's plan. There was a reason for it—and neither Barber, baseball, nor America would ever be the same.

A t the end of that pleasant luncheon meeting in Bronxville, Rickey said he was going to count on me. He said, too, "You think I don't know much about you. But there is more about you that I know than you have any idea." He said, "You have a potential for civic value that has not been touched."

I look back now and I realize that up to then I had never been involved, or been asked to get involved, in any sort of fund-raising campaign or even been asked to solicit for any, not even for the Community Fund on my own block. I had never even thought about it. But when Rickey told me I had a civic value that had not been touched, he added, "And I'm going to do something about it." I don't know exactly what he did, but before long things began to jump and I was right in the middle. Sometime I'll take my shirt off and show the backful of scars I got trying to raise money for the Red Cross, for the Episcopalian Church, for St. Barnabas house, for the new St. Christopher's on Key Biscayne.

But that was all right. Rickey was at Brooklyn, and we had a warm relationship, and that meant much to me. After I became Fund Raising Chairman for the Brooklyn Red Cross, he became *my* public relations man. One day during the war there was a Red Cross meeting in the office of John Cashmore, the borough president of Brooklyn. It began in the late morning, and like so many meetings, especially those populated largely by volunteers, it dragged on. Volunteers like to be heard, and at this particular meeting all the volunteers wanted to say something. They spoke and they were heard, and as a result the meeting did not break up until considerably after lunchtime.

Mr. Rickey and I left Cashmore's office in Borough Hall and walked around to Joe's Restaurant, which was an old landmark in Brooklyn. It was just around the corner from the Dodger offices at 215 Montague Street. When we went in the place, it was practically empty because it was well past the luncheon period. Mr. Rickey walked to a table way in the back of the restaurant, and I followed. We sat down and gave our order, and the waiter left. We were completely alone.

I recall very distinctly that he picked up a hard roll and broke it into pieces, and that he kept jabbing his knife into the butter and dabbing the butter onto the pieces of roll and then eating them.

He said, "I'm going to tell you something. I'm going to tell you something that even my board of directors doesn't know. No one knows outside of the family."

He chewed another piece of roll and then he said, "When I was baseball coach at the University of Michigan—I coached baseball there while I was getting my law degree—the best player I had one year was a catcher. He was a splendid young man. He was a Negro from Upper Michigan, and his family was the only Negro family in that area. When he came to Ann Arbor he was, by and large, unaware that he was a Negro in a white world. He had had no unpleasant experiences.

"Early in the season we went down to South Bend, Indiana, to play Notre Dame. We were staying at the Oliver Hotel. I stood at the desk registering my players, saying this is so-and-so, and this is so-and-so, and getting their room keys for them and sending them off to their rooms. When the catcher came up, the room clerk pulled back the register and he said, 'We do not take Negroes here.'

"I was stunned, and the boy didn't know what hit him. I explained to the room clerk that this was the catcher for the University of Michigan team, and that the University of Michigan team had complete reservations. We were guests of the University of Notre Dame.

"The room clerk was blunt and rude and vocally firm. He said they did not register Negroes, and that they were not going to register this one, and he didn't care if it was the University of Michigan baseball team or football team, or what. Quite a crowd had gathered around by now, listening and watching. I said to the room clerk, 'Well, now. We have to have some way out of this. He has to have a place to sleep. Would you object if he slept in the extra bed in my room, as long as you don't have to register him?' And the clerk said, 'All right. You can do that.'

"He turned and got the key and handed it to me, and I gave it to my catcher. I said, 'Now you go up to the room, and you stay there until I come up. I'll be up just as soon as I can finish registering the rest of the team. It won't be but a couple of minutes. You go ahead.'

"When I finished registering the rest of the team, I went up to the room, pushed open the door, and went inside. And there was this fine young man, sitting on the edge of a chair, crying. He was crying as though his heart would break. His whole body was racked with sobs. He was pulling frantically at his hands, pulling at his hands, pulling at his hands. He looked at me and he said, 'It's my skin. If I could just tear it off, I'd be like everybody else. It's my skin. It's my skin, Mr. Rickey.' "

There in Joe's Restaurant in Brooklyn, this bear-shaped man with the dark, bushy eyebrows broke another hard roll, spilled crumbs all over the place, jabbed at the butter. He was angry all over again. He was back in the Oliver Hotel in South Bend.

Then he leaned forward across the table and said "You know, I have formed a Negro baseball team called the Brooklyn Brown Dodgers."

I said, "Is that the team that's going to go into the Negro League?"

He said, "Yes. I have all my Dodger scouts out looking for Negro players. They're scouting them all over the Caribbean. They're scouting them all over the United States. I've got Sukey [he meant Clyde Sukeforth, who was his best scout] and all the others out working on this. They are scouting Negro players only."

He chewed on a piece of roll. "They think they're scouting them for the Brown Dodgers."

I didn't react at all. I really didn't understand what he was talking about.

Abruptly, he said, "I have never been able to shake the picture of that fine young man tearing at his hands, and telling me that it was his skin, and that if he could just tear it off he would be like everybody else. As the years have come and gone, this has hurt me inside. And I have made up my mind that before I pass on I am going to do something about it."

He looked at me. "What I am telling you is this: there is a Negro ballplayer coming to the *Dodgers,* not the Brown Dodgers. I don't know who he is, and I don't know where he is, and I don't know when he's coming. But he is *coming.* And he is coming soon, just as soon as we can find him."

Again, I didn't say a word. I couldn't.

"Needless to say," he went on, "I have taken you into my confidence in telling you this. I have talked about it only with my family. Jane is utterly opposed to my doing it. The family is dead set against it. But I have got to do it. I must do it. I will do it. I *am* doing it. And now you know it."

This was a year before I heard the name Robinson. It was a full year later—Rickey never talked to me about it again—that I picked up the paper and saw that Jackie Robinson had been signed and was going to play that season with Montreal, Brooklyn's number one farm team. I said to myself, "Well, he said he was going to do it."

I have often wondered why this man told *me* about his earth-shaking project that afternoon in Joe's Restaurant. You could argue that the thing had become so much a part of him, and the opposition of his family was so complete, and he was carrying all of this inside himself, that he had to have some human being to speak out loud to, that he had to have some other human being hear him say what was inside him. You could say he paid me a high compliment in choosing me as the human being that he would trust to listen to him and respect his confidence.

But Rickey's strength was such that he could walk his way alone. I don't think he needed me as his confessor. And, certainly, when he spoke to me about it, I gave him back no support. I gave him back 100 per cent silence, because he had shaken me. He had shaken me to my heels.

And I think *that* is why he told me, because he knew it would shake me. He always told me that I was the most valuable person in Brooklyn to him and the ball club. He never let me forget that I had a great public relations worth to him and the Dodgers, and that I was doing valuable work. He saw to it that I was left alone, that I was free to do my job the way I wanted to do it. I don't believe anyone was able to go to Rickey and say something critical of my broadcasting. He stopped them. He wouldn't listen to them. He would say, "You don't know his job and his problems. He does. He handles things in his own way. You leave him alone."

Rickey saw to it, in other words, that I had sole occupancy of the cat-bird seat, but he shook me that afternoon in Joe's Restaurant. He needed me in Brooklyn, or he *wanted* me in Brooklyn, which is more accurate. But he knew that the coming of a Negro ballplayer could disturb me, could upset me. I believe he told me about it so far in advance so that I could have time to wrestle with the problem, live with it, solve it. I was born in Mississippi. I grew up in Florida. My father was from North Carolina. My mother's people were long-time Mississippians. My entire heredity and environment was of the Deep South. Florida is not Deep South in the sense that Mississippi, Alabama, Georgia and South Carolina would be considered Deep South—Florida has always been a more cosmopolitan state—but make no mistake about it, it is still a southern state. So I was raised southern. I was raised by wonderful, tolerant people who taught me never to speak unkindly to anyone or to take advantage of anyone. The Negroes who came and went through our lives were always treated with the utmost respect and a great deal of warmth and a great deal of affection. But there was a line drawn, and that line was always there.

I know that it gave me great pause when I first went to Cincinnati, the first time I went north to live. I wondered how I could get along in a northern city. Well, I got along all right, because I tended strictly to my own business. But what Mr. Rickey told me in Joe's Restaurant meant that this was now part of my business. I would still be broadcasting baseball, with all its closeness and intimate friendships and back-and-forth and give-and-take, but now a Negro player would be part of all that. And if he meant one Negro player, he meant more than one. He meant that the complexion (and this is no play on words) in the dugout and the clubhouse was going to be drastically and permanently changed.

I went home that night to Scarsdale and as soon as I got in the house I told my wife what Mr. Rickey had said. (That was in no sense a violation of confidence: Rickey believed in wives and husbands sharing each other's lives.) I told her about it, and I said to her, "I'm going to quit. I don't think I want— I don't know whether I can— I'm going to quit."

She said, "Well, it's your job and you're the one who's going to have to make the decision. But it's not immediate. You don't have to do anything about it right now. Why don't we have a martini? And then let's have dinner."

So time went by and, as I said, Mr. Rickey never referred to it again. But the thing was gnawing on me. It tortured me. I finally found myself doing something I had never really done before. I set out to do a deep self-examination. I attempted to find out who I was. This did not come easily, and it was not done lightly.

I had to face the economic side of things. That was a great job in Brooklyn and, other things being equal, I did not want to leave it. I was very happy in my work, very happy at Brooklyn. (That's why I left in 1953, when I found I could not be happy broadcasting in Brooklyn under Walter O'Malley—the happiness that I had in Ebbets Field was too precious to me to dilute and vitiate, so I left.) Even so, when I was thinking about the impending arrival of the man who turned out to be Jackie Robinson and saying to myself, "Don't be in such a hurry to walk away from a great job," I wasn't afraid of leaving. I was only thirty-seven years old. I still had the confidence of youth. I have always felt that I could make a living. My father used to tell me, "Son, don't let anybody ever tell you that the job you have is the *only* job you can have. And don't ever let a man make you afraid of your job." My father told me that when I was a boy, and he repeated it during my adolescence, and whenever anybody has threatened me, his words come back and I react rather strongly. So it wasn't so much the loss of the job itself. It was leaving something I loved.

But then I had to ask myself, what is it that is so upsetting about the prospect of working with a Negro ballplayer? Or broadcasting the play of a Negro ballplayer? Or traveling with a Negro ballplayer? What is it that has me so stirred up? Why did I react the way I did when Rickey told me he was bringing in a Negro player? Why did I go straight home and tell my wife I was going to quit?

Well, I said, I'm southern. I'm trained. Of course, that answer came to me more clearly some years later when I saw *South Pacific;* I didn't know it at the time I was struggling to find the answer. In that great show there was a song, "You've Got To Be Carefully Taught." That was my problem. I had been carefully taught, and not just by my parents. I had been taught by everybody I had been around. I had been carefully taught by Negroes and whites alike. I was a product of a civilization: that line that was always there was indelible. All right, I said, I'm southern.

And then—I don't know why the thought came to my mind—I asked myself the basic question that a human being, if he is fair, ought to ask. How much control did I have over the parents I was born to? The answer was immediate: I didn't have any. By an accident of birth I was born to Selena and William Barber, white, Protestant, in Columbus, Mississippi, February 17, 1908. And due to circumstances over which I had no control, I stayed in Columbus, Mississippi, until I was ten and then I stayed in Florida until I was a grown man. The first time I had something to do with what I was doing was when I left Sanford and went up to work my way through the University of Florida. For the rest of it, I had some vote in the matter.

Then, of course, I worked out that but for an accident of birth I could have been born to black parents. I could have been born to any parents. Then I figured out that I didn't have anything to be so proud of after all, this accident of the color of my skin.

Just about that time, the rector of the church of St. James the Less in Scarsdale asked me to do a radio talk for him out in Westchester County. You look back and you say to yourself, how marvelous it is the way things synchronize in your life, how they fit and mesh together, the timing. I had been brought up in a family that believed in religion. I had gone to Sunday School as a regular thing, and later, as a young man, I taught Sunday School briefly myself. But I lost the habit of going to church after I got involved in broadcasting, and it wasn't until after the birth of our daughter Sarah that I became interested again. My father was a Baptist and my mother was a Presbyterian, but I married an Episcopalian and when I went back to church I went back as an Episcopalian. And so, while I was trying to work out this thing of who I am, and this accident of birth, and losing a lot of false pride, the Reverend Harry Price, an Episcopal clergyman I had gotten to know, asked me to do this radio talk. The talk, built on a sentence from St. Paul, was to be called "Men and Brothers." And what the rector wanted me to talk about was a problem that was coming to a head then. It was just about the time that it was beginning to get attention, and later it got to be quite serious and it hasn't diminished. It was the problem of the relationship between the Jews and the non-Jews in the wealthy community of Scarsdale, New York. It was going pretty good—and it still is. A lot of people forgot that Jesus was a Jew. Some embarrassingly sickening things were beginning to happen. Sad things were being said. Things were being done to children. And so the rector asked me to talk about men and brothers, with the idea being that whether you were a Jew or a Christian, you were brothers. You were men, and you were men and brothers together, and you should get along together.

Well, when I worked out that talk I suddenly found that I wasn't nearly so interested in the relationship between Christians and Jews, Jews and Christians, as I was about the relationship between one white southern broadcaster and one unknown Negro ballplayer, who was coming. That talk—working it out, preparing it, giving it—I don't know how much help it gave to anyone who was listening, but it helped me a great deal. What was my job? What was my function? What was I supposed to do as I broadcast baseball games? As I worked along on that line, I remembered something about Bill Klem, the great umpire. Klem always said, "All there is to umpiring is umpiring the ball." When you think about it, that is the one thing you must tell a fellow who wants to umpire. Just umpire the ball. There are a couple of other technicalities that you have to know, of course, but the ball is the basic thing. Is the ball foul or fair? Is the ball a good pitch or a bad pitch? Did the ball get to the base before the runner did, or did it not? Did the ball stick in the fielder's glove, or did it bounce out? An umpire doesn't care anything about how big the crowd is or which team is ahead or who the runner is on third or whether this is the winning run that is approaching the plate. All he does is umpire the ball. It doesn't matter whether the man at bat is a great star or a brand new rookie. It doesn't even matter what color he is.

I took that and worked over it a little bit, and I said, "Well, isn't that what I'm supposed to do? Just broadcast the ball? Certainly, a broadcaster is concerned with who is at the plate—you're deeply concerned. You're concerned about the score, and the excitement of the crowd, and the drama of the moment. You do care if this is the winning run approaching the plate. But still, basically, primarily, beyond everything else, you broadcast the ball—*what* is happening to it. All you have to do is tell the people what is going on."

I got something else in my head then. I understood that I was not a sociologist, that I was not Mr. Rickey, that I was not building the ball club, that I was not putting players on the field, that I was not involved in a racial experiment, that I did not care what anybody else said, thought, or did about this Negro player who was coming and whose name I still did not know. All I had to do when he came—and I didn't say *if* he came, because after Mr. Rickey talked to me I *knew* he was coming—all I had to do when he came was treat him as a man, a fellow man, treat him as a ballplayer, broadcast the ball.

I had this all worked out before I ever read that Jackie Robinson was signed and going to Montreal. And when he did come, I didn't broadcast Jackie Robinson, I broadcast what Jackie Robinson did. Sometimes it was quite interesting. But it was what *he* did that made it interesting. All I did was broadcast it, which was my job.

There was another Mississippian involved in Jackie's start. When Robinson reported to the Montreal ball club, the manager of the Royals at that time was Clay Hopper, from Mississippi. Rickey had told Clay, "He's coming," and I don't suppose Hopper was any happier about the idea than I had been. But Rickey put it to him flatly: "You can manage correctly, or you can be unemployed." That's all he said. He didn't waste any time gentling Hopper, who was a professional manager. Rickey just said, "You manage this fellow the way *I* want him managed, and you figure out *how* I want him managed." And Hopper said, "Yes, Mr. Rickey."

Clay told me that he first saw Jackie when Robinson reported at the minor league camp Rickey had set up for his farm teams at an old naval air training station at De Land, Florida. It was 1946, the year the Dodgers trained at Daytona Beach. The minor league camp was an area that they could get inside of and spread around in, and the unregenerate southerners outside could look the other way and pretend it wasn't happening. Robinson reported at a moment when Hopper had the Montreal team in the clubhouse, getting ready to go over something with them. The door opened, and Jackie came in. Clay told me later, "I didn't need an introduction when he came through that door. I said to myself, 'Well, when Mr. Rickey picked one he sure picked a black one.'"

And yet the relationship between Hopper and Robinson was splendid. Jackie told me so. Hopper was fair. Jackie was surprised, he said, but pleased. He found that Hopper was a *fair* man. When you get around to life, isn't that what it's all supposed to be? Be a *fair* man?

I believe that's what I came around to in my own mind when I was wrestling with myself. If I did do anything constructive in the Robinson situation, it was simply in accepting him the way I did—as a man, as a ballplayer. I didn't resent him, and I didn't crusade for him. I broadcast the ball.

It was a sensitive, even delicate, situation. After all, I had the microphone, and I had the southern accent, and I had millions of people listening to every word I said. And this thing was not something that you were suddenly confronted with one day, and then didn't have to worry about any more. It had to be handled inning by inning, game by game, month by month. It was there all the time because when Robinson came, he came to stay.

I think I did it the right way. I know that Jack told me he appreciated what I did, and Mr. Rickey said he thoroughly approved. Other people were kind in their comments, too. It's been written about in newspapers and magazines and in a couple of books. I never had any backlash from my listeners, to use a word that has come into popular use but which no one ever thought of using in that context then. To my knowledge, the Brooklyn broadcasts never had any backlash, either white or black, in the slightest degree. I know I never heard of any.

And so am I proud—in that meaning of self-respect—of this. But I would like to say something else. While I deeply appreciate it when Jackie Robinson thanks me, I know that if I have achieved any understanding or tolerance in my life, if I have been able to implement in any way St. Paul's dictum of men and brothers, if I have been able to follow a little better the second great commandment, which is to love thy neighbor, it all stems from this. That word "love," in the Biblical sense, comes from the Greek word, *agape*. In Greek, the language that the New Testament was written in, the word *agape* means "to have concern for." That is the sense in which Christ used it when he said the second great commandment was like the first—the first was to love God, and the second was to love your fellow man. It means that far from "loving" him, you can hate his guts, but if he's hurting, you're to help him. You don't have to like him. It has nothing to do with love in the romantic, physical sense. Jesus dramatized this in his story about the Good Samaritan. A man was jumped on and beaten and robbed by thugs and left lying in a road. A rich man, of the same racial strain, came along and saw the wounded man and ignored him, left him lying there. A priest, a priest of the man's own religion, passed him by. But a fellow who was foreign and of a different religion and of a different color skin—there was fear and bitter hatred between the different peoples there in the Holy Land, and it continues to this day—when this fellow saw the man lying there he turned back from where he was going, helped the man to an inn, and had him bandaged and fed and put to bed. He told the innkeeper to take care of him and whatever the bill was, he would pay it. That is concern, that is love. It is a great thing to have.

So, if I have been able to implement to any degree the second great commandment, to have concern. . . . Well, what I am trying to say is, if there is any thanks involved, any appreciation, I thank Jackie Robinson. He did far more for me than I did for him.

A Mickey Mantle Koan

DAVID JAMES DUNCAN

There must have been something of the Zen master in Mickey Mantle because he sure doled out his share of koans.

One of the guys I used to play ball with when I lived in Los Angeles had grown up, like me, on the outskirts of New York. He worshiped Mickey Mantle. When my friend Josh graduated from high school in the 1960s, he sent The Mick his autograph book to sign. Josh waited. And waited. When the book finally arrived, he anxiously paged through it. There was no Mickey Mantle autograph anywhere.

Josh eventually joined the Marines, and was badly wounded in Vietnam. Needing to touch a piece of home during a hospitalization in the Philippines, he asked his parents to send him the autograph book. Going through it more carefully this time, he noticed two pages stuck together. What he found when he separated them remains as emotionally overwhelming when Josh tells the story today as it must have been back in that hospital bed. Mantle *had* signed the book. The koan? How did the signature know not to reveal itself until the precise moment it would be most beneficial?

Novelist, essayist, and short-story master David James Duncan—*River Teeth, The Brothers K, My Story as Told by Water*—had his own "Mickey Mantle Koan" to confront. He wrestled with its riddle in this 1991 piece from *Harper's* magazine.

On April 6, 1965, my brother, Nicholas John Duncan, died of what his surgeons called "complications" after three unsuccessful open-heart operations. He was seventeen at the time—four years my elder to the very day. He'd been the fastest sprinter in his high school class until the valve in his heart began to close, but he was so bonkers about baseball that he'd preferred playing a mediocre JV shortstop to starring at varsity track. As a ballplayer he was a competent fielder, had a strong and fairly accurate arm, and stole bases with ease—when he could reach them. But no matter how much he practiced or what stances, grips, or self-hypnotic tricks he tried, he lacked the hand/eye magic that consistently lays bat-fat against ball, and remained one of the weakest hitters on his team.

John lived his entire life on the outskirts of Portland, Oregon—637 miles from the nearest major league team. In franchiseless cities in the Fifties and early Sixties there were two types of fans: those who thought the Yankees stood for everything right with America, and those who thought they stood for everything wrong with it. My brother was an extreme manifestation of the former type. He conducted a one-man campaign to notify the world that Roger Maris's sixty-one homers in '61 came in three fewer at bats than Babe Ruth's sixty in '27. He maintained—all statistical evidence to the contrary— that Clete Boyer was a better third baseman than his brother, Ken, simply be- cause Clete was a Yankee. He may not have been the only kid on the block who considered Casey Stengel the greatest sage since Solomon, but I'm sure he was the only one who considered Yogi Berra the second greatest. And, of course, Mickey Mantle was his absolute hero, but his tragic hero. The Mick, my brother maintained, was the greatest raw talent of all time. He was one to whom great gifts were given, from whom great gifts had been ripped away; and the more scarred his knees became, the more frequently he fanned, the more flagrant his limp and apologetic his smile, the more John revered him. And toward this single Yankee I, too, was able to feel a touch of reverence, if only because on the subject of scars I considered my brother an unimpeach- able authority: he'd worn one from the time he was eight, compliments of the Mayo Clinic, that wrapped clear around his chest in a wavy line, like stitching round a clean white baseball.

Yankees aside, John and I had more in common than a birthday. We bickered regularly with our middle brother and little sister, but almost never with each other. We were both bored, occasionally to insurrection, by school- going, churchgoing, and any game or sport that didn't involve a ball. We both preferred, as a mere matter of style, Indians to cowboys, hoboes to business- men, Buster Keaton to Charlie Chaplin, Gary Cooper to John Wayne, deadbeats to brownnosers, and even brownnosers to Elvis Presley. We shared a single cake on our joint birthday, invariably annihilating the candle flames with a tandem blowing effort, only to realize that we'd once again forgotten to make a wish. And when the parties were over or the house was stuffy, the parents cranky or the TV shows insufferably dumb, whenever we were restless, punchy, or just feeling as if there was nothing to do, catch—with a hard ball—is what John and I did.

We were not exclusive, at least not by intention: our father and middle brother and an occasional cousin or friend would join us now and then. But something in most everyone else's brain or bloodstream sent them bustling off to less contemplative endeavors before the real rhythm of the thing ever took hold. Genuine catch-playing occurs in a double limbo between busyness and idleness, and between what is imaginary and what is real. Also, as with any contemplative pursuit, it takes time, and the ability to forget time, to slip into this dual limbo and to discover (i.e., lose) oneself in the music of the game.

It helps to have a special place to play. Ours was a shaded, ninety-foot corridor between one neighbor's apple orchard and the other's stand of old-growth Douglas firs, on a stretch of lawn so lush and mossy it sucked the heat out of even the hottest grounders. I always stood in the north, John in the south. We might call balls and strikes for an imaginary inning or two, or maybe count the number of errorless catches and throws we could make (300s were common, and our record was high in the 800s). But the deep shade, the 200-foot firs, the mossy footing and fragrance of apples all made it a setting more conducive to mental vacationing than to any kind of disciplined effort. During spring-training months our catch occasionally started as a drill—a grounder, then a peg; another grounder, a peg. But as our movements became fluid and the throws brisk and accurate, the pretense of practice would inevitably fade, and we'd just aim for the chest and fire, *hisssss pop! hisssss pop!* until a meal, a duty, or total darkness forced us to recall that this was the real world in which even timeless pursuits come to an end.

Our talk must have seemed strange to eavesdroppers. We lived in our bodies during catch, and our minds and mouths, though still operative, were just along for the ride. Most of the noise I made was with the four or five pieces of Bazooka I was invariably working over, though when the gum turned bland, I'd sometimes narrate our efforts in a stream-of-doggerel play-by-play. My brother's speech was less voluminous and a bit more coherent, but of no greater didactic intent: he just poured out idle litanies of Yankee worship or even idler braggadocio à la Dizzy Dean, all of it artfully spiced with spat sunflower-seed husks.

But one day when we were sixteen and twelve, respectively, my big brother surprised me out there in our corridor. Snagging a low throw, he closed his mitt round the ball, stuck it under his arm, stared off into the trees, and got serious with me for a minute. All his life, he said, he'd struggled to be a shortstop and a hitter, but he was older now, and had a clearer notion of what he could and couldn't do. It was time to get practical, he said. Time to start developing obvious strengths and evading flagrant weaknesses. "So I've decided," he concluded, "to become a junk pitcher."

I didn't believe a word of it. My brother had been a "slugger worshiper" from birth. He went on embellishing his idea, though, and even made it sound rather poetic: to foil some muscle-bound fence-buster with an off-speed piece of crap that blupped off his bat like cow custard—this, he maintained, was the pluperfect pith of an attribute he called Solid Cool.

I didn't recognize until months later just how carefully considered this new junk-pitching jag had been. That John's throwing arm was better than his batting eye had always been obvious, and it made sense to exploit that. But there were other factors he didn't mention: like the sharp pains in his chest every time he took a full swing, or the new ache that half-blinded and sickened him whenever he ran full speed. Finding the high arts of slugging and base stealing physically impossible, he'd simply lowered his sights enough to keep his baseball dreams alive. No longer able to emulate his heroes, he set out to bamboozle those who thought they could. To that end he'd learned a feeble knuckler, a roundhouse curve, a submarine fastball formidable solely for its lack of accuracy, and was trashing his arm and my patience with his attempts at a screwball, when his doctors informed our family that a valve in his heart was rapidly closing. He might live as long as five years if we let it go, they said, but immediate surgery was best, since his recuperative powers were greatest now. John said nothing about any of this. He just waited until the day he was due at the hospital, snuck down to the stable where he kept his horse, saddled her up, and galloped away. He rode about twenty miles, to the farm of a friend, and stayed there in hiding for nearly two weeks. But when he snuck home one morning for clean clothes and money, my father and a neighbor caught him, and first tried to force him but finally convinced him to have the operation and be done with it.

Once in the hospital he was cooperative, cheerful, and unrelentingly courageous. He survived second, third, and fourth operations, several stoppings of the heart, and a nineteen-day coma. He recovered enough at one point, even after the coma, to come home for a week or so. But the overriding "complication" to which his principal surgeon kept making oblique references turned out to be a heart so ravaged by scalpel wounds that an artificial valve had nothing but shreds to be sutured to. Bleeding internally, pissing blood, John was moved into an oxygen tent in an isolated room, where he remained fully conscious, and fully determined to heal, for two months after his surgeons had abandoned him. And, against all odds, his condition stabilized, then began to improve. The doctors reappeared and began to discuss, with obvious despair, the feasibility of a fifth operation.

Then came the second "complication": staph. Overnight, we were reduced from genuine hope to awkward pleas for divine intervention. We invoked no miracles. Two weeks after contracting the infection, my brother died.

At his funeral, a preacher who didn't know John from Judge Kenesaw Mountain Landis eulogized him so lavishly and inaccurately that I was moved to a state of tearlessness that lasted for four years. It's an unenviable task to try to make public sense of a private catastrophe you know little about. But had I been in that preacher's shoes, I would have mentioned one or two of my brother's actual attributes, if only to reassure late-arriving mourners that they hadn't wandered into the wrong funeral. The person we were endeavoring to miss had, for instance, been a C student all his life, had smothered everything he ate with ketchup, had diligently avoided all forms of work that didn't involve horses, and had frequently gone so far as to wear sunglasses indoors in the relentless quest for Solid Cool. He'd had the disconcerting habit of sound-testing his pleasant baritone voice by bellowing *"Beeeeeee-Ooooooooooo!"* down any alley or hallway that looked like it might contain an echo. He'd had an interesting, slangy obliviousness to proportion: any altercation, from a fistfight to a world war, was "a rack"; any authority, from our mother to the head of the U.N., was "the Brass"; any pest, from the kid next door to Khrushchev, was "a buttwipe"; and any kind of ball, from a BB to the sun, was "the orb." He was brave: whenever anybody his age harassed me, John warned them once and beat them up the second time, or got beat up trying. He was also unabashedly, majestically vain. He referred to his person, with obvious pride, as "the Bod." He was an immaculate dresser. And he loved to stare at himself, publicly or privately—in mirrors, windows, puddles, chrome car-fenders, upside-down in teaspoons—and to solemnly comb his long auburn hair over and over again, like his hero, Edd ("Kookie") Byrnes, on *77 Sunset Strip.*

His most astonishing attribute, to me at least, was his never-ending skein of girlfriends. He had a simple but apparently efficient rating system for all female acquaintances: he called it "percentage of Cool versus percentage of Crud." A steady girlfriend usually weighed in at around 95 percent Cool, 5 percent Crud, and if the Crud level reached 10 percent it was time to start quietly looking elsewhere. Only two girls ever made his "100 percent Cool List," and I was struck by the fact that neither was a girlfriend and one wasn't even pretty: whatever "100 percent Cool" was, it was not skin-deep. No girl ever came close to a "100 percent Crud" rating, by the way: my brother was chivalrous.

John was not religious. He believed in God, but passively, with nothing like the passion he had for the Yankees. He seemed a little more friendly with Jesus. "Christ is cool," he'd say, if forced to show his hand. But I don't recall him speaking of any sort of goings-on between them until he casually mentioned, a day or two before he died, a conversation they'd just had, there in the oxygen tent. And even then John was John: what impressed him even more than the fact of Christ's presence or the consoling words He spoke was the natty suit and tie He was wearing.

On the morning after his death, April 7, 1965, a small brown-paper package arrived at our house, special delivery from New York City, addressed to John. I brought it to my mother and leaned over her shoulder as she sat down to study it. Catching a whiff of antiseptic, I thought at first that it came from her hair: she'd spent the last four months of her life in a straightback chair by my brother's bed, and hospital odors had permeated her. But the smell grew stronger as she began to unwrap the brown paper, until I realized it came from the object inside.

It was a small, white, cylindrical, cardboard bandage box. "Johnson & Johnson," it said in red letters. "12 inches × 10 yards," it added in blue. Strange. Then I saw it had been split in half by a knife or a scalpel and bound back together with adhesive tape: so there was another layer, something hiding inside.

My mother smiled as she began to rip the tape away. At the same time, tears were landing in her lap. Then the tape was gone, the little cylinder fell away, and inside, nested in tissue, was a baseball. Immaculate white leather. Perfect red stitching. On one cheek, in faint green ink, the signature of American League president Joseph Cronin and the trademark REACH. THE SIGN OF QUALITY. And on the opposite cheek, with bright blue ballpoint ink, a tidy but flowing hand had written, *To John—My Best Wishes. Your Pal, Mickey Mantle. April 6, 1965.*

The ball dwelt upon our fireplace mantel—an unintentional pun on my mother's part. We used half the Johnson & Johnson box as a pedestal, and for years I saved the other half, figuring that the bandage it once contained had held Mantle's storied knee together for a game.

Even after my mother explained that the ball came not out of the blue but in response to a letter, I considered it a treasure. I told all my friends about it, and invited the closest to stop by and gawk. But gradually I began to see that the public reaction to the ball was disconcertingly predictable. The first response was usually, "Wow! Mickey Mantle!" But then they'd get the full story: "Mantle signed it the day he died? Your brother never even *saw* it?" And that made them uncomfortable. This was not at all the way an autographed baseball was supposed to behave. How could an immortal call himself your "Pal," how could you be the recipient of The Mick's "Best Wishes," and still just lie back and die?

I began to share the discomfort. Over the last three of my thirteen years I'd devoured scores of baseball books, all of which agreed that a bat, program, mitt, or ball signed by a big-league hero was a sacred relic, that we *should* expect such relics to have magical properties, and that they *would* prove pivotal in a young protagonist's life. Yet here I was, the young protagonist. Here was my relic. And all the damned thing did, before long, was depress and confuse me.

I stopped showing the ball to people, tried ignoring it, found that this was impossible, tried instead to pretend that the blue ink was an illegible scribble and that the ball was just a ball. But the ink *wasn't* illegible: it never stopped saying just what it said. So finally I picked the ball up and studied it, hoping to discover exactly why I found it so troublesome. Feigning the cool rationality I wished I'd felt, I told myself that a standard sports hero had received a letter from a standard distraught mother, had signed, packaged, and mailed off the standard ingratiatingly heroic response, had failed to think that the boy he inscribed the ball to might be dead when it arrived, and so had mailed his survivors a blackly comic non sequitur. I then told myself, "That's all there is to it"—which left me no option but to pretend that I hadn't expected or wanted any more from the ball than I got, that I'd harbored no desire for any sort of sign, any imprimatur, any flicker of recognition from an Above or a Beyond. I then began falling to pieces for lack of that sign.

Eventually, I got honest about Mantle's baseball: I picked the damned thing up, read it once more, peered as far as I could inside myself, and admitted for the first time that I was *pissed*. As is always the case with arriving baseballs, timing is the key—and this cheery little orb was inscribed on the day its recipient lay dying and arrived on the day he was being embalmed! This was *not* a harmless coincidence: it was the shabbiest, most embittering joke that Providence had ever played on me. My best friend and brother was dead, dead, dead, and Mantle's damned ball and best wishes made that loss even less tolerable, and *that,* I told myself, really was all there is to it.

I hardened my heart, quit the baseball team, went out for golf, practiced like a zealot, cheated like hell, kicked my innocuous, naive little opponents all over the course. I sold the beautiful outfielder's mitt that I'd inherited from my brother for a pittance.

But, as is usual in baseball stories, that wasn't all there was to it.

I'd never heard of Zen koans at the time, and Mickey Mantle is certainly no roshi. But baseball and Zen are two pastimes that Americans and Japanese have come to revere almost equally: roshis are men famous for hitting things hard with a big wooden stick; a koan is a perfectly nonsensical or nonsequacious statement given by an old pro (roshi) to a rookie (layman or monk); and the stress of living with and meditating upon a piece of mind-numbing nonsense is said to eventually prove illuminating. So I know of no better way to describe what the message on the ball became for me than to call it a koan.

In the first place, the damned thing's batteries just wouldn't run down. For weeks, months, *years,* every time I saw those nine blithely blue-inked words they knocked me off balance like a sudden shove from behind. They were an emblem of all the false assurances of surgeons, all the futile prayers of preachers, all the hollowness of Good-Guys-Can't-Lose baseball stories I'd ever heard or read. They were a throw I'd never catch. And yet . . . REACH, the ball said. THE SIGN OF QUALITY.

So year after year I kept trying, kept hoping to somehow answer the koan.

I became an adolescent, enrolling my body in the obligatory school of pain-without-dignity called "puberty," nearly flunking, then graduating almost without noticing. I discovered in the process that some girls were nothing like 95 percent Crud. I also discovered that there was life after baseball, that America was not the Good Guys, that God was not a Christian, that I preferred myth to theology, and that, when it came to heroes, the likes of Odysseus, Rama, and Finn MacCool meant incomparably more to me than the George Washingtons, Davy Crocketts, and Babe Ruths I'd been force-fed. I discovered (sometimes prematurely or overabundantly, but never to my regret) metaphysics, wilderness, Europe, black tea, high lakes, rock, Bach, tobacco, poetry, trout streams, the Orient, the novel, my life's work, and a hundred other grown-up tools and toys. But amid these maturations and transformations there was one unwanted constant: in the presence of that confounded ball, I remained thirteen years old. One peek at the "Your Pal" koan and whatever maturity or wisdom or equanimity I possessed was repossessed, leaving me as irked as any stumped monk or slumping slugger.

It took four years to solve the riddle on the ball. It was autumn when it happened—the same autumn during which I'd grown older than my brother would ever be. As often happens with koan solutions, I wasn't even thinking about the ball at the time. As is also the case with koans, I can't possibly describe in words the impact of the response, the instantaneous healing that took place, or the ensuing sense of lightness and release. But I'll say what I can.

The solution came during a fit of restlessness brought on by a warm Indian summer evening. I'd just finished watching the Miracle Mets blitz the Orioles in the World Series, and was standing alone in the living room, just staring out at the yard and the fading sunlight, feeling a little stale and fidgety, when I realized that this was *just* the sort of fidgets I'd never had to suffer when John was alive—because we'd always work our way through them with a long game of catch. With that thought, and at that moment, I simply saw my brother catch, then throw a baseball. It occurred neither in an indoors nor an outdoors. It lasted a couple of seconds, no more. But I saw him so clearly, and he then vanished so completely, that my eyes blurred, my throat and chest ached, and I didn't need to see Mantle's baseball to realize exactly what I'd wanted from it all along:

From the moment I'd first laid eyes on it, all I'd wanted was to take that immaculate ball out to our corridor on an evening just like this one, to take my place near the apples in the north, and to find my brother waiting beneath the immense firs to the south. All I'd wanted was to pluck that too-perfect ball off its pedestal and proceed, without speaking, to play catch so long and hard that the grass stains and nicks and the sweat of our palms would finally obliterate every last trace of Mantle's blue ink, until all he would have given us was a grass-green, earth-brown, beat-up old baseball. Beat-up old balls were all we'd ever had anyhow. They were all we'd ever needed. The dirtier they were, and the more frayed the skin and stitching, the louder they'd hissed and the better they'd curved. And remembering this—recovering in an instant the knowledge of how little we'd needed in order to be happy—my grief for my brother became palpable, took on shape and weight, color and texture, even an odor. The measure of my loss was precisely the difference between one of the beat-up, earth-colored, grass-scented balls that had given us such happiness and this antiseptic-smelling, sad-making, icon-ball on its bandage-box pedestal. And as I felt this—as I stood there palpating my grief, shifting it around like a throwing stone in my hand—I fell through some kind of floor inside myself, landing in a deeper, brighter chamber just in time to feel something or someone tell me: *But who's to say we need even an old ball to be happy? Who's to say we couldn't do with less? Who's to say we couldn't still be happy—with no ball at all?*

And with that, the koan was solved.

I can't explain why this felt like such a complete solution. Reading the bare words, two decades later, they don't look like much of a solution. But a koan answer is not a verbal, or a literary, or even a personal experience. It's a spiritual experience. And a boy, a man, a "me," does not have spiritual experiences; only the spirit has spiritual experiences. That's why churches so soon become bandage boxes propping up antiseptic icons that lose all value the instant they are removed from the greens and browns of grass and dirt and life. It's also why a good Zen monk always states a koan solution in the barest possible terms. *"No ball at all!"* is, perhaps, all I should have written—because then no one would have an inkling of what was meant and so could form no misconceptions, and the immediacy and integrity and authority of the experience would be safely locked away.

This is getting a bit iffy for a sports story. But jocks die, and then what? The brother I played a thousand games of catch with is dead and so will I be, and unless you're one hell of an athlete so will you be. In the face of this fact, I find it more than a little consoling to recall how clearly and deeply it was brought home to me, that October day, that there is something in us which needs absolutely *nothing*—not even a dog-eared ball—in order to be happy. From that day forward the relic on the mantel lost its irksome overtones and became a mere autographed ball—nothing more, nothing less. It lives on my desk now, beside an old beater ball my brother and I wore out, and it gives me a satisfaction I can't explain to sit back, now and then, and compare the two— though I'd still gladly trash the white one for a good game of catch.

As for the ticklish timing of its arrival, I only recently learned a couple of facts that shed some light. First, I discovered—in a copy of the old letter my mother wrote to Mantle—that she'd made it quite clear that my brother was dying. So when The Mick wrote what he wrote, he knew perfectly well what the situation might be when the ball arrived. And second, I found out that my mother actually went ahead and showed the ball to my brother. True, what was left of him was embalmed. But what was embalmed wasn't all of him. And I've no reason to assume that the unembalmed part had changed much. It should be remembered, then, that while he lived my brother was more than a little vain, that he'd been compelled by his death to leave a handsome head of auburn hair behind, and that when my mother and the baseball arrived at the funeral parlor, that lovely hair was being prepared for an open-casket funeral by a couple of cadaverous-looking yahoos whose oily manners, hair, and clothes made it plain that they didn't know Kookie from Roger Maris or Solid Cool from Kool-Aid. What if this pair took it into their heads to spruce John up for the hereafter with a Bible camp cut? Worse yet, what if they tried to show what sensitive, accommodating artists they were and decked him out like a damned Elvis the Pelvis *greaser?* I'm not trying to be morbid here. I'm just trying to state the facts. "The Bod" my brother had very much enjoyed inhabiting was about to be seen for the last time by all his buddies, his family, and a girl-friend who was only 1.5 percent Crud, and the part of the whole ensemble he'd been most fastidious about—the coiffure—was completely out of his control! He *needed* best wishes. He needed a pal. Preferably one with a comb.

Enter my stalwart mother, who took one look at what the two rouge-and-casket wallahs were doing to the hair, said, "No, no, no!", produced a snap-shot, told them, "He wants it *exactly* like this," sat down to critique their efforts, and kept on critiquing until in the end you'd have thought John had dropped in to groom himself.

Only then did she ask them to leave. Only then did she pull the auto-graphed ball from her purse, share it with her son, read him the inscription.

As is always the case with arriving baseballs, timing is the key. Thanks to the timing that has made The Mick a legend, my brother, the last time we all saw him, looked completely himself.

I return those best wishes to my brother's pal.

The Catch

ARNOLD HANO

On September 29, 1954, fate conspired to give Arnold Hano the best seat in the house to view one of baseball's most storied moments: Willie Mays' over-the-shoulder catch—forever after, just The Catch. Hano preserved that memorable afternoon in *A Day in the Bleachers,* his reverse-angle record of that defensive gem and so much more.

A workhorse of the sporting press, Hano was a regular in the pages of *Sport* magazine, and penned several baseball biographies—Mays's, Roberto Clemente's, and Sandy Koufax's, among them. As dedicated a contributor off the page as on it, he joined the Peace Corps in the early 1990s. He was in his seventies at the time.

Now it was Liddle, jerking into motion as Wertz poised at the plate, and then the motion smoothed out and the ball came sweeping in to Wertz, a shoulder-high pitch, a fast ball that probably would have been a fast curve, except that Wertz was coming around and hitting it, hitting it about as hard as I have ever seen a ball hit, on a high line to dead center field.

For whatever it is worth, I have seen such hitters as Babe Ruth, Lou Gehrig, Ted Williams, Jimmy Foxx, Ralph Kiner, Hack Wilson, Johnny Mize, and lesser-known but equally long hitters as Wally Berger and Bob Seeds send the batted ball tremendous distances. None, that I recall, ever hit a ball any harder than this one by Wertz in my presence.

And yet I was not immediately perturbed. I have been a Giant fan for years, twenty-eight years to be exact, and I have seen balls hit with violence to extreme center field which were caught easily by Mays, or Thomson before him, or Lockman or Ripple or Hank Leiber or George Kiddo Davis, that most marvelous fly catcher.

I did not—then—feel alarm, though the crack was loud and clear, and the crowd's roar rumbled behind it like growing thunder. It may be that I did not believe the ball would carry as far as it did, hard hit as it was. I have seen hard-hit balls go a hundred feet into an infielder's waiting glove, and all that one remembers is crack, blur, spank. This ball did not alarm me because it was hit to dead center field—Mays' territory—and not between the fielders, into those dread alleys in left-center and right-center which lead to the bullpens.

And this was not a terribly high drive. It was a long low fly or a high liner, whichever you wish. This ball was hit not nearly so high as the triple Wertz struck earlier in the day, so I may have assumed that it would soon start to break and dip and come down to Mays, not too far from his normal position.

Then I looked at Willie, and alarm raced through me, peril flaring against my heart. To my utter astonishment, the young Giant center fielders—the inimitable Mays, most skilled of outfielders, unique for his ability to scent the length and direction of any drive and then turn and move to the final destination of the ball—Mays was turned full around, head down, running as hard as he could, straight toward the runway between the two bleacher sections.

I knew then that I had underestimated—badly underestimated—the length of Wertz's blow.

I wrenched my eyes from Mays and took another look at the ball, winging its way along, undipping, unbreaking, forty feet higher than Mays' head, rushing along like a locomotive, nearing Mays, and I thought then: it will beat him to the wall.

Through the years I have tried to do what Red Barber has cautioned me and millions of admiring fans to do: take your eye from the ball after it's been hit and look at the outfielder and the runners. This is a terribly difficult thing to learn; for twenty-five years I was unable to do it. Then I started to take stabs at the fielder and the ball, alternately. Now I do it pretty well. Barber's advice pays off a thousand times in appreciation of what is unfolding, of what takes some six or seven seconds—that's all, six or seven seconds—and of what I can see in several takes, like a jerking motion picture, until I have enough pieces to make nearly a whole.

There is no perfect whole, of course, to a play in baseball. If there was, it would require a God to take it all in. For instance, on such a play, I would like to know what Manager Durocher is doing—leaping to the outer lip of the sunken dugout, bent forward, frozen in anxious fear? And Lopez—is he also frozen, hope high but too anxious to let it swarm through him? The coaches—

have they started to wave their arms in joy, getting the runners moving, or are they half-waiting, in fear of the impossible catch and the mad scramble that might ensue on the base paths?

The players—what have they done? The fans—are they standing, or half-crouched, yelling (I hear them, but since I do not see them, I do not know who makes that noise, which of them yells and which is silent)? Has activity stopped in the Giant bullpen where Grissom still had been toiling? Was he now turned to watch the flight of the ball, the churning dash of Mays?

No man can get the entire picture; I did what I could, and it was painful to rip my sight from one scene frozen forever on my mind, to the next, and then to the next.

I had seen the ball hit, its rise; I had seen Mays' first backward sprint; I had again seen the ball and Mays at the same time, Mays still leading. Now I turned to the diamond—how long does it take the eyes to sweep and focus and telegraph to the brain?—and there was the vacant spot on the hill (how often we see what is not there before we see what is there) where Liddle had been and I saw him at the third-base line, between home and third (the wrong place for a pitcher on such a play; he should be behind third to cover a play there, or behind home to back up a play there, but not in between).

I saw Doby, too, hesitating, the only man, I think, on the diamond who now conceded that Mays might catch the ball. Doby is a center fielder and a fine one and very fast himself, so he knows what a center fielder can do. He must have gone nearly halfway to third, now he was coming back to second base a bit. Of course, he may have known that he could jog home if the ball landed over Mays' head, so there was no need to get too far down the line.

Rosen was as near to second as Doby, it seemed. He had come down from first, and for a second—no, not that long, nowhere near that long, for a hundred-thousandth of a second, more likely—I thought Doby and Rosen were Dark and Williams hovering around second, making some foolish double play on this ball that had been hit three hundred and thirty feet past them. Then my mind cleared; they were in Cleveland uniforms, not Giant, they were Doby and Rosen.

And that is all I allowed my eyes on the inner diamond. Back now to Mays—had three seconds elapsed from the first ominous connection of bat and ball?—and I saw Mays do something that he seldom does and that is so often fatal to outfielders. For the briefest piece of time—I cannot shatter and compute fractions of seconds like some atom gun—Mays started to raise his head and turn it to his left, as though he were about to look behind him.

Then he thought better of it, and continued the swift race with the ball that hovered quite close to him now, thirty feet high and coming down (yes, finally coming down) and again—for the second time—I knew Mays would make the catch.

In the Polo Grounds, there are two square-ish green screens, flanking the runway between the two bleacher sections, one to the left-field side of the runway, the other to the right. The screens are intended to provide a solid dark background for the pitched ball as it comes in to the batter. Otherwise he would be trying to pick out the ball from a far-off sea of shirts of many colors, jackets, balloons, and banners.

Wertz's drive, I could see now, was not going to end up in the runway on the fly; it was headed for the screen on the right-field side.

The fly, therefore, was not the longest ball ever hit in the Polo Grounds, not by a comfortable margin. Wally Berger had hit a ball over the left-field roof around the four-hundred foot marker. Joe Adcock had hit a ball into the center-field bleachers. A Giant pitcher, Hal Schumacher, had once hit a ball over the left-field roof, about as far out as Berger's. Nor—if Mays caught it—would it be the longest ball ever caught in the Polo Grounds. In either the 1936 or 1937 World Series—I do not recall which—Joe DiMaggio and Hank Leiber traded gigantic smashes to the foot of the stairs within that runway; each man had caught the other's. When DiMaggio caught Leiber's, in fact, it meant the third out of the game. DiMaggio caught the ball and barely broke step to go up the stairs and out of sight before the crowd was fully aware of what had happened.

So Mays' catch—if he made it—would not necessarily be in the realm of the improbable. Others had done feats that bore some resemblance to this.

Yet Mays' catch—if, indeed, he was to make it—would dwarf all the others for the simple reason that he, too, could have caught Leiber's or DiMaggio's fly, whereas neither could have caught Wertz's. Those balls had been towering drives, hit so high the outfielder could run forever before the ball came down. Wertz had hit his ball harder and on a lower trajectory. Leiber—not a fast man—was nearing second base when DiMaggio caught his ball; Wertz—also not fast—was at first when . . .

When Mays simply slowed down to avoid running into the wall, put his hands up in cup-like fashion over his left shoulder, and caught the ball much like a football player catching leading passes in the end zone.

He had turned so quickly, and run so fast and truly that he made this impossible catch look—to us in the bleachers—quite ordinary. To those reporters in the press box, nearly six hundred feet from the bleacher wall, it must have appeared far more astonishing, watching Mays run and run until he had become the size of a pigmy and then he had run some more, while the ball diminished to a mote of white dust and finally disappeared in the dark blob that was Mays' mitt.

Old Well-Well

ZANE GREY

Think Zane Grey (1872–1939) and you think westerns. The prolific author of *Riders of the Purple Sage* virtually invented the genre. But before he romanced the west, he was flirting pretty heavily with baseball.

He'd been a star on the sandlots of Ohio growing up, then a reliable outfielder and pitcher at the University of Pennsylvania. He played four years of minor league ball, and, by accounts of the day, had a good shot at making the majors. He became a dentist instead.

In time, he would exchange that for the writer's life, interspersing his westerns with a trio of baseball books. The best remains *The Redheaded Outfield and Other Baseball Stories.* Published in 1920, it included "Old Well-Well," one of the finest of all fictional portraits of a baseball fan.

Baseball was a family affair for the Greys, by the way. Zane's younger brother was the model for one of those redheaded outfielders. In 1903, Reddy Grey collected a pair of hits in six at-bats with the Pittsburgh Pirates.

He bought a ticket at the 25-cent window, and edging his huge bulk through the turnstile, laboriously followed the noisy crowd toward the bleachers. I could not have been mistaken. He was Old Well-Well, famous from Boston to Baltimore as the greatest baseball fan in the East. His singular yell had pealed into the ears of five hundred thousand worshippers of the national game and would never be forgotten.

At sight of him I recalled a friend's baseball talk. "You remember Old Well-Well? He's all in—dying, poor old fellow! It seems young Burt, whom the Phillies are trying out this spring, is Old Well-Well's nephew and protege. Used to play on the Murray Hill team; a speedy youngster. When the Philadelphia team was here last, Manager Crestline announced his intention to play Burt in center field. Old Well-Well was too ill to see the lad get his tryout. He was heartbroken and said: 'If I could only see one more game!' "

The recollection of this random baseball gossip and the fact that Philadelphia was scheduled to play New York that very day, gave me a sudden desire to see the game with Old Well-Well. I did not know him, but where on earth were introductions as superfluous as on the bleachers? It was a very easy matter to catch up with him. He walked slowly, leaning hard on a cane and his wide shoulders sagged as he puffed along. I was about to make some pleasant remark concerning the prospects of a fine game, when the sight of his face shocked me and I drew back. If ever I had seen shadow of pain and shade of death they hovered darkly around Old Well-Well.

No one accompanied him; no one seemed to recognize him. The majority of that merry crowd of boys and men would have jumped up wild with pleasure to hear his well-remembered yell. Not much longer than a year before, I had seen ten thousand fans rise as one man and roar a greeting to him that shook the stands. So I was confronted by a situation strikingly calculated to rouse my curiosity and sympathy.

He found an end seat on a row at about the middle of the right-field bleachers and I chose one across the aisle and somewhat behind him. No players were yet in sight. The stands were willing up and streams of men were filing into the aisles of the bleachers and piling over the benches. Old Well-Well settled himself comfortably in his seat and gazed about him with animation. There had come a change to his massive features. The hard lines had softened; the patches of gray were no longer visible; his cheeks were ruddy; something akin to a smile shone on his face as he looked around, missing no detail of the familiar scene.

During the practice of the home team Old Well-Well sat still with his big hands on his knees; but when the gong rang for the Phillies, he grew restless, squirming in his seat and half rose several times. I divined the importuning of his old habit to greet his team with the yell that had made him famous. I expected him to get up; I waited for it. Gradually, however, he became quiet as a man governed by severe self-restraint and directed his attention to the Philadelphia center fielder.

At a glance I saw that the player was new to me and answered the newspaper description of young Burt. What a lively looking athlete! He was tall, lithe, yet sturdy. He did not need to chase more than two fly balls to win me. His graceful, fast style reminded me of the great Curt Welch. Old Well-Well's face wore a rapt expression. I discovered myself hoping Burt would make good; wishing he would rip the boards off the fence; praying he would break up the game.

It was Saturday, and by the time the gong sounded for the game to begin the grandstand and bleachers were packed. The scene was glittering, colorful, a delight to the eye. Around the circle of bright faces rippled a low, merry murmur. The umpire, grotesquely padded in front by his chest protector, announced the batteries, dusted the plate, and throwing out a white ball, sang the open sesame of the game: "Play!"

Then Old Well-Well arose as if pushed from his seat by some strong propelling force. It had been his wont always when play was ordered or in a moment of silent suspense, or a lull in the applause, or a dramatic pause when hearts beat high and lips were mute, to bawl out over the listening, waiting multitude his terrific blast: "Well-Well-Well!"

Twice he opened his mouth, gurgled and choked, and then resumed his seat with a very red, agitated face; something had deterred him from his purpose, or he had been physically incapable of yelling.

The game opened with White's sharp bounder to the infield. Wesley had three strikes called on him, and Kelly fouled out to third base. The Phillies did no better, being retired in one, two, three order. The second inning was short and no tallies were chalked up. Brain hit safely in the third and went to second on a sacrifice. The bleachers began to stamp and cheer. He reached third on an infield hit that the Philadelphia shortstop knocked down but could not cover in time to catch either runner. The cheer in the grandstand was drowned by the roar in the bleachers. Brain scored on a fly-ball to left. A double along the right foul line brought the second runner home. Following that the next batter went out on strikes.

In the Philadelphia half of the inning young Burt was the first man up. He stood left-handed at the plate and looked formidable. Duveen, the wary old pitcher for New York, to whom this new player was an unknown quantity, eyed his easy position as if reckoning on a possible weakness. Then he took his swing and threw the ball. Burt never moved a muscle and the umpire called strike. The next was a ball, the next a strike; still Burt had not moved.

"Somebody wake him up!" yelled a wag in the bleachers. "He's from Slumbertown, all right, all right!" shouted another.

Duveen sent up another ball, high and swift. Burt hit straight over the first baseman, a line drive that struck the front of the right-field bleachers.

"Peacherino!" howled a fan.

Here the promise of Burt's speed was fulfilled. Run! He was fleet as a deer. He cut through first like the wind, settled to a driving stride, rounded second, and by a good, long slide beat the throw in to third. The crowd, who went to games to see long hits and daring runs, gave him a generous handclapping.

Old Well-Well appeared on the verge of apoplexy. His ruddy face turned purple, then black; he rose in his seat; he gave vent to smothered gasps; then he straightened up and clutched his hands into his knees.

Burt scored his run on a hit to deep short, an infielder's choice, with the chances against retiring a runner at the plate. Philadelphia could not tally again that inning. New York blanked in the first of the next. For their opponents, an error, a close decision at second favoring the runner, and a single to right tied the score. Bell of New York got a clean hit in the opening of the fifth. With no one out and chances for a run, the impatient fans let loose. Four subway trains in collision would not have equalled the yell and stamp in the bleachers. Maloney was next to bat and he essayed a bunt. This the fans derided with hoots and hisses. No teamwork, no inside ball for them.

"Hit it out!" yelled a hundred in unison.

"Home run!" screamed a worshipper of long hits.

As if actuated by the sentiments of his admirers Maloney lined the ball over short. It looked good for a double; it certainly would advance Bell to third; maybe home. But no one calculated on Burt. His fleetness enabled him to head the bounding ball. He picked it up cleanly, and checking his headlong run, threw toward third base. Bell was halfway there. The ball shot straight and low with terrific force and beat the runner to the bag.

"What a great arm!" I exclaimed, deep in my throat. "It's the lady's day! He can't be stopped."

The keen newsboy sitting below us broke the amazed silence in the bleachers.

"Wot d'ye tink o' that?"

Old Well-Well writhed in his seat. To him it was a one-man game, as it had come to be for me. I thrilled with him; I gloried in the making good of his protege; it got to be an effort on my part to look at the old man, so keenly did his emotion communicate itself to me.

The game went on, a close, exciting, brilliantly fought battle. Both pitchers were at their best. The batters batted out long flies, low liners, and sharp grounders; the fielders fielded these difficult chances without misplay. Opportunities came for runs, but no runs were scored for several innings. Hopes were raised to the highest pitch only to be dashed astonishingly away.

The crowd in the grandstand swayed to every pitched ball; the bleachers tossed like surf in a storm.

To start the eighth, Stranathan of New York tripled along the left foul line. Thunder burst from the fans and rolled swellingly around the field. Before the hoarse yelling, the shrill hooting, the hollow stamping had ceased Stranathan made home on an infield hit. Then bedlam broke loose. It calmed down quickly, for the fans sensed trouble between Binghamton, who had been thrown out in the play, and the umpire who was waving him back to the bench.

"You dizzy-eyed old woman, you can't see straight!" called Binghamton.

The umpire's reply was lost, but it was evident that the offending player had been ordered out of the grounds.

Binghamton swaggered along the bleachers while the umpire slowly returned to his post. The fans took exception to the player's objection and were not slow in expressing it. Various witty enconiums, not to be misunderstood, attested to the bleachers' love of fair play and their disgust at a player's getting himself put out of the game at a critical stage.

The game proceeded. A second batter had been thrown out. Then two hits in succession looked good for another run. White, the next batter, sent a single over second base. Burt scooped the ball on the first bounce and let drive for the plate. It was another extraordinary throw. Whether ball or runner reached home base first was most difficult to decide. The umpire made his sweeping wave of hand and the breathless crowd caught his decision.

"Out!"

In action and sound the circle of bleachers resembled a long curved beach with a mounting breaker thundering turbulently high.

"Rob–b–ber–r!" bawled the outraged fans, betraying their marvelous inconsistency.

Old Well-Well breathed hard. Again the wrestling of his body signified an inward strife. I began to feel sure that the man was in a mingled torment of joy and pain, that he fought the maddening desire to yell because he knew he had not the strength to stand it. Surely, in all the years of his long following of baseball he had never had the incentive to express himself in his peculiar way that rioted him now. Surely, before the game ended he would split the winds with his wonderful yell.

Duveen's only base on balls, with the help of a bunt, a steal, and a scratch hit, resulted in a run for Philadelphia, again tying the score. How the fans raged at Fuller for failing to field the lucky scratch.

"We had the game on ice!" one cried.

"Get him a basket!"

New York men got on bases in the ninth and made strenuous efforts to cross the plate, but it was not to be. Philadelphia opened up with two scorching hits and then a double steal. Burt came up with runners on second and third. Half the crowd cheered in fair appreciation of the way fate was starting the ambitious young outfielder; the other half, dyed-in-the-wool home-team fans, bent forward in a waiting silent gloom of fear. Burt knocked the dirt out of his spikes and faced Duveen. The second ball pitched he met fairly and it rang like a bell.

No one in the stands saw where it went. But they heard the crack, saw the New York shortstop stagger and then pounce forward to pick up the ball and speed it toward the plate. The catcher was quick to take the incoming runner, and then snap the ball to first base, completing a double play.

When the crowd fully grasped this, which was after an instant of bewilderment, a hoarse crashing roar rolled out across the field to bellow back in loud echo from Coogan's Bluff. The grandstand resembled a colored corn field waving in a violent wind; the bleachers lost all semblance of anything. Frenzied, flinging action—wild chaos—shrieking cries—manifested sheer insanity of joy.

When the noise subsided, one fan, evidently a little longer-winded than his comrades, cried out hysterically:

"O-h! I don't care what becomes of me—now-w!"

Score tied, three to three, game must go ten innings—that was the shibboleth; that was the overmastering truth. The game did go ten innings— eleven—twelve, every one marked by masterly pitching, full of magnificent catches, stops and throws, replete with reckless base-running and slides like flashes in the dust. But they were unproductive of runs. Three to three! Thirteen innings!

"Unlucky thirteenth," wailed a superstitious fan.

I had got down to plugging, and for the first time, not for my home team. I wanted Philadelphia to win, because Burt was on the team. With Old Well-Well sitting there so rigid in his seat, so obsessed by the playing of the lad, I turned traitor to New York.

White cut a high twisting bounder inside the third base, and before the ball could be returned he stood safely on second. The fans howled with what husky voice they had left. The second hitter batted a tremendously high fly toward center field. Burt wheeled with the crack of the ball and raced for the ropes. Onward the ball soared like a sailing swallow; the fleet fielder ran with his back to the stands. What an age that ball stayed in the air! Then it lost its speed, gracefully curved and began to fall. Burt lunged forward and up-wards; the ball lit in his hands and stuck there as he plunged over the ropes into the crowd. White had leisurely trotted halfway to third; he saw the catch, ran back to touch second and then easily made third on the throw-in. The ap-plause that greeted Burt proved the splendid spirit of the game. Bell placed a safe little hit over short, scoring White. Heaving, bobbing bleachers—wild, broken, roar on roar!

Score four to three—only one half inning left for Philadelphia to play—how the fans rooted for another run! A swift double-play, however, ended the inning.

Philadelphia's first hitter had three strikes called on him.

"Asleep at the switch!" yelled a delighted fan.

The next batter went out on a weak pop-up fly to second.

"Nothin' to it!"

"Oh, I hate to take this money!"

"All-l o-over!"

Two men at least of all that vast assemblage had not given up victory for Philadelphia. I had not dared to look at Old Well-Well for a long while. I dreaded the next portentious moment. I felt deep within me something like clairvoyant force, an intangible belief fostered by hope.

Magoon, the slugger of the Phillies, slugged one against the left-field bleachers, but, being heavy and slow, he could not get beyond second base. Cless swung with all his might at the first pitched ball, and instead of hitting it a mile as he had tried, he scratched a mean, slow, teasing grounder down the third-base line. It was as safe as if it had been shot out of a cannon. Magoon went to third.

The crowd suddenly awoke to ominous possibilities; sharp commands came from the players' bench. The Philadelphia team was bowling and hopping on the side lines, and had to be put down by the umpire.

An inbreathing silence fell upon stands and field, quiet, like a lull be-fore a storm.

When I saw young Burt start for the plate and realized it was his turn at bat, I jumped as if I had been shot. Putting my hands on Old Well-Well's shoulder I whispered: "Burt's at bat: He'll break up this game! I know he's going to lose one!"

The old fellow did not feel my touch; he did not hear my voice; he was gazing toward the field with an expression on his face to which no human speech could render justice. He knew what was coming. It could not be denied him in that moment.

How confidently young Burt stood up to the plate! None except a natural hitter could have had his position. He might have been Wagner for all he showed of the tight suspense of that crisis. Yet there was a tense alert poise to his head and shoulders which proved he was alive to his opportunity.

Duveen plainly showed he was tired. Twice he shook his head to his catcher, as if he did not want to pitch a certain kind of ball. He had to use extra motion to get his old speed, and he delivered a high straight ball that Burt fouled over the grandstand. The second ball met a similar fate. All the time the crowd maintained that strange waiting silence. The umpire threw out a glistening white ball, which Duveen rubbed in the dust and spat upon. Then he wound himself up into a knot, slowly unwound, and swinging with effort, threw for the plate.

Burt's lithe shoulders swung powerfully. The meeting of ball and bat fairly cracked. The low driving hit lined over second a rising glittering streak, and went far beyond the center fielder.

Bleachers and stands uttered one short cry, almost a groan, and then stared at the speeding runners. For an instant, approaching doom could not have been more dreaded. Magoon scored. Cless was rounding second when the ball lit. If Burt was running swiftly when he turned first he had only got started, for then his long sprinter's stride lengthened and quickened. At second he was flying; beyond second he seemed to merge into a gray flitting shadow.

I gripped my seat strangling the uproar within me. Where was the applause? The fans were silent, choked as I was, but from a different cause. Cless crossed the plate with the score that defeated New York; still the tension never laxed until Burt beat the ball home in as beautiful a run as ever thrilled an audience.

In the bleak dead pause of amazed disappointment Old Well-Well lifted his hulking figure and loomed, towered over the bleachers. His wide shoulders spread, his broad chest expanded, his breath whistled as he drew it in. One fleeting instant his transfigured face shone with a glorious light. Then, as he threw back his head and opened his lips, his face turned purple, the muscles of his cheeks and jaw rippled and strung, the veins on his forehead swelled into bulging ridges. Even the back of his neck grew red.

"Well!—Well!—Well!!!"

Ear-splitting stentorian blast! For a moment I was deafened. But I heard the echo ringing from the cliff, a pealing clarion call, beautiful and wonderful, winding away in hollow reverberation, then breaking out anew from building to building in clear concatenation.

A sea of faces whirled in the direction of that long unheard yell. Burt had stopped statue-like as if stricken in his tracks; then he came running, darting among the spectators who had leaped the fence.

Old Well-Well stood a moment with slow glance lingering on the tumult of emptying bleachers, on the moving mingling colors in the grandstand, across the green field to the gray-clad players. He staggered forward and fell.

Before I could move, a noisy crowd swarmed about him, some solicitous, many facetious. Young Burt leaped the fence and forced his way into the circle. Then they were carrying the old man down to the field and toward the clubhouse.

I waited until the bleachers and field were empty. When I finally went out there was a crowd at the gate surrounding an ambulance. I caught a glimpse of Old Well-Well. He lay white and still, but his eyes were open, smiling intently. Young Burt hung over him with a pale and agitated face. Then a bell clanged and the ambulance clattered away.

His Most Prized Possession
Was That '54 Eddie

RON SHELTON

Just before Christmas of 2000, I drove up to New York from our home in the country beyond Philadelphia to have dinner with Ron Shelton. I met Ron just before the opening of *Bull Durham,* and we've been friends ever since. Through the years, his movie has become a certified classic, the best baseball movie ever made. Funny as it is, it brilliantly probes the ethos of the game be-cause Ron, once a second baseman in the Orioles' system, lived that ethos, his own baseball dream ending a heartbreaking hop from the majors with the Rochester Red Wings in Triple-A.

At first, my plan was to insert in these pages the delicious opening monologue Ron wrote for Annie Savoy. A few cocktails into dinner, I sus-pected I'd revise the lineup. Ron was weaving a mesmerizing tale about him-self, his father, religion, television, and hometown hero, Eddie Mathews, the Braves' Hall of Fame third baseman. I urged him to write it. He did—sadly—when Mathews died not long after.

Great baseball stories have a way of reaching into our lives, taking hold, and telling us who we are. This one does precisely that.

E ddie died Sunday. He was "Eddie" to all of us growing up in Santa Barbara, where he was a god, where his exploits on the football and baseball fields inspired a generation of young boys. I was one of those boys.

In the early '50s when Eddie broke in with the Boston Braves, my father would drive me to the small house west of the highway where Mathews grew up. His mother would wave.

"Just came to see Eddie's house," my old man would say. His father wasn't around—something about a problem with the bottle, though I wouldn't know what that meant until years later.

Then came '54, a year that to most men of my generation meant one thing—Willie Mays' catch of Vic Wertz's screaming line drive to deep center at the Polo Grounds. Giants in four. I mean, what else happened in '54?

Well, the first-ever issue of *Sports Illustrated* was published in '54 and Eddie was on the cover, caught in mid-swing during a night game at Milwaukee's County Stadium. My father brought it home and presented it like a religious icon. What a swing he had—Ty Cobb himself called it the best in baseball. "His swing was so pretty he even looked good striking out," it was said.

If you lived in Santa Barbara—or Milwaukee, because the Braves moved there from Boston—you knew early on that two young hitting stars were about to become the most potent 1-2 home-run combination in baseball history. Two kids, really. Henry Aaron and Eddie Mathews. With one "t", Mathews—that was a big thing for us kids. Spell his name right. He's our guy.

My brother named his cat Ralph Kiner. I named mine Eddie Mathews.

That, '54, also was the year we started collecting baseball cards. Every kid I knew had two to three hundred before I could convince my father to drive me to Dave's Market to buy my first pack—everybody knew that Dave's Market had the best cards. The curious thing was that nobody yet had collected an Eddie Mathews. Did Topps Chewing Gum Co. intentionally restrict the number of Eddies distributed in Santa Barbara so that we kids would keep forking over the nickels as a kind of madness swept through the 8-year-olds, a feeding frenzy in our search for the first Eddie? We knew nothing of price fixing or corporate stock manipulations. But we knew something was up.

Then one day my father just pulled over to Dave's Market and accompanied me inside, announcing to Dave that "this was my son's first pack of baseball cards and we expect Eddie will be in the pack." I was embarrassed. I knew that wasn't how it worked. You couldn't demand or expect that anybody would be in a pack and, in fact, most of my friends had collected a dozen or so Bob Oldis cards (he was a backup catcher somewhere or other) to every Stan Musial. We were sure the decks were stacked with utility guys. We kind of understood that was the way the world worked.

It was like having your father show up on your first date, and then having him announce it was time for the girl to kiss you. We paid our nickel and my father insisted we open the pack right there, in front of God and Dave himself. I knew the face of Bob Oldis or Solly Hemus or Thornton Kipper or Dave Jolly would greet me. But no, there he was.

Eddie. Right on top, under the powdery gum. Eddie against a light blue background. The 1954 Topps card design, the greatest baseball card design ever. Eddie, powder-blue sky, the Braves logo . . .

"There," my father said, "Eddie."

Kids from all over town came to see my Eddie. Stared at it. Tried to touch it, but I wouldn't let them. They had Willie and Whitey and Mickey. But I had Eddie. He was our guy.

He was my guy.

The next year, '55, means only one thing to baseball people. The Dodgers at last won the Series. To me it also was the year Eddie got arrested for drunk driving for the first time. It was a somber night at our dinner table and my father brought up the subject first in a kind of preemptive strike—he knew I'd read about it in the sports page when the evening paper arrived.

"Eddie did a bad thing," my father said with the gravity of sharing a family death. "He had too much to drink and went out driving. He has a little trouble with the bottle, ya know." I think we prayed for him. But we remained his loyal followers and I learned a lesson early. Certain people can teach us certain things—nobody can teach us everything. Your athletic heroes should be just that, no more, no less—and that is plenty. I would later grow to understand what having a "little trouble with the bottle" meant.

And then, in '57, when I was 12, a kind of Road to Damascus reverse conversation took place. And Eddie was at the center.

We didn't have a television until that year. We couldn't afford one and didn't need one—until the Braves were in the World Series against the Yankees. We hated the Yankees—other than the Braves, we were a Dodger family. My father bought a television from Ott's, the local department store. "Always buy local," he said.

The first great religious crisis of my life came Sunday, Game 4. The Braves trailed the series, 2–1, and Game 4 was scheduled during Sunday church. We never missed Sunday school or church. Never, ever, wherever we were.

We went to Sunday school and, afraid even to think about the game, headed into the First Baptist Church sanctuary for the 11 A.M. service, dreading as always the boring, endless, dry sermons and hymns sung out of key.

But no, my father whisked us away, tossed us in the old Buick station wagon with my mother and drove straight home to watch the game. Nobody spoke.

The illicitness of the act cannot be overstated. The guilt. The danger. We were skipping church to watch a baseball game. We were skipping God for Eddie, a guy who had a little problem with the bottle.

We watched the game in virtual silence. Had lightning struck our house, we would not have been surprised. We would have gone to hell and deserved it. My father was rarely nervous in those days, but on this day, he fidgeted, paced, sweated.

And in the 10th inning Eddie hit one deep over the right center field fence and the Braves won. A few days later our Eddie made a great backhand play off the bat of Moose Skowron and the Braves were champions of the world.

We had been liberated from the iron grip of an angry God by Eddie, a man who probably never had been in a church. Our Sundays became more relaxed, and a couple years later, my father couldn't be found in a Sunday morning church service.

"I got my own church," he began saying. And we listened.

Five years later in high school, I won the batting title at Santa Barbara High and was awarded the Eddie Mathews Bat, which was the school's trophy for best batting average. Of all the trophies, plaques and honors I've received, this is the only one I can actually locate. It's the only trophy you can carry out to the backyard and take a few cuts with.

I never hit any balls close to where Eddie hit them in high school—up on the barranca near the swimming pool, there's a spot that old-timers point to—but one year, at least, I earned a bat with his name on it.

The great Henry Aaron said in his autobiography that Eddie used to deck anyone making a racial remark in Aaron's direction. Eddie wasn't making a statement about race, but about teams. If you were on Mathews' team, he'd kill for you. If you were on the opposing team, well, good luck.

"I believe in the church of baseball" was a line I wrote 30 years after his home run freed us from evangelical prison. Scouting my first movie as a director in Durham, N.C., I saw Eddie sitting in an empty dugout, clearly hung over, dragging on a cigarette. He was a long-time member of the Hall of Fame by then, and hanging on as a minor league scout for the Braves.

The bottle had taken its toll, the cigarettes were endless. Finishing a career in small motels in small towns in the South, just as he had started. But now he was watching young players, filing reports, spending more nights in bars in towns like Asheville and Lynchburg and Bluefield.

I wanted to go over and tell him all this, but I didn't. Who was I but another guy who batted .500 in high school but couldn't handle a professional breaking ball? I had another career now, another life. Let him sit there, alone, in whatever peace he'd found.

I wanted to go over and try to explain about the Road to Damascus and Pauline Doctrine and that powder-blue background and ask him if he understood the significance of his home run in Game 4 of the '57 Series.

But he'd have just said, "Hell, the guy hung a curveball, I caught it pretty good. Can I buy you a beer, kid?"

In a flash, it's 1954 and I can see the guy at Dave's Market looking up at my father when Eddie's face appears on top in the pack of cards. That little smile, those matinee-idol good looks, and, of course, the powdered-blue background.

Eddie was my guy.

Keith

PETE HAMILL

In May of 1988, I was sitting with three friends in the front row of the mezzanine section of Dodger Stadium above third base when Mets first-baseman Keith Hernandez stepped in against reliever Alejandro Pena. It was the sixth inning of a close game. I have no recollection of how the at-bat ended, who won, or what the final score was, but that at-bat remains my most personally thrilling moment as a fan.

Hernandez had sprayed three or four pitches around the stands before launching one in our direction. From the moment the ball left his bat, I knew it was mine—if I could just get my paws out far enough. The ball kept curving toward us, and the friend next to me—realizing I had the angle—wrapped his arms around my waist and told me to go for it. I reached out of the stands, my arms fully extended. The ball found my bare hands.

I had always sworn that if I ever caught a foul ball—this was my first and, to date, only—I would sit down graciously, as if it were just another moment at the yard.

Not a chance.

I held up my prize, waved like a three-year-old, high-fived my friends, and accepted the pats of people I'd never seen before. And that would normally be the end of the story, except . . .

There was a phone booth in the aisle just behind our seats. One of my buddies suggested I call my father. He'd probably have the game on back in New York.

"Dad, Dad," I exploded when he picked up the receiver, "you watching the game?"

"Yeah," he answered. "A guy looks just like you just caught a foul ball."

It was a streamlined moment, and this is a streamlined piece—written for *The Village Voice*—about a streamlined player by one of New York's most streamlined writers. Whether observing baseball, boxing, Vietnam, art, the rich and famous, or the voiceless and downtrodden, Pete Hamill has been a pillar of passion, conscience, and poetic prose since his start at *The New York Post* in the 1960s. Novelist, memoirist, and screenwriter, Hamill has never strayed too far from the blue-collar ethos of newsprint; in 2001 he returned to the *New York Daily News,* which he once edited, his name again atop a column.

The ball, by the way, sits in a plastic cube on a shelf above the computer on my desk.

I

It is morning in the clubhouse at Huggins-Stengel Field in St. Petersburg and Keith Hernandez is moving from locker to locker, handing out schedules. He is the player rep of the world champion New York Mets; this is one of his duties. Still dressed in street clothes and sneakers, he says little as he hands the sheets to each of the players. At 33, he is young in the world of ordinary men; in baseball, especially on this young ball club, he is middle-aged. Kids and veterans nod and study the mimeographed sheets, which tell them when the bus will leave for the afternoon game and how many tickets they can expect for wives and friends. Hernandez explains nothing; he was out late the night before with a woman down from New York. "Too much goddamned wine," he says. And besides, he has been here before, through 13 major league seasons; this is a time for ease, the careful steady retrieval of the skills of the summer game.

"It's all about getting back in a kind of groove," Hernandez says. "Not about getting in shape. Most of the guys are in shape, or they get in shape before coming down. I worked out with weights all winter, the first time I ever did that, 'cause I'm getting old." He smiles, shakes his head. "At the Vertical Club in New York. Jesus, don't go there at five o'clock. It's fucking insane, a social—No, this is about getting your stroke right. About getting back your concentration. I don't worry about it much until the last 10 games before the season starts. If I'm having trouble *then,* then I worry."

In the clubhouse, Hernandez wanders among those who have made it to The Show and those who desperately want to. They all move with that coiled and practiced indolence that is unique to baseball, the style of a game where the most exciting action seems to explode out of the greatest calm. A large table is spread with food; there are boxes of Dubble Bubble and sugarless gum. Some players nibble as they dress; others knead and work new gloves, bad-mouth each other, talk about women, read newspapers and sports magazines, all the while stripping off street clothes and pulling on jocks and T-shirts and uniforms.

Keven McReynolds, new to the team after a winter trade from San Diego, stares into space. Darryl Strawberry isn't here yet (two weeks before the great alarm clock rhubarb); neither is Dwight Gooden. Hernandez leaves the mimeographed sheets on the small benches in front of their lockers and moves on. When he's finished, he dumps the leftovers in a trash can, sits down at his own locker, lights a Winston and reaches for the *New York Times* crossword puzzle.

"We'll talk later," he says, takes a drag, and stares at the puzzle while unbuttoning his shirt. Hernandez examines the words the way fans examine stats. His own stats are, of course, extraordinary. One of the most consistent hitters in the game, in three full seasons as a Met, he has averaged .311, .309, and .310. Against left-handed pitching last year, he hit .312; against right-handers, .309. He hit .310 at home and .311 on the road. Last year, he had 13 game-winning RBIs, and his career total of 107 is the most in National League history.

It seemed that every time you looked up last season, Hernandez was on base; this wasn't an illusion; he tied with Tim Raines for the lead in on-base percentage (.413), with 94 walks added to 171 hits. Although he has never been much of a power hitter (his career high was 16 home runs for the Cardinals in 1980), when there are men on base there is nobody you'd rather have at bat. "I can't stand leading off an inning," he says. "It's so goddamned boring." Hernandez hit safely in 10 of the 13 postseason games. That's what he's paid to do.

"Keith is the kind of consistent clutch hitter who relies on 'big' RBI production as compared with 'multi' RBI production," says the astute Mets announcer Tim McCarver in the new book he wrote with Ray Robinson, *Oh, Baby, I Love It!* "As an example, a lot of one-run games are won by key hits in the middle innings rather than by big three-run home runs late in the game. Keith is a spectacular middle-inning hitter. . . . You've heard the baseball adage 'Keep 'em close, I'll think of something'? Well, the something the Mets think of is usually Keith Hernandez."

The fielding stats are even more extraordinary. Last year, he won his ninth straight Gold Glove Award at first base—the most of any player in history—with only five errors in the season, for a .996 average. Those stats don't even begin to tell the story of what Hernandez does on the field; like all great glove men, he makes difficult plays look easy.

But more important, Hernandez can still dazzle you with the play that follows no rule. In the 12th inning of a game with Cincinnati last July 22, the Reds had runners on first and second with none out. Carl Willis dropped a splendid bunt down the third base line, and suddenly, there was Keith, all the way over from first. He threw to Gary Carter, who was playing third, and Carter went back to first for the double play. The Mets won 6–3 in the 14th inning. McCarver, who calls Hernandez "the Baryshnikov of first basemen," writes: "Baseball is a game where, if you do the routine things spectacularly, you win more games than doing the spectacular things routinely—because few athletes have the talent to do spectacular things routinely. Keith has that kind of talent."

In spring training, of course, all players spend their mornings doing the routine things routinely. And on this day, after the cigarette and the crossword, Hernandez is suited up. He makes a quick visit to the john. And then he joins the other players as they move out onto the field. To a visitor who believes the phrase "spring training" is the loveliest in the American language, the view is suddenly beautiful, the bright blue and orange of the Mets' uniforms instantly transforming the great sward of fresh green grass.

After more than 130 days without baseball, it's beginning again. The wan sun abruptly breaks through the clouds and the young men jog out to the far reaches of the outfield and then back. They line up in rows, and then an instructor leads them through 15 minutes of stretching exercises. There is something wonderfully appealing about the clumsiness of the players during this drill; thrown out of their accustomed positions and stances, they don't look like professional athletes at all. Instead, the field now looks like part of some peculiar kind of boot camp, stocked with raw recruits. Jesse Orosco glances at Doug Sisk to see if he's doing the exercise correctly; Lenny Dykstra says something to Carter, who laughs; Backman does a push-up when the others are twisting through sit-ups. Hernandez leads with his left leg when everyone else is leading with the right. You can see more athletic workouts at the New York Health & Racquet Club.

But then it's over and they're all up and reaching for gloves. The players pair off, playing catch, loosening up, while the sun begins to dry the wet grass. Hernandez is throwing with Roger McDowell. The ease and grace and economy of movement are obvious; it's as if he is on a morning stroll. He chatters away with other players (as he does with opposing players who reach first base during the season, a tactical matter that is less about conviviality than it is about distracting the enemy). Dykstra slides a package of Red Man from his hip pocket and bites off a chunk and Hernandez says something we can't hear and Dykstra tries to laugh with his mouth shut. On the sidelines, Davey Johnson has emerged to watch his charges. His coaches—Buddy Harrelson, Bill Robinson, Vern Hoscheit, Sam Perlozzo, and Mel Stottlemyre—are on the side, glancing indifferently at the players, talking about famous assholes they've known. The list is fairly long and each new name brings a guffaw and a story. Harrelson turns to a visitor and says, "That's *all* off the record." And laughs. On the field, Hernandez is working out of a pitcher's windup. He throws a strike. "You think Mex can make this team?" Perlozzo says. Stottlemyre smiles. "He already did."

Then the players amble over to the batting cage, where Perlozzo will be throwing. There's a wire fence beside the cage and fans have assembled behind it, some wearing Mets jackets, caps, and T-shirts. A few are old, the stereotypical snowbirds of spring training; but more are young. They've arranged vacations to come down to see the ballplayers. A few are screaming for autographs. Hernandez waits to bat, says, "Jesus Christ, *listen* to them. . . ." The kids among them seem in awe, and are not screaming. "These are supposed to be *grown-ups*." Two of the middle-aged fans are waving baseballs to be signed. I mention to Hernandez what Warren Spahn had said at a banquet the night before in St. Petersburg: "Baseballs were never meant to be written on. Kids ought to play with 'em. They ought to throw 'em, hit 'em. I hope someday they develop a cover you can't write on." Hernandez says, "Ain't that the truth."

But the fans are persistent and I remember waiting outside Ebbets Field with my brother Tom one late afternoon long ago and seeing Carl Furillo come out, dressed in a sports shirt. His arms looked like the thickest, most powerful arms in the known universe. I wanted to ask him for an autograph but didn't know how; a mob of other kids chased after him and he got in a car with Jackie Robinson and Roy Campanella, and I wondered how he had ever been able to sign the petition at spring training in 1947 saying he couldn't play with a black man. Years later, I learned that Leo Durocher told the protesting players (Dixie Walker, Hugh Casey, Kirby Higbe, Bobby Bragan, Furillo, among others) to go and "wipe your ass" with the petition. Durocher was the manager and Robinson was on the team and there was nothing else to say except play ball. Standing at the batting cage, while Hernandez took his swings and the fans demanded to be authenticated with signatures, I realized again how much of the adult response to baseball is about the accretion of memory and the passage of time.

"Christ, I hate spring training," Hernandez said at one point. "It's so goddamned *boring.*"

But for the rest of us, spring training is something else: the true beginning of the year, a kind of preliminary to the summer festival, another irreversible mark in time. On the field and in the clubhouse, kid players come over to Hernandez. "Hey, Mex, lemme ask you something. . . ." They are talking to him about the present and the future. But we who don't play also see the past; it helps us measure accomplishment, skill, potential. Don Mattingly is another Musial; Wally Backman is another Eddie Stanky. At spring training, somewhere in the Florida afternoons, we always hear the voice of Red Barber and know that in a few weeks we'll be playing the Reds at Crosley Field and the Cardinals in Sportsman's Park and we could lose one in the late innings if that goddamned Slaughter lifts one over the pavilion roof. This is not mere sentiment; it's history and lore, part of the baggage of New York memory.

New Yorkers don't easily accept ballplayers. They almost always come from somewhere else, itinerants and mercenaries, and most of them are rejected. We look at Darryl Strawberry and unfairly compare him to Snider, DiMaggio, Mays, Mantle. We question his desire, his heart, his willingness under pressure to risk everything in one joyful and explosive moment. Since he is young, we reserve judgment, but after four seasons, he still seems a stranger in the town. Those who are accepted seem to have been part of New York forever. Hernandez is one of them.

II

He was born on October 20, 1953, in San Francisco. Although his teammates call him Mex, he isn't Mexican at all. His grandparents on his father's side immigrated from Spain in 1907; his mother's side is Scotch-Irish. Keith's father, John, was a fine high school player (batting .650 in his senior year) and was signed by the Brooklyn Dodgers for a $1000 bonus in 1940. According to William Nack in *Sports Illustrated,* John Hernandez was badly beaned in a minor league night game just before the war; his eyesight was ruined, and though he played with Musial and others in some Navy games, when the war was over, John Hernandez knew he couldn't play again. He became a San Francisco fireman, moved to suburban Pacifica, and started the process of turning his sons, Gary and Keith, into the ballplayers he could never be. They swung at a balled-up sock attached to a rope in the barn; both playing first base, they learned to field ground balls, thousands of ground balls, millions.

From the time Keith was eight, he and his brother were given baseball quizzes, questions about tactics and strategy, *the fundamentals.* His mother,

Jackie, took home movies at Little League games, and they would be carefully studied, analyzed for flaws. John Hernandez was not the first American father to do such things; he will not be the last. But he did the job well. Perhaps too well.

"My father taught me how to hit," Keith says. "He made us swing straight at the ball, not to undercut it, golf it. A straight swing, an even stroke. He really knew."

But Nack, and other writers, have described the relationship of father and son as a mixed blessing. In brief, John Hernandez is said to be unable to leave his son alone; Keith is one of the finest players in the game, an acknowledged leader of a splendid world championship team, the father of three daughters of his own; but too often, his father still treats him as if he were the kid behind the barn, learning to hit the slider. When Keith goes into a slump (and he has one almost every year, usually in midseason), his father is on the phone with advice. As Nack wrote, "Keith knows that no one can help him out of a slump as quickly as his father can, and so, throughout his career, he has often turned to his father for help. At the same time, he has felt the compelling need to break away from his father and make it on his own, to be his own man."

Obviously it would be a mistake to think that Keith Hernandez is the mere creation of his father. His brother, Gary, was trained the same way, went to Berkeley on an athletic scholarship, but didn't make it to the majors. Keith had his own drive, his own vision. At Capuchino High (where he hit .500 one season), he also starred on the football and basketball teams, and says that football was particularly good training. "I was a quarterback, and I had to make choices all the time, to move guys around, read the other teams' defenses. But I was 5-11, 175 pounds then and that was too small, even for college. I went down to Stanford for a tryout, saw the size of these guys, and decided baseball was for me."

Major league scouts were watching him in high school, but in his senior year he quit the team after an argument with the manager. Most of the scouts vanished. Until then, it had been expected that Keith would be a first-round draft pick in the June 1971 free agent draft; instead, he was chosen by the Cardinals in the 40th round. He had always been a fairly good student, and was accepted at Berkeley, but when the Cardinals offered a $30,000 bonus, he decided to head for professional ball.

There are hundreds of stories about minor league phenoms who burn up the leagues and fizzle in the majors; Hernandez had the opposite experience. He has always hit better for average in the majors than he did starting out in A ball at St. Petersburg in 1972 (.256) or AAA ball at Tulsa in the same year (.241). He found his groove in Tulsa in '73 and '74, and was brought up for 14 games in St. Louis in 1974. He hit .294 in those games, was soon being described as the next Musial, started the 1975 season at first, couldn't get going, was sent down again, and brought up again the following year, this time to stay.

That first full year with the Cardinals, he hit .289, the next year .291. Still, he didn't feel secure. In 1978, the year he met and married Sue Broecker, he slumped to .255. "I didn't feel I was *really* here until '79," he says. That year, he hit .344, with a career-high 210 hits. He won the batting championship, and shared the Most Valuable Player award with Willie Stargell, who hit .281.

"Yeah, you get better," he said one afternoon in St. Petersburg. "You know more. You watch, you see, you learn. You know something about pacing yourself too. One of the most important things about the minors is learning how to play every day. In high school, college ball, you play maybe twice a week. You don't know what it's like to do it day in and day out. . . . In the majors, you're seeing guys over and over. You look at a guy like Steve Carlton for 11 or 12 years. You know how hard he throws, you know how his breaking ball is, you know how he likes to pitch you. And you know the catchers too, how they see you, what kind of game they like to call."

Hernandez is one of those players who seem totally involved in the game. On deck, his concentration is ferocious. After an at-bat, including those in which he fails ("a great hitter, a guy who hits .300, fails seven out of 10 times"), he is passing on information about pitchers.

"I look for patterns," he says. "I usually only look at the way a pitcher pitches to left-handed hitters. I don't pay much attention to the right-handed hitters. What does he like to do when he's in trouble? Does he go to the breaking ball, or the fastball, does he like to come in or stay away? I look for what you can do to hurt him. There are very few pitchers that are patternless. Of course, there are a few guys—Seaver, Don Sutton—who don't have a pattern. They pitch you different every time. That's why they have 500 wins between them, why they're future Hall of Famers."

Hernandez is known as a generous player; he will talk about hitting with anyone on the team "except pitchers, 'cause they might get traded." Pitchers themselves are a notoriously strange breed (a player once described his team as being made up of blacks, whites, and pitchers), and though Hernandez is friendly with all of them, and was amazingly valuable to the young Mets staff in the 1984 season (Gary Carter didn't arrive until '85), he still maintains a certain distance.

"Most pitchers . . . can't relate to hitting because they can't hit, they've never hit. They don't know how. And there's very few that know how to *pitch*. But it's not so simple. Some guys you can hit off, some you can't. I was always successful against Carlton, and he was a great pitcher. And then there's some sub-.500 pitcher, and you can't get a hit off him. It's one of the inexplicable mysteries of baseball."

Hernandez clearly loves talking about the craft of baseball. But there are some subjects he won't discuss. One is his ruined marriage to Sue Broecker. There have been various blurry published reports about this messy soap opera. How Keith played around a lot after the marriage, particularly on the road. How they broke up after the All-Star game in 1980, then reconciled and had a baby. How Keith liked his booze after games, and later started dabbling with cocaine. She got fed up, one version goes, and then demanded most of his $1.7 million a year salary as reparations. In my experience, the truth about anybody else's marriage is unknowable; thousands struggle to understand their own.

Hernandez, by all accounts, loves his children; he dotes on them when he is with them, even took a few days out of spring training to take them to Disney World. Marriages end; responsibility does not. Hernandez says that he would like to marry again someday and raise a family, but not until he's finished with baseball. One sign of maturity is the realization that you can't have everything.

He also won't discuss cocaine anymore. At one point, he told writer Joe Klein what it was like around the major leagues in the late '70s. "All of a sudden, it was everywhere. In the past, you might be in a bar and someone would say, 'Hey, Keith, wanna smoke a joint?' Now it was 'Wanna do a line?' People I'd never met before were offering; people I didn't know. *Everywhere* you went. It was like a wave: it came, and then people began to realize that cocaine could really hurt you, and they stopped."

Nobody has ever disputed Hernandez's claim that his cocaine use was strictly recreational; he never had to go into treatment (as teammate Lonnie Smith did); his stats remained consistent. But when Hernandez was traded to the Mets in June 1983 for Neil Allen and Rick Ownbey, the whispering was all over baseball. Cards manager Whitey Herzog would not have traded Hernandez for such mediocre players if the first baseman didn't have some monstrous drug problem. It didn't matter that Hernandez almost immediately transformed the Mets into a contender, giving them a professional core, setting an example for younger players, inspiring some of the older men. The whispering went on.

Then, deep into the 1985 season, Hernandez joined the list of professional ballplayers who testified in the Curtis Strong case in Pittsburgh, and the whole thing blew open. In his testimony, Hernandez described cocaine as a demon that got into him, but that was now gone; he had stopped well before the trade to the Mets. He wasn't the only player named in the Strong case, but he seemed to get most of the ink. When he rejoined the team the next day in Los Angeles, he did the only thing he knew how to do: he went five for five.

When the Mets finally came home to Shea Stadium, Hernandez was given a prolonged standing ovation during his first at-bat. It was as if the fans were telling him that all doubt was now removed: he was a New Yorker forever. Flawed. Imperfect. Capable of folly. But a man who had risen above his own mistakes to keep on doing what he does best. That standing ovation outraged some of the older writers and fans but it moved Hernandez almost to tears. He had to step out of the box to compose himself. Then he singled to left.

Last spring, as Hernandez was getting ready for the new season, baseball commissioner Peter Ueberroth made his decision about punishing the players who had testified in the Strong case. Hernandez was to pay a fine of 10 per cent of his salary (roughly $180,000, to be donated to charity), submit to periodic drug testing, and do 100 hours of community service in each of the next two years. Most of the affected players immediately agreed; Hernandez did not. He objected strongly to being placed in Group 1, those players who "in some fashion facilitated the distribution of drugs in baseball." In the new afterword to his book *If at First . . .,* Hernandez insists: "I never sold drugs or dealt in drugs and didn't want that incorrect label for the rest of my life."

There were some obvious constitutional questions. (Hernandez and the other players were given grants of immunity, testified openly, and were punished anyway—by the baseball commissioner—even though they had the absolute right to plead the Fifth Amendment in the first place.) There was also something inherently unfair about punishing a man who came clean. Hernandez threatened to file a grievance, conferred with friends, lawyers, his brother. After a week of the resulting media shitstorm, Hernandez reluctantly agreed to comply, still saying firmly, "The only person I hurt was myself."

Last year, he took a certain amount of abuse. A group of Chicago fans showed up with dollar bills shoved up their noses. Many Cardinal fans, stirred up by the local press, were unforgiving. And I remember being at one game at Shea Stadium, where a leather-lunged guy behind me kept yelling at Hernandez, "Hit it down da white line, Keith. Hit it down da white line." Still, Hernandez refused to grovel, plead for forgiveness, appear on the Jimmy Swaggart show, or kiss anyone's ass. He just played baseball. The Mets won the division, the playoffs, and the World Series, and they couldn't have done it without him. When *The New York Times* did a roundup piece a few weeks ago about how the players in the Pittsburgh case had done their community service, Hernandez was the only ballplayer to refuse an interview. His attitude is clear: I did it, it's over, let's move on. He plays as hard as he can (slowed these days by bad ankles that get worse on Astroturf) and must know that the Drug Thing might prevent him from ever managing in the major leagues—and could even keep him out of the Hall of Fame.

"I like playing ball," he says. "That's where I'm almost always happy."

III

Now it's the spring and everything lies before him. The sports pages are full of questions: what's the matter with Gooden and why isn't Dykstra hitting and will the loss of Ray Knight change everything and why does McReynolds look so out to lunch. Nobody writes much about Hernandez; his career and his style don't provoke many questions. He will tell you that he thinks Don Mattingly is "the best player in the game today," but admits that he seldom watches American League games and isn't even interested in playing American League teams in spring. The next day, for example, the Mets are scheduled to play the Blue Jays in nearby Dunedin. "I'd rather not even go," says Hernandez. "It's a shit park and we're never gonna play these guys, so why?"

In the clubhouse, nothing even vaguely resembles a headline; Hernandez does talk in an irritated way about Strawberry, as if the sight of such natural gifts being inadequately used causes him a kind of aesthetic anger. "Last year, he finally learned how to separate his offense from his defense and that's a major improvement," Hernandez says. "Before, if he wasn't hitting, he'd let it affect his fielding. Not last year."

His locker is at the opposite end of the clubhouse from that of Gary Carter, who is the other leader of the club. I'm told that some players are Carter men, some Hernandez men. There could not be a greater difference in style. Carter is Mister Good Guy America, right out of the wholesome Steve Garvey mold. You can imagine him as a Los Angeles Dodger—but not a Brooklyn Dodger. He smiles most of the time and even his teeth seem to have muscles; he radiates fair-haired good health; if a demon has ever entered him, he shows no signs of the visit.

You can see Carter on a horse, or kicking up dust with a Bronco on some western backcountry road or strolling toward you on the beach at Malibu. Hernandez is dark, reflective, analytical, urban. Through the winter, you see him around the saloons of the city, sometimes with friends like Phil McConkey of the Giants, other times with beautiful women. His clothes are carefully cut. He reads books, loves history, buys art for his apartment on the East Side. Carter is the king of the triumphant high-fives; Hernandez seems embarrassed by them. In a crisis, Carter might get down on a knee and have a prayer meeting; Hernandez advocates a good drunk. Between innings, Carter gives out with the rah-rah on the bench; Hernandez is in the runway smoking a cigarette.

They are friendly, of course, in the casual way that men on the same team are friendly. But it's hard to imagine them wandering together through the night. Hernandez speaks about his personal loneliness and fear; Carter smiles through defeat and promises to be better tomorrow. Both are winners. In some odd way, they were forever joined, forever separated, during the Greatest Game Ever Played (well, one of them): the 6th playoff game against Houston. In the 14th inning, Billy Hatcher hit a home run off Jesse Orosco to tie the game. There was a hurried conference on the mound. Hernandez later said he told Carter, "If you call another fastball, I'll fight you right here." Carter insists that the words were never uttered, telling Mark Ribowsky of *Inside Sports:* "Keith *never* said that, he just told the press that he did out of the tension of the game. I call the pitches and *I* decided not to throw anything after that but Jesse's slider, his best pitch. Let's get that straight once and for all."

That was last season. This is the new season, and in the cool mornings of the Florida spring, they are all still thousands of pitches away from the fierce tests of August, the terrors of September. There will be crises, dramas, fights, slumps, failures, disappointments, along with giddy joyous triumphs. There are perils up ahead. The Cardinals might get themselves together again; the Phillies had a great second half last year and could come on strong. When you're a champion, you have to defend what you've won. But for now, they are all months away from discussions of such arcane phenomena as the All Important Loss Column. Up ahead lies the season of the summer game and it remains a mystery, a maybe, a perhaps.

On another morning, Hernandez was waiting to take his swings, 10 hits apiece, and two young women were standing behind the fence, chewing gum. "They've gotta be from New York," Keith said. "Every girl in New York chews gum. Everywhere. All the time. In restaurants. In bed. Drives me crazy." He laughs. He looks at a foam rubber pad he wears in BP to protect his left thumb, which was hurt when Vida Blue jammed him in a game years ago. Then he steps in and takes his swings, the straight level strokes his father taught him, always making contact, intense in his concentration. That day, he wasn't playing in the team game, and the field was almost empty. When he was finished hitting, he and Backman helped pick up all the balls and handed them to Perlozzo. Dave Magadan was ready to hit. Hernandez leaned down and touched his toes. "I'd like to go back to bed," he said. "But I can't do that anymore. I'm getting old. . . ."

With that he walked out onto the empty field, and then began to jog easily and gracefully through the lumpy grass, and then to run, out around the edges of the field, under the palm trees beside the fence, a lone small figure in a lush and verdant place.

Baseball Players Called Her Ma

JAMES T. FARRELL

The bard of Chicago's South Side, James T. Farrell (1904–1979) captured the gritty realism of his hometown in the three muscular novels of the '30s that comprise his "Studs Lonigan" trilogy. A lifelong White Sox fan and a fine second baseman in his youth, Farrell often wove strands of the National Pastime through his narratives. He was transfixed by baseball—"I understood the game and could follow the plays," he once wrote, "before I could read and write"; it became one of the constancies in his artistically and politically turbulent life.

In 1957, Farrell published *My Baseball Diary,* a panoramic collection of essays, journalism, reminiscences, and excerpts from his fiction. It included this affectionate recollection of Ma McCuddy and the players whose whistles she was always happy to wet.

One day in 1912, the late Charles A. Comiskey, then owner of the Chicago White Sox, took a boy in his late teens across the street from Comiskey Park to a frame house next door to a saloon on West Thirty-fifth Street. He spoke to a Chicago-born woman of Italian descent, more or less as follows:

"Ma, this is Ray Schalk, and I want you to feed him and take care of him."

At the time, Schalk was a country boy in the big city, and looked so juvenile that he could have been more easily taken for a bat boy rather than the great catcher he was quickly to become. When the White Sox were playing at home, Schalk would report to this woman for lunch every day before he went across the street to put on his uniform for the game. He would sit out in her garden eating big plates of food, and finding a substitute sense of home in the glow of her warmth and hospitality. They became life-long friends.

The woman is Mrs. Elizabeth McCuddy, and she still lives in the same frame house. The neighborhood has changed but she has not moved. It is home to her. About two years or so ago, the house was almost destroyed by fire. She had it repaired and was happy to return to it as quickly as she could. She lives there with her son, her daughter and two dogs. She has many memories. For years, she has seen the crowds flow by to go to the White Sox ball games, and sometimes the roar of the crowds can be heard in her home. In other days, there were the crowds, and the roar. Then, the cheers would be for Babe Ruth, Ty Cobb, Joe Jackson, Buck Weaver, Harry Heilmann. She was their friend, she saw them often and most of the ball players called her "Ma."

"Mother," Babe Ruth often used to say to her, "you're the best woman in the world."

Two years ago, Ray Schalk took me to meet Ma McCuddy. When we entered, she had a mild and affectionate reprimand for him, he had not phoned her of late. He apologized and said that he would phone her more often. We sat down to talk. The home was warm, cozy and its atmosphere seemed especially hospitable with a blizzard raging outside. There was the Christmas tree, a dog by a stove, a puppy penned up in the kitchen and full of life, two daughters talking and buzzing about to get us things, and Mrs. McCuddy sitting and rocking, talking with Schalk about the old days when he was young and ac-knowledged as the greatest catcher in baseball.

Mrs. McCuddy is now gray, slender and medium sized, but she still looks youthful for her age. She has a clear skin, soft hazel eyes, and enjoys good health.

Her husband owned a saloon next door to the family home on Thirty-fifth Street, but he died over thirty years ago. She raised and supported a family of three girls and a boy, washed towels for the White Sox ball club, held open house for baseball players, fed them, washed for them, boarded their sons, loaned them money, listened to them when they needed a friendly ear, and sat there amidst them when they would let off steam in boyish release. They knocked at her door day and night but it was always open. Today the tav-ern which her husband once owned is back in the family, it is clean and well kept and her son and her two daughters run it. On summer days and nights when the crowds pour by for the ball game, many fans stop in for a glass of beer and for McCuddy hot dogs. Some fans will not buy hot dogs at the ball park, preferring the ones that Ma and her daughters make.

"Two seasons ago," one of her daughters said, "a man with his hair getting gray stopped at the bar with a boy and told me that when he was a boy, his father stopped in with him for a glass of beer and bought him a root-beer. He wanted to do this now with his own son."

"Yes, but it's a new crowd now," Mrs. McCuddy said. "We had good times. And Ray, I remember you when Mr. Comiskey brought you to me. You were just a skinny kid."

"I can remember it as if it were yesterday," Schalk said. "Those were good meals, I used to sit out in your garden and eat and I never ate better meals, Ma."

"We gave you what we had. The players always took pot luck and sat down to the table with us, and ate what we ate. Ray, I got a Christmas card from Nick Altrock."

Ray Schalk asked of Altrock's health. They had both heard that he had been ill.

"He said that he was well," Mrs. McCuddy said. There was a sense of pleasure and affection in her voice.

She likes to hear from the old-time ball players and is gratified when they remember her.

"I washed Nick's shirt." A daughter told the story. During the last War, Altrock was in Chicago with a group of old-timers for a War Bond Rally. The Washington Nationals were playing the White Sox and a coach was dropped. Altrock was ordered to stay with the team until there was a replacement of another coach, and he had only one nylon shirt with him.

"Every day at four o'clock he sent that shirt over to me to be washed."

In the kitchen spaghetti was on the stove. Charles A. Comiskey II, grandson of the Old Roman, and others in the White Sox office had phoned over to the McCuddys for spaghetti for lunch. Now and then, Mrs. McCuddy reminded her daughters to watch the stove, or would look to me and say:

"Give the man something!"

We talked more of Altrock.

"He came to see me often. He used to be Santa Claus for my children. He would dress up for it and he looked the part. But he fell on my Johnny's train one Christmas. We were giving Johnny a train that year and when Nick came dressed up he sat right down on it. But we were able to get the train fixed."

Later I saw Nick Altrock in Florida. He was reminiscing about his early days in baseball. I mentioned Mrs. McCuddy and his eyes filled with a warm glow of memory, and his smile, so familiar to baseball fans, grew charming.

"Did she ever tell you that I was Santa Claus for her children?" he asked.

And he wanted to know how she was and also wanted her to know that he was well.

"We used to have fun and good times at her place," he said.

"Yes, Nick Altrock came here," Mrs. McCuddy told me. "They all did. They were good men. They were all good men. And you couldn't find anyone who looked more like Santa Claus than Nick. Did I tell you, Ray, that he sent me a Christmas card?"

The previous summer, Ed Walsh had been in Chicago for an old-timer's game. He had been one of her favorites.

"He looks young. He hasn't a gray hair on his head. I don't know why he doesn't come back here and live. I told him he ought to.

"There used to be good times here," she continued. "But sometimes, they used to play ball and golf in my house. I came home one day and the rug was pulled back. The furniture was pushed into corners and they were playing a ball game here. They broke some of my furniture."

That was a day in the 1920's. When the White Sox were rained out and several of the young ball players wanted to play, they brought a bat and indoor ball over to the McCuddy's and went to it in the living room. The house was really wrecked.

"And golf—they played golf in here. I had a special putter they used. Babe Ruth used to come over here and use it. He and the others ruined one of my rugs and I had to buy a new one. He was a big, fine man. I liked Babe Ruth. He could eat. He ate here with us."

Sometimes when Babe Ruth was playing in Chicago, he would send a message across the street.

"Tell Ma to put six bottles of beer on ice—it's two out in the ninth."

"We had good times when he was here. There was fun. There was a poor little boy. Nobody knew his name. They called him Teddy Bear. I can still see Teddy Bear. He didn't know who Babe Ruth was and you know how the kids were with him. Babe Ruth was good to them. He gave Teddy Bear one of his gloves. And poor little Teddy Bear didn't know what it was worth. A man wanted to give him a dollar for it. I said 'No.' I told Teddy Bear to get five dollars for it. He might as well have gotten something. He was such a poor little kid. I don't know what happened to Teddy Bear. Babe Ruth liked him and was good to little Teddy Bear."

Another time, Babe came with his first wife after a game. He left her outside on the sidewalk talking with a fellow in white pants. Babe socialized, talked with Ma, drank some beer, and every once in a while looked out. His wife was still there.

"She likes White Pants," Babe said.

Then he left.

Johnny Mostil, one-time fleet-footed White Sox center fielder, knocked at the door. He had come for the spaghetti dinner being cooked for the staff at the White Sox offices. He was invited to sit down and have a bite to eat. He was in a hurry but did have a cup of coffee.

"How is Chuckie?" he was asked.

"Chuckie" is Charles Comiskey II, the present vice-president of the White Sox.

"We had him when he was a baby. We took him out every Sunday," Ma said.

"You never come and see me, anymore," Ma told Mostil.

He apologized and said that he would drop by very soon.

"But that's all right. I see you waving to me when you go by on Thirty-fifth Street."

Mostil left with the spaghetti and Ray Schalk spoke of Kid Gleason.

"He was good to us ball players."

"He used to come over here, too. He was a fine man, one of the finest men. He came over here one day to me and told me one of my daughters was misbehaving. She was sitting near the White Sox bench and causing trouble. 'I'll soon put a stop to that,' I told him. But next day, Kid Gleason was back here. He asked me why I had let my daughter go back to the ball game. She had misbehaved even more. It wasn't my daughter at all but one of the girls in the neighborhood. We had given this girl some dresses and Kid Gleason had recognized the dresses. But what I liked about him is that he came to me."

The name of George Uhle, the one-time Cleveland pitching star, was mentioned.

"Remember Uhle and the pig, Mother?" one of the daughters asked.

"I do," she said. "Uhle was a good man, too."

Uhle was once pitching in an exhibition game at Comiskey Park. Harry Heilmann and other stars were also playing.

"And they bought a big pig for me to cook for them after the game. I put it on the fire and went to see the ball game myself. In the second inning, Uhle said he was sick. He said he had stomach trouble. Oh, he looked sick, and he had to leave the game. He came over here to lay down. When we got here after the game, there he was at the table, eating pig and he wasn't sick at all. He seemed like he was figuring to eat the whole pig himself. He had grease on his hands and face, and looked up at me and asked me, 'Ma, do I look like a pig?' "

Fans may remember Art Shires, who came up with the White Sox and who was much in the newspapers for a brief spell. He styled himself "The Great Guy" and he was constantly getting into trouble and scrapes.

"He wasn't bad. He was just wild," Ma remarked. "I remember him the first day he came. He knocked here at my door, and looked like a country boy. I asked him what he was looking for and he said he was looking for Comiskey Park."

" 'Why boy,' " I told him, " 'it's right in front of you.' "

"Old Mr. Comiskey liked Shires. Shires took my daughters downtown that very day. He needed luggage. He didn't ask about prices and picked out fancy valises. He bought hats and bags to match for my daughters. When he was asked for the money, he said he was a ball player and to send the bill to Mr. Comiskey. There was a lot of worry, but Mr. Comiskey, he liked Shires and the bill was paid.

"Some of them used to come to me and tell me that Art Shires was a bad one and advised me not to loan him money. But I did. When he needed money he came to me. Once he wired me from some place in Pennsylvania for two hundred dollars, and I sent it. But he always paid me back."

On a subsequent visit which I paid to her, she talked more of old ball players.

"There was that Italian from San Francisco, what was his name? A quiet man, he's dead now? Tony Lazzeri. He was a quiet one. He wrote me once from California, to buy him an electric toaster he wanted to give as a wedding present to someone. I wondered why he wanted an electric toaster shipped all the way to California when he could buy one there. But then, I remembered he always had thrifty habits and I used to get gifts for the boys wholesale.

"They all came here. They'd leave a five or a twenty-dollar bill on the table and eat as much as they wanted and talk. We'd have friends, and politicians and business men coming and I treated them all the same. One night, Nick Altrock was here and he talked to a Monsignor. Well, you know Nick and the way he talks. But the Monsignor liked him and they went on talking. He didn't mind the way Nick did a little cursing. And Joe Jackson was a good man. He was simple. He didn't talk much. He used to come here sometimes and he'd sit here and take his shoes off."

She was a good friend of the late Harry Grabiner, one-time Secretary of the Chicago White Sox.

"After my husband died, I had to support my children. I washed towels for the White Sox for twenty years. I was ready to quit, but Harry Grabiner said to me, 'Ma, you've done this for twenty years, you might as well do it for twenty-five years.' So I did it for five more years before I stopped.

"And they all came here. They had fun. We had good times. Ty Cobb, I knew him. He came here. They were all good men, fine men."

She mentioned an old-time star.

"His son was a bad one, though. He was wild. I boarded him." She shook her head from side to side. "He used to tear the house up. He destroyed things. I was glad when he left. One day, one of my daughters wanted to take a bath. And so did he. He was big, so he picked her up and dumped her in a bathtub full of water and said, 'There, you had your bath.' He locked her out of the bathroom. He was a wild one, always destroying furniture, but I boarded him. He went to college. He wasn't a ball player.

"And the young Comiskey. Did I tell you, we had him every Sunday? My daughters wheeled him in his baby buggy. The other day after we had a snow storm, I was outside seeing about my sidewalk, and he was across the street in front of the ball park, doing the same thing. He was getting together a ground crew to shovel off the sidewalk. It was only nine o'clock in the morning. He tends to his business. He saw me and waved and called over to me.

" 'Ma, don't forget that you saw your grandson out at work early this morning.'

"I like that about him. He tends to business."

Mrs. McCuddy is a woman of warmth, character and courage. At almost any gathering of old ball players, one can find among them, a player who fondly remembers her home, her hospitality and good times he had at her place. And stories are sometimes told of her. A few years ago, after the tavern was closed, a drunk rang her bell. Baseball players used to do this at all hours. But this was a stranger. She told him that the tavern was closed. He put one foot in her door and insisted that he be admitted and given a drink. She grabbed two revolvers and chased him along Thirty-fifth Street. He was last seen fleeing across Thirty-fifth Street and Wentworth Avenue as fast as his legs would carry him.

Not many of the modern players seem to know Mrs. McCuddy. It is the old-timers she knew, and it is they whom she remembers with a kind of maternal warmth. It was they whom she fed, and for whom she held open house. Now they are like ghosts of the past. Across the street the new crowds roar for Minnie Minoso, Nellie Fox, Mickey Mantle and the other players of the moment. Many of the old-timers are dead. But they are alive in Mrs. McCuddy's memory and in her feelings for the past when taking some care of them was part of her business. Still young in heart and enjoying good health, she rocks in her chair and remembers them. To her, they were good men who sometimes had to be fed, and taken care of, and given a passing or wayside home to come to, to sit in and talk and play and be themselves. The social history of baseball cannot be told or written without mention of Ma McCuddy and her family. Baseball players called her "Ma" with real affection because she was for several decades, a mother to many of them. She created a little way station where there was love, kindness, good cheer, fun and understanding. She has meant much to some of these players, and hence to the game itself. It is no exaggeration to characterize her as one of the living legends of baseball.

The Pitcher and the Plutocrat

P. G. WODEHOUSE

Associate a ball with P. G. Wodehouse (1881–1975) and it will, without question, be dimpled; his golf stories, featuring the club's Oldest Living Member, are some of the funniest and most-enduring ever teed up on a typewriter. But the English-born Wodehouse wrote so much—some ninety books, twenty film scripts, and more than thirty plays and musical comedies—that mere chance would dictate he'd at least stumble onto baseball. In "The Pitcher and the Plutocrat," written in 1910 soon after he arrived in America to live, Wodehouse doesn't stumble at all. Given the game's novelty for him, he covers the bases quite splendidly.

The main difficulty in writing a story is to convey to the reader clearly yet tersely the natures and dispositions of one's leading characters. Brevity, brevity—that is the cry. Perhaps, after all, the playbill style is the best. In this drama of love, baseball, frenzied finance, and tainted millions, then, the principals are as follows, in their order of entry:

Isabel Rackstraw (a peach)
Clarence Van Puyster (a Greek god)
Old Man Van Puyster (a proud old aristocrat)
Old Man Rackstraw (a tainted millionaire)

More about Clarence later. For the moment let him go as a Greek god. There were other sides, too, to Old Man Rackstraw's character; but for the moment let him go as a Tainted Millionaire. Not that it is satisfactory. It is too mild. He was *the* Tainted Millionaire. The Tainted Millions of other Tainted Millionaires were as attar of roses compared with the Tainted Millions of Tainted Millionaire Rackstraw. He preferred his millions tainted. His attitude toward an untainted million was that of the sportsman toward the sitting bird. These things are purely a matter of taste. Some people like Limburger cheese.

It was at a charity bazaar that Isabel and Clarence first met. Isabel was presiding over the Billiken, Teddy Bear, and Fancy Goods stall. There she stood, that slim, radiant girl, buncoing the Younger Set out of its father's hard-earned with a smile that alone was nearly worth the money, when she observed, approaching, the handsomest man she had ever seen. It was—this is not one of those mystery stories—it was Clarence Van Puyster. Over the heads of the bevy of gilded youths who clustered round the stall their eyes met. A thrill ran through Isabel. She dropped her eyes. The next moment Clarence had bucked center; the Younger Set had shredded away like a mist; and he was leaning toward her, opening negotiations for the purchase of a yellow Teddy Bear at sixteen times its face value.

He returned at intervals during the afternoon. Over the second Teddy Bear they became friendly; over the third, intimate. He proposed as she was wrapping up the fourth Golliwog, and she gave him her heart and the parcel simultaneously. At six o'clock, carrying four Teddy Bears, seven photograph frames, five Golliwogs, and a Billiken, Clarence went home to tell the news to his father.

Clarence, when not at college, lived with his only surviving parent in an old red-brick house at the north end of Washington Square. The original Van Puyster had come over in Governor Stuyvesant's time in one of the then fashionable ninety-four-day boats. Those were the stirring days when they were giving away chunks of Manhattan Island in exchange for trading-stamps; for the bright brain which conceived the idea that the city might possibly at some remote date extend above Liberty Street had not come into existence. The original Van Puyster had acquired a square mile or so in the heart of things for ten dollars cash and a quarter interest in a pedler's outfit. "The Columbus Echo and Vespucci Intelligencer" gave him a column and a half under the heading: "Reckless Speculator. Prominent Citizen's Gamble in Land." On the proceeds of that deal his descendants had led quiet, peaceful lives ever since. If any of them ever did a day's work, the family records are silent on the point. Blood was their long suit, not Energy. They were plain, homely folk, with a refined distaste for wealth and vulgar hustle. They lived simply, without envy of their richer fellow citizens, on their three hundred thousand dollars a year.

They asked no more. It enabled them to entertain on a modest scale; the boys could go to college, the girls buy an occasional new frock. They were satisfied.

Having dressed for dinner, Clarence proceeded to the library, where he found his father slowly pacing the room. Silver-haired old Vansuyther Van Puyster seemed wrapped in thought. And this was unusual, for he was not given to thinking. To be absolutely frank, the old man had just about enough brain to make a jay-bird fly crooked, and no more.

"Ah, my boy," he said, looking up as Clarence entered. "Let us go in to dinner. I have been awaiting you for some little time now. I was about to inquire as to your whereabouts. Let us be going."

Mr. Van Puyster always spoke like that. This was due to Blood.

Until the servants had left them to their coffee and cigarettes, the conversation was desultory and commonplace. But when the door had closed, Mr. Van Puyster leaned forward.

"My boy," he said quietly, "we are ruined."

Clarence looked at him inquiringly.

"Ruined much?" he asked.

"Paupers," said his father. "I doubt if when all is over, I shall have much more than a bare fifty or sixty thousand dollars a year."

A lesser man would have betrayed agitation, but Clarence was a Van Puyster. He lit a cigarette.

"Ah," he said calmly. "How's that?"

Mr. Van Puyster toyed with his coffee-spoon.

"I was induced to speculate—rashly, I fear—on the advice of a man I chanced to meet at a public dinner, in the shares of a certain mine. I did not thoroughly understand the matter, but my acquaintance appeared to be well versed in such operations, so I allowed him to—and, well, in fact, to cut a long story short, I am ruined."

"Who was the fellow?"

"A man of the name of Rackstraw. Daniel Rackstraw."

"Daniel Rackstraw!"

Not even Clarence's training and traditions could prevent a slight start as he heard the name.

"Daniel Rackstraw," repeated his father. "A man, I fear, not entirely honest. In fact it seems that he has made a very large fortune by similar transactions. Friends of mine, acquainted with these matters, tell me his behavior toward me amounted practically to theft. However, for myself I care little. We can rough it, we of the old Van Puyster stock. If there is but fifty thousand a year left, well—I must make it serve. It is for your sake that I am troubled, my poor boy. I shall be compelled to stop your allowance. I fear you will be obliged to adopt some profession." He hesitated for a moment. "In fact, work," he added.

Clarence drew at his cigarette.

"Work?" he echoed thoughtfully. "Well, of course, mind you, fellows *do* work. I met a man at the club only yesterday who knew a fellow who had met a man whose cousin worked."

He reflected for a while.

"I shall pitch," he said suddenly.

"Pitch, my boy?"

"Sign on as a professional ballplayer."

His father's fine old eyebrows rose a little.

"But, my boy, er—the—ah—family name. Our—shall I say *noblesse oblige?* Can a Van Puyster pitch and not be defiled?"

"I shall take a new name," said Clarence. "I will call myself Brown." He lit another cigarette. "I can get signed on in a minute. McGraw will jump at me."

This was no idle boast. Clarence had had a good college education, and was now an exceedingly fine pitcher. It was a pleasing sight to see him, poised on one foot in the attitude of a Salome dancer, with one eye on the batter, the other gazing coldly at the man who was trying to steal third, uncurl abruptly like the main spring of a watch and sneak over a swift one. Under Clarence's guidance a ball could do practically everything except talk. It could fly like a shot from a gun, hesitate, take the first turning to the left, go up two blocks, take the second to the right, bound in mid-air like a jack-rabbit, and end by dropping as the gentle dew from heaven upon the plate beneath. Briefly, there was class to Clarence. He was the goods.

Scarcely had he uttered these momentous words when the butler entered with the announcement that he was wanted by a lady at the telephone.

It was Isabel.

Isabel was disturbed.

"Oh, Clarence," she cried, "my precious angel wonder-child, I don't know how to begin."

"Begin just like that," said Clarence approvingly. "It's fine. You can't beat it."

"Clarence, a terrible thing has happened. I told papa of our engagement, and he wouldn't hear of it. He was furious. He c-called you a b-b-b—

"A p-p-p—"

"That's a new one on me," said Clarence, wondering.

"A b-beggarly p-pauper. I knew you weren't well off, but I thought you had two or three millions. I told him so. But he said no, your father had lost all his money."

"It is too true, dearest," said Clarence. "I am a pauper. But I'm going to work. Something tells me I shall be rather good at work. I am going to work with all the accumulated energy of generations of ancestors who have never done a hand's turn. And some day when I—"

"Good-by," said Isabel hastily, "I hear papa coming."

The season during which Clarence Van Puyster pitched for the Giants is destined to live long in the memory of followers of baseball. Probably never in the history of the game has there been such persistent and widespread mortality among the more distant relatives of office-boys and junior clerks. Statisticians have estimated that if all the grandmothers alone who perished between the months of April and October that year could have been placed end to end they would have reached considerably further than Minneapolis. And it was Clarence who was responsible for this holocaust. Previous to the opening of the season skeptics had shaken their heads over the Giants' chances for the pennant. It had been assumed that as little new blood would be forthcoming as in other years, and that the fate of Our City would rest, as usual, on the shoulders of the white-haired veterans who were boys with Lafayette.

And then, like a mentor, Clarence Van Puyster had flashed upon the world of fans, bugs, chewing-gum, and nuts (pea and human). In the opening game he had done horrid things to nine men from Boston; and from then onward, except for an occasional check, the Giants had never looked back.

Among the spectators who thronged the bleachers to watch Clarence perform there appeared week after week a little, gray, dried-up man, insignificant except for a certain happy choice of language in moments of emotion and an enthusiasm far surpassing that of the ordinary spectator. To the trained eye there is a subtle but well-marked difference between the fan, the bug, and—the last phase—the nut of the baseball world. This man was an undoubted nut. It was writ clear across his brow.

Fate had made Daniel Rackstraw—for it was he—a tainted millionaire, but at heart he was a baseball spectator. He never missed a game. His baseball museum had but one equal, that of Mr. Jacob Dodson of Detroit. Between them the two had cornered, at enormous expense, the curio market of the game. It was Rackstraw who had secured the glove worn by Neal Ball, the Cleveland shortstop, when he made the only unassisted triple play in the history of the game; but it was Dodson who possessed the bat which Hans Wagner used as a boy. The two men were friends, as far as rival connoisseurs can be friends; and Mr. Dodson, when at leisure, would frequently pay a visit to Mr. Rackstraw's country home, where he would spend hours gazing wistfully at the Neal Ball glove buoyed up only by the thought of the Wagner bat at home.

Isabel saw little of Clarence during the summer months, except from a distance. She contented herself with clipping photographs of him from the evening papers. Each was a little more unlike him than the last, and this lent variety to the collection. Her father marked her new-born enthusiasm for the national game with approval. It had been secretly a great grief to the old buccaneer that his only child did not know the difference between a bunt and a swat, and, more, did not seem to care to know. He felt himself drawn closer to her. An understanding, as pleasant as it was new and strange, began to spring up between parent and child.

As for Clarence, how easy it would be to cut loose to practically an unlimited extent on the subject of his emotions at this time. One can figure him, after the game is over and the gay throng has dispersed, creeping moodily—but what's the use? Brevity. That is the cry. Brevity. Let us on.

The months sped by. August came and went, and September; and soon it was plain to even the casual follower of the game that, unless something untoward should happen, the Giants must secure the National League pennant. Those were delirious days for Daniel Rackstraw. Long before the beginning of October his voice had dwindled to a husky whisper. Deep lines appeared on his forehead; for it is an awful thing for a baseball nut to be compelled to root, in the very crisis of the season, purely by means of facial expression. In this time of affliction he found Isabel an ever-increasing comfort to him. Side by side they would sit at the Polo Grounds, and the old man's face would lose its drawn look, and light up, as her clear young soprano pealed out above the din, urging this player to slide for second, that to knock the stitching off the ball; or describing the umpire in no uncertain voice as a reincarnation of the late Mr. Jesse James.

Meanwhile, in the American League, Detroit had been heading the list with equal pertinacity; and in far-off Michigan Mr. Jacob Dodson's enthusiasm had been every whit as great as Mr. Rackstraw's in New York. It was universally admitted that when the championship series came to be played, there would certainly be something doing.

But, alas! How truly does Epictetus observe: "We know not what awaiteth us around the corner, and the hand that counteth its chickens ere they be hatched ofttimes graspeth but a lemon." The prophets who anticipated a struggle closer than any on record were destined to be proved false.

It was not that their judgment of form was at fault. By every law of averages the Giants and the Tigers should have been the two most evenly matched nines in the history of the game. In fielding there was nothing to choose between them. At hitting the Tigers held a slight superiority; but this was balanced by the inspired pitching of Clarence Van Puyster. Even the keenest supporters of either side were not confident. They argued at length, figuring out the odds with the aid of stubs of pencils and the backs of envelopes, but they were not confident. Out of all those frenzied millions two men alone had no doubts. Mr. Daniel Rackstraw said that he did not desire to be unfair to Detroit. He wished it to be clearly understood that in their own class the Tigers might quite possibly show to considerable advantage. In some rural league down South, for instance, he did not deny that they might sweep all before them. But when it came to competing with the Giants—Here words failed Mr. Rackstraw, and he had to rush to Wall Street and collect several tainted millions before he could recover his composure.

Mr. Jacob Dodson, interviewed by the Detroit "Weekly Rooter," stated that his decision, arrived at after a close and careful study of the work of both teams, was that the Giants had rather less chance in the forthcoming tourney than a lone gumdrop at an Eskimo tea party. It was his carefully considered opinion that in a contest with the Avenue B juniors the Giants might, with an effort, scrape home. But when it was a question of meeting a live team like Detroit—Here Mr. Dodson, shrugging his shoulders despairingly, sank back in his chair, and watchful secretaries brought him round with oxygen.

Throughout the whole country nothing but the approaching series was discussed. Wherever civilization reigned, and in Jersey City, one question alone was on every lip: Who would win? Octogenarians mumbled it. Infants lisped it. Tired business men, trampled under foot in the rush for the West Farms express, asked it of the ambulance attendants who carried them to hospital.

And then, one bright, clear morning, when all Nature seemed to smile, Clarence Van Puyster developed mumps.

New York was in a ferment. I could have wished to go into details to describe in crisp, burning sentences the panic that swept like a tornado through a million homes. A little encouragement, the slightest softening of the editorial austerity, and the thing would have been done. But no. Brevity. That was the cry. Brevity. Let us on.

The Tigers met the Giants at the Polo Grounds, and for five days the sweat of agony trickled unceasingly down the corrugated foreheads of the patriots who sat on the bleachers. The men from Detroit, freed from the fear of

Clarence, smiled grim smiles and proceeded to knock holes through the fence. It was in vain that the home fielders skimmed like swallows around the diamond. They could not keep the score down. From start to finish the Giants were a beaten side.

Broadway during that black week was a desert. Gloom gripped Lobster Square. In distant Harlem red-eyed wives faced silently scowling husbands at the evening meal, and the children were sent early to bed. Newsboys called the extras in a whisper.

Few took the tragedy more nearly to heart than Daniel Rackstraw. Each afternoon found him more deeply plunged in sorrow. On the last day, leaving the ground with the air of a father mourning over some prodigal son, he encountered Mr. Jacob Dodson of Detroit.

Now, Mr. Dodson was perhaps the slightest bit shy on the finer feelings. He should have respected the grief of a fallen foe. He should have abstained from exulting. But he was in too exhilarated a condition to be magnanimous. Sighting Mr. Rackstraw, he addressed himself joyously to the task of rubbing the thing in. Mr. Rackstraw listened in silent anguish.

"If we had had Brown—" he said at length.

"That's what they all say," whooped Mr. Dodson. "Brown! Who's Brown?"

"If we had had Brown, we should have—" He paused. An idea had flashed upon his overwrought mind. "Dodson," he said, "listen here. Wait till Brown is well again, and let us play this thing off again for anything you like a side in my private park."

Mr. Dodson reflected.

"You're on," he said. "What side bet? A million? Two million? Three?"

Mr. Rackstraw shook his head scornfully.

"A million? Who wants a million? I'll put on my Neal Ball glove against your Hans Wagner bat. The best of three games. Does that go?"

"I should say it did," said Mr. Dodson joyfully. "I've been wanting that glove for years. It's like finding it is one's Christmas stocking."

"Very well," said Mr. Rackstraw. "Then let's get it fixed up."

Honestly, it is but a dog's life, that of the short-story writer. I particularly wished at this point to introduce a description of Mr. Rackstraw's country home and estate, featuring the private ballpark with its fringe of noble trees. It would have served a double purpose, not only charming the lover of nature, but acting as a fine stimulus to the youth of the country, showing them the sort of home they would be able to buy some day if they worked hard and saved their money. But no. You shall have three guesses as to what was the cry. You give it up? It was "Brevity! Brevity!" Let us on.

The two teams arrived at the Rackstraw house in time for lunch. Clarence, his features once more reduced to thier customary finely chiseled proportions, alighted from the automobile with a swelling heart. He could see nothing of Isabel, but that did not disturb him. Letters had passed between the two. Clarence had warned her not to embrace him in public, as McGraw would not like it; and Isabel accordingly had arranged a tryst among the noble trees which fringed the ballpark.

I will pass lightly over the meeting of the two lovers. I will not describe the dewy softness of their eyes, the catching of their breath, their murmured endearments. I could, mind you. It is at just such descriptions that I am particularly happy. But I have grown discouraged. My spirit is broken. It is enough to say that Clarence had reached a level of emotional eloquence rarely met with among pitchers of the National League, when Isabel broke from him with a startled exclamation, and vanished behind a tree; and, looking over his shoulder, Clarence observed Mr. Daniel Rackstraw moving toward him.

It was evident from the millionaire's demeanor that he had seen nothing. The look on his face was anxious, but not wrathful. He sighted Clarence, and hurried up to him.

"Say, Brown," he said. "I've been looking for you. I want a word with you."

"A thousand, if you wish it," said Clarence courteously.

"Now, see here," said Mr. Rackstraw. "I want to explain to you just what this ball game means to me. Don't run away with the idea I've had you fellows down to play an exhibition game just to keep me merry and bright. If the Giants win today, it means that I shall be able to hold up my head again and look my fellow man in the face, instead of crawling around on my stomach and feeling like thirty cents. Do you get that?"

"I am hep," replied Clarence with simple dignity.

"And not only that," went on the millionaire. "There's more to it. I have put up my Neal Ball glove against Mr. Dodson's Wagner bat as a side bet. You understand what that means? It means that either you win or my life is soured for keeps. See?"

"I have got you," said Clarence.

"Good. Then what I wanted to say was this. Today is your day for pitching as you've never pitched before. Everything depends on whether you make good or not. With you pitching like mother used to make it, the Giants are some nine. Otherwise they are Nature's citrons. It's one thing or the other. It's all up to you. Win, and there's twenty thousand dollars waiting for you above what you share with the others."

Clarence waved his hand deprecatingly.

"Mr. Rackstraw," he said, "keep your dough. I care nothing for money."

"You don't?" cried the millionaire. "Then you ought to exhibit your-self in a dime museum."

"All I ask of you," proceeded Clarence, "is your consent to my engage-ment to your daughter."

Mr. Rackstraw looked sharply at him.

"Repeat that," he said. "I don't think I quite got it."

"All I ask is your consent to my engagement to your daughter."

"Young man," said Mr. Rackstraw, not without a touch of admiration, "you have gall."

"My friends have sometimes said so," said Clarence.

"And I admire gall. But there is a limit. That limit you have passed so far that you'd need to look for it with a telescope."

"You refuse your consent."

"I never said you weren't a clever guesser."

"Why?"

Mr. Rackstraw laughed. One of those nasty, sharp, metallic laughs that hit you like a bullet.

"How would you support my daughter?"

"I was thinking that you would help to some extent."

"You were, were you?"

"I was."

"Oh?"

Mr. Rackstraw emitted another of those laughs.

"Well," he said, "it's off. You can take that as coming from an authorita-tive source. No wedding-bells for you."

Clarence drew himself up, fire flashing from his eyes and a bitter smile curving his expressive lips.

"And no Wagner bat for you!" he cried.

Mr. Rackstraw started as if some strong hand had plunged an auger into him.

"What!" he shouted.

Clarence shrugged his superbly modeled shoulders in silence.

"Say," said Mr. Rackstraw, "you wouldn't let a little private difference like that influence you any in a really important thing like this ball game, would you?"

"I would."

"You would hold up the father of the girl you love?"

"Every time."

"Her white-haired old father?"

"The color of his hair would not affect me."

"Nothing would move you?"

"Nothing."

"Then, by George, you're just the son-in-law I want. You shall marry Isabel; and I'll take you into partnership this very day. I've been looking for a good, husky bandit like you for years. You make Dick Turpin look like a preliminary three-round bout. My boy, we'll be the greatest team, you and I, that ever hit Wall Street."

"Papa!" cried Isabel, bounding happily from behind her tree.

Mr. Rackstraw joined their hands, deeply moved, and spoke in low, vibrant tones:

"Play ball!"

Little remains to be said, but I am going to say it, if it snows. I am at my best in these tender scenes of idyllic domesticity.

Four years have passed. Once more we are in the Rackstraw home. A lady is coming down the stairs, leading by the hand her little son. It is Isabel. The years have dealt lightly with her. She is still the same stately, beautiful creature whom I would have described in detail long ago if I had been given half a chance. At the foot of the stairs the child stops and points at a small, wooden object in a glass case.

"Wah?" he said.

"That?" says Isabel. "That is the bat Mr. Wagner used to use when he was a little boy."

She looks at a door on the left of the hall, and puts a finger to her lip.

"Hush!" she says. "We must be quiet. Daddy and grandpa are busy in there cornering wheat."

And softly mother and child go out into the sunlit garden.

One Down, 713 to Go

DAMON RUNYON

Every once in a while the planets line up just right, the universe resonates, and the harmonic convergence that results echoes ever after. On May 6, 1915, two giants of the sporting scene crossed paths; neither, at the time, could have the slightest inkling that one would be making history while the other was recording it.

Damon Runyon (1880–1946) went out to the Polo Grounds that day to watch the Yankees host the Red Sox. Nothing unusual there. Years before he would populate stories with characters like Nathan Detroit, Sky Masterson, Sorrowful Jones and Baseball Hattie, Runyon had become one of the most important sportswriters in the capital city of American sports. He had a game to cover. This account would run in the next day's *New York American*.

It was a good game, certainly, but that's not why it's here. It's here because in the third inning, a twenty-year-old Red Sox pitcher named Ruth hit his first Major League home run. He'd hit 713 more before he was through, which makes this a significant moment in baseball history, though at the time, it was just another of the countless moments Runyon would regularly filter through his typewriter.

Ruth, by the way, posted an 18–8 record in 1915, his first full season in the majors. He also hit three more home runs.

There is not enough of Hughy High to make one good-sized hero for our story this morning, and so we add to him Luther Cook and thus compile a sufficient subject. Hughy and Luther, bunched together, make something to talk about. They assisted this community in taking a notable decision over the municipality of Boston, Mass., yesterday afternoon.

The shades of the thirteenth inning were falling fast up at the Polo Grounds, and the Wild Yanks and the Boston Red Sox, champs-presumptive of the Amur-r-r-ick-kin League, as Ban Johnson calls it, were clustered in a tie. The count was three all, with Will Evans, the gesticulator, eagerly scanning the horizon for evidence of nightfall, when Hughy and Luther amalgamated and broke up the pastime, the final tally being 4 to 3 in favor of the grand old Empire State.

In our own garrulous way we shall now endeavor to tell you just how it happened, omitting only such details as we deem unfit for publication.

Hughy High, small, but efficient, opened that thirteenth with a single to centre. Walter Pipp struck out, Hughy High stole second. Luther Cook singled over Heine Wagner's head, just out of Heine Wagner's reach and mid the mad mumble of the multitude. Hughy High came tumbling in across the h. p. with the winning run. How was that for High?

Having described the most important incident of the game, we now feel constrained to warn the compositors to clear away all obstructions below, and to either side, so we can run right on down this column, and over into the next, in telling about the goings-on prior to the moment mentioned, beginning with that hour in the ninth when we boys tied 'er up.

Luther Cook figured in that, too. One was out in the ninth, when George Ruth struck Luther with a pitched baseball. George pitched the baseball left-handed, and by giving it the body-follow-through, he succeeded in raising a tumor on Luther's shoulder. Cap'n Roger Peckinpaugh subsided without a struggle, while Luther tarried at first, rubbing his wounded torso, and glaring at George Ruth. That made two out, and it looked as this story would have to open with sighs, when Luther Boone—but by all means a separate paragraph for Luther.

Luther Boone doubled to right, a solid, smacking, soulful double that knocked the bleacherites back on the butt of their spines from the crouch that precedes the rush for the exits, and which scored Luther Cook with the tying tally.

A moment later Luther Boone went on to third, when George Ruth made a bad throw trying to catch him off second, but Leslie Nunamaker could not bring him in, and the game passed on into extra innings and to the big punch in the story as outlined above.

Well, it was quite a pastime. Everybody said it was a great game to win. Everybody was so delighted that they almost forgot about Dominick Mullaney, who was cast for the character of the bad guy in this tale. Not that we intend to make Dominick out, because you know the size of Dominick. The day that we blacken the character of Dominick is the day after Dominick leaves town, and gets well beyond the confines of this newspaper's circulation.

In the seventh inning, with we 'uns needing a run to tie, Luther Cook singled. Peckinpaugh was duly expunged, and Boone hit the right field wall with a blow which put cook [sic] on third. The ball hopped back off the razor-backed sign in right into Hooper's hands, and Hooper threw to first, instead of second, as Boone anticipated.

Boone had taken "that old turn" after hitting first, in accordance with the advice of all the coachers, and was several feet off the bag when Hoblitzel got the ball. Dominick said he was out, and the rally bogged down right there.

The crowd discussed Dominick in audible tones on account of that decision, and some thought it might be a good thing to assassinate him at once, but no action was taken on account of Dominick's size, and the presence of Ban Johnson.

We have been wondering ever since the season opened why Wild Bill Donovan has been keeping little Jack Warhop warmed up down there in right field, and the reason developed yesterday. It was for the purpose of having Jack pitch this game, and Jack pitched very well indeed while he was pitching, proving the efficacy of warming-up.

In the eighth inning, Charles Mullen batted for Jack, but nothing came of it, as Mike McNally, the Sox's new third baser, and the noisiest man in the whole world, next to Baumgartner, the Phil pitcher, made a smashing play on Charley's drive. Fritz Maisel got an infield hit that inning, stole second, moved to third on Carrigan's bad throw, and scored on Hartzell's out.

Cyrus Pieh finished the game for the Yanks, and this story would be wholly incomplete without an eulogy of Cyrus. Tall, thin and very interesting, Cyrus would have a column all to himself did space permit. He compiled a masterly finish. Pieh had the crust, as you might say, to use a slow curve on some of the sluggers of the Sox, and he made them appear mighty futile and inefficient.

In the eleventh he gathered up Scott's slow roller and made a two-base bad chuck to Pipp. Then he fanned McNally. Henricksen, who once broke up a world's series pastime on Chris Mathewson—long and long ago, that seems—batted for Cyrus Pieh any time he feels that way about it.

Henricksen singled and Scott took third, Henricksen moving to second on the throw in. Then Cyrus Pieh fanned Ruth and Hooper. How was that for Peih?

Fanning this Ruth is not as easy as the name and occupation might indicate. In the third frame Ruth knocked the slant out of one of Jack Warhop's underhanded subterfuges, and put the baseball in the right field stand for a home run.

Ruth was discovered by Jack Dunn in a Baltimore school a year ago when he had not yet attained his lefthanded majority, and was adopted, and adapted, by Jack for the uses of the Orioles. He is now quite a pitcher and a demon hitter—when he connects.

In our boys' end of the eleventh, Pipp led off with a single, but Wild Bill had Cook up there trying to sacrifice, and after failing in two attempts to bunt, Cook struck out. Whereupon he flung his bat far from him and took on an expression of intense disgust. Evidently the only way Luther likes to bunt is from his shoe cleats.

It was in that inning that Luther Boone was purposely passed for the first time in his brief career. In other days pitchers would have passed the whole batting order to get at Luther, but yesterday Ruth let him go to fire at Nunamaker, and Leslie did not betray Ruth's confidence. He lifted a fly to Hooper.

Roger Maris

JIMMY CANNON

It's still hard to reconcile the affection showered on Mark McGwire's chase of Roger Maris with the vitriol Maris had to absorb in his own chase of Babe Ruth. All Maris was was a ballplayer, but, with Ruth as a shadow and Mantle a teammate, that never really cut it, not with the fans, and not with the press.

Like his mentor Damon Ruynon, Jimmy Cannon (1910–1973) was a fixture in a bygone world of New York journalism that colorfully straddled sports and Broadway. As the big gun at the *New York Post* and then the *Journal-American,* he perfected a rat-a-tat style that grouped together short, disparate observations and opinions under the rubric of "Nobody Asked Me, But . . ." He also wrote whole columns in the second person with uncanny effect.

Like this one on Maris during the 1967 World Series.

Cannon couldn't let go of the fact that Maris declined an interview request in the spring after hitting 61. When Cannon fired this fusillade, the resentment was still simmering.

Y ou're Roger Maris who isn't Babe Ruth. In St. Louis they allowed you to drop out of history. You're just a competent outfielder playing well for the Cards in the World Series against the Red Sox. The only contest is the one between you and the pitcher. You're not competing with a beloved dead man and Mickey Mantle who was cherished by the Yankees.

People expected you to be like Ruth when you hit the 61 home runs in 1961. He was regarded as a national resource. He was flattered by crowds and responded to adulation. You shrank from all that. It was as if you didn't believe it. Yet you had turned in one of the great achievements of baseball.

Sometimes it seemed you were being attacked by a man already in the grave. Old-timers rapped you because a .269 batter had hit one more home run than Ruth. You didn't break Ruth's record because you had your cuts across a schedule of 162 games. He struck 60 in a tournament of 154 games. The pitcher threw the ball, and you hit it. It was what Ruth did. But they wanted you to have more style. Fame became drudgery for you. It all went sour.

It was you up against Mickey Mantle. But your real opponent was Ruth. Even on your own team most of the players weren't pulling for you. A couple of guys who had played with you on the Kansas City ballclub were your partisans with the Yankees. The majority wanted Mantle to do it. He, just as Ruth and Joe DiMaggio were before him, is the Yankees. They believed he was entitled to it. All over baseball they favored Mantle. But he dropped out, after hanging on until late in the season. He hit 54 home runs for .317. They made a point of that. The sports journalists put pressure on you. It was their assignment. But you seemed to believe they were trying to persecute you.

Small things irritated you. Some reporters were rude and unsympathetic. But you didn't help your case. In Detroit you hit a home run that bounced back on the field. Al Kaline threw it to the Yankee dugout. He wanted you to have it as a souvenir.

A writer asked you if you didn't think it was a pleasant gesture. You replied that anyone would do it. It had all come down on you. Maybe that's what made you cranky. But it sounded nasty. Some guys tried to make it easier for you. It didn't matter. There were a few who felt sorry for you. It would be hard to convince you of that.

You batted third. Mantle hit fourth. They couldn't walk you, or they'd get Mantle. Guys who hit over .300 with power get more respect than a .260 batter even if history has a piece of him. There were printed theories that if you and Mantle had exchanged places in the lineup, he would have hit more home runs. But he didn't, you did. You still had to get your bat on the baseball and lift it over the wall.

That spring you sounded like Dean Rusk. Have you heard about my new policy? you asked. You would give no interviews. Too many reporters had ripped you. It went for all of them. You wanted no part of any of them. There were arguments and a lot of harmful stories. You hit 33 home runs the next year, and your average was .256. But you were still a valuable player who could do a lot of things on a ball field.

New York was never your town. You didn't bring your family there during the baseball season. You belong in a smaller place. Injuries crippled you. Mantle is a legend of perseverance who plays in great pain. You were unjustly compared with him. It was obvious the Yankees had to trade you. You yearned to be somewhere else.

Once other clubs would have tapped out to get you. But you had been laid up too much. The Cardinals put up Charlie Smith who had been a Met. It provoked a lot of unkind stories. But you were glad. You were out of New York. You still drew a large salary. No one in St. Louis thought Babe Ruth was coming to town.

The home runs don't fall in often anymore. You only hit nine this year. Sometimes you were platooned with Bobby Tolan but you hit when the Cards were in trouble during the early scuffle for the pennant. You carried your share of the burden. You had your family with you. You were in a different town which you found agreeable. The newspapermen were after guys like Orlando Cepeda who is the Cards' important man.

In the Series guys like Lou Brock and Bob Gibson get the play. But inconspicuously you are playing fine baseball although your throw in Monday's game staked the Red Sox to a harmless run. You have hit a home run, driven in six runs and you're batting over .300. And the Series commutes between St. Louis and Boston and doesn't play New York where the Met fans boo you when you come up for the Cards. You're Roger Maris who isn't Babe Ruth.

Home Run Fever

GARY SMITH

In a recent poll of Associated Press editors from around the country, Gary Smith took home an accolade any sportswriter would covet; they voted him the one sportswriter they'd most like to hire. Whenever his work shows up in *Sports Illustrated,* the reason is clear.

By mid-July of 1998, Smith, like most of the rest of the country, was bit by the bug of "Home Run Fever." His antidote? He'd exhaust it—and himself—by chasing the chase, achieving something of a personal best in the process.

Y ou're out of it, pal. You're hungry, and the kitchen's closed. You don't live in St. Louis or Seattle or Chicago, where *the* story of this American summer of 1998 is cooking, nor in the other big cities where the dailies bring it piping hot to the breakfast table every dawn. You live a five-and-a-half-hour drive from the nearest big league ballpark, and your newspaper's serving it up like bulletins from the front in World War I—GRIFFEY HITS 39th; SOSA'S 36th LEADS CUBS; McGWIRE MASHES 2 MORE—followed by a bare-bones sentence or two, and cripes, there's not even *SportsCenter* to fill your belly because your wife bears a deep grudge against TV and sneers whenever you creep down the stairs at 7 a.m. to turn it on.

But you're a sportswriter, and people assume you know. "What do ya think?" they ask. "Is Maris's record gonna fall? Which one's gonna do it? What kind of guy's McGwire? Who do you like?" You don't know who you like. Never met any of the three men in your life. It's scary, not being able to answer the water-cooler question.

So you get this idea. It's too good to be true, but you ask your boss anyway. How about letting you chase the chase? Three cities, three nights, three men—go on a long-ball bender, a four-bag jag. Enter the bubble to feel what it's like to be one of them right now, belting homers and stalking legends. Then become one of the mob up in the seats, rising to snag history. Big Mac in San Diego on Monday, Junior in St. Petersburg on Tuesday, Slammin' Sammy in Chicago on Wednesday, back-to-back-to-back . . . pretty please?

Sure, says your boss. Why not?

Hot damn! You're going . . . going . . . *gone!*

It's only when you're up in the air at dawn, a week ago Monday, blinking on four hours' sleep and staring at the travel schedule you've scribbled out, that you start thinking, Man, this is lunacy, and what are the odds you'll actually see any of the big boys launch? Two flights, 2,500 miles and 14 hours later you're sitting in a football locker room next to the visitors' clubhouse at Qualcomm Stadium, waiting for the press conference that Mark McGwire holds on his first day in each city when he's on the road. You remember reading about the media horde that swallowed Roger Maris in 1961. Ten to 15 reporters would converge on him before and after each game. That was in September, when Maris had 55, 56, 57. Today is July 20. McGwire has 42. There are 30 of us. There were 50 on the last road trip, in Cincinnati, a writer tells you.

McGwire walks in, St. Louis Cardinals cap tugged low on his head, dressed for battle. He sees the four cameras aimed at a chair and a table holding a half-dozen microphones. He shakes his head in disgust. "I'm not gonna sit down," he says. "This is informal stuff, so. . . ." He leans against one of the lockers, his green eyes blinking like those of a cornered ox as the humans and their hardware close in. Someone takes pity on him, lobs him a lollipop about his team instead of about what everyone's here for. He shakes his head grimly again. "This is for Mark McGwire home run questions," he says. "That's the only reason I'm doing this. I talk about the team after the game."

Haltingly, the questions come. You have this feeling that if you ask the wrong question, he might chomp your head off, and you would absolutely deserve it, so you wait for someone else to ask it. "I don't know how anybody can get used to this," McGwire says. "I don't play the game for this. I'm sick of seeing my mug. I've always believed that the more people know about you, the more they get sick of you. The media sets this up like it's going to happen . . . so how are they going to write it if it doesn't happen? I assume people want this record to be broken. So let's use some sense. Why not wait until somebody gets close to breaking the record? If people want to see something done, it makes sense to do this in a way that won't wear the person down."

Is he having any fun? "Between the lines, I have a lot of fun," he says. What does he think of Mexican pitchers? He rolls his eyes.

The cameras and microphones reap the 20-second snips they need and begin peeling away, the crowd dwindles to a dozen men with notepads. McGwire's stiff, mammoth body loosens—the cornered ox is gone. He looks every questioner in the eye and answers earnestly. He wraps an arm around the divider between two locker stalls, lets it have some of his 250 pounds and smiles. "I wish every player could feel what I've felt in visiting ballparks," he says. "The receptions I've received. . . . It's blown me away. It's absolutely remarkable."

After the All-Star break, he says, he pulled the shutters over the looking glass. No more *SportsCenter*—his finger clicks right past it on the remote control. No more sports pages—he extracts that section from newspapers, folds it and drops it in the trash. No more reading the mail.

You follow him into the Cardinals clubhouse, feeling bad because now you like him, and your eyes feel like cameras. There it is, blaring from the television that hangs from the ceiling and faces all the lockers—an ESPN segment on the home-run-swinging styles of McGwire, Ken Griffey Jr. and Sammy Sosa, the crack of McGwire's bat and the bark of his name coming over and over. You watch how swiftly he walks past the screen to retrieve something from his stall and then strides back to remain on the TV's dark side until it's time for batting practice, ferrying his bat to the trainer's room, to the manager's office, to the corridor outside, the look in his eye that of a man on his way to do something very important, so no one will stop him with more questions. You can't help feeling that here's a guy who wishes to hell he could do this without expectations, without the dread of letting people down.

A teammate, pitcher Todd Stottlemyre, watches him hurry by. "It's like a starting pitcher in the seventh inning of a no-hitter," Stottlemyre says. "We don't say anything to him anymore about home runs. We can tell he doesn't want us to talk about it, and nobody's gonna question him, because it's too damn big."

You're startled, as you follow McGwire down the tunnel to the dugout, to hear the cries begin even before he emerges. "McGwire! *McGwire!*" He walks past the bleating fans, never looks up. Every head, every camera is on him. His face is a mask, eyes gripping a nothingness before him. He lifts his arms overhead to stretch. A woman with a tiny camera taps his armpit with her fingernail, asking him to turn and pose. He never looks at her. She doesn't exist.

Two hours before game time, the leftfield stands are choked with people wearing mitts. The air crackles. Foul territory is thick with writers and photographers and special guests—a hundred, easy. Every few minutes McGwire's eyes meet those of someone he knows. Immediately the mask vanishes, the eyes and lips become animated; you see how grateful he is to be human again. There's Scott LaRose, his comedian buddy who tells you that McGwire cackles so loud at comedy clubs that he brings a towel with him to bite on rather than draw attention to himself. There's George Will and his two sons. "It's not about the pennant races anymore," Will tells you. "It's about the home run race. You'd think I'd want Sosa, because I grew up a Cubs fan, but I'm rooting for McGwire. The base of achievement is there—he's earned this. He's got the swing down, it never varies, so he won't have any long periods of mechanical trouble. But all three of them seem to be nice human beings. There's not a Sprewell in the house."

Three of them? Or is it four now? You look up, and there's San Diego Padres outfielder Greg Vaughn standing 10 feet away. His 34th home run, yesterday, has brought him within two of Sosa, to the lip of the volcano, and since you're here, hell, why not nudge him in too? He gives you a big, warm, no-way-in-hell grin and says, "I won't even think about it. I don't want to hear or see anybody blowin' smoke up my butt. It's so far-fetched, so unrealistic, it hasn't even entered my mind. Man, McGwire's a monster. He's got *Nintendo* numbers! Junior, he was born to play baseball and be a superstar, and Sammy, he's like a little kid having fun. I love to watch those guys go over the top."

As if to prove he doesn't belong, he goes homerless his first four rounds of batting practice and exits the cage with a sorrowful shake of his head. "Got the worst BP swing in baseball," Vaughn laments. Then, looking over your shoulder, he cracks up. "McGwire just called over to me. Says he wants to rub me, I'm so hot. Imagine that!"

Vaughn trots to McGwire's side, spilling laughter. Nobody back home has ever even asked you about Vaughn, but for pure warmth alone, maybe he's the dark horse you should pull for.

Big Mac walks toward the dugout. He reaches above it to sign a few autographs, looking at no one as he signs, his face a blank. The crush of people mashes a redheaded little boy against the railing atop the dugout. The boy breaks into sobs. His father and a security guard shove and shout to set him free.

McGwire strides to the plate for BP. You park yourself right at the rope that keeps noncombatants back from the cage. Everyone's on his feet. A couple of grounders, *ohhhh,* a couple of fly balls, *ahhhh,* and then the thunder, *whoooooah!* Twenty-two compact swings in all, seven bullets into the sea of begging bare and leathered hands. Just before McGwire finishes, a boy runs out to the cage in a Cardinals uniform with McGwire's name and number on the back—Mark's son, Matthew, reporting for duty as batboy and Nation's Luckiest Child. Big Mac grins, slaps five and hugs the boy, then heads back to the clubhouse.

You go up into the stands, buy a soda and a hot dog and grab an empty seat near the Cardinals' dugout. Along the way, in three conversations, you hear men explaining to their women about Ruth's 60 and Maris' 61 and the history afoot here tonight. Big Mac approaches the plate in the top of the first to a standing O. He's not a Cardinal anymore. He's on everyone's team.

Lord, those thighs. In McGwire's knock-kneed stance, they scream to burst out of his pants, and as he takes those swift little warm-up swipes, his 33 ounces of northern white ash becomes a toothpick. With distance, up here in the crowd, you can see the appetite for legend that he's feeding. He's the caricature that a children's artist would draw of a home run slugger; he's Bunyan swinging an ax, the gentle giant whose charity for abused children everybody you'll meet tonight is amazingly quick to point out. Camera flashes pop all around the concrete bowl. McGwire lashes a white-blur single to left, Little Mac gallops out grinning to collect his daddy's shin guard, and you're thinking, Damn, wouldn't it be nice if your son could be beside you to see this, and how can you not root for this guy?

Bottom of the second. Vaughn launches number 35, which goes 433 feet to dead left. Look out, people tell you. Here comes Vaughny. Sitting on the third-base side, watching that home run descend, you know where you need to go—on the double.

Up in the leftfield seats, everybody wants McGwire to take the record and snap it in half over one of those thighs. Junior? "Great player, the best, but . . . a little arrogant . . . kinda smug." That's what you're hearing. Sammy? "He won't last." Big Mac is their choice because of the sexually-abused kids he's helping. Because of his humility and respect for the game. And most of all: "Because he's so extravagant, so monstrous," says Daria Zanoi, a 24-year-old nurse who examines sexual-assault victims, of all things, and who's giving McGwire the I'm-not-worthy bow as he steps in and singles once more. "It's like he should be on his own team because he doesn't match anyone else. I just want him to break the record, nobody else. That would make it even more special."

Second deck, that's too obvious. For Mac's third at-bat, in the fifth, you guess first row, lower deck, pure rope, and man your battle station. Fool!

There she goes—good God, they really *are* as long as you've read—a 458-foot bomb into the second tier in left center, the second-deepest one since distances were first recorded in this ballpark. You jump to your feet with everyone else, jam your notepad under your arm and pound your hands together, hardly believing your good luck. You've got to find who snagged that baby, but when you get up there, it looks like a hospital tent at Shiloh. A silver-haired man is holding a wet folded paper towel to an ugly red welt high on his forehead. A seat away, a man with a Padres hat tugged over unruly blond hair is wincing and fingering a humdinger of his own on his left cheek. "We're victims of McGwire!" cries Bob Colwell, a 46-year-old machine operator from Ocean Beach, California.

"McGwire did this?" you ask. "To both of you?"

"To both of us!" shouts Colwell. "Can you believe it? I'm up here during batting practice explaining to her"—he jabs a thumb at his girlfriend, Dawn Mariani, a dispatcher for the San Diego police—"about Roger and the Babe, and she's barely listening, she's reading *Sphere* by Michael Crichton. All of a sudden I see McGwire hit one that's coming straight for me, and it's like a scene from *The Natural,* it's surreal, and I'm wearing a glove, which I haven't worn in twenty years, thinking, I've got a chance! I reach up, but everybody bumps me, and it hits the top of my glove and then hits my cheek, and there I am bumming out, bleeding profusely, when I turn and . . . there's my honey holding the ball! Thank God, thank God! Then what happens? Lightning strikes twice! The home run McGwire just hit? It comes right up here again! And this guy, who I didn't know before tonight"—the factory worker reaches across Dawn to thump attorney James Conway on the back—"this time he gets nailed! Do a story on us! Victims of McGwire!"

So who got number 43? you ask. They point to the row behind, where a thick 49-year-old high school football coach named Robert Byers Jr., from Moreno Valley, California, took it on the ricochet off Conway's noggin. "As I watched it coming, I just kept telling myself what I always tell my receivers," Byers says. "*Soft hands, soft hands.* I just turned down an offer of seven hundred dollars for this ball."

Big Mac goes 4 for 4, with a walk. Cards win 13–1. What you want to do right now is go get a cold one with James and Robert and Bob, but there's no time for that. Junior's waiting back on the other side of the country. The only way to get there in time for batting practice tomorrow in Florida is to take the red-eye, but it's 11 p.m., too late to catch the last flight to the East Coast out of San Diego, so you've got to drive two hours up I-5 to catch the 1:55 a.m. out of L.A. and change planes in Dallas.

You can die in the dinger wringer. This occurs to you an hour north of San Diego, after your second Coca-Cola's gone and the rumble of the lane dividers has just snapped your eyes open for the third time and your body realizes it's gone 24 hours without sleep. You roll down the windows, crank up the radio, scream with The Who and Jethro Tull at the top of your lungs for the next 45 minutes—that's how you reel into L.A. International and live to see Griffey swing his black bat.

Only nine of your kind surround Junior in the clubhouse when he looks up, stick of red licorice poking out of his mouth, eyes cool, voice distant. You can touch the tension again, glimpse the cliff edge these three sluggers must walk. If they play along with your questions, if they ignore teammates' glances in a clubhouse where code dictates that no player steps above the other 24, if they reveal their deepest cravings for immortality, they're inviting free fall and ridicule from within and without should they fall short of 61. If they don't play along, if they ask to be left alone when they hear the same question for the 23rd straight day, or if they give the *Dogpatch Gazette* reporter's question the glare and bark it deserves, they risk ruining their reputation forever even as they lay claim to the most acclaimed individual sports record in America. How's Junior going to play this game before the game?

"I don't like to talk about myself," he says. "Hard to believe, isn't it? I'm not going to talk about home runs. I just want to win. I'm not going to talk about McGwire and Sosa. They don't help this team win. It's hard for people to believe that Roger Maris's record isn't important to me, but it's not." Nine of you clutch empty notepads, all your questions about McGwire, Sosa, Maris, home runs and Griffey himself just blown away in the top of the first, so now what do you do? Play cat and mouse, of course. Ask Junior 20 questions about why he *won't* talk about McGwire, Sosa, Maris, home runs or himself. In no time Junior's sitting on an equipment chest, feet propped up, grinning and spinning the nine of you wherever he wants, in no hurry at all to leave. He's the cat, you're the mice, and as long as that's clear, he enjoys the attention.

A journalist uses the word *chase.* Junior won't have it. "Only thing I wanna chase is my kids," he says. Nobody's going to pigeon-hole him as a home run hitter when he's clearly the finest all-around player in the game. Nobody's going to make him pant after a goal that 270 million *others* have set for him.

"That's all people want to talk about," he says, "but fifty home runs will probably win you only twelve games a season. I think more about the little things, like playing defense, getting guys over—that might win you forty games. I think about wanting to be the last guy on the field at the end of the season, spraying free champagne all over my teammates. I just wasn't brought up to talk about myself. Growing up, my dad [former Cincinnati Reds star Ken Griffey] would probably bop me on the head if I bragged. He's got three rings, and I want a couple for myself. If someone doesn't like me because I don't want to talk about myself or home runs, that's their problem."

Strikes you as odd, then, Junior's answer to one of the last questions: Which of the Reds, whose clubhouse he rattled around in as a boy, impressed him most as a player? "George Foster," he says.

"That surprises me," says the questioner, obviously expecting Junior to say Pete Rose, Joe Morgan or Johnny Bench. "Why Foster?"

"Fifty-two home runs," Junior replies.

"But with all their great players. . . ."

"None of the others hit fifty-two home runs in a season," says Junior. Hmmm.

There's no BP buzz at domed Tropicana Field. Maybe it's because everything, from the grass under your feet to the canopy overhead, is artificial. Maybe it's because the Tampa Bay Devil Rays are going down the toilet without a gurgle, and maybe it's because an appearance at the ballpark here is just an outing, not a subpoena from the heart. A half-dozen signs and the loudest applause are for junior, but it's just polite, backside-buried-in-the-seat clapping from the 30,298 in the house.

Still, everyone you approach is thrilled when you raise the question. Yessir, here's your tip for the awkward and lonely of this land, those whose every pickup line has failed. Sidle up to any stranger and ask, "Who you pullin' for? Big Mac, Junior or Sammy?" Everyone wants to chime in, even when your press credential's in your pocket and your notepad's stashed away. Everyone, when he finds out what you're doing, howls, "Oh, man! Can you take me?" Everyone's dying to get into the clubhouse to meet the mashers, not realizing how much better it is out here. Everyone's mainlining *SportsCenter*. Everyone knows all the ins and outs, can't wait to point out that of the three, Junior's surrounded by the most dangerous hitters, making him the least likely to be pitched around, while Big Mac's got the least cover and a history of second-half declines and Sammy sits at the mercy of the wind direction at Wrigley Field. Everyone wants to know who *you're* pulling for, but you say you're not going to decide until your escapade's done.

Now you've got another tip, for those who haven't decided yet whom to lay their money on. If Maris's record is going to fall to the man whose muscle tissue stays loosest before he walks to the plate in the dry-mouth months of August and September, then it's going to fall to Junior. That's what you know after you catch his first at-bat from field level. Griffey gazes into the crowd from the on-deck circle, makes eye contact with people shouting to him and then rags on a photographer: "I know you got a better camera than that." Then he sweet-swings a run-scoring double down the leftfield line.

Whew, you almost blow it. Just before the fourth, you grab a slice of pizza and rush back in when you realize Junior's fixing to hit. *Crack!* Number 40 goes screaming over the 407 sign in center, and the fans finally come off their cans to scream too. You drop your pizza box and almost pinch yourself—counting Vaughn you're 3 for 3!—and head to the rightfield seats with five innings left because when you're on a roll, you never know.

You plunk yourself down next to a 32-year-old man wearing glasses, a blue cap and a glove, who is flanked by an eight-year-old nephew and a nine-year-old son at his first big league game. The man is an Air Force staff sergeant named Ralph Thomas who pored over seating charts for this game as if he were preparing for war. Had to be seats where Griffey's natural swing would most likely send a ball, he tells you, but also seats near enough to Junior's centerfield position to make the thing he had been telling his son R. J. for weeks come true: that when you sit near the great ones, some of their greatness jumps out and comes into you. It took them nine hours to drive here from Panama City, Florida, through torrential rains and frightening funnel clouds, but nothing was going to stand between them and Junior's siege of Maris, and when they finally arrived, too late for batting practice, dammit, the boy sat there in his Griffey hat and Griffey shirt staring wordlessly at his man in centerfield for 10 long minutes, letting the spiritual transfer occur.

"See how Junior's smiling?" Sergeant Thomas points out to his son. "See how he throws everything on a line, even when he's just playing catch before the inning starts? Remember Rule 1 and Rule 2?"

"Have fun and always try your best," replies the boy.

"That's right!" says the father. "Junior *never* forgets those two things!"

Maybe it's as simple as that, you're thinking. Maybe you should root for Junior because of Rule 1 and Rule 2.

Sergeant Thomas sure is smiling, too, because nine hours of coming and nine more of going back are nothing compared with the impending joy of ramming his eyewitness account of number 40 down the gullet of his boss, Capt. Roger Scott—Cardinals fan extraordinaire, Big Mac lover and namesake of Roger Maris himself, a former Cardinal!

"Can't wait, can't wait," Sergeant Thomas keeps crowing as the Mariners lock up an 8–3 breezer. "Cap'n's always sticking McGwire articles and pictures on my desk, and I do the same to him with Griffey stuff—but now I got *this.* I *told* him Junior would catch McGwire by the end of July! McGwire can't take the media and the pressure. And like I told Cap'n, doesn't matter if the ball goes one inch over the fence or three miles over—you can't add that extra distance to the next hit. *Love* telling Cap'n that—nothing he can say!"

The five ladies at poolside must think you're daft the next morning, Day 3, swimming those 46 laps in that little L-shaped hotel pool before you hightail it to the airport to fly to Chicago. It's the only way you know to knife through the fatigue, now that you're too juiced and jet-lagged to sleep. Slammin' Sammy's next. The wild card in the deck. Holding at 36, he has jacked just one in the last 11 days, but just might hit 20 in the next month, as he did in June.

As your plane wings toward O'Hare and everyone around you is reading about the home run chase, you're wondering: Could you possibly go 4 for 4? Then you land, and the dark skies start spitting rain on your rental-car windshield, and a flutter runs through your belly. No, God, please. What if you and Sammy get washed out?

You enter the clubhouse three and a half hours before the Cubs-Montreal Expos game and find Sosa swaying to Latin music. "I'll take care of you," he tells you. "Just wait?" You take a stool at a table five feet from his locker, back turned to him, delighted that you're going to speak to him alone and that this all seems so easy, just like the p.r. man promised . . . till Sammy shoos you away, tells you to go camp somewhere else. Over an hour you wait, and when you finally get the nod, Sammy opens a magazine of local real-estate listings. Uh-oh. . . .

Even for Sammy, who's never been a household name, the novelty's gone. He'll light up when he has an audience, but one-on-one with you and other reporters who follow, he answers questions lifelessly, eyes rarely lifting from photographs of houses with circular driveways and swimming pools. He says the media don't bother him. He admits it's nice to be part of the big story. He admits he's been overswinging again lately, his evil habit of old. He admits he doesn't know what position Roger Maris played. He says 18 minutes is enough. You resist recommending the brick colonial. What right do you have to be miffed? Jeez, isn't each one of these guys entitled to his own little way of hiding right in front of everyone's eyes?

When you exit the clubhouse, the sky's clear, the temperature's perfect, the sun's showering pinks and golds on the earth's most beautiful ballpark, and you decide, what the hell. It's the final night of your tater tear, so why not go drink a few cold ones with those bare-chested kids in the first row of the rightfield bleachers?

They're a whole different herd from the people you've met in San Diego and St. Petersburg. Everybody up here's got wit, everybody's got beer, everybody's got a desperate clear-eyed love for his team and an astonishing intimacy with it. Everybody's trying to decide whether he'll betray rightfield—family—and sneak over to left when Big Mac comes to town next month, and mulling how to stash an extra ball somewhere so that if Mac sends one into his palms, God willing, he'll have something to hurl back on the field when the mob chants, as it always does for visitors' home runs, "Throw it back! Throw it back!"

Nobody, *nobody,* thinks Sammy's got a prayer to bust Maris's record, not even the Sosa Boys, each of whom wears a letter of Sammy's surname in dripping blue paint across his bare chest. "Wore Sammy's number in high school," says Jake Abel, who's a letter S. "Got two dogs, named Wrigley and Sammy. But Griffey's gonna do it."

"Sammy won't even break Hack Wilson's team record of fifty-six," declares Chris Ramirez, a bartender and rightfield diehard. "Sammy thinks about it a little too much."

"That's exactly why he's never hit a grand slam," chimes in Linda Eisenberg, a 48-year-old rightfield regular for 20 years. "Not once. He can't resist swinging for the fences. He's better about it this year, but still. . . . See that bare spot he dug out with his spikes? That's so he'll remember where to stand. He and [shortstop] Manny Alexander share a brain. That's why we're always asking Sammy how many outs there are. We're doing it to make sure *he* knows."

"Aw, don't ask *them,*" says Ramirez. "That's the anti-Sammy faction. Let's talk about *you.* Man, is it true? Did you *really* see McGwire and Vaughn hit one on Monday and Griffey hit one last night? And they *pay* you for that job? Don't worry, Sammy's gonna hit one for you, too. How 'bout a beer?"

Here comes Sammy to take his position, bolting out of the dugout like a pitchforked bull, veering sharply at the warning track and acknowledging the bleacher bums' *Sam-my! Sam-my!* chant with a fist thump on his heart and a kiss to his fingers. It's been 16 days since the second-place Cubs have been home, and when Ramirez cries, "Ahhhh, it's good to be home, Sammy!" the rightfielder turns immediately, nods and flashes him a clenched fist.

Amazing, how everything changes up here. With words out of the way, Sammy's pure heart comes shining through—he's the faithful mute using hand and body language to keep up a steady patter of appreciation for the legions behind him. Clenched fists, heart thumps, peace signs, finger kisses and hip wiggles come in relentless sequences, conveying a message after each event on the field that everyone around you understands, and always, the big forefinger stabbing up or the pinkie and the thumb when the mob cries, "How many outs, Sammy?" Shouldn't *he* be the one you pull for?

In the fifth Sammy singles home the run that knots the game at 2–2, and George Shields, a grad student sitting one row down and two seats over, turns and tells you, with embers in his eyes, that he would cut off his finger, honest to God, if it meant these Cubs would get into the '98 World Series. You buy rounds for the Sosa Boys, along with Ramirez and his two pals, union laborer Marty Crowley and air-conditioning mechanic Jeff Cline. "Don't worry," Ramirez keeps telling you as the sixth and seventh innings pass. "Sammy's gonna wait till his last at-bat to give you your homer."

Sammy steps to the plate for his last poke in the home eighth, Cubs up 5–3. You look across the stadium to the poor guys sitting on their hands up in the press box and ask yourself why—if you ever cover a ball game again—you would do it from there. It's nuts here tonight, fans heaving balls at Expos players, fans racing on the field and dodging the diving tackles of security guards, fans raining beer cups on the field. Now there are runners on the corners, wind blowing to right, fans waving fishnets and thumping HIT IT HERE, SAMMY T-shirts, packed house on its feet, and you right there with them, thinking, No, these sluggers have already given you three homers and a combined 9 for 14—you can't ask for more.

Then more comes. Across the night sky it comes—impossibly, Sammy's 37th, straight at you. You're watching it, feeling the beer splash across your neck and the regulars closing around you like a fist. George Shields throws up his hand in front of you—there's the finger he swore he'd trade for a shot at the Series—and the ball smacks off the heel of his palm and bounces into the green mesh basket along the lip of the wall. Now it's a dogpile of flesh at your feet, everybody you've been drinking beer with diving and clawing and grunting. Crowley, the union leader, wants it most. He goes headfirst into the basket, legs flying up before you, wrenches it from the Sosa Boys and comes up whooping.

You? You just stand there like a happy idiot as Ramirez pounds you on the back and bellows, "You did it! Three nights in a row! This is incredible! You sure you're not coming back tomorrow?"

No . . . no, you're not. You're on an 8 a.m. flight home the next morning, looking like something the cat dragged in, wondering who it is you finally want to break the record. Your eyelids begin to sag, and a smile comes to your lips as it dawns on you.

You've got the record. Nobody on the planet's ever going to see all four of the men assaulting history hit home runs on three straight nights—just let 'em try. Go to sleep, you tell yourself. . . . You've got it. . . . You've got it in the bag.

Woman Whiffs Ruth and Gehrig

WILLIAM E. BRANDT

Remember Ila Borders?

She was the pitcher who caused a sensation in the mid 1990s when she made the men's baseball team at Southern California College. A few years later, she signed a contract with the St. Paul Pioneers of the independent Northern League. Her signature may have made her, quite literally, a Pioneer, but it didn't make her the first.

Or even the second.

Her spiritual ancestors—pitchers, too—were both signed to minor league contracts, in part, because they were women, and, in part, because of their skills. Each of their careers in organized ball ended quickly for one reason only: prejudice.

Which is why—Tom Hanks and *A League of Their Own* notwithstanding—there *should* be crying in baseball.

Lizzie Arlington, the first to cross the gender line, pitched—in four innings, she gave up three unearned runs—played second base and got two hits in one game for the Philadelphia Reserves in 1898. Following her performance, Atlantic League president Edward G. Barrow signed her to his league's club in Reading. She pitched a single, scoreless inning for them, but was released after the game when the novelty of her presence hadn't tripled the gate. Some years later, Barrow conceded that he'd signed her as a stunt, but also admitted, quite seriously, that she had the goods. "I'm not so sure," he said, "she couldn't win a spot somewhere in organized ball if she were in her prime today."

Maybe selling hot dogs. Barrow knew organized ball wouldn't have let her play.

Nor would it let Jackie Mitchell.

Some three decades after Arlington, Mitchell, a crafty left-hander, was mowing down men in the Chattanooga sandlots with wicked off-speed breaking stuff. As a kid, she'd been coached by future Hall of Famer Dazzy Vance; he taught her well. By her teens, she was a phenom.

In 1931, the Chattanooga Lookouts of the Double-A Southern Association, signed Mitchell, just seventeen, to a contract. Team owner Joe Engel, once a starter alongside Walter Johnson in Washington, wasted no time in capitalizing on her publicity value, his reason for signing her in the first place. Engel announced he would throw her in against the mighty Yankees—coincidentally, Ed Barrow was then running their front office—when they barnstormed through town on their way north a few days later. The four thousand fans who showed up weren't disappointed.

The two pieces here mark the event. The first, by William E. Brandt, is a straight account of the game—mistakenly referring to her as "organized baseball's first girl pitcher"—from the next day's *New York Times*. The second, unsigned, ran a day later on the editorial page, the *Times* deeming Mitchell's accomplishment significant enough to weigh in on.

Speculation bubbled that Mitchell's appearance was just a stunt. It was—she put the Lookouts in the national spotlight—and it wasn't—she really could play. But could she whiff two of the heaviest hitters in baseball? Well, pitchers don't need to overpower hitters to strike them out, do they? They just need to upset hitters' timing, which was what Mitchell designed her repertoire to do.

Might Ruth and Gehrig have just been playing along? Ruth perhaps, Gehrig doubtful. Personally, I think Ruth was cagey enough to realize his hammy exhibition at the plate established his best defense against having to explain how he could have been fanned by a female.

Not surprisingly, Commissioner Kenesaw Mountain Landis was unamused by the episode. He raised his red flag, voiding Mitchell's contract, banning her from organized ball. Baseball, he insisted, was "too strenuous" for a lady.

For the record, both Arlington and Mitchell continued to let baseball strain them. Arlington latched on with a series of "Bloomer Girl" squads. Mitchell toured with men's semi-pro teams, including the fabled House of David, beyond the reach of Judge Landis's jurisdiction. She later supported the movement for women's rights.

CHATTANOOGA, Tenn., April 2.—Jackie Mitchell, organized baseball's first girl pitcher, struck out Babe Ruth and Lou Gehrig in the first inning today. Then she faltered and walked Tony Lazzeri, so Manager Bert Niehoff substituted one of his regular pitchers, Clyde Barfoot.

Thereupon the Yanks went to work with their war clubs, running their total to fourteen hits and scoring a 14-to-4 victory over the Lookouts, local entrants in the Southern Association pennant race.

Barfoot took the mound at the start of the game. Combs doubled and Lary scored him with a single. Then Ruth came to bat. Barfoot retired to the bench temporarily and Miss Mitchell, who had been testing her pitching arm in front of the rightfield bleachers, marched to the pitching tee.

The crowd of about 4,000 cheered the local girl athlete heartily as she faced the Sultan of Swat. The Babe performed his role very ably. He swung hard at two pitches, then demanded that Umpire Owens inspect the ball, just as batters do when utterly baffled by a pitcher's delivery.

Then the 17-year-old left-hander shot a third strike over the plate. The Babe didn't swing, but when Umpire Owens called him out he flung his bat away in high disdain and trudged to the bench, registering disgust with his shoulders and chin.

Gehrig took three hefty swings as his contribution to the occasion. Lazzeri tried to bunt the first ball pitched, then merely stood languidly in the batter's box while Miss Mitchell served four wide ones.

That completed the day's work for Pitcher Mitchell. She retired amid cheers and the Yankees went to work in dead earnest, getting ten hits and five runs off Barfoot before the end of the fifth, and whacking Pat Simmons, former Boston Red Sox hurler, for nine more runs in the last four rounds.

Dusty Cooke achieved the goal all the Yanks were aiming for when he poled a home run onto the roof of the pavillion in left field. A watch was the prize for the day's first homer.

Cooke got quick delivery, too. His homer drove in the last three runs of the Yankees' big sixth inning. When he came to bat in the eighth the manager of a jewelry company marched to the plate and presented him with the prize.

★   ★   ★   ★   ★

A Pearl Among Pitchers

The Chattanooga baseball club may not win the Southern Association pennant this year. But people who won't know the identity of the winning club will know about the Chattanooga Lookouts. The reason is Miss JACKIE MITCHELL, "organized baseball's first girl pitcher." Already envious Memphis has sought to exchange two outfielders for her. Overtures are expected from Nashville and Birmingham. Her advertising value is worth two Chambers of Commerce. And if doubt of her pitching ability be expressed by envious rivals in the association, her record will show that she struck out two leading batsmen, RUTH and GEHRIG.

The 4,000 Chattanoogans who witnessed that feat Thursday will not soon forget it. When RUTH came to bat, the lady pitcher was called in. The Babe swung at two, missed them and let a third strike spin across the plate. GEHRIG fanned hard at three in succession. If Miss MITCHELL'S control had lasted, she might have added LAZZERI to her bag. But she tossed him four wide ones, and her work was over for that glorious day.

Cynics may contend that on the diamond as elsewhere it is *place aux dames*. Perhaps Miss JACKIE hasn't quite enough on the ball yet to bewilder RUTH and GEHRIG in a serious game. But there are no such sluggers in the Southern Association, and she may win laurels this season which cannot be ascribed to mere gallantry. The prospect grows gloomier for misogynists.

The Silent Season of a Hero

GAY TALESE

A giant of New Journalism, Gay Talese helped kick down the wall between the art of fiction and the craft of reporting by incorporating the techniques of a novelist into his already formidable arsenal of nonfiction skills. Across a distinguished career, he found ways, often astonishing ways, to get into—and under—the skins of institutions as disparate as *The New York Times,* the Mafia, Frank Sinatra, and, of course, Joe DiMaggio.

I say "of course" because more than thirty years after this stunning, chilling, hypnotic profile of the Yankee Clipper appeared in Esquire, it continues to cast a daunting shadow. David Halberstam chose it to lead off his hefty anthology, "Best American Sportswriting of the Century." I think it's among the best writing of the century—period—and I'm not alone in the supposition.

The main dissenter? That would have been DiMaggio himself.

"I would like to take the great DiMaggio fishing," the old man said. "They say his father was a fisherman. Maybe he was as poor as we are and would understand."
—Ernest Hemingway, *The Old Man and the Sea*

It was not quite spring, the silent season before the search for salmon, and the old fishermen of San Francisco were either painting their boats or repairing their nets along the pier or sitting in the sun talking quietly among themselves, watching the tourists come and go, and smiling, now, as a pretty girl paused to take their picture. She was about twenty-five, healthy and blue-eyed and wearing a red turtle-neck sweater, and she had long, flowing blonde hair that she brushed back a few times before clicking her camera. The fishermen, looking at her, made admiring comments but she did not understand because they spoke a Sicilian dialect; nor did she notice the tall grey-haired man in a dark suit who stood watching her from behind a big bay window on the second floor of DiMaggio's Restaurant that overlooks the pier.

He watched until she left, lost in the crowd of newly arrived tourists that had just come down the hill by cable car. Then he sat down again at the table in the restaurant, finishing his tea and lighting another cigarette, his fifth in the last half hour. It was eleven-thirty in the morning. None of the other tables was occupied, and the only sounds came from the bar where a liquor salesman was laughing at something the headwaiter had said. But then the salesman, his briefcase under his arm, headed for the door, stopping briefly to peek into the dining room and call out, "See you later, Joe." Joe DiMaggio turned and waved at the salesman. Then the room was quiet again.

At fifty-one, DiMaggio was a most distinguished-looking man, aging as gracefully as he had played on the ball field, impeccable in his tailoring, his nails manicured, his six-foot-two-inch body seeming as lean and capable as when he posed for the portrait that hangs in the restaurant and shows him in Yankee Stadium swinging from the heels at a pitch thrown twenty years ago. His grey hair was thinning at the crown, but just barely, and his face was lined in the right places, and his expression, once as sad and haunted as a matador's, was more in repose these days, though, as now, tension had returned and he chain-smoked and occasionally paced the floor and looked out the window at the people below. In the crowd was a man he did not wish to see.

The man had met DiMaggio in New York. This week he had come to San Francisco and had telephoned several times but none of the calls had been returned because DiMaggio suspected that the man, who had said he was doing research on some vague sociological project, really wanted to delve into DiMaggio's private life and that of DiMaggio's former wife, Marilyn Monroe. DiMaggio would never tolerate this. The memory of her death is still very painful to him, and yet, because he keeps it to himself, some people are not sensitive to it. One night in a supper club a woman who had been drinking approached his table, and when he did not ask her to join him, she snapped:

"All right, I guess I'm *not* Marilyn Monroe."

He ignored her remark, but when she repeated it, he replied, barely controlling his anger, "No—I wish you were, but you're not."

The tone of his voice softened her, and she asked, "Am I saying something wrong?"

"You already have," he said. "Now will you please leave me alone?"

His friends on the wharf, understanding him as they do, are very careful when discussing him with strangers, knowing that should they inadvertently betray a confidence he will not denounce them but rather will never speak to them again; this comes from a sense of propriety not inconsistent in the man who also, after Marilyn Monroe's death, directed that fresh flowers be placed on her grave "forever."

Some of the older fishermen who have known DiMaggio all his life remember him as a small boy who helped clean his father's boat, and as a young man who sneaked away and used a broken oar as a bat on the sandlots nearby. His father, a small mustachioed man known as Zio Pepe, would become infuriated and call him *lagnuso,* lazy, *meschino,* good-for-nothing, but in 1936 Zio Pepe was among those who cheered when Joe DiMaggio returned to San Francisco after his first season with the New York Yankees and was carried along the wharf on the shoulders of the fishermen.

The fishermen also remember how, after his retirement in 1951, DiMaggio brought his second wife, Marilyn, to live near the wharf, and sometimes they would be seen early in the morning fishing off DiMaggio's boat, the *Yankee Clipper,* now docked quietly in the marina, and in the evening they would be sitting and talking on the pier. They had arguments, too, the fishermen knew, and one night Marilyn was seen running hysterically, crying as she ran, along the road away from the pier, with Joe following. But the fishermen pretended they did not see this; it was none of their affair. They knew that Joe wanted her to stay in San Francisco and avoid the sharks in Hollywood, but she was confused and torn then—"She was a child," they said—and even today DiMaggio loathes Los Angeles and many of the people in it. He no longer speaks to his onetime friend, Frank Sinatra, who had befriended Marilyn in her final years, and he also is cool to Dean Martin and Peter Lawford and Lawford's former wife, Pat, who once gave a party at which she introduced Marilyn Monroe to Robert Kennedy, and the two of them danced often that night, Joe heard, and he did not take it well. He was very possessive of her that year, his close friends say, because Marilyn and he had planned to remarry; but before they could she was dead, and DiMaggio banned the Lawfords and Sinatra and many Hollywood people from her funeral. When Marilyn Monroe's attorney complained that DiMaggio was keeping her friends away, DiMaggio answered coldly, "If it weren't for those friends persuading her to stay in Hollywood she would still be alive."

Joe DiMaggio now spends most of the year in San Francisco, and each day tourists, noticing the name on the restaurant, ask the men on the wharf if they ever see him. Oh yes, the men say, they see him nearly every day; they have not seen him yet this morning, they add, but he should be arriving shortly. So the tourists continue to walk along the piers past the crab vendors, under the circling sea gulls, past the fish 'n' chip stands, sometimes stopping to watch a large vessel steaming toward the Golden Gate Bridge which, to their dismay, is painted red. Then they visit the Wax Museum, where there is a life-size figure of DiMaggio in uniform, and walk across the street and spend a quarter to peer through the silver telescopes focused on the island of Alcatraz, which is no longer a Federal prison. Then they return to ask the men if DiMaggio has been seen. Not yet, the men say, although they notice his blue Impala parked in the lot next to the restaurant. Sometimes tourists will walk into the restaurant and have lunch and will see him sitting calmly in a corner signing autographs and being extremely gracious with everyone. At other times, as on this particular morning when the man from New York chose to visit, DiMaggio was tense and suspicious.

When the man entered the restaurant from the side steps leading to the dining room he saw DiMaggio standing near the window talking with an elderly maître d' named Charles Friscia. Not wanting to walk in and risk intrusion, the man asked one of DiMaggio's nephews to inform Joe of his presence. When DiMaggio got the message he quickly turned and left Friscia and disappeared through an exit leading down to the kitchen.

Astonished and confused, the visitor stood in the hall. A moment later Friscia appeared and the man asked, "Did Joe leave?"

"Joe who?" Friscia replied.

"Joe DiMaggio!"

"Haven't seen him," Friscia said.

"You haven't *seen* him! He was standing right next to you a second ago!"

"It wasn't me," Friscia said.

"You were standing next to him. I saw you. In the dining room."

"You must be mistaken," Friscia said, softly, seriously. "It wasn't me."

"You *must* be kidding," the man said, angrily, turning and leaving the restaurant. Before he could get to his car, however, DiMaggio's nephew came running after him and said, "Joe wants to see you."

He returned expecting to see DiMaggio waiting for him. Instead he was handed a telephone. The voice was powerful and deep and so tense that the quick sentences ran together.

"You are invading my rights, I did not ask you to come, I assume you have a lawyer, you must have a lawyer, get your lawyer!"

"I came as a friend," the man interrupted.

"That's beside the point," DiMaggio said. "I have my privacy, I do not want it violated, you'd better get a lawyer. . . ." Then, pausing, DiMaggio asked, "Is my nephew there?"

He was not.

"Then wait where you are."

A moment later DiMaggio appeared, tall and red-faced, erect and beautifully dressed in his dark suit and white shirt with the grey silk tie and the gleaming silver cuff links. He moved with big steps toward the man and handed him an airmail envelope, unopened, that the man had written from New York.

"Here," DiMaggio said. "This is yours."

Then DiMaggio sat down at a small table. He said nothing, just lit a cigarette and waited, legs crossed, his head held high and back so as to reveal the intricate construction of his nose, a fine sharp tip above the big nostrils and tiny bones built out from the bridge, a great nose.

"Look," DiMaggio said, more calmly. "I do not interfere with other people's lives. And I do not expect them to interfere with mine. There are things about my life, personal things, that I refuse to talk about. And even if you asked my brothers they would be unable to tell you about them because they do not know. There are things about me, so many things, that they simply do not know. . . ."

"I don't want to cause trouble," the man said. "I think you're a great man, and . . ."

"I'm not great," DiMaggio cut in. "I'm not great," he repeated, softly. "I'm just a man trying to get along."

Then DiMaggio, as if realizing that he was intruding upon his own privacy, abruptly stood up. He looked at his watch.

"I'm late," he said, very formal again. "I'm ten minutes late. *You're* making me late."

The man left the restaurant. He crossed the street and wandered over to the pier, briefly watching the fishermen hauling their nets and talking in the sun, seeming very calm and contented. Then, after he had turned and was headed back toward the parking lot, a blue Impala stopped in front of him and Joe DiMaggio leaned out the window and asked, "Do you have a car?" His voice was very gentle.

"Yes," the man said.

"Oh," DiMaggio said. "I would have given you a ride."

Joe DiMaggio was not born in San Francisco but in Martinez, a small fishing village twenty-five miles northeast of the Golden Gate. Zio Pepe had settled there after leaving Isola delle Femmine, an islet off Palermo where the DiMaggios had been fishermen for generations. But in 1915, hearing of the luckier waters off San Francisco's wharf, Zio Pepe left Martinez, packing his boat with furniture and family, including Joe who was one year old.

San Francisco was placid and picturesque when the DiMaggios arrived, but there was a competitive undercurrent and struggle for power along the pier. At dawn the boats would sail out to where the bay meets the ocean and the sea is rough, and later the men would race back with their hauls, hoping to beat their fellow fishermen to shore and sell it while they could. Twenty or thirty boats would sometimes be trying to gain the channel shoreward at the same time, and a fisherman had to know every rock in the water, and later know every bargaining trick along the shore, because the dealers and restaurateurs would play one fisherman off against the other, keeping the prices down. Later the fishermen became wiser and organized, predetermining the maximum amount each fisherman would catch, but there were always some men who, like the fish, never learned, and so heads would sometimes be broken, nets slashed, gasoline poured onto their fish, flowers of warning placed outside their doors.

But these days were ending when Zio Pepe arrived, and he expected his five sons to succeed him as fishermen, and the first two, Tom and Michael, did; but a third, Vincent, wanted to sing. He sang with such magnificent power as a young man that he came to the attention of the great banker, A. P. Giannini, and there were plans to send him to Italy for tutoring and the opera. But there was hesitation around the DiMaggio household and Vince never went; instead he played ball with the San Francisco Seals and sportswriters misspelled his name.

It was *De*Maggio until Joe, at Vince's recommendation, joined the team and became a sensation, being followed later by the youngest brother, Dominic, who was also outstanding. All three later played in the big leagues and some writers like to say that Joe was the best hitter, Dom the best fielder, Vince the best singer, and Casey Stengel once said: "Vince is the only player I ever saw who could strike out three times in one game and not be embarrassed. He'd walk into the clubhouse whistling. Everybody would be feeling sorry for him, but Vince always thought he was going good."

After he retired from baseball Vince became a bartender, then a milkman, now carpenter. He lives forty miles north of San Francisco in a house he partly built, has been happily married for thirty-four years, has four grandchildren, has in the closet one of Joe's tailor-made suits that he has never had altered to fit, and when people ask if he envies Joe he always says, "No, maybe

Joe would like to have what I have. He won't admit it, but he just might like to have what I have." The brother Vince most admired was Michael, "a big earthy man, a dreamer, a fisherman who wanted things but didn't want to take from Joe, or to work in the restaurant. He wanted a bigger boat, but wanted to earn it on his own. He never got it." In 1953, at the age of forty-four, Michael fell from his boat and drowned.

Since Zio Pepe's death at seventy-seven in 1949, Tom, at sixty-two the oldest brother—two of his four sisters are older—has become nominal head of the family and manages the restaurant that was opened in 1937 as Joe DiMaggio's Grotto. Later Joe sold out his share and now Tom is the co-owner of it with Dominic. Of all the brothers, Dominic, who was known as the "Little Professor" when he played with the Boston Red Sox, is the most successful in business. He lives in a fashionable Boston suburb with his wife and three children and is president of a firm that manufactures fiber-cushion materials and grossed more than $3,500,000 last year.

Joe DiMaggio lives with his widowed sister, Marie, in a tan stone house on a quiet residential street not far from Fisherman's Wharf. He bought the house almost thirty years ago for his parents, and after their death he lived there with Marilyn Monroe; now it is cared for by Marie, a slim and handsome dark-eyed woman who has an apartment on the second floor, Joe on the third. There are some baseball trophies and plaques in the small room off DiMaggio's bedroom, and on his dresser are photographs of Marilyn Monroe, and in the living room downstairs is a small painting of her that DiMaggio likes very much: it reveals only her face and shoulders and she is wearing a very wide-brimmed sun hat, and there is a soft sweet smile on her lips, an innocent curiosity about her that is the way he saw her and the way he wanted her to be seen by others—a simple girl, "a warm bighearted girl," he once described her, "that everybody took advantage of."

The publicity photographs emphasizing her sex appeal often offended him, and a memorable moment for Billy Wilder, who directed her in *The Seven Year Itch,* occurred when he spotted DiMaggio in a large crowd of people gathered on Lexington Avenue in New York to watch a scene in which Marilyn, standing over a subway grating to cool herself, had her skirts blown high by a sudden wind below. "What the hell is going on here?" DiMaggio was overheard to have said in the crowd, and Wilder recalled, "I shall never forget the look of death on Joe's face."

He was then thirty-nine, she was twenty-seven. They had been married in January of that year, 1954, despite disharmony in temperament and time: he was tired of publicity, she was thriving on it; he was intolerant of tardiness, she was always late. During their honeymoon in Tokyo an American general had introduced himself and asked if, as a patriotic gesture, she would visit the troops in Korea. She looked at Joe. "It's your honeymoon," he said, shrugging, "go ahead if you want to."

She appeared on ten occasions before 100,000 servicemen, and when she returned she said, "It was so wonderful, Joe. You never heard such cheering."

"Yes I have," he said.

Across from her portrait in the living room, on a coffee table in front of a sofa, is a sterling-silver humidor that was presented to him by his Yankee teammates at a time when he was the most talked-about man in America, and when Les Brown's band had recorded a hit that was heard day and night on the radio:

> . . . From Coast to Coast, that's all you hear
> Of Joe the One-Man Show
> He's glorified the horsehide sphere,
> Jolting Joe DiMaggio . . .
> Joe . . . Joe . . . DiMaggio . . . we
> want you on our side. . . .

The year was 1941, and it began for DiMaggio in the middle of May after the Yankees had lost four games in a row, seven of their last nine, and were in fourth place, five-and-a-half games behind the leading Cleveland Indians. On May 15th, DiMaggio hit only a first-inning single in a game that New York lost to Chicago, 13–1; he was barely hitting .300, and had greatly disappointed the crowds that had seen him finish with a .352 average the year before and .381 in 1939.

He got a hit in the next game, and the next, and the next. On May 24th, with the Yankees losing 6–5 to Boston, DiMaggio came up with runners on second and third and singled them home, winning the game, extending his streak to ten games. But it went largely unnoticed. Even DiMaggio was not conscious of it until it had reached twenty-nine games in mid-June. Then the newspapers began to dramatize it, the public became aroused, they sent him good-luck charms of every description, and DiMaggio kept hitting, and radio announcers would interrupt programs to announce the news, and then the song again: *"Joe . . . Joe . . . DiMaggio . . . we want you on our side . . ."*

Sometimes DiMaggio would be hitless his first three times up, the tension would build, it would appear that the game would end without his getting another chance—but he always would, and then he would hit the ball against the left-field wall, or through the pitcher's legs, or between two leaping infielders. In the forty-first game, the first of a double-header in Washington, DiMaggio tied an American League record that George Sisler had set in 1922. But before the second game began a spectator sneaked onto the field and into the Yankees' dugout and stole DiMaggio's favorite bat. In the second game, using another of his bats, DiMaggio lined out twice and flied out. But in the seventh inning, borrowing one of his old bats that a teammate was using, he singled and broke Sisler's record, and he was only three games away from surpassing the major-league record of forty-four set in 1897 by Willie Keeler while playing for Baltimore when it was a National League franchise.

An appeal for the missing bat was made through the newspapers. A man from Newark admitted the crime and returned it with regrets. And on July 2, at Yankee Stadium, DiMaggio hit a home run into the left-field stands. The record was broken.

He also got hits in the next eleven games, but on July 17th in Cleveland, at a night game attended by 67,468, he failed against tow pitchers, Al Smith and Jim Bagby, Jr., although Cleveland's hero was really its third baseman, Ken Keltner, who in the first inning lunged to his right to make a spectacular backhanded stop of a drive and, from the foul line behind third base, he threw DiMaggio out. DiMaggio received a walk in the fourth inning. But in the seventh he again hit a hard shot at Keltner, who again stopped it and threw him out. DiMaggio hit sharply toward the shortstop in the eighth inning, the ball taking a bad hop, but Lou Boudreau speared it off his shoulder and threw it to the second baseman to start a double play and DiMaggio's streak was stopped at fifty-six games. But the New York Yankees were on their way to winning the pennant by seventeen games, and the World Series too, and so in August, in a hotel suite in Washington, the players threw a surprise party for DiMaggio and toasted him with champagne and presented him with this Tiffany silver humidor that is now in San Francisco in his living room. . . .

Marie was in the kitchen making toast and tea when DiMaggio came down for breakfast; his grey hair was uncombed but, since he wears it short, it was not untidy. He said good-morning to Marie, sat down and yawned. He lit a cigarette. He wore a blue wool bathrobe over his pajamas. It was eight a.m. He had many things to do today and he seemed cheerful. He had a conference with the president of Continental Television, Inc., a large retail chain in California of which he is a partner and vice-president; later he had a golf date, and then a big banquet to attend, and, if that did not go on too long and he were not too tired afterward, he might have a date.

Picking up the morning paper, not rushing to the sports page, DiMaggio read the front-page news, the people-problems of '66: Kwame Nkrumah was overthrown in Ghana, students were burning their draft cards (DiMaggio shook his head), the flu epidemic was spreading through the whole state of California. Then he flipped inside through the gossip columns, thankful they did not have him in there today—they had printed an item about his dating "an electrifying airline hostess" not long ago, and they also spotted him at dinner with Dori Lane, "the frantic frugger" in Whiskey à Go Go's glass cage—and then he turned to the sports page and read a story about how the injured Mickey Mantle may never regain his form.

It had all happened so quickly, the passing of Mantle, or so it seemed; he had succeeded DiMaggio as DiMaggio had succeeded Ruth, but now there was no great young power hitter coming up and the Yankee management, almost desperate, had talked Mantle out of retirement; and on September 18, 1965, they gave him a "day" in New York during which he received several thousand dollars' worth of gifts—an automobile, two quarter horses, free vacation trips to Rome, Nassau, Puerto Rico—and DiMaggio had flown to New York to make the introduction before 50,000: it had been a dramatic day, an almost holy day for the believers who had jammed the grandstands early to witness the canonization of a new stadium saint. Cardinal Spellman was on the committee, President Johnson sent a telegram, the day was officially proclaimed by the Mayor of New York, an orchestra assembled in center field in front of the trinity of monuments to Ruth, Gehrig, Huggins; and high in the grandstands, billowing in the breeze of early autumn, were white banners that read: "Don't Quit Mick," "We Love the Mick."

The banners had been held by hundreds of young boys whose dreams had been fulfilled so often by Mantle, but also seated in the grandstands wre older men, paunchy and balding, in whose middle-aged minds DiMaggio was still vivid and invincible, and some of them remembered how one month before, during a pre-game exhibition at Old-timers' Day in Yankee Stadium, DiMaggio had hit a pitch into the left-field seats, and suddenly thousands of people had jumped wildly to their feet, joyously screaming—the great DiMaggio had returned, they were young again, it was yesterday.

But on this sunny September day at the Stadium, the feast day of Mickey Mantle, DiMaggio was not wearing No. 5 on his back nor a black cap to cover his greying hair; he was wearing a black suit and white shirt and blue tie, and he stood in one corner of the Yankees' dugout waiting to be introduced by Red Barber, who was standing near home plate behind a silver microphone. In the outfield Guy Lombardo's Royal Canadians were playing soothing soft music; and moving slowly back and forth over the sprawling green grass between the left-field bullpen and the infield were two carts driven by groundskeepers and containing dozens and dozens of large gifts for Mantle—a six-foot, one-hundred-pound Hebrew National salami, a Winchester rifle, a mink coat for Mrs. Mantle, a set of Wilson golf clubs, a Mercury 95-horse-power outboard motor, a Necchi portable, a year's supply of Chunky Candy. DiMaggio smoked a cigarette, but cupped it in his hands as if not wanting to be caught in the act by teen-aged boys near enough to peek down into the dugout. Then, edging forward a step, DiMaggio poked his head out and looked up. He could see nothing above except the packed towering green grandstands that seemed a mile high and moving, and he could see no clouds, or blue sky, only a sky of faces. Then the announcer called out his name—*"Joe DiMaggio!"*—and suddenly there was a blast of cheering that grew louder and louder, echoing and reechoing within the big steel canyon, and DiMaggio stomped out his cigarette and climbed up the dugout steps and onto the soft green grass, the noise resounding in his ears, he could almost feel the breeze, the breath of 50,000 lungs upon him, 100,000 eyes watching his every move and for the briefest instant as he walked he closed his eyes.

Then in his path he saw Mickey Mantle's mother, a smiling elderly woman wearing an orchid, and he gently reached out for her elbow, holding it as he led her toward the microphone next to the other dignitaries lined up on the infield. Then he stood, very erect and without expression, as the cheers softened and the Stadium settled down.

Mantle was still in the dugout, in uniform, standing with one leg on the top step, and lined on both sides of him were the other Yankees who, when the ceremony was over, would play the Detroit Tigers. Then into the dugout, smiling, came Senator Robert Kennedy, accompanied by two tall curly-haired young assistants with blue eyes, Fordham freckles. Jim Farley was the first on the field to notice the Senator, and Farley muttered, loud enough for others to hear, "Who the hell invited *him?*"

Toots Shor and some of the other committeemen standing near Farley looked into the dugout, and so did DiMaggio, his glance seeming cold, but he remaining silent. Kennedy walked up and down within the dugout shaking hands with the Yankees, but he did not walk onto the field.

"Senator," said the Yankees' manager, Johnny Keane, "why don't you sit down?" Kennedy quickly shook his head, smiled. He remained standing, and then one Yankee came over and asked about getting relatives out of Cuba, and Kennedy called over one of his aides to take down the details in a notebook.

On the infield the ceremony went on, Mantle's gifts continued to pile up—a Mobilette motor bike, a Sooner Schooner wagon barbecue, a year's supply of Chock Full O'Nuts coffee, a year's supply of Topps Chewing Gum—and the Yankee players watched, and Maris seemed glum.

"Hey, Rog," yelled a man with a tape recorder, Murray Olderman, "I want to do a thirty-second tape with you."

Maris swore angrily, shook his head.

"It'll only take a second," Olderman said.

"Why don't you ask Richardson? He's a better talker than me."

"Yes, but the fact that it comes from you. . . ."

Maris swore again. But finally he went over and said in an interview that Mantle was the finest player of his era, a great competitor, a great hitter.

Fifteen minutes later, standing behind the microphone at home plate, DiMaggio was telling the crowd, "I'm proud to introduce the man who succeeded me in center field in 1951," and from every corner of the Stadium the cheering, whistling, clapping came down. Mantle stepped forward. He stood with his wife and children, posed for the photographers kneeling in front. Then he thanked the crowd in a short speech, and, turning, shook hands with the dignitaries standing nearby. Among them now was Senator Kennedy, who had been spotted in the dugout five minutes before by Red Barber, and been called out and introduced. Kennedy posed with Mantle for a photographer, then shook hands with the Mantle children, and with Toots Shor and James Farley and others. DiMaggio saw him coming down the line and at the last second he backed away, casually, hardly anybody noticing it, and Kennedy seemed not to notice it either, just swept past shaking more hands. . . .

Finishing his tea, putting aside the newspaper, DiMaggio went upstairs to dress, and soon he was waving good-bye to Marie and driving toward his business appointment in downtown San Francisco with his partners in the retail television business. DiMaggio, while not a millionaire, has invested wisely and has always had, since his retirement from baseball, executive positions with big companies that have paid him well. He also was among the organizers of the Fisherman's National Bank of San Francisco last year, and, though it never came about, he demonstrated an acuteness that impressed those businessmen who had thought of him only in terms of baseball. He has had offers to manage big-league baseball teams but always has rejected them, saying, "I have enough trouble taking care of my own problems without taking on the responsibilities of twenty-five ballplayers."

So his only contact with baseball these days, excluding public appearances, is his unsalaried job as a batting coach each spring in Florida with the New York Yankees, a trip he would make once again on the following Sunday, three days away, if he could accomplish what for him is always the dreaded responsibility of packing, a task made no easier by the fact that he lately has fallen into the habit of keeping his clothes in two places—some hang in his closet at home, some hang in the back room of a saloon called Reno's.

Reno's is a dimly-lit bar in the center of San Francisco. A portrait of DiMaggio swinging a bat hangs on the wall, in addition to portraits of other star athletes, and the clientele consists mainly of the sporting crowd and newspapermen, people who know DiMaggio quite well and around whom he speaks freely on a number of subjects and relaxes as he can in few other places. The owner of the bar is Reno Barsocchini, a broad-shouldered and handsome man of fifty-one with greying hair who began as a fiddler in Dago Mary's tavern thirty-five years ago. He later became a bartender there and elsewhere, including DiMaggio's Restaurant, and now he is probably DiMaggio's closest friend. He was the best man at the DiMaggio-Monroe wedding in 1954, and when they separated nine months later in Los Angeles, Reno rushed down to help DiMaggio with the packing and drive him back to San Francisco. Reno will never forget the day.

Hundreds of people were gathered around the Beverly Hills home that DiMaggio and Marilyn had rented, and photographers were perched in the trees watching the windows, and others stood on the lawn and behind the rose bushes waiting to snap pictures of anybody who walked out of the house. The newspapers that day played all the puns—"Joe Fanned on Jealousy"; "Marilyn and Joe—Out at Home"—and the Hollywood columnists, to whom DiMaggio was never an idol, never a gracious host, recounted instances of incompatibility, and Oscar Levant said it all proved that no man could be a success in two national pastimes. When Reno Barsocchini arrived he had to push his way through the mob, then bang on the door for several minutes before being admitted. Marilyn Monroe was upstairs in bed, Joe DiMaggio was downstairs with his suitcases, tense and pale, his eyes bloodshot.

Reno took the suitcases and golf clubs out to DiMaggio's car, and then DiMaggio came out of the house, the reporters moving toward him, the lights flashing.

"Where are you going?" they yelled. "I'm driving to San Francisco," he said, walking quickly.

"Is that going to be your home?"

"That *is* my home and always has been."

"Are you coming back?"

DiMaggio turned for a moment, looking up at the house.

"No," he said, "I'll never be back."

Reno Barsocchini, except for a brief falling out over something he will not discuss, has been DiMaggio's trusted companion ever since, joining him whenever he can on the golf course or on the town, otherwise waiting for him in the bar with other middle-aged men. They may wait for hours sometimes, waiting and knowing that when he arrives he may wish to be alone; but it does not seem to matter, they are endlessly awed by him, moved by the mystique, he is a kind of male Garbo. They know that he can be warm and loyal if they are sensitive to his wishes, but they must never be late for an appointment to meet him. One man, unable to find a parking place, arrived a half-hour late once and DiMaggio did not talk to him again for three months. They know, too, when dining at night with DiMaggio, that he generally prefers male companions and occasionally one or two young women, but never wives; wives gossip, wives complain, wives are trouble, and men wishing to remain close to DiMaggio must keep their wives at home.

When DiMaggio strolls into Reno's bar the men wave and call out his name, and Reno Barsocchini smiles and announces, "Here's the Clipper!", the "Yankee Clipper" being a nickname from his baseball days.

"Hey, Clipper, Clipper," Reno had said two nights before, "where you been, Clipper? . . . Clipper, how 'bout a belt?"

DiMaggio refused the offer of a drink, ordering instead a pot of tea, which he prefers to all other beverages except before a date, when he will switch to vodka.

"Hey, Joe," a sportswriter asked, a man researching a magazine piece on golf, "why is it that a golfer, when he starts getting older, loses his putting touch first? Like Snead and Hogan, they can still hit a ball well off the tee, but on the greens they lose the strokes. . . ."

"It's the pressure of age," DiMaggio said, turning around on his bar stool. "With age you get jittery. It's true of golfers, it's true of any man when he gets into his fifties. He doesn't take chances like he used to. The younger golfer, on the greens, he'll stroke his puts better. The older man, he becomes hesitant. A little uncertain. Shaky. When it comes to taking chances the younger man, even when driving a car, will take chances that the older man won't."

"Speaking of chances," another man said, one of the group that had gathered around DiMaggio, "did you see that guy on crutches in here last night?"

"Yeah, had his leg in a cast," a third said. "Skiing."

"I would never ski," DiMaggio said. "Men who ski must be doing it to impress a broad. You see these men, some of them forty, fifty, getting onto skis. And later you see them all bandaged up, broken legs. . . ."

"But skiing's a very sexy sport, Joe. All the clothes, the tight pants, the fireplace in the ski lodge, the bear rug—Christ, nobody goes to ski. They just go out there to get it cold so they can warm it up. . . ."

"Maybe you're right," DiMaggio said. "I might be persuaded."

"Want a belt, Clipper?" Reno asked.

DiMaggio thought for a second, then said, "All right—first belt tonight."

Now it was noon, a warm sunny day. DiMaggio's business meeting with the television retailers had gone well; he had made a strong appeal to George Shahood, president of Continental Television, Inc., which has eight retail outlets in Northern California, to cut prices on color television sets and increase the sales volume, and Shahood had conceded it was worth a try. Then DiMaggio called Reno's bar to see if there were any messages, and now he was in Lefty O'Doul's car being driven along Fisherman's Wharf toward the Golden Gate Bridge en route to a golf course thirty miles upstate. Lefty O'Doul was one of the great hitters in the National League in the early Thirties, and later he managed the San Francisco Seals when DiMaggio was the shining star. Though O'Doul is now sixty-nine, eighteen years older than DiMaggio, he nevertheless possesses great energy and spirit, is a hard-drinking, boisterous man with a big belly and roving eye; and when DiMaggio, as they drove along the highway toward the golf club, noticed a lovely blonde at the wheel of a car nearby and exclaimed, "Look at *that* tomato!" O'Doul's head suddenly spun around, he took his eyes off the road, and yelled, "Where, *where?*" O'Doul's golf game is less than what it was—he used to have a two-handicap—but he still shoots in the 80's, as does DiMaggio.

DiMaggio's drives range between 250 and 280 yards when he doesn't sky them, and his putting is good, but he is distracted by a bad back that both pains him and hinders the fullness of his swing. On the first hole, waiting to tee off, DiMaggio sat back watching a foursome of college boys ahead swinging with such freedom. "Oh," he said with a sigh, "to have *their* backs."

DiMaggio and O'Doul were accompanied around the golf course by Ernie Nevers, the former football star, and two brothers who are in the hotel and movie-distribution business. They moved quickly up and down the green hills in electric golf carts, and DiMaggio's game was exceptionally good for the first nine holes. But then he seemed distracted, perhaps tired, perhaps even reacting to a conversation of a few minutes before. One of the movie men was praising the film *Boeing, Boeing,* starring Tony Curtis and Jerry Lewis, and the man asked DiMaggio if he had seen it.

"No," DiMaggio said. Then he added, swiftly, "I haven't seen a film in eight years."

DiMaggio hooked a few shots, was in the woods. He took a No. 9 iron and tried to chip out. But O'Doul interrupted DiMaggio's concentration to remind him to keep the face of the club closed. DiMaggio hit the ball. It caromed off the side of his club, went skipping like a rabbit through the high grass down toward a pond. DiMaggio rarely displays any emotion on a golf course, but now, without saying a word, he took his No. 9 iron and flung it into the air. The club landed in a tree and stayed up there.

"Well," O'Doul said, casually, "there goes *that* set of clubs."

DiMaggio walked to the tree. Fortunately the club had slipped to the lower branch and DiMaggio could stretch up on the cart and get it back.

"Every time I get advice," DiMaggio muttered to himself, shaking his head slowly and walking toward the pond, "I shank it."

Later, showered and dressed, DiMaggio and the others drove to a banquet about ten miles from the golf course. Somebody had said it was going to be an elegant dinner, but when they arrived they could see it was more like a county fair; farmers were gathered outside a big barn-like building, a candidate for sheriff was distributing leaflets at the front door, and a chorus of homely ladies were inside singing *You Are My Sunshine.*

"How did we get sucked into this?" DiMaggio asked, talking out of the side of his mouth, as they approached the building.

"O'Doul," one of the men said. "It's his fault. Damned O'Doul can't turn *anything* down."

"Go to hell," O'Doul said.

Soon DiMaggio and O'Doul and Ernie Nevers were surrounded by the crowd, and the woman who had been leading the chorus came rushing over and said, "Oh, Mr. DiMaggio, it certainly is a pleasure having you."

"It's a pleasure being here, ma'am," he said, forcing a smile.

"It's too bad you didn't arrive a moment sooner, you'd have heard our singing."

"Oh, I heard it," he said, "and I enjoyed it very much."

"Good, good," she said. "And how are your brothers Dom and Vic?"

"Fine. Dom lives near Boston. Vince is in Pittsburgh."

"Why, *hello* there, Joe," interrupted a man with wine on his breath, patting DiMaggio on the back, feeling his arm. "Who's gonna take it this year, Joe?"

"Well, I have no idea," DiMaggio said.

"What about the Giants?"

"Your guess is as good as mine."

"Well, you can't count the Dodgers out," the man said.

"You sure can't," DiMaggio said.

"Not with all that pitching."

"Pitching is certainly important," DiMaggio said.

Everywhere he goes the questions seem the same, as if he has some special vision into the future of new heroes, and everywhere he goes, too, older men grab his hand and feel his arm and predict that he could still go out there and hit one, and the smile on DiMaggio's face is genuine. He tries hard to remain as he was—he diets, he takes steam baths, he is careful; and flabby men in the locker rooms of golf clubs sometimes steal peeks at him when he steps out of the shower, observing the tight muscles across his chest, the flat stomach, the long sinewy legs. He has a young man's body, very pale and little hair; his face is dark and lined, however, parched by the sun of several seasons. Still he is always an impressive figure at banquets such as this—an *immortal*, sportswriters called him, and that is how they have written about him and others like him, rarely suggesting that such heroes might ever be prone to the ills of mortal men, carousing, drinking, scheming; to suggest this would destroy the myth, would disillusion small boys, would infuriate rich men who own ball clubs and to whom baseball is a business dedicated to profit and in pursuit of which they trade mediocre players' flesh as casually as boys trade players' pictures on bubble-gum cards. And so the baseball hero must always act the part, must preserve the myth, and none does it better than DiMaggio, none is more patient when drunken old men grab an arm and ask, "Who's gonna take it this year, Joe?"

Two hours later, dinner and the speeches over, DiMaggio is slumped in O'Doul's car headed back to San Francisco. He edged himself up, however, when O'Doul pulled into a gas station in which a pretty red-haired girl sat on a stool, legs crossed, filing her fingernails. She was about twenty-two, wore a tight black skirt and tighter white blouse.

"Look at *that*," DiMaggio said.

"Yeah," O'Doul said.

O'Doul turned away when a young man approached, opened the gas tank, began wiping the windshield. The young man wore a greasy white uniform on the front of which was printed the name "Burt." DiMaggio kept looking at the girl, but she was not distracted from her fingernails. Then he looked at Burt, who did not recognize him. When the tank was full, O'Doul paid and drove off. Burt returned to his girl; DiMaggio slumped down in the front seat and did not open his eyes again until they'd arrived in San Francisco.

"Let's go see Reno," DiMaggio said.

"No, I gotta go see my old lady," O'Doul said. So he dropped DiMaggio off in front of the bar, and a moment later Reno's voice was announcing in the smoky room, "Hey, here's the Clipper!" The men waved and offered to buy him a drink. DiMaggio ordered a vodka and sat for an hour at the bar talking to a half dozen men around him. Then a blonde girl who had been with friends at the other end of the bar came over, and somebody introduced her to DiMaggio. He bought her a drink, offered her a cigarette. Then he struck a match and held it. His hands were unsteady.

"Is that me that's shaking?" he asked.

"It must be," said the blonde. "I'm calm."

Two nights later, having collected his clothes out of Reno's back room, DiMaggio boarded a jet; he slept crossways on three seats, then came down the steps as the sun began to rise in Miami. He claimed his luggage and golf clubs, put them into the trunk of a waiting automobile, and less than an hour later he was being driven into Fort Lauderdale, past palm-lined streets, toward the Yankee Clipper Hotel.

"All my life it seems I've been on the road traveling," he said, squinting through the windshield into the sun. "I never get a sense of being in any one place."

Arriving at the Yankee Clipper Hotel, DiMaggio checked into the largest suite. People rushed through the lobby to shake hands with him, to ask for his autograph, to say, "Joe, you look great." And early the next morning, and for the next thirty mornings, DiMaggio arrived punctually at the baseball park and wore his uniform with the famous No. 5, and the tourists seated in the sunny grandstands clapped when he first appeared on the field each time, and then they watched with nostalgia as he picked up a bat and played "pepper" with the younger Yankees, some of whom were not even born when, twenty-five years ago this summer, he hit in fifty-six straight games and became the most celebrated man in America.

But the younger spectators in the Fort Lauderdale park, and the sportswriters, too, were more interested in Mantle and Maris, and nearly every day there were news dispatches reporting how Mantle and Maris felt, what they did, what they said, even though they said and did very little except walk around the field frowning when photographers asked for another picture and when sportswriters asked how they felt.

After seven days of this, the big day arrived—Mantle and Maris would swing a bat—and a dozen sportswriters were gathered around the big batting cage that was situated beyond the left-field fence; it was completely enclosed in wire, meaning that no baseball could travel more than thirty or forty feet before being trapped in rope; still Mantle and Maris would be swinging, and this, in spring, makes news.

Mantle stepped in first. He wore black gloves to help prevent blisters. He hit right-handed against the pitching of a coach named Vern Benson, and soon Mantle was swinging hard, smashing line drives against the nets, going *ahhh ahhh* as he followed through with his mouth open.

Then Mantle, not wanting to overdo it on his first day, dropped his bat in the dirt and walked out of the batting cage. Roger Maris stepped in. He picked up Mantle's bat.

"This damn thing must be thirty-eight ounces," Maris said. He threw the bat down into the dirt, left the cage and walked toward the dugout on the other side of the field to get a lighter bat.

DiMaggio stood among the sportswriters behind the cage, then turned when Vern Benson, inside the cage, yelled, "Joe, wanna hit some?"

"No chance," DiMaggio said.

"Com'on, Joe," Benson said.

The reporters waited silently. Then DiMaggio walked slowly into the cage and picked up Mantle's bat. He took his position at the plate but obviously it was not the classic DiMaggio stance; he was holding the bat about two inches from the knob, his feet were not so far apart, and, when DiMaggio took a cut at Benson's first pitch, fouling it, there was none of that ferocious follow through, the blurred bat did not come whipping all the way around, the No. 5 was not stretched full across his broad back.

DiMaggio fouled Benson's second pitch, then he connected solidly with the third, the fourth, the fifth. He was just meeting the ball easily, however, not smashing it, and Benson called out, "I didn't know you were a choke hitter, Joe."

"I am now," DiMaggio said, getting ready for another pitch.

He hit three more squarely enough, and then he swung again and there was a hollow sound.

"Ohhh," DiMaggio yelled, dropping his bat, his fingers stung, "I was waiting for that one." He left the batting cage rubbing his hands together. The reporters watched him. Nobody said anything. Then DiMaggio said to one of them, not in anger nor in sadness, but merely as a simply stated fact, "There was a time when you couldn't get me out of there."

A Native Son's Thoughts

RICHARD BEN CRAMER

Richard Ben Cramer's *Philadelphia Inquirer* dispatches from the Middle East won the Pulitzer Prize for international reporting in 1979, and he's been a well-travelled journalist ever since. What makes this 1996 *Sports Illustrated* snapshot of Cal Ripken on the march to the magic number of 2130 so remarkable is not just the writing, but how clearly its subject is developed without Cramer ever doing anything but observing. The Ripken who comes into such sharp focus in the piece's highly cinematic ending serves as a thankful antidote to another baseball icon held up to the light by Cramer in the tour-de-force biography, *Joe DiMaggio: The Hero's Life.*

It's a stinkin'-hot night at the ballpark—near 100 degrees, the air is code red—and the Orioles are playing the cellar-dwelling Blue Jays. Still, it's got to be a big night; it's Coca-Cola/Burger King Cal Ripken Fotoball Night. That is, it's the sort of ersatz event that is a staple of baseball now that payrolls are fat, attendance is slim, and the game—well, no one trusts the game to be enough. These new Orioles yield to no club in the promotional pennant race. There's Floppy Hat Night, Squeeze Bottle Night, Cooler Bag Night. There's an item called the NationsBank Orioles Batting Helmet Bank, and there's the highly prized Mid-Atlantic Milk Marketing Cal Ripken Growth Poster. They are all a stylistic match for the graphics on the scoreboard that tell you when to clap or the shlub whose bodily fluids are draining into his fake-fur Bird Suit while he dances on the dugouts for reasons known only to him.

Still, as a celebration of the Hardest-Workin' Man in Baseball, the hero of this Old-Fashioned Hardworkin' Town, the Cal Ripken Fotoball is my personal favorite, perfect in every detail. There is the *F* in the name—gives it klass, and it's korrect, because there's no photo on the ball. There's a line drawing of Cal's face, with a signature across the neck. The signature is of the artist who made the genuine-original line drawing from a genuine-official photo of Cal. And then there's the plastic wrapper—says it's all Made in China. I like that in a baseball. And one key word: NONPLAYABLE. In other words, don't throw or hit it, or this footbooger will come apart.

Hours before game time, I wanted to ask Cal about his Fotoball. I wanted to ask how it feels to be the icon for baseball and Baltimore. But he's hard to catch in the locker room. He has his locker way off in the corner, where his dad used to dress as a coach. The official-and-genuine Oriole explanation is that the corner affords him room for two lockers—one extra to pile up all the stuff fans send him. But it's also unofficially helpful that there's an exit door in that corner, and anyway it makes Cal plain hard to get to. (One day early in the season I was blocked entirely by the richly misshapen and tattooed flesh of Sid Fernandez.) And if you're lucky enough to catch Cal, you're still not home free: Even local writers—guys Cal knows—find that out. "Angle your story," he might say, without looking at the writer, his eyes still on the socks in his hand. "Yeah . . . but what's the angle?"

So the writer must explain what he *means* to write. "Cal, it's just about all the second basemen you've had to play with—you know, 30 different guys to get used to."

"No," Cal says to his socks. "Doesn't do me any good to answer that."

See, these days, just a handful of games from Lou Gehrig's record of 2,130 consecutive starts, he's playing writers like he always plays defense, on the balls of his feet, cutting down the angles: *How is this gonna come at me? Where should I play it?* Positioning (forethought, control) has always been his game. And streak or no streak, Cal still has to play the game *his way*—that is, correctly: He's got to click with his second baseman.

This new locker room defense is the only effect Cal permits himself to show as he surfs the hype wave into the record books. That and maybe some testiness toward umpires. Just a couple of nights before Fotoball, the second base ump missed Cal's tag on a runner, and for the next ten minutes obscenities and spittle flew out of Ripken's mouth. (Of course, Cal did it the right way, facing home plate while he manned his position, never turning his head, so the ump wouldn't be shown up and have to toss Cal out. Ripken, being Ripken, has to throw even imprecations correctly.)

The point is, the umps, the writers, even the Streak itself, they all get in the way of the goal—always the same goal—which is to play the game *just right*. The umps make mistakes. The writers don't care; they want controversy. Cal doesn't like controversy. And the writers take time. Cal doesn't have time, not now. He's got his wife and kids in the big country house; he doesn't get enough time with them already. He's got fans, he gives autographs—thousands of signatures. He's got press conferences at ballparks across the country and big, scheduled media hits—the *New York Times, Prime Time Live, TV Guide,* the cover of *Sports Illustrated.* He's got endorsement deals, his old ones (local hot dogs and milk) and new ones: Chevy Trucks, Coca-Cola, Nike, Franklin Glove, the Adventureland theme park, and assorted memorabilia, including a bobble-head doll. (You can't establish a deathless baseball record without a bobble-head doll.) It's not easy being an icon—when it *has to be done just right*.

And time before a game . . . well, forget it. That's sacred. That's Cal's time to prepare. He's in his routine—the silence, the planning, the discussion. And he wants to hit, take batting practice, correctly: first, a bunt, then a ground ball to the right side (move that runner to third), then a fly to the outfield (bring that runner home) and then swing away, swing away, swing away. He wants to take grounders—has to take grounders—but correctly: You don't grab the ball any which way and close your mitt around it; you catch the grounder with an open glove, to get your throwing hand in. You catch it in position to throw. That's all part of catching the grounder correctly. See, Cal's dad, who taught him, has these sayings—said them all a million times—like: *If you want to play the game properly, you have to get ready to play.*

Or there's this one:

You have to know what you want to do before you can do it.

And even more often, there's this one:

Practice doesn't make perfect. PERFECT practice makes perfect.

So there's Cal on the Camden Yards ball field, trying to practice perfectly to get ready to be perfect, and I'm lurking in the dugout—*I wanna ask about the Fotoball.* That's the funny thing that happened to Cal: He landed in all this hype and distraction, the reporters and the shoe deals and about a thousand plaintive kids screaming, "Cal!" "Cal, pleeze!" "Mr. Ripken!" "*Caaal!*" He's got hungry little Baltimore to feed with esteem. He's got Powerade and Fotoball. He's got me to deal with, and every other sideshow in the whole Hoopla Nation . . . because he was raised to pay attention to the game.

Here's the funniest thing that happened to Ripken: Now that the calendar, luck and stubbornness have made him Baltimore's hero, the team, the media and the city's nabobs have decided he's got to be a blue-collar hero.

Oh, young Cal . . . he was raised a Baltimore, you know. . . .

That's how the local song begins.

. . . So he grabbed his lunchbucket and went to work every day—the way guys do in this hardworkin' town. He did his job 13 years straight—like the fellas on the swing shift at Crown Cork 'n' Seal. . . .

Well, a workin'-class hero is something to be. But it just doesn't happen to be . . . him.

At $6 million a year, Cal Ripken Jr. lives in a house the size of a Wall-Mart, near the ninth jump of the Maryland Hunt Cup, in steeplechase country, the Greenspring Valley, along with the other rulers of Baltimore. Ripken goes to work in a chartered plane or in the Orioles' fashionably retro theme park.

And the town? Well, that's a complicated story—one that goes well beyond the Camden Yards theme park and the surrounding Inner Harbor theme park, with its rows of shoppees selling $20 T-shirts or crabs at $35 a dozen. None of that is meant for the man on the swing shift. In fact, there is no more swing shift. Crown Cork and Seal closed up its plants, like all the other big manufacturers.

The ball yard, Harborplace, the gleaming insurance and banking towers looming over the gleaming water—they were all designed (with forethought, control) to replace the blue-collar Baltimore that was crumbling like an empty row house. Or at least to distract attention: Here the rulers of the town would build the Baltimore you're *supposed* to see; they would stock it with family attractions—the shoppees, tall ships, an aquarium (Hey! How 'bout *baseball?*) . . . and plenty of parking, so the white people could jump into their cars and go back to the suburbs to sleep. They wanted the kind of place that *Good Morning America* would visit. *If you build it, Joan and Charlie will come!* And so they did! That worked like a charm. In fact, that's what they called Baltimore: Charm City.

But somehow that name never really stuck. See, the schools still didn't work, crime's a problem, taxes are murder. And even those new towers shining out there, beyond the centerfield fence, they're going empty. This town is literally shrinking up. Somehow, all the Disneyfication of the downtown didn't win for Baltimore the label that the rulers really wanted: big league. Now they've given up on the catch nicknames. They've just mounted Cal up front, like a hood ornament, to symbolize what Baltimore's all about.

The truth is, Cal wasn't raised a Baltimore—nor even a true son of Aberdeen, Maryland, the town thirty-three miles up the highway where his parents still keep their house. When Cal was growing up, the Ripkens' home was baseball. Young Cal was raised an Oriole.

You have to understand what it meant. When Cal was growing up, the Orioles were the best club in the game. There were pennants: '66 (world champs) and '69, then '70 (world champs again) and '71. There were playoff teams in '73 and '74 and a pennant again in '79. These Orioles were stars on the mound: Jim Palmer, Dave McNally, Mike Cuellar. They were sluggers at the plate: Frank Robinson, Boog Powell. They were stars with the glove: Mark Belanger, Paul Blair . . . and for twenty-three years at third base, Brooks Robinson.

The great thing was not what they won but how they did it. This wasn't the richest club. As a business, it wasn't even good. The Orioles had to win pennants to draw a million fans. Any evening you could leave work at 7:15 and drive like a bandit through the neighborhood in northeast Baltimore that had as its centerpiece Memorial Stadium. Everybody had his own route through those tight streets. Everybody knew a kid who parked cars in his alley or his driveway. And for five bucks at the window, you could stroll through this comfy concrete pile and settle yourself to watch the greatest right-hander to hit the league in thirty years, Palmer, mow down some visiting lesser lights. By midgame, if you had the wit and nerve, you could spot an empty seat in the second or third row . . . you could sit, for god's sake, a foot and a half behind the bald owner, Jerry Hoffberger, hard by the third base dugout, where it looked like Brooks was gonna dive straight into your lap for that ball. "Way to dig it out, Brooksie!" some fan would yell. Brooks would look up to see if he knew him. These were ball fans. They would hoot an outfielder out of the park if he threw some rainbow over the cutoff man's head. The Orioles were all about defense. Sometimes they made brilliant plays. But they always made the routine plays right. That was the Oriole Way.

There was actually a book. It had all the plays: where the cutoff men stood, who backed up where, all the bunt plays, the pickoff plays. . . . This was the codification of the Oriole Way. And this text was taught at every spring training and through the summer, in every ballpark throughout the organization. In Stockton, Knoxville, and Elmira, they did everything the Oriole Way, down to the dress code (on the street), full uniform (on the field), batting practice (*first the bunt . . . one to move the runner over . . . one to bring the runner in . . . then swing away, swing away, swing away*). The Orioles couldn't afford to *buy* pennants. When they had a hole, they had to fill it from the farm. But when those kids came up, they were Orioles already. The only thing manager Earl Weaver had to tell them was the curfew. On the field, they knew how to make the plays right.

And that's where the old man came in. Cal Ripken Sr. was a catcher whose playing career (1957–62) arced short of the majors. Then he was, for almost fifteen years, a coach and manager in the bushes, teaching the gospel to fledgling Orioles. For all the years of his famous son's life, Senior was preaching the Oriole Way. Living it, in fact, in Ashville, Rochester, or some other town where his wife, Vi, would rent a house and make a home for the four children during the summer. Wherever home was, the ballpark was the Ripkens' second home. Dad would set the kids to work in the clubhouse or hit grounders to them (Dad could run a perfect infield)—100 grounders, 150, as many as they wanted—unless they started screwing around, grabbing at the ball, hotdogging throws, in which case he would pick up the ball bag and walk off. (*PERFECT practice makes perfect.*)

Cal Jr. didn't live in Aberdeen full-time till high school, in '75. (Senior didn't come up to the big club, as a coach, till '76.) But young Cal was already an Oriole. From the time he was able to read, the box score from Baltimore held names he knew—they'd been kids on his father's teams. (*Hey! Bumbry went 3 for 4! Junior had shined his shoes in the Ashville clubhouse!*) When Junior was drafted in '78—and made it through the system, the Oriole Way, by '81—he was just rejoining family.

And it *was* like family, the way the guys would go out after road games—or in Baltimore, they would babysit one another's kids, watch 'em all together in somebody's pool. Or everyone would go out to Hoffberger's house after Sunday doubleheaders: cookouts and laughter, players and ex-players, kids and wives, stadium ushers and secretaries, Weaver and the old coaches—Bamberger, Hunter, Ripken—grinning half-lit on National Bohemian beer (that was Hoffberger's brewery), saying (like they always did), "It's great to be young and an Oriole!" And it would go from just after the game to . . . well, when the last guest left. Even on a weekday night Cal Jr. would come off the field, and there would be Dad at the table in the locker room, holding court—Senior never liked to leave too quickly after a game. And he would take apart that game, too, for a couple of hours sometimes, and you could learn some baseball. Cal Jr. liked to hang around like Dad. And even if he stayed for two hours, he'd still see guys—Palmer, Elrod Hendricks—in the parking lot, fans around their cars. Autographs were mostly for kids. When that was over, they could talk baseball.

And the baseball was splendid. In '82, Cal Jr.'s first full year, the Orioles took the pennant race to the final weekend against Milwaukee. That was the most exciting thing Junior had ever felt in his life. The next year they took it up a notch and won the pennant in the playoffs in Chicago. Attendance was sky-high. All of Baltimore was on a roll. There was a working mayor in those days—guy named Schaefer, he was kind of the Oriole Way of mayors—and he'd walk into some business in town and tell 'em, flat out, they had to buy season tickets. That's when he wasn't busy building somewhere. (Hell, he was rebuilding the whole Inner Harbor, said it was going to save the city!) It was exciting just to be there. And when the O's beat the Phillies in five games in October, and Schaefer had a parade through the streets, and the fans came out by the tens of thousands, yelling, "*Cal M-V-P, Cal M-V-P!*" . . . then everything seemed perfect. Nobody knew it was over.

No one had marked as a disaster the moment three years earlier that Hoffberger sold the team. (The new owner, attorney Edward Bennett Williams, was already whining about the tight streets around the ballpark. Fer crissakes, it took him *an hour* to get home to Washington.) No one knew the mayor was running for his last reelection; he was building his last towers, selling his last tickets. No one—certainly not Cal Jr.—knew that would be his last pennant, last Series, last parade. No one saw it was the end of the Oriole Way— not even Senior, keeper of the code—until four years later, when Williams gave him a thoroughly diminished team to manage and then fired him because he didn't win.

Sure enough, it's a big crowd for Fotoball. No surprise: Camden Yards is always near-sold-out. The field level is almost all season tickets. The club level, above that, is all bought up by businessmen who send young waitresses to fetch their crab cakes and designer beer. And it's big business in the skyboxes, where buffets and TVs are arrayed in cool darkness, behind plate glass. The rulers of Baltimore built this pleasure playground for themselves.

In the rest of the yard it's family entertainment—parents cajoling little Kim, Lee, and Ashley to keep their Fotoballs in the Oriole (promo) sports bag so they won't get cotton candy or frozen yogurt on them. It's a prosperous crowd, overwhelmingly white. The P.A. man, Rex Barney, yells his single, aged joke—"*Give that fan a contract!*"—whenever a customer catches a foul ball. There's the Bird dweeb, dancing with the ball girl down the left-field line. There's the Jumbotron in centerfield, flashing trivia quizzes (JeopBirdie) or guess-the-attendance or a picture of the player at bat, along with some cheery bio factoid: *Chris had 3 HR in one game with Columbus.* (Big deal.) The whole show is paced like a Saturday-morning cartoon: something has to happen every thirty seconds, or else.

Oh, there is a game, too.

It isn't a very good game—though Cal puts the O's on the board with a home run in the second inning. That revs the crowd for a while. They're up in their seats, rooting . . . till the third out, and then the P.A. speakers whine to life with a female voice like treacle: *Noo-body does it better. . . .* It's the theme song for the Jumbotron video on Cal: Cal hitting, Cal sliding, Cal high-fiving, Cal in the pivot, Cal as a kid, Cal with his kids, Cal getting a plaque, Cal in gauzy sunshine waving his cap. *Noo-body doezzz it bettttter. Bayyyy-bee yerrrrr the besssst!* The boys in marketing must have put that splendid tribute together. No one is rooting at all—they're just watching TV. Cal is already the favorite with all the suburban children. They wear jerseys with the big number 8 on the back and ORIOLES across the chest. (No official-and-genuine Oriole jersey, not even the road uniform, says BALTIMORE anymore. Regionalism is a Key Marketing Concept.)

Meanwhile, the O's are giving the game away—handing it over to a last-place club. On the mound Jamie Moyer has already walked in two Toronto runs. Now, two ground balls that the second baseman can't play and an error in left field turn into three more runs. The nearly 42,000 in attendance watch in murmurous passivity. They make noise when they're told to—though they did stand to cheer for Bobby Bonilla on the occasion of his first Oriole hit; he was o-fer his first two games. Still, everyone seems sure Bonilla will put the O's over the top. He's worth millions! They're pleased with the team's owner, Peter Angelos (another lawyer). *At least he's not afraid to spend!* (And isn't it great? All they had to give up for Bonilla was a couple of farmhands—just two of their best outfield prospects. Minor leaguers!)

Middle innings: Toronto now has six runs. It's always disturbing to this crowd when their team of hired millionaires doesn't win. And it's always somewhat mysterious.

The front-row box next to the dugout, right on third base, is now held by Ripken's agent, Ron Shapiro. Those seats have a splendid view of Toronto runners rounding third, but Shapiro couldn't be in a better mood. He's gorgeous in his warmth—the kind of fellow who'll reach over and hold your arm with his hand while he tells you something nice about yourself. He's a lawyer by training, sports agent by trade; he's the man who set up Cal's charity foundation and created the Tufton Group, which handles demands on Cal in this year of the Streak. As Cal's father is father to Cal's game, so is Shapiro father to Cal's iconhood.

"To me," says Shapiro, "the bonding between a player and his community is what it's all about." Ripken, he says, has made a conscious choice to stay in Baltimore for his entire career. Yes, Cal is committed to working with Baltimore. "He wants to be appreciated for his totality as a human being . . . as a thoughtful, caring, committed and community human being." Shapiro is thoroughly hip to the great divide in the ballpark—the family crowd, the corporate crowd—and alive to the possibilities this presents for Cal. "Because, remember," says Shapiro, "they'll all come out for Cal. Both constituencies." He sounds like an operative sizing up a prime piece of political horseflesh. Politics is another of Shapiro's games. He is the finance chairman for the current mayor's reelection campaign. Ron Shapiro is going to remain a ruler of Baltimore.

The Blue Jays have the bases loaded (again!) when their batter, Alex Gonzalez, raps a clean hit to left . . . except it never gets through. Ripken was moving before the bat hit the ball. He is so far in the hole, it looks as if his weight will carry him into foul ground. But he picks the ball on the bounce, backhand, with his body somehow already turning, with his right hand already sweeping up to meet his glove at his hip. He is backpedaling, almost falling toward third, when he plants his big right leg, which lifts him into the air, whence he fires the ball in a white streak to second base. And the runner is out—inning over. It is the kind of play that stays in your head as a picture. At Camden Yards, no one yells. Polite applause. The fans are waiting for the next thing to happen. "Dad. . . . *Dad!* . . . DAD!" This is a kid on my left. He wears a T-shirt that says CHICAGO BULLS. His father turns. "Cal's gotta hit another home run! Dad! Can we get ice cream?"

This current mayor, guy named Schmoke, made a new slogan for the city: *Baltimore. The City That Reads.* No one knows what that's supposed to mean. But about the same time, Cal set up his own foundation and its literacy program: Reading, Runs and Ripken. Shapiro keeps everybody on the same page of the hymnal. Cal's always been willing to sing along.

Now that Blue Collar Cal's so famous across the nation, everybody's trying to pick up the tune. *Would you say there's something special about this town? Hardworkin' people?* It was one of those man-on-the-street ads, supposed to thump the tub for local Channel 11. They wanted to bill themselves as the Hard-Working News Team. Of course, it seemed like a small-minded play on Cal's streak—collusive, self-satisfied, and small-town. That's Baltimore too.

Though he'll never talk about it, Cal remembers clearly those times when the town chorus turned against him. There was '88, that awful year when his father was fired (the O's started 0–6 under Cal Sr., then Frank Robinson came in, and they lost 15 more in a row). And there was '92, when the team and the town gave up on his little brother, Billy (Cal's favorite second baseman, but of course he can't say that, either). In fact, every time Cal's hitting went south, those hardworkin' airwaves were filled with captious comment. People said Cal ought to sit down. Take a rest. Stop acting like Superman. *Stop putting his own streak ahead of the team!*

It hurt him. Confused him. In '88, when Brady Anderson joined the O's, he found Cal one day leaning alone against the left-field fence. "What's goin' on?" Brady said.

Cal just waved him away: "Not now."

Brady insisted. "No, c'mon. Tell me. What's wrong?"

Then Cal asked this near-rookie, this *kid,* "What does the Streak mean to you?"

What Cal couldn't figure was: How could they criticize *the best thing about him?* He always came to play. What was wrong with that? That's the way he was. Was there something wrong with him?

Still, he signed two contracts after that. Even in the middle of negotiations, he never made a threat to leave. That didn't have to do with Baltimore's values. It had to do with his values. He thought if you say you're willing to leave—if you declare for free agency—then you have to be willing to go. He wasn't.

And that's his real link with this town, with the people in the row houses. City councilman Martin O'Malley (who is to local politics what Cal was to baseball as Rookie of the Year) represents those old, tight streets around the silent Memorial Stadium. "People here don't care where he lives," O'Malley says. "Or how. They don't want him to be blue collar. And they're not waiting with bated breath for him to pass Lou Gehrig. You know, the city can ebb and flow. We've got racial divisions. We're best known for *Homicide* on TV. The population's at its lowest point since World War I. But number 8's still trottin' out to shortstop. People see that. He never gave up on them."

Cal does hit another home run. Two dingers on Fotoball Night—how 'bout that? but it isn't enough, not when the rest of the lineup hits nothin', and the O's give away three or four runs. Toronto 6, O's 3—final. The Orioles have departed second place, heading south.

It promises to be a somber clubhouse scene when the writers are admitted ten minutes after the O's last strikeout. The pack makes for the manager's interview room. I am hunting Cal, still with my Fotoball, still without avail. Often after games he'll sit for a while in the lounge—players only—to talk about the game. But tonight it looks like the rest of the guys are getting dressed, heading out. Coaches, too. It is almost eleven o'clock. I watch Cal's corner. A camera crew, for mysterious reasons, is filming his locker, shining a minicam spotlight onto his shoes, his chair, his uniform shirts. (Maybe it's another Jumbotron tribute. Maybe they'll make this one scratch-'n'-sniff.)

"Check the field." This is whispered in my ear in the locker room. "He's out there. You better check it out."

I go out through the tunnel, under the empty stands. Except they aren't empty. There are thousands of people, all standing, looking down at the rail where Cal Ripken is signing Fotoballs.

Cal has one foot on the rubberized warning track, one foot on the padding of the rail. He has his own felt-tip. And he is signing—correctly, of course, down to the *Jr* and the period after his name. (Then he blows on his signature to make sure it won't smudge.) There are city cops around him and two dozen ushers to keep the crowd in line. But mostly they just stand there grinning. This is just Cal and the fans.

"Cal, would you put 'From B.J. to Kristin'?"

"Kristin with a *K*?"

"K-R-I-S-T-I-N. . . . Thanks, Cal."

"You're welcome," Cal says.

He signs their Fotoballs and then their programs—or their shirts, ticket stubs, popcorn boxes, whatever they want, as many as they want. If they want him to use their pens, he caps his and signs with theirs. (One guy's pen doesn't work, so Cal rubs the point on his palm till it satisfactorily marks up his hand.) If they don't ask him something, Cal asks them, "Favorite hat?" Cal says as he bends to sign one kid's sweaty headgear.

"It is now," says one of the cops.

Cal never lets a kid leave without a word from him. "You ready for bed?" Cal says to a yawning little girl. "I feel that way, too."

But he doesn't look ready for bed at all—stoked up is more like it, in high enjoyment. He doesn't just hold out his hand for the next ball and the next ball . . . he looks up and fixes each fan with the shock of his light blue eyes and a greeting. The cops warn him a couple of times that fans are still piling into line in the concourse—the line stretches now from the right side of home plate halfway to the left-field corner. "That's O.K.," Cal says. He keeps signing and talking.

"How'd you break your arm?" he says to a boy as he signs his cast, then his Fotoball, then his hat. "Your bike? Jumpin' a couple of cars? Or you just fell off. . . . How long you got to have it on? . . . Well, that's O.K. You can still play other games, can't you?" (The kid just shakes his head, mute with awe.)

The grown-ups, who didn't get Fotoballs, bring Ripken whatever they have. One woman hands over her shoe. "I'd like to sign it inconspicuously," says Cal, turning it over, "so you can still wear it." Says the woman: "I'll wear it." Maybe a hundred parents push kids forward and then back away, making motions of entreaty with their cameras. Each time, Cal leans in next to the kid— "Cheese," he says. ("Oh, didn't wind? Try again. Cheese and crackers.") Teenage girls are in that breathless, open-mouthed, near-tears state known to doctors as Deep Elvis. They want to kiss him. Cal demurs. They want to hug him. Cal leans in. "Not too close," he'll say. "I'm all sweaty." (They don't mind.)

At midnight it is still near 90 degrees on the field. The rest of the vast yard is silent and empty, in a strange surfeit of light. The grounds crew has finished with the mound, home plate and infield. The rest of the stands are clean and bare. Supper has long since been cleared in the clubhouse. The locker room is also empty save for a couple of attendants cleaning, putting laundry away. Still there are fans, stretched in a line down the concourse. And Cal keeps signing: "Is that Katie with an *i-e?*"

The polite lieutenant, Russell Shea, leans in behind Cal. "I'll be the bad guy, O.K.?" he says. Cal nods but keeps signing and talking. Shea calls Cal "the finest gentleman I've met, bar none—and I've been stadium commander for two years." So he lets Cal make the schedule. He leans in again: "You want anything? Cold drink?" Cal shakes his head. He is still in full uniform, his forearms shining with sweat, his ankles still taped. For most of the last hour and a half, he has stood on one leg while he propped each ball, photograph, or program on his left knee—so he could sign just right. Shea, unbidden, brings a bottle of Powerade. Cal keeps signing.

"Let me stretch out your shirt, so I can sign it right."

"Yeah, this picture's rookie year. You want me to sign on his leg?"

The way Cal describes it, he's too pumped up after a game to leave. His family's asleep . . . and the fans want so little—a picture, a handshake, a signature, to remember the night. He likes it when they ask him to write their names too—or when they bring pure trash for him to sing (some lemon-ice wrapper that has been on the floor). That way, he knows: they never mean to sell it. (The one piece he won't sign is a pair of uniform pants brought down by a collector. The guy would have sold the pants for a fortune.) He likes it when fans ask if he remembers them or they bring up some name he's supposed to know. ("Do you know Pat Francis?" asks a big-haired blonde. "She useta babysitcha." Cal fixes the woman with an elfin smile. "We used to tie up our babysitters sometimes. We outnumbered 'em." And the woman is giggling.) The way Cal describes it, if he can talk with a thousand Baltimore fans, he'll find out he knows most of them. That isn't true. But it pleases him to think it's true.

It leases him to see the excitement on their faces—and their shock. (*He talked to us! He was so nice!*) It pleases him to do this correctly. It pleases him, this power to give some bit of himself (as the kids yell to one another, as they run with their autographs: *We got Cal! We GOT CAL!*). This is a heady power: On this night or any night, at any hour, midnight or after . . . by his act alone, by his attention for one minute, by a stroke of his pen, he can give value to trash. He can make a night, or a town, feel big league. he can make even Fotoball something real.

Quarter after twelve. What he can't do is stop. Not easily. Not tonight. There are hundreds left in the concourse when Cal murmurs, "Pen's going." That means he is going—soon. But he signs a few more, till the collector with the pants show up again. ("I didn't come to argue. Cal! just these pictures!")

"I'm done," Cal says. He caps his pen.

"CAL! Ooooowww!" It is a moan of near-physical pain from a mother-with-son behind the collector—a kinda-cute mom, with curly brown hair. "Pleeeese, oh, god!" She's been waiting with her hyperweary kid for hours.

"I'm done," Cal says. "Sorry. I can't do any more." He is heading down the dugout steps. She is going to cry—you can see it. "But how 'bout if I give you my cap? Is that all right?"

The mother doesn't get it. She looks at her stunned son to see if that is all right. Cal ducks in the dugout and surreptitiously signs the bill. Then he pops up the steps, puts it in the kid's hands. The mother is still staring at her kid: *is it all right?*

But the kid can't look up. He is staring at this . . . *thing.* As if a meteorite had landed in his hands. Cal is already in the tunnel when the boy looks up—not at the mom but at the dark heavens—and says, "Whoa! YESSS!"

K as in Koufax

VIN SCULLY

Most of us talk in phrases. Some of us talk in sentences. A few of us can even talk in paragraphs.

Vin Scully talks in stories.

The voice of the Dodgers, he is baseball's Homer, building an oral history one game at a time. His call of the final three outs of Sandy Koufax's perfecto—27 up, 27 down—against the Cubs in 1965 is a model of narrative virtue. It is filled with such tension, description, information, and zest—building to an unforgettable climax and conclusion—that it's hard to believe this could be on-the-spot, off-the-cuff play-by-play. For five decades, Scully's great art has rested in never letting us see how much sweat actually goes into achieving the brilliance of what he pulls off day after day, season after season.

On the subject of brilliance, Koufax's fourth no-hitter in four years cast a total eclipse over the stellar performance thrown against him. In a heartbreaking 1–0 loss, Cubs pitcher Bob Hendley tossed a dandy one-hitter. Sadly for him, the best performance of his career was simply no match against perfection. It wound up as just another loss in the record book.

Three times in his sensational career has Sandy Koufax walked out to the mound to pitch a fateful ninth when he turned in a no-hitter. But tonight, September 9th, 1965, he made the toughest walk of his career, I'm sure, because through eight innings he has pitched a perfect game. He has struck out eleven, has retired 24 consecutive batters.

And the first man he will look at is catcher Chris Krug—big, right-handed hitter—flied to center, grounded to short.

Dick Tracewski is now at second base; and Koufax ready—and delivers: curve ball for a strike—0-and-1 the count to Chris Krug.

Out on deck to pinch-hit is one of the men we mentioned as a "possible": Joe Amalfitano. Here's the strike-one pitch: fast ball, swung on and missed, strike two.

And you can almost taste the pressure now. Koufax lifted his cap, ran his fingers through his black hair, and pulled the cap back down, fussing at the bill. Krug must feel it too, as he backs out, heaves a sigh, took off his helmet, put it back on, and steps back up to the plate.

Tracewski is over to his right to fill up the middle. Kennedy is deep to guard the line. The strike-two pitch on the way: fast ball outside, ball one. Krug started to go after it but held up, and Torborg held the ball high in the air trying to convince Vargo, but Eddy said, "No, sir."

One-and-two the count to Chris Krug. It is 9:41 P.M. on September the ninth. The 1-2 pitch on the way: curve ball tapped foul off to the left of the plate. The Dodgers defensively in this spine-tingling moment: Sandy Koufax and Jeff Torborg—the boys who will try to stop anything hit their way: Wes Parker, Dick Tracewski, Maury Wills and John Kennedy—the outfield of Lou Johnson, Willie Davis and Ron Fairly.

There are 29,000 people in the ball park and a million butterflies; 29,139 paid. Koufax into his windup and the 1-2 pitch: fast ball, fouled back out of play.

In the Dodger dugout Al Ferrara gets up and walks down near the runway and it begins to get tough to be a teammate and sit in the dugout and have to watch.

Sandy back of the rubber now, toes it. All the boys in the bullpen straining to get a better look as they look through the wire fence in left field. One-and-two the count to Chris Krug. Koufax, feet together, now to his windup, and the 1-2 pitch: ball, outside, ball two. [*The crowd boos.*]

A lot of people in the ball park now are starting to see the pitches with their hearts. The pitch was outside. Torborg tried to pull it in over the plate, but Vargo, an experienced umpire, wouldn't go for it. Two-and-two the count to Chris Krug. Sandy reading signs. Into his windup, 2-2 pitch: fast ball got him swinging! Sandy Koufax has struck out twelve. He is two outs away from a perfect game.

Here is Joe Amalfitano to pinch-hit for Don Kessinger. Amalfitano is from southern California, from San Pedro. He was an original bonus boy with the Giants. Joey's been around, and as we mentioned earlier, he has helped to beat the Dodgers twice. And on deck is Harvey Kuenn.

Kennedy is tight to the bag at third. The fast ball for a strike: 0-and-1 with one out in the ninth inning, 1 to 0 Dodgers.

Sandy ready, into his windup, and the strike-one pitch: curve ball tapped foul, 0-and-2, and Amalfitano walks away and shakes himself a little bit, and swings the bat. And Koufax, with a new ball, takes a hitch at his belt and walks behind the mound. I would think that the mound at Dodger Stadium right now is the loneliest place in the world. Sandy, fussing, looks in to get his sign; 0-and-2 to Amalfitano—the strike-two pitch to Joe: fast ball, swung on and missed, strike three!

He is one out away from the promised land, and Harvey Kuenn is coming up. So Harvey Kuenn is batting for Bob Hendley. The time on the scoreboard is 9:44, the date September the ninth, 1965. And Koufax working on veteran Harvey Kuenn.

Sandy into his windup, and the pitch: fast ball for a strike. He has struck out, by the way, five consecutive batters, and this has gone unnoticed.

Sandy ready, and the strike-one pitch: very high, and he lost his hat. He really forced that one. That was only the second time tonight where I have had the feeling that Koufax threw instead of pitched, trying to get that little extra, and that time he tried so hard his hat fell off. He took an extremely long stride toward the plate, and Torborg had to go up to get it. One-and-one to Harvey Kuenn. Now he's ready: fast ball high, ball two.

You can't blame the man for pushing just a little bit now. Sandy backs off, mops his forehead, runs his left index finger along his forehead, dries it off on his left pants-leg. All the while, Kuenn just waiting.

Now Sandy looks in. Into his windup, and the 2-1 pitch to Kuenn: swung on and missed, strike two. It is 9:46 P.M. Two-and-two to Harvey Kuenn—one strike away.

Sandy into his windup. Here's the pitch: *swung on and missed, a perfect game! [Long wait as crowd noise takes over.]*

On the scoreboard in right field it is 9:46 P.M. in the city of the angels, Los Angeles, California, and a crowd of 29,139 just sitting in to see the only pitcher in baseball history to hurl four no-hit, no-run games. He has done it four straight years, and now he capped it: on his fourth no-hitter, he made it a perfect game.

And Sandy Koufax, whose name will always remind you of strikeouts, did it with a flourish. He struck out the last six consecutive batters. So, when he wrote his name in capital letters in the record book, the "K" stands out even more than the "O-U-F-A-X."

The Rocky Road of Pistol Pete

W. C. HEINZ

Every time I sit down with Bill Heinz's wrenching 1958 profile of Pete Reiser, I start to hear "What I Did for Love," the song from *A Chorus Line,* bouncing around inside my cranium. This is a story about what a ballplayer did for love, and what he did for love almost killed him. But he knew no other way.

Heinz told the tale, which ran in *True* magazine, with perfect pitch. He didn't romanticize athletes, he humanized them. His clean prose, his ear for conversation, and his eye for detail presaged the New Journalism that the next generation of writers—Gay Talese, Tom Wolfe, Jimmy Breslin—would give form to.

In the early 1950s, Heinz left daily journalism to stretch out, writing for magazines like *True, Look, Colliers, Sport, Esquire* and *The Saturday Evening Post.* His first novel, *The Professional,* about boxing, was embraced by Hemingway, and his next, *MASH,* co-written with Dr. H. Richard Hornberger, spawned a classic movie and one of the most honored series in television history. At eighty-six, he thankfully found time to collect some of his observations on our athletes and their games into a single volume; *What a Time It Was: The Best of W. C. Heinz on Sports* was published in the spring of 2001.

O ut in Los Angeles," says Garry Schumacher, who was a New York baseball writer for 30 years and is now assistant to Horace Stoneham, president of the San Francisco Giants, "they think Duke Snider is the best center fielder they ever had. They forget Pete Reiser. The Yankees think Mickey Mantle is something new. They forget Reiser, too."

267

Maybe Pete Reiser was the purest ballplayer of all time. I don't know. There is no exact way of measuring such a thing, but when a man of incomparable skills, with full knowledge of what he is doing, destroys those skills and puts his life on the line in pursuit of his endeavor as no other man in his game ever has, perhaps he is the truest of them all.

"Is Pete Reiser there?" I said on the phone.

This was last season, in Kokomo. Kokomo has a population of about 50,000 and a ball club, now affiliated with Los Angeles and called the Dodgers, in the Class D Midwest League. Class D is the bottom of the barrel of organized baseball, and this was the second season that Pete Reiser had managed Kokomo.

"He's not here right now," the woman's voice on the phone said. "The team played a double-header yesterday in Dubuque, and they didn't get in on the bus until 4:30 this morning. Pete just got up a few minutes ago, and he had to go to the doctor's."

"Oh?" I said. "What has he done now?"

In two and a half years in the minors, three seasons of Army ball and ten years in the majors, Pete Reiser was carried off the field 11 times. Nine times he regained consciousness either in the clubhouse or in hospitals. He broke a bone in his right elbow, throwing. He broke both ankles, tore a cartilage in his left knee, ripped the muscles in his left leg, sliding. Seven times he crashed into outfield walls, dislocating his left shoulder, breaking his right collarbone and, five times, ending up in an unconscious heap on the ground. Twice he was beaned, and the few who remember still wonder today how great he might have been.

"I didn't see the old-timers," Bob Cooke, who is sports editor of the New York *Herald Tribune,* was saying recently, "but Pete Reiser was the best ballplayer I ever saw."

"We don't know what's wrong with him," the woman's voice on the phone said now. "He has a pain in his chest and he feels tired all the time, so we sent him to the doctor. There's a game tonight, so he'll be at the ball park about 5 o'clock."

Pete Reiser is 39 years old now. The Cardinals signed him out of the St. Louis Municipal League when he was 15. For two years, because he was so young, he chauffeured for Charley Barrett, who was scouting the Midwest. They had a Cardinal uniform in the car for Pete, and he used to work out with the Class C and D clubs, and one day Branch Rickey, who was general manager of the Cardinals then, called Pete into his office in Sportsman's Park.

"Young man," he said, "you're the greatest young ballplayer I've ever seen, but there is one thing you must remember. Now that you're a professional ballplayer you're in show business. You will perform on the biggest stage in the world, the baseball diamond. Like the actors on Broadway, you'll be expected to put on a great performance every day, no matter how you feel, no matter whether it's too hot or too cold. Never forget that."

Rickey didn't know it at the time, but this was like telling Horatius that, as a professional soldier, he'd be expected someday to stand his ground. Three times Pete sneaked out of hospitals to play. Once he went back into the lineup after doctors warned him that any blow on the head would kill him. For four years he swung the bat and made the throws when it was painful for him just to shave and to comb his hair. In the 1947 World Series he stood on a broken ankle to pinch hit, and it ended with Rickey, then president of the Dodgers, begging him not to play and guaranteeing Pete his 1948 salary if he would just sit that season out.

"That might be the one mistake I made," Pete says now. "Maybe I should have rested that year."

"Pete Reiser?" Leo Durocher, who managed Pete at Brooklyn, was saying recently. "What's he doing now?"

"He's managing Kokomo," Lindsey Nelson, the TV sportcaster, said.

"Kokomo?" Leo said.

"That's right," Lindsey said. "He's riding the buses to places like Lafayette and Michigan City and Mattoon."

"On the buses," Leo said, shaking his head and then smiling at the thought of Pete.

"And some people say," Lindsey said, "that he was the greatest young ballplayer they ever saw."

"No doubt about it," Leo said. "He was the best I ever had, with the possible exception of Mays. At that, he was even faster than Willie." He paused. "So now he's on the buses."

The first time that Leo ever saw Pete on a ball field was in Clearwater that spring of '39. Pete had played one year of Class D in the Cardinal chain and one season of Class D for Brooklyn. Judge Kenesaw Mountain Landis, who was then Baseball Commissioner, had sprung Pete and 72 others from what they called the "Cardinal Chain Gang," and Pete had signed with Brooklyn for $100.

"I didn't care about money then," Pete says. "I just wanted to play."

Pete had never been in a major-league camp before, and he didn't know that at batting practice you hit in rotation. At Clearwater he was grabbing any bat that was handy and cutting in ahead of Ernie Koy or Dolph Camilli or one of the others, and Leo liked that.

One day Leo had a chest cold, so he told Pete to start at shortstop. His first time up he hit a homer off the Cards' Ken Raffensberger, and that was the beginning. He was on base his first 12 times at bat that spring, with three homers, five singles and four walks. His first time against Detroit he homered off Tommy Bridges. His first time against the Yankees he put one over the fence off Lefty Gomez.

Durocher played Pete at shortstop in 33 games that spring. The Dodgers barnstormed North with the Yankees, and one night Joe McCarthy, who was managing the Yankees, sat down next to Pete on the train.

"Reiser," he said, "you're going to play for me."

"How can I play for you?" Pete said. "I'm with the Dodgers."

"We'll get you," McCarthy said. "I'll tell Ed Barrow, and you'll be a Yankee."

The Yankees offered $100,000 and five ballplayers for Pete. The Dodgers turned it down, and the day the season opened at Ebbets Field, Larry MacPhail, who was running things in Brooklyn, called Pete on the clubhouse phone and told him to report to Elmira.

"It was an hour before game time," Pete says, "and I started to take off my uniform and I was shaking all over. Leo came in and said: 'What's the matter? You scared?' I said: 'No. MacPhail is sending me to Elmira.' Leo got on the phone and they had a hell of a fight. Leo said he'd quit, and MacPhail said he'd fire him—and I went to Elmira.

"One day I'm making a throw and I heard something pop. Every day my arm got weaker and they sent me to Johns Hopkins and took X rays. Dr. George Bennett told me: 'Your arm's broken.' When I came to after the operation, my throat was sore and there was an ice pack on it. I said: 'What happened? Your knife slip?' They said: 'We took your tonsils out while we were operating on your arm.' "

Pete's arm was in a cast from the first of May until the end of July. His first two weeks out of the cast he still couldn't straighten the arm, but a month later he played ten games as a left-handed outfielder until Dr. Bennett stopped him.

"But I can't straighten my right arm," Pete said.

"Take up bowling," the doctor said.

When he bowled, though, Pete used first one arm and then the other. Every day that the weather allowed he went out into the back yard and practiced throwing a rubber ball left-handed against a wall. Then he went to Fairgrounds Park and worked on the long throw, left-handed, with a baseball.

"At Clearwater that next spring," he says, "Leo saw me in the outfield throwing left-handed, and he said: 'What do you think you're doin'?' I said: 'Hell, I had to be ready. Now I can throw as good with my left arm as I could with my right.' He said: 'You can do more things as a right-handed ballplayer. I can bring you into the infield. Go out there and cut loose with that right arm.' I did and it was okay, but I had that insurance."

So at 5 o'clock I took a cab from the hotel in Kokomo to the ball park on the edge of town. It seats about 2,200, 1,500 of them in the white-painted fairgrounds grandstand along the first base line, and the rest in chairs behind the screen and in bleachers along the other line.

I watched them take batting practice; trim, strong young kids with their dreams, I knew, of someday getting up there where Pete once was, and I listened to their kidding. I watched the groundskeeper open the concession booth and clean out the electric popcorn machine. I read the signs on the outfield walls, advertising the Mid-West Towel and Linen Service, Basil's Nite Club, the Hoosier Iron Works, UAW Local 292 and the Around the Clock Pizza Café. I watched the Dubuque kids climbing out of their bus, carrying their uniforms on wire coat hangers.

"Here comes Pete now," I heard the old guy setting up the ticket box at the gate say.

When Pete came through the gate he was walking like an old man. In 1941 the Dodgers trained in Havana, and one day they clocked him, in his baseball uniform and regular spikes, at 9.8 for 100 yards. Five years later the Cleveland Indians were bragging about George Case and the Washington Senators had Gil Coan. The Dodgers offered to bet $1,000 that Reiser was the fastest man in baseball, and now it was taking him forever to walk to me, his shoulders stooped, his whole body heavier now, and Pete just slowly moving one foot ahead of the other.

"Hello," he said, shaking hands but his face solemn. "How are you?"

"Fine," I said, "but what's the matter with you?"

"I guess it's my heart," he said.

"When did you first notice this?"

"About eleven days ago. I guess I was working out too hard. All of a sudden I felt this pain in my chest and I got weak. I went into the clubhouse and lay down on the bench, but I've had the same pain and I'm weak ever since."

"What did the doctor say?"

"He says it's lucky I stopped that day when I did. He says I should be in a hospital right now, because if I exert myself or even make a quick motion I might go—just like that."

He snapped his fingers. "He scared me," he said. "I'll admit it. I'm scared."

"What are you planning to do?"

"I'm going home to St. Louis. My wife works for a doctor there, and he'll know a good heart specialist."

"When will you leave?"

"Well, I can't just leave the ball club. I called Brooklyn, and they're sending a replacement for me, but he won't be here until tomorrow."

"How will you get to St. Louis?"

"It's about 300 miles," Pete says. "The doctor says I shouldn't fly or go by train, because if anything happens to me they can't stop and help me. I guess I'll have to drive."

"I'll drive you," I said.

Trying to get to sleep in the hotel that night I was thinking that maybe, standing there in that little ball park, Pete Reiser had admitted out loud for the first time in his life that he was scared. I was thinking of 1941, his first full year with the Dodgers. He was beaned twice and crashed his first wall and still hit .343 to be the first rookie and the youngest ballplayer to win the National League batting title. He tied Johnny Mize with 39 doubles, led in triples, runs scored, total bases and slugging average, and they were writing on the sports pages that he might be the new Ty Cobb.

"Dodgers Win On Reiser HR," the headlines used to say. "Reiser Stars As Brooklyn Lengthens Lead."

"Any manager in the National League," Arthur Patterson wrote one day in the New York *Herald Tribune*, "would give up his best man to obtain Pete Reiser. On every bench they're talking about him. Rival players watch him take his cuts during batting practice, announce when he's going to make a throw to the plate or third base during outfield drill. They just whistle their amazement when he scoots down the first base line on an infield dribbler or a well-placed bunt."

He was beaned the first time at Ebbets Field five days after the season started. A sidearm fast ball got away from Ike Pearson of the Phillies, and Pete came to at 11:30 that night in Peck Memorial Hospital.

"I was lying in bed with my uniform on," he told me once, "and I couldn't figure it out. The room was dark, with just a little night light, and then I saw a mirror and I walked over to it and lit the light and I had a black eye and a black streak down the side of my nose. I said to myself: 'What happened to me?' Then I remembered.

"I took a shower and walked around the room, and the next morning the doctor came in. He looked me over, and he said: 'We'll keep you here for five or six more days under observation.' I said: 'Why?' He said: 'You've had a serious head injury. If you tried to get out of bed right now, you'd fall down.' I said: 'If I can get up and walk around this room, can I get out?' The doc said: 'All right, but you won't be able to do it.' "

Pete got out of bed, the doctor standing ready to catch him. He walked around the room. "I've been walkin' the floor all night," Pete said.

The doctor made Pete promise that he wouldn't play ball for a week, but Pete went right to the ball park. He got a seat behind the Brooklyn dugout and Durocher spotted him.

"How do you feel?" Leo said.

"Not bad," Pete said.

"Get your uniform on," Leo said.

"I'm not supposed to play," Pete said.

"I'm not gonna play you," Leo said. "Just sit on the bench. It'll make our guys feel better to see that you're not hurt."

Pete suited up and went out and sat on the bench. In the eighth inning it was tied, 7–7. The Dodgers had the bases loaded, and there was Ike Pearson again, coming in to relieve.

"Pistol," Leo said to Pete, "get the bat."

In the press box the baseball writers watched Pete. They wanted to see if he'd stand right in there. After a beaning they are all entitled to shy, and many of them do. Pete hit the first pitch into the center-field stands, and Brooklyn won, 11 to 7.

"I could just barely trot around the bases," Pete said when I asked him about it. "I was sure dizzy."

Two weeks later they were playing the Cardinals, and Enos Slaughter hit one and Pete turned in center field and started to run. He made the catch, but he hit his head and his tail bone on that corner near the exit gate.

His head was cut, and when he came back to the bench they also saw blood coming through the seat of his pants. They took him into the clubhouse and pulled his pants down and the doctor put a metal clamp on the cut.

"Just don't slide," he told Pete. "You can get it sewed up after the game."

In August of that year big Paul Erickson was pitching for the Cubs and Pete took another one. Again he woke up in a hospital. The Dodgers were having some pretty good beanball contests with the Cubs that season, and Judge Landis came to see Pete the next day.

"Do you think that man tried to bean you?" he asked Pete.

"No sir," Pete said. "I lost the pitch."

"I was there," Landis said, "and I heard them holler: 'Stick it in his ear.' "

"That was just bench talk," Pete said. "I lost the pitch."

He left the hospital the next morning. The Dodgers were going to St. Louis after the game, and Pete didn't want to be left in Chicago.

Pete always says that the next year, 1942, was the year of his downfall, and the worst of it happened on one play. It was early July and Pete and the Dodgers were tearing the league apart. In a fourth-game series in Cincinnati he got 19 for 21. In a Sunday double-header in Chicago he went 5 for 5 in the first game, walked three times in the second game and got a hit the one time they pitched to him. He was hitting .381, and they were writing in the papers that he might end up hitting .400.

When they came into St. Louis the Dodgers were leading by ten and a half games. When they took off for Pittsburgh they left three games of that lead and Pete Reiser behind them.

"We were in the twelfth inning, no score, two outs and Slaughter hit it off Whit Wyatt," Pete says. "It was over my head and I took off. I caught it and missed that flagpole by two inches and hit the wall and dropped the ball. I had the instinct to throw it to Peewee Reese, and we just missed gettin' Slaughter at the plate, and they won, 1–0.

"I made one step to start off the field and I woke up the next morning in St. John's Hospital. My head was bandaged, and I had an awful headache."

Dr. Robert Hyland, who was Pete's personal physician, announced to the newspapers that Pete would be out for the rest of the season. "Look, Pete," Hyland told him. "I'm your personal friend. I'm advising you not to play any more baseball this year."

"I don't like hospitals, though," Pete was telling me once, "so after two days I took the bandage off and got up. The room started to spin, but I got dressed and I took off. I snuck out, and I took a train to Pittsburgh and I went to the park.

"Leo saw me and he said: 'Go get your uniform on, Pistol.' I said: 'Not tonight, Skipper.' Leo said: 'Aw, I'm not gonna let you hit. I want these guys to see you. It'll give 'em that little spark they need. Besides, it'll change the pitching plans on that other bench when they see you sittin' here in uniform'."

In the fourteenth inning the Dodgers had a runner on second and Ken Heintzelman, the left-hander, came in for the Pirates. He walked Johnny Rizzo, and Durocher had run out of pinch hitters.

"Damn," Leo was saying, walking up and down. "I want to win this one. Who can I use? Anybody here who can hit?"

Pete walked up to the bat rack. He pulled out his stick. "You got yourself a hitter," he said to Leo.

He walked up there and hit a line drive over the second baseman's head that was good for three bases. The two runs scored, and Pete rounded first base and collapsed.

"When I woke up I was in a hospital again," he says. "I could just make out that somebody was standin' there and then I saw it was Leo. He said: 'You awake?' I said: 'Yep.' He said: 'By God, we beat 'em! How do you feel?' I said: 'How do you think I feel?' He said: 'Aw, you're better with one leg, and one eye than anybody else I've got.' I said: 'Yeah, and that's the way I'll end up—on one leg and with one eye.'

"I'd say I lost the pennant for us that year," Pete says now, although he still hit .310 for the season. "I was dizzy most of the time and I couldn't see fly balls. I mean balls I could have put in my pocket, I couldn't get near. Once in Brooklyn when Mort Cooper was pitching for the Cards I was seeing two baseballs coming up there. Babe Pinelli was umpiring behind the plate, and a couple of times he stopped the game and asked me if I was all right. So the Cards beat us out the last two days of the season."

The business office of the Kokomo ball club is the dining room of a man named Jim Deets, who sells insurance and is also the business manager of the club. His wife, in addition to keeping house, mothering six small kids, boarding Pete, an outfielder from Venezuela and a shortstop from the Dominican Republic, is also the club secretary.

"How do you feel this morning?" I asked Pete. He was sitting at the dining-room table, in a sweat shirt and a pair of light-brown slacks, typing the game report of the night before to send it to Brooklyn.

"A little better," he said.

Pete has a worn, green 1950 Chevy, and it took us eight and a half hours to get to St. Louis. I'd ask him how the pain in his chest was and he'd say that it wasn't bad or it wasn't so good, and I'd get him to talking again about

Durocher or about his time in the Army. Pete played under five managers at Brooklyn, Boston, Pittsburgh and Cleveland, and Durocher is his favorite.

"He has a great mind, and not just for baseball," Pete said. "Once he sat down to play gin with Jack Benny, and after they'd played four cards Leo read Benny's whole hand to him. Benny said: 'How can you do that?' Leo said: 'If you're playin' your cards right, and I give you credit for that, you have to be holding those others.' Benny said: 'I don't want to play with this guy.'

"One spring at Clearwater there was a pool table in a room off the lobby. One night Hugh Casey and a couple of other guys and I were talking with Leo. We said: 'Gee, there's a guy in there and we've been playin' pool with him for a couple of nights, but last night he had a real hot streak.' Leo said: 'How much he take you for?' We figured it out and it was $2,000. Leo said: 'Point him out to me.'

"We went in and pointed the guy out and Leo walked up to him and said: 'Put all your money on the table. We're gonna shoot for it.' The guy said: 'I never play like that.' Leo said: 'You will tonight. Pick your own game.' Leo took him for $4,000, and then he threw him out. Then he paid us back what we'd gone for, and he said: 'Now, let that be a lesson. That guy is a hustler from New York. The next time it happens I won't bail you out.' Leo hadn't had a cue in his hands for years."

It was amazing that they took Pete into the Army. He had wanted to enlist in the Navy, but the doctors looked him over and told him none of the services could accept him. Then his draft board sent him to Jefferson Barracks in the winter of 1943, and the doctors there turned him down.

"I'm sittin' on a bench with the other guys who've been rejected," he was telling me, "and a captain comes in and says: 'Which one of you is Reiser?' I stood up and I said: 'I am.' In front of everybody he said: 'So you're trying to pull a fast one, are you? At a time like this, with a war going on, you came in here under a false name. What do you mean, giving your name as Harold Patrick Reiser? Your name's Pete Reiser, and you're the ballplayer, aren't you?' I said: 'I'm the ballplayer and they call me Pete, but my right name is Harold Patrick Reiser.' The captain says: 'I apologize. Sergeant, fingerprint him. This man is in.'"

They sent him to Fort Riley, Kansas. It was early April and raining and they were on bivouac, and Pete woke up in a hospital. "What happened?" he said.

"You've got pneumonia," the doctor said. "You've been a pretty sick boy for six days. You'll be all right, but we've been looking you over. How did you ever get into this Army?"

"When I get out of the hospital," Pete was telling me, "I'm on the board for a discharge and I'm waitin' around for about a week, and still nobody there knows who I am. All of a sudden one morning a voice comes over the bitch box in the barracks. It says: 'Private Reiser, report to headquarters immediately.' I think: 'Well, I'm out now.'

"I got over there and the colonel wants to see me. I walk in and give my good salute and he says: 'Sit down, Harold.' I sit down and he says: 'Your name really isn't Harold, is it?' I say: 'Yes, it is, sir.' He says: 'But that isn't what they call you where you're well known, is it? You're Pete Reiser the ballplayer, aren't you?' I say: 'Yes, sir.' He says: 'I thought so. Now, I've got your discharge papers right there, but we've got a pretty good ball club and we'd like you on it. We'll make a deal. You say nothing, and you won't have to do anything but play ball. How about it?' I said: 'Suppose I don't want to stay in?'

"He picked my papers up off his desk," Pete was saying, "and he tore 'em right up in my face. I can still hear that 'zip' when he tore 'em. He said: 'You see, you have no choice.'

"Then he picked up the phone and said something and in a minute a general came in. I jumped up and the colonel said: 'Don't bother to salute, Pete.' Then he said to the general: 'Major, this is Pete Reiser, the great Dodger ballplayer. He was up for a medical discharge, but he's decided to stay here and play ball for us.'

"So, the general says: 'My, what a patriotic thing for you to do, young man. That's wonderful. Wonderful.' I'm sittin' there, and when the general goes out the colonel says: 'That major, he's all right.' I said: 'But he's a general. How come you call him a major?' The colonel says: 'Well, in the regular Army he's a major and I'm a full colonel. The only reason I don't outrank him now is that I've got heart trouble. He knows it, but I never let him forget it. I always call him major.' I thought: 'What kind of an Army am I in?' "

Joe Gantenbein, the Athletics' outfielder, and George Scharein, the Phillies' infielder, were on that team with Pete, and they won the state and national semipro titles. By the time the season was over, however, the order came down to hold up all discharges.

The next season there were 17 major-league ballplayers on the Fort Riley club, and they played four nights a week for the war workers in Wichita. Pete hit a couple of walls, and the team made such a joke of the national semipro tournament that an order came down from Washington to break up the club.

"Considering what a lot of guys did in the war," Pete says, "I had no complaints, but five times I was up for discharge, and each time something happened. From Riley they sent me to Camp Livingston. From there they sent me to New York Special Services for twelve hours and I end up in Camp Lee, Virginia, in May of 1945.

"The first one I meet there is the general. He says: 'Reiser, I saw you on the list and I just couldn't pass you up.' I said: 'What about my discharge?' He says: 'That will have to wait. I have a lot of celebrities down here, but I want a good baseball team.'"

Johnny Lindell, of the Yankees, and Dave Philley, of the White Sox, were on the club and Pete played left field. Near the end of the season he went after a foul fly for the third out of the last inning, and he went right through a temporary wooden fence and rolled down a 25-foot embankment.

"I came to in the hospital, with a dislocated right shoulder," he says, "and the general came over to see me and he said: 'That was one of the greatest displays of courage I've ever seen, to ignore your future in baseball just to win a ball game for Camp Lee.' I said: 'Thanks.'

"Now it's November and the war is over, but they're still shippin' guys out, and I'm on the list to go. I report to the overseas major, and he looks at my papers and says: 'I can't send you overseas. With everything that's wrong with you, you shouldn't even be in this Army. I'll have you out in three hours.' In three hours, sure enough, I've got those papers in my hand, stamped, and I'm startin' out the door. Runnin' up to me comes a Red Cross guy. He says: 'I can get you some pretty good pension benefits for the physical and mental injuries you've sustained.' I said: 'You can?' He said: 'Yes, you're entitled to them.' I said: 'Good. You get 'em. You keep 'em. I'm goin' home.'"

When we got to St. Louis that night I drove Pete to his house and the next morning I picked him up and drove him to see the heart specialist. He was in there for two hours, and when he came out he was walking slower than ever.

"No good," he said. "I have to go to the hospital for five days for observation."

"What does he think?"

"He says I'm done puttin' on that uniform. I'll have to get a desk job."

Riding to the hospital I wondered if that heart specialist knew who he was tying to that desk job. In 1946, the year he came out of the Army, Pete led the league when he stole 34 bases, 13 more than the runner-up Johnny Hopp of the Braves. He also set a major-league record that still stands, when he stole home eight times.

"Nine times," he said once. "In Chicago I stole home and Magerkurth hollered: 'You're out!' Then he dropped his voice and he said: '_____, I missed it.' He'd already had his thumb in the air. I had nine out of nine."

I suppose somebody will beat that some day, but he'll never top the way Pete did it. That was the year he knocked himself out again trying for a diving catch, dislocated his left shoulder, ripped the muscles in his left leg and broke his left ankle.

"Whitey Kurowski hit one in the seventh inning at Ebbets Field," he was telling me. "I dove for it and woke up in the clubhouse. I was in Peck Memorial for four days. It really didn't take much to knock me out in those days. I was comin' apart all over. When I dislocated my shoulder they popped it back in, and Leo said: 'Hell, you'll be all right. You don't throw with it anyway.' "

That was the year the Dodgers tied with the Cardinals for the pennant and dropped the play-off. Pete wasn't there for those two games. He was in Peck Memorial again.

"I'd pulled a Charley horse in my left leg," Pete was saying. "It's the last two weeks of the season, and I'm out for four days. We've got the winning run on third, two outs in the ninth and Leo sends me up. He says: 'If you don't hit it good, don't run and hurt your leg.'

"The first pitch was a knockdown and, when I ducked, the ball hit the bat and went down the third base line, as beautiful a bunt as you've ever seen. Well, Ebbets Field is jammed. Leo has said: 'Don't run.' But this is a big game. I take off for first, and we win and I've ripped the muscles from my ankle to my hip. Leo says: 'You shouldn't have done it.'

"Now it's the last three days of the season and we're a game ahead of the Cards and we're playin' the Phillies in Brooklyn. Leo says to me: 'It's now or never. I don't think we can win it without you.' The first two up are outs and I single to right. There's Charley Dressen, coachin' on third, with the steal sign. I start to get my lead, and a pitcher named Charley Schanz is workin' and he throws an ordinary lob over to first. My leg is stiff and I slide and my heel spike catches the bag and I hear it snap.

"Leo comes runnin' out. He says: 'Come on. You're all right.' I said: 'I think it's broken.' He says: 'It ain't stickin' out.' They took me to Peck Memorial, and it was broken."

We went to St. Luke's Hospital in St. Louis. In the main office they told Pete to go over to a desk where a gray-haired, semistout woman was sitting at a typewriter. She started to book Pete in, typing his answer on the form. "What is your occupation, Mr. Reiser?" she said.

"Baseball," Pete said.

"Have you ever been hospitalized before?"

"Yes," Pete said.

In 1946 the Dodgers played an exhibition game in Springfield, Missouri. When the players got off the train there was a young radio announcer there, and he was grabbing them one at a time and asking them where they thought they'd finish that year.

"In first place," Reese and Casey and Dixie Walker and the rest were saying. "On top" . . . "We'll win it."

"And here comes Pistol Pete Reiser!" the announcer said. "Where do you think you'll finish this season, Pete?"

"In Peck Memorial Hospital," Pete said.

After the 1946 season Brooklyn changed the walls at Ebbets Field. They added boxes, cutting 40 feet off left field and dropping center field from 420 to 390 feet. Pete had made a real good start that season in center, and on June 5 the Dodgers were leading the Pirates by three runs in the sixth inning when Culley Rikard hit one.

"I made my turn and ran," Pete says, "and, where I thought I still had that thirty feet, I didn't."

"The crowd," Al Laney wrote the next day in the New York *Herald Tribune,* "which watched silently while Reiser was being carried away, did not know that he had held onto the ball . . . Rikard circled the bases, but Butch Henline, the umpire, who ran to Reiser, found the ball still in Reiser's glove. . . . Two outs were posted on the scoreboard after play was resumed. Then the crowd let out a tremendous roar."

In the Brooklyn clubhouse the doctor called for a priest, and the Last Rites of the Church were administered to Pete. He came to, but lapsed into unconsciousness again and woke up at 3 A.M. in Peck Memorial.

For eight days he couldn't move. After three weeks they let him out, and he made that next western trip with the Dodgers. In Pittsburgh he was working out in the outfield before the game when Clyde King, chasing a fungo, ran into him and Pete woke up in the clubhouse.

"I went back to the Hotel Schenley and lay down," he says. "After the game I got up and had dinner with Peewee. We were sittin' on the porch, and I scratched my head and I felt a lump there about as big as half a golf ball. I told Peewee to feel it and he said: 'Gosh!' I said: 'I don't think that's supposed to be like that.' He said: 'Hell, no!' "

Pete went up to Rickey's room and Rickey called his pilot and had Pete flown to Johns Hopkins in Baltimore. They operated on him for a blood clot.

"You're lucky," the doctor told him. "If it had moved just a little more you'd have been gone."

Pete was unable to hold even a pencil. He had double vision and, when he tried to take a single step, he became dizzy. He stayed for three weeks and then went home for almost a month.

"It was August," he says, "and Brooklyn was fightin' for another pennant. I thought if I could play the last two months it might make the difference, so I went back to Johns Hopkins. The doctor said: 'You've made a remarkable recovery.' I said: 'I want to play.' He said: 'I can't okay that. The slightest blow on the head can kill you.'"

Pete played. He worked out for four days, pinch hit a couple of times and then, in the Polo Grounds, made a diving catch in left field. They carried him off, and in the clubhouse he was unable to recognize anyone.

Pete was still having dizzy spells when the Dodgers went into the 1947 Series against the Yankees. In the third game he walked in the first inning, got the steal sign and, when he went into second, felt his right ankle snap. At the hospital they found it was broken.

"Just tape it, will you?" Pete said.

"I want to put a cast on it," the doctor said.

"If you do," Pete said, "they'll give me a dollar-a-year contract next season."

The next day he was back on the bench. Bill Bevens was pitching for the Yankees and, with two out in the ninth, it looked like he was going to pitch the first no-hitter in World Series history.

"Aren't you going to volunteer to hit?" Burt Shotton, who was managing Brooklyn, said to Pete.

Al Gionfriddo was on first and Bucky Harris, who was managing the Yankees, ordered Pete walked. Eddie Miksis ran for him, and when Cookie Lavagetto hit that double, the two runs scored and Brooklyn won, 3–2.

"The next day," Pete says, "the sports writers were second-guessing Harris for putting me on when I represented the winning run. Can you imagine what they'd have said if they knew I had a broken ankle?"

At the end of that season Rickey had the outfield walls at Ebbets Field padded with one-inch foam rubber for Pete, but he never hit them again. He had headaches most of the time and played little. Then he was traded to

Boston, and in two season there he hit the wall a couple of times. Twice his left shoulder came out while he was making diving catches. Pittsburgh picked Pete up in 1951, and the next year he played into July with Cleveland and that was the end of it.

Between January and September of 1953, Pete dropped $40,000 in the used-car business in St. Louis, and then he got a job in a lumber mill for $100 a week. In the winter of 1955 he wrote Brooklyn asking for a part-time job as a scout, and on March 1, Buzzy Bavasi, the Dodger vice-president, called him on the phone.

"How would you like a manager's job?" Buzzy said.

"I'll take it," Pete said.

"I haven't even told you where it is. It's Thomasville, Georgia, in Class D."

"I don't care," Pete said. "I'll take it.

At Vero Beach that spring, Mike Gaven wrote a piece about Pete in the New York *Journal American.*

"Even in the worn gray uniform of the Class D Thomasville, Georgia, club," Mike wrote, "Pete Reiser looks, acts and talks like a big leaguer. The Dodgers pitied Pete when they saw him starting his comeback effort after not having handled a ball for two and a half years. They lowered their heads when they saw him in a chow line with a lot of other bushers, but the old Pistol held his head high. . . ."

The next spring, Sid Friedlander, of the New York *Post,* saw Pete at Vero and wrote a column about him managing Kokomo. The last thing I saw about him in the New York papers was a small item out of Tipton, Indiana, saying that the bus carrying the Kokomo team had collided with a car and Pete was in a hospital in Kokomo with a back injury.

"Managing," Pete was saying in that St. Louis hospital, "you try to find out how your players are thinking. At Thomasville one night one of my kids made a bad throw. After the game I said to him: 'What were you thinking while that ball was coming to you?' He said: 'I was saying to myself that I hoped I could make a good throw.' I said: 'Sit down.' I tried to explain to him the way you have to think. You know how I used to think?"

"Yes," I said, "but you tell me."

"I was always sayin': 'Hit it to me. Just hit it to me. I'll make the catch. I'll make the throw.' When I was on base I was always lookin' over and sayin': 'Give me the steal sign. Give me the sign. Let me go.' That's the way you have to think."

"Pete," I said, "now that it's all over, do you ever think that if you hadn't played it as hard as you did, there's no telling how great you might have been or how much money you might have made?"

"Never," Pete said. "It was my way of playin'. If I hadn't played that way I wouldn't even have been whatever I was. God gave me those legs and the speed, and when they took me into the walls that's the way it had to be. I couldn't play any other way."

A technician came in with an electrocardiograph. She was a thin, dark-haired woman and she set it up by the bed and attached one of the round metal disks to Pete's left wrist and started to attach another to his left ankle.

"Aren't you kind of young to be having pains in your chest?" she said.

"I've led a fast life," Pete said.

On the way back to New York I kept thinking how right Pete was. To tell a man who is this true that there is another way for him to do it is to speak a lie. You cannot ask him to change his way of going, because it makes him what he is.

Three days after I got home I had a message to call St. Louis. I heard the phone ring at the other end and Pete answered. "I'm out!" he said.

"Did they let you out, or did you sneak out again?" I said.

"They let me out," he said. "It's just a strained heart muscle, I guess. My heart itself is all right."

"That's wonderful."

"I can manage again. In a couple of days I can go back to Kokomo."

If his voice had been higher he would have sounded like a kid at Christmas.

"What else did they say?" I said.

"Well, they say I have to take it easy."

"Do me a favor," I said.

"What?"

"Take their advice. This time, please take it easy."

"I will," he said. "I'll take it easy."

If he does it will be the first time.

One Vote for Morganna

RED SMITH

The summer that I graduated from high school, my father began to bring home at my request Women's Wear Daily, the fashion-industry newspaper, several times a week. I had no interest in the rag business. I was just devoted to its sports columnist.

I began reading Red Smith (1905–1982), the most elegant of sports stylists, on the sports pages of the *New York Herald Tribune* in the early 1960s. He became habit. And then when the *Trib* and its successor, the *World Journal Tribune,* disappeared from New York in 1967, so did Smith's byline . . . until *Women's Wear Daily* picked up his nationally syndicated column a year later. The pages of *WWD* became his New York home until the *New York Times* brought him in from the cold in 1971. I haven't touched a copy of *WWD* since.

The second sports columnist to win a Pulitzer Prize, Smith liked to say that writing was easy; you just open a vein and bleed. He gave enough blood to transfuse a few generations of readers; his clear, smooth prose read effortlessly. He was so consistent, so superb for so long, that to pick an appropriate sample of his work, all I had to do was throw everything he'd ever written on baseball into a hat, reach in, and go with whatever I picked out. If this column featuring an encounter between Reds catcher Johnny Bench and Morganna, the Kissing Bandit, seems a bit out of left field, it's just proof of how versatile the incomparable Smith could be.

Cincinnati—the game was one putout old and Tom Seaver had missed the strike zone with a pitch to Carl Yastrzemski when Morganna the Wild One (44–23–37) vaulted out of the grandstand in short left field. A private cop named Thomas Burton caught her like a pop foul and they went to the mat with his arms wrapped around 37.

As they struggled to their feet, a clutch of Cincinnati's Finest swooped. Morganna was blindsided by one of the fuzz who wound the long arms of the law around 44, found a firm handhold, and did not let go.

Kicking and squirming under callused male hands, the helpless bit of fluff was hustled to an exit, yet another victim of police brutality. All the sweet thing wanted was to kiss Seaver's catcher, John Bench, through his mask. Yet they treated her like a common felon.

There will be repercussions, for this is one case where the Administration cannot plead ignorance. Sitting right there watching with a mouthful of teeth was Richard Milhous Nixon himself, and he did not lift a finger. Neither did Pat nor Julie nor David nor Rep. Robert Taft, Jr., nor Bowie Kuhn nor president Joe Cronin of the American League nor president Chub Feeney of the National League nor Chub's predecessor Warren Giles nor the hundred or so Secret Service men and six umpires who witnessed the sorry affair.

For the benefit of readers on Mars, it should be explained that Morganna Roberts is a stripper who has been undressing in a joint across the Ohio River in Newport, Ky. She is a shy, timorous creature whose distaste for publicity drives her into baseball parks where she has smooched Pete Rose of the Reds, Clete Boyer of the Braves, Wes Parker of the Dodgers, Billy Cowan of the Angels, Frank Howard of the Senators, and a roundball player named Bob Verga.

Ads in the local papers had promised that she would be in Riverfront Stadium last night to ornament the 41st All-Star Game and—if the vernacular may be forgiven—she did indeed shape up. She wore a tousled black wig and dark glasses, with her interesting contours encased in a green sweatshirt and brown bell-bottoms.

Her trouble, and that of most of the batters on the field, was overeagerness. Through the early innings the batters twitched and lunged and swung and missed, especially when Seaver or Jim Merritt or Jim Palmer or Sam McDowell was pitching.

Like them, Morganna simply couldn't wait. She should have held her fire until, say, the eighth inning when punishing heat and smothering boredom had put the crowd of 51,838 into a somnolent stupor. At that point the show needed her desperately and she would have been cheered to the sultry skies.

Instead, she chose to make her pitch soon after the arrival of the Presidential party when security forces were still on the alert for infiltrating Democrats.

Due in part to the misfeasance of Cincinnati deities, the first eight innings were tedious and tidy. "Tricky Dick loves the big red machine," read one of the bedsheet banners that festooned the new playpen in celebration of Cincinnati's 10-game lead in the National League West. But over the normal nine-inning distance, the only contributions from Tony Perez, Pete Rose, and John Bench, all cogs in the machine, were seven strikeouts.

It was enough to make Nixon burn his card of honorary membership in the Baseball Writers Association of America, but he contented himself by explaining the game to the baseball commissioner and shaking hands. In the fifth inning when there were no unshaken paws left within reach, Ed Roush, who made the Hall of Fame as a Cincinnati outfielder, was brought to the royal box to have his knuckles clutched. In the ninth the President risked a hernia hanging over the rail to press the flesh of Al Barlick, the plate umpire.

At this point the Americans led, 4–1, and could taste their first victory in eight year. Bud Harrelson, the littlest Met, had singled and scored the Nationals' only run. In the ninth the Giants' Dick Dietz smashed a home run, Harrelson singled again, and by the time the side was out the score was tied.

Not until the 12th inning did Rose score the Nationals' winning run. The job required three suffocating hours and 19 sweltering minutes. Few husbands would be surprised to hear that Mrs. Nixon mentioned the time of game later when she inspected the seat of her pretty red plaid frock.

Yastrzemski made four hits, scored a run, drove in another, and was chosen most valuable player in a pressbox poll.

Morganna got one vote and Mr. Nixon none, even though he wore his arm out throwing a firstball to Bill Freehan for the American League, a first ball to Bench for the National League, and three balls for deserving Republicans in the second deck of stands.

Considering how much grimacing effort he put into his performance, this must have been his most galling defeat since the California gubernatorial election of 1962. He is expected to call a news conference when the soreness leaves his shoulder and turn in his baseball writer's card. He will, informed sources report, tell the writers:

"You won't have Nixon to kick around anymore."

Yogi

ROY BLOUNT, JR.

Even as a kid, I knew my position. It was behind the plate.

I had no choice. My father, a pretty good pitcher in industrial and semi-pro leagues around New York, needed someone to throw to when he got home from work. I was that someone. That I could handle his stuff became the prime link, beyond genetics, that connected us.

At first, I hated catching—the hot, sweaty mask; the oppressiveness of chest protector and shin guards; the foul tips; the collisions—but I grew, over time, to love the job as I, growing up, grew with it. I loved the authority. The control. The opportunity to look out while everyone else on the field in the same uniform was looking in. The toughness ascribed to it. The respect that toughness engendered. Yogi Berra. The "8" I would wear on my back because that number was Yog's. Of course, I had no idea back in my halcyon days how deeply rooted I'd be planting the seeds of my mid-life arthritis; every Yin has its Yang. As Yog himself might have explained the catcher's life, "It gets late early out there."

When Yogi returned to manage the Yankees in 1984, *Sports Illustrated* asked humorist Roy Blount, Jr. to assess the import. Berra and Blount? It was a match made in Nirvana.

★　　★　　★　　★　　★

> *Yoga consists in the stopping of spontaneous activities of the mind-stuff.*
> —YOGI PANTANJALI

> *How can you think and hit at the same time?*
> —YOGI BERRA

I s the new manager of the New York Yankees a true yogi?

That may seem an odd question. Lawrence Peter Berra is the most widely known Yogi in the world, or at least in those parts of the world where baseball is played. (When the Yankees appeared in Tokyo in 1955, "the biggest ovation, including screams from bobby-soxers, went to Yogi Berra," according to the Associated Press.) He loves to sit around reflecting in his undershorts. He almost never loses his cool, except in ritual observances with umpires, during which he has been seen to levitate several inches. And he's being counted on to bring peace and unity—*yoga* is Sanskrit for union—to baseball's most rancorous team.

Yet, yogis don't tend to appear in a form that is 5′7 1/2″tall and weighs 190 pounds. Jimmy Cannon, the late sportswriter, said Berra was built like a bull penguin. When Larry MacPhail, the Yankee president from 1945 to 1947, first saw Berra, he was reminded of "the bottom man on an unemployed acrobatic team."

Whereas yoga springs from Hinduism, Berra is a Roman Catholic who tries to attend Mass every Sunday and who once visited the Pope. Yogi told of his meeting with Pope John XXIII in a now-famous interview:

Reporter: "I understand you had an audience with the Pope."

Yogi: "No, but I saw him."

Reporter: "Did you get to talk to him?"

Yogi: "I sure did. We had a nice little chat."

Reporter: "What did he say?"

Yogi: "You know, he must read the papers a lot, because he said, 'Hello, Yogi.' "

Reporter: "And what did you say?"

Yogi: "I said, 'Hello, Pope.' "

Yoga is an Eastern study, and Berra is Midwestern Italian. Once, at a dinner held so Japanese journalists could get together with American baseball stars, a Tokyo newspaper editor was ceremoniously reading off a list of Japanese delicacies that he was sure his American guests would enjoy. "Don't you have any bread?" Berra interrupted.

Berra's parents were born in Italy. (On his passport, Yogi is Lorenzo Pietro.) He was born in St. Louis, and his sayings are in the American grain. For instance, after visiting the Louvre and being asked whether he liked the paintings there, Berra said, "Yeah, if you like paintings." Another time, after attending a performance of *Tosca* in Milan, he said, "It was pretty good. Even the music was nice." These remarks are less in the tradition of the *Bhagavad-Gita* than in that of Mark Twain, who observed that the music of Richard Wagner was "better than it sounds." Berra is also supposed to have said, after someone mentioned that a Jewish lord mayor had been elected in Dublin, "Yeah. Only in America can a thing like this happen."

Berra hasn't followed the traditional regimen of a person who gives his life over to yoga. He has never attempted to assume the Lotus, the Plough, the Fish or the touching-the-top-of-your-head-with-the-soles-of-your-feet position. In his playing days, it's true, he so mastered the Bat Swing and the Crouch that he's now in the Baseball Hall of Fame. And this spring, in the Yankees' new flexibility program, he stretched, bent and folded himself pretty well for a man of 58. But when he's asked whether he knows the body toning postures of yoga, he says, "Nahhh. A couple of people wrote me, 'What exercises do you give?' thinking I was a, you know. . . . Ahhh, I don't do no exercises."

In traditional yoga, the practice of meditation is of central importance. But Berra says, "Guys talk about doing this meditating when they go up to the plate. If I'd done that I'd've been worse. I went up there thinking about something else."

And yet there's something inscrutable about a man who said, when he saw the late Steve McQueen in a movie on television, "He must have made that before he died." There's something mystic about a man who said, "You got to be very careful if you don't know where you're going, because you might not get there." And there's something wise about a man who said, "Slump? I ain't in no slump. I just ain't hitting."

Although yoga is "a definite science," the Yogi Paramahansa Yogananda has written, "There are a number of great men, living today in American or European or other non-Hindu bodies, who, though they may have never heard the words *yogi* or *swami,* are yet true exemplars of those terms. Through their disinterested service to mankind, or through their mastery over passions and thoughts . . . or through their great powers of concentration, they are, in a sense, yogis; they have set themselves the goal of yoga—self-control."

★ ★ ★ ★ ★

By dispelling that ignorance of the true self
he has realized the Changeless Total Universal Self
as his own true form, and through this realization
ignorance has been destroyed.
—THE VEDANTASARA
a 15th-century Brahmanical text

I'd be pretty dumb if all of a sudden
I started being something I'm not.
—YOGI BERRA

★ ★ ★ ★ ★

The dynastic Yankees of the 1940s, '50s and '60s knew exactly who they were. They weren't a projection of their owner's ego. "In those days, to be a Yankee, in New York," says Berra, who was the Yankees' best or at least, after Mickey Mantle, next-best immortal of the '50s, "you were treated like a god." Yankees were united by aplomb and *esprit de corps*. Yoga, wrote Jung, is a "method of fusing body and mind together so that they form a unity which is scarcely to be questioned. This unit creates a psychological disposition which makes possible intuitions that transcend consciousness."

★ ★ ★ ★ ★

Levitate your consciousness to total nothingness.
—YOGI BHAJAN

In baseball, you don't know nothing.
—YOGI BERRA

★ ★ ★ ★ ★

Anyone who has followed the Yankees over the last 20 years—since 1964, when Berra was fired as manager although New York won a pennant in its first season under him—knows that the franchise has a karma problem: a festering buildup of the consequences of past actions.

"The Yankees made the biggest mistake in their whole career, firing Yogi," says Berra's old teammate Whitey Ford. It took them 12 years to win another pennant, and although they have won four in the last eight seasons, those years have been an Era of Ill Feeling.

"I don't want to play for George Steinbrenner," said star reliever Goose Gossage last December, before he forsook the Yankees for the Padres. Steinbrenner, New York's principal owner since 1973, has fired 11 managers and alienated player after player. It's about as uplifting to go over his wrangles with Billy Martin, whom he fired for the third time after last season, as it is to replay the Watergate tapes. Bad karma accrues when your manager calls your owner a liar or punches out a marshmallow salesman, both of which Martin did. Also when your owner gets into a fight either in an elevator, as Steinbrenner claimed, or with an elevator, as skeptics suggested.

Just this spring training the Yankees captain, Graig Nettles, decried Steinbrenner's "big mouth" and demanded to be traded. Dave Winfield, New York's best player, who has had various run-ins with Steinbrenner that still rankle on both sides, predicted that 1984 will see more of the same: "Afternoon soaps will have nothing on us. I think people are tired of that. They want to see baseball."

Ah. Yogi is baseball all over. Says his wife, Carmen, "Everything except baseball seems small to him." That "everything" would seem to include himself. There's not much I in Yogi, whom people often call Yog. Perhaps the true meaning of "In baseball, you don't know nothing" is that baseball is a game that humbles those who presume to be authoritative, as Martin and Steinbrenner have done. "Yogi is perfect for this club right now," said pitcher Dave LaRoche in camp this spring. "Billy always wanted to be the center of attention. Yogi is satisfied to be a wallflower type."

★   ★   ★   ★   ★

The iron filings of karma are attracted only where
a magnet of the personal ego still exists.
—YOGI PARAMAHANSA YOGANANDA

A good ball club.
—YOGI BERRA
when asked what makes a good manager

★   ★   ★   ★   ★

Since 1960, the Yankees and their fellow New Yorkers, the Mets, have won 11 pennants. Yogi, who served with the Mets as coach from 1965 through '71 and as manager from '72 through part of '75, is the only person who has been a player or a coach or a manager on every one of those pennant-winning teams. When he was fired by the Yankees after losing to St. Louis in the '64 World Series and also when he was fired by the Mets in '75 although his '73 team had won a pennant, Yogi's critics said he had lost control of his players. But a yogi doesn't try to control others. "Every individual," says the Maharishi Mahesh Yogi, "is responsible for his own development in any field." Were the Maharishi a baseball fan, he would add "and at the plate." A yogi attempts to control himself.

Too nice a guy, Yogi's detractors have said of him. But "gentleness of mind is an attribute of a yogi, whose heart melts at all suffering," said the Yogi B.K.S. Iyengar. Robert Burnes, a St. Louis baseball writer, once went with Berra to a church father-and-son banquet. Every son received a bat and a ball and came up to have Yogi autograph them. At a corner table were some kids from a local orphanage. They sat there with no balls or bats. "Aren't they getting anything?" Yogi asked. An organizer of the banquet told him that a couple of balls were being sent to the home for the orphans' use. "We think it's enough of a thrill for them just to be here," the man added.

Yogi got up from the head table, went to the orphans' table, sat down and began autographing whatever the orphans had. Someone at the head table finally said, "Yogi, we'd like you to come back up here and say a few words."

"Go on with the program," Yogi snapped. "I'm busy. I'm talking to some friends." And he stayed with the orphans the rest of the evening. As he and Burnes left, Yogi said, "I'll never forget that as long as I live."

When Yogi was promoted to manager this winter—he'd rejoined the Yankees as a coach in '76—Boston sports talk show host Eddie Andelman said that what the Yankees were actually getting was a "designated schmoo." Yogi's shape and good nature may resemble a schmoo's, but he may be more than that. He may be the man of the hour.

★   ★   ★   ★   ★

The time is now and now is the time.
—YOGI BHAJAN

You mean right now?
—YOGI BERRA
when someone asked him what time it was

★   ★   ★   ★   ★

To speak of the history of the Steinbrenner Yankees is difficult, because who wants to wade through all that again? To speak of Berra's history is difficult because so much of what's said about him—no one, including Yogi, seems to know how much—is legend.

Berra has little inclination to dwell upon the past. "I'm sure glad I don't live in them days," he once said, after watching a bloody movie called *The Vikings.* Or he may have said that. He's said to have said it. Trying to establish which of Yogi's famous sayings he actually said is an interesting, but hopeless, endeavor.

Sometimes diligent research pays off. For instance, there's the story about what Yogi told a young Met hitter who had adopted Frank Robinson's batting stance but still wasn't hitting. "If you can't imitate him," Yogi is supposed to have advised, "don't copy him."

But on Jan. 11, 1964, right after Berra had been named Yankee manager and a year before he got to the Mets, a long tape-recorded telephone colloquy between Berra, Casey Stengel and reporter Robert Lipsyte appeared, in transcript, in *The New York Times.* In it Stengel says to Yogi, "If you can't imitate anybody, don't copy him. That's the best advice I can give a new manager." Conceivably, Berra later passed that adage on to a Met, but because Berra spent several minutes one morning this spring chuckling over the kind of things Stengel used to say and wishing he could remember even a few of them specifically, that seems unlikely.

Why not ask Berra himself whether he said various things he's supposed to have said? Well, I did that. It confused matters. For instance, if I hadn't consulted Yogi, I'd be able to report that I had pinned down the origin of "Nobody ever goes there anymore; it's too crowded" once and for all. I'd always been told that Yogi said that about a place called Charlie's in Minneapolis. On the other hand, I read somewhere that back in the late '40s Dorothy Parker had said it about Chasen's in Beverly Hills. Then I read that John McNulty had written it in a short story. And sure enough, in the Feb. 20, 1943 issue of *The New Yorker,* in a McNulty story entitled *Some Nights When Nothing Happens Are the Best Nights in This Place,* there occurs this passage:

". . . a speakeasy, you could control who comes in and it was more homelike and more often not crowded the way this saloon is now. Johnny, one of the hackmen outside, put the whole thing in a nutshell one night when they were talking about a certain hangout and Johnny said, 'Nobody goes there any more. It's too crowded.' "

Because in 1943 Yogi was 18 and playing in Norfolk, Va., we can assume that neither McNulty nor some New York cabdriver stole the line from Yogi.

However. Before I tracked that short story down I discussed Berraisms with Yogi and Carmen. We were relaxing over vodka on the rocks in their nicely appointed parlor in Montclair, N.J. After their three boys grew up, the Berras sold the enormous Tudor house about which Yogi once said proudly, "It's nothing but rooms," and moved into a smaller but still substantial gray-shingled house a few blocks away. It's a home filled with fine antiques, with dropping-by children and grandchildren and with Berraisms which, however, the Berras don't preserve as carefully as they do furniture.

"The kids are always telling me, 'There you go, you said another one,' " Yogi said with a chuckle.

"He said one the other day," said Carmen. "I thought, 'That's a classic. I've got to write that one down.' But I forgot."

"How about the one I said, 'If I didn't wake up, I'd still be sleeping,' " said Yogi. "I was almost late someplace," he explained. "Another one . . . ," he added, and he said something else that I didn't quite catch.

"No, that one wasn't funny," said Carmen.

"Oh," said Yogi affably.

"How about the one about the restaurant being so crowded nobody ever goes there?" I asked. "You didn't really say that, did you"

Yogi smiled. "Yeah! I said that one," he assured me.

"You did?" I said. "About Charlie's in Minneapolis?"

"Nahhh, it was about Ruggeri's in St. Louis. When I was headwaiter there." That would have been in 1948.

"No," said Carmen, "you said that in New York."

"St. Louis," Yogi said firmly.

So there you are.

"My favorite Yogi story," says Yankee first baseman Roy Smalley, "is about the time he went to a reception at Gracie Mansion [the residence of New York's mayor]. It was a hot day and everybody was sweating, and Yogi strolled in late wearing a lime-green suit. Mayor Lindsay's wife, Mary, saw Yogi and said, 'You certainly look cool,' and he said, 'Thanks. You don't look so hot yourself.' If that isn't true, I don't want to know it isn't."

Nor do I. I feel bound to report, however, that there's at least one other version of the story. Same dialogue, only between Yogi and someone it would be hard for witnesses to confuse with Mary Lindsay: umpire Hank Soar.

Bill Veeck once maintained that "Yogi is a completely manufactured product. He is a case study of this country's unlimited ability to gull itself and be gulled. . . . You say 'Yogi' at a banquet, and everybody automatically laughs, something Joe Garagiola discovered to his profit many years ago."

What Berra says about his sayings, in general, is "I always say I said half of them, and Joe said the other half." This is apt but untrue. Certainly Garagiola, who grew up with Berra in St. Louis on what was known then as Dago Hill and who is working on a book about those days, has done as much for Berra's legend as the Beatles did for the Maharishi's. For one thing, as Berra says, "Joe can remember stories better than I can. I can't remember them." It follows that Yogi isn't the best authority for what he actually said. (And nobody else is, either.) Sometimes he will say, "I could've probably said that." Sometimes he will say he never said things that you wish he wouldn't deny saying. For instance, he claims he never said, "How can you think and hit at the same time?" It's a cold-blooded historian indeed who's willing to take Berra's word for that.

It may even be that Berra did think and hit at the same time. "Any hitter as good as Yogi was had to have an idea up there," says Yankee coach Mickey Vernon, who played against him for years. But when you ask Berra if it's true that he always hit high pitches well, he says, "They told me I did. I didn't know. If I could see it good, I'd hit it. Some of them I'd swing at, and some of them I wouldn't because I didn't see them good." Berra's old teammate Phil Rizzuto claims, "I've seen him hit them on the bounce; I've seen him leave his feet to hit them."

There's no doubt that Berra thought about other people's hitting. Ted Williams says Berra would notice subtle shifts of an opposing batter's feet that no other catcher would notice. "Berra knows how to pitch to everybody in the league except himself," said Stengel. But then, nobody knew how to pitch to Berra. "He could pull anything inside," says Vernon. "They'd try to throw him two pitches inside and hope he'd pull them foul, and then they'd go outside on him. And he'd take that to the opposite field."

Yankee player-coach Lou Piniella, who says, "When I'm feeling good I'm a player, when I'm feeling bad I'm a coach," studies hitting mechanics meticulously with the aid of videotape. He insists that thinking and hitting are thoroughly compatible. However, he concedes that "the paramount thing is to see the damn baseball." And New York outfielder Steve Kemp says, "Baseball is a game that if you think too much, it'll eat you up."

Let us remind ourselves that if Berra did say what he says he didn't say about thinking and hitting, he didn't say you can't think and hit at the same time. He just raised the eternal question, "How can you?" And even if he didn't say it, he deserves to be credited with saying it because he's such a great example of the athlete who doesn't distract himself. Berra was so attuned to his Batting Self that he didn't consciously have to focus his mind on hitting. Asked if he ever studied his swing on videotape, he cringes. "I don't like seeing myself on television," he says. "I don't like it."

★   ★   ★   ★   ★

Concentration is the narrowing of the field
of attention, the fixing of the mental eye upon a chosen object.
—ERNEST WOOD
Seven Schools of Yoga

You only got one guy to concentrate
on. He throws the ball.
—YOGI BERRA

★   ★   ★   ★   ★

Many putative Berraisms are clearly bogus. Jim Piersalll, a player of Berra's era, tells banquet audiences that someone once asked Berra, "Why don't you get your kids an encyclopedia?" Yogi answered, "Listen here, buddy, when I went to school, I walked. So can they." In the *New York Mirror* in 1959 Dan Parker wrote that someone once said to Yogi, "Why, you're a fatalist," and Yogi answered, "You mean I save postage stamps? Not me."

There were plenty of firsthand witnesses, however, to Berra's famous remark on the occasion of Yogi Berra Night at Sportsman's Park in 1947: "I want to thank all those who made this night necessary." Isn't that a perfect expression of the ambivalence of one who sincerely feels honored but hates playing the role of honoree? A poetic slip.

Some Berraisms transcend logic because they are simpler than logic. "I'm wearing these gloves for my hands," he said one cold spring-training day.

Others express something too subtle for logic. There was the time when some sportswriters urged Berra to go with them to a dirty movie. "Nahhh," he said, "I don't want to see no dirty movie. I'm going to see *Airport.*"

"Come on, Yog, come with us. Let's go see the dirty movie."

"Nahhh. I'm not interested."

"Come on. You can see *Airport* anytime. Let's go see this dirty picture."

"Well," said Yogi, "who's in it?"

Isn't that a trenchant comment on pornography? Dirty movies don't have anyone in them.

There are many stories about Yogi on radio shows. He's supposed to have laid down this ground rule once: "If you ask me anything I don't know, I'm not going to answer." Would that everyone on radio followed that policy.

But my radio favorite is the one about the interviewer who told Berra before the broadcast, "We're going to do free association. I'm going to throw out a few names, and you just say the first thing that pops into your mind."

"O.K.," said Berra.

They went on the air. "I'm here tonight with Yogi Berra," said the host, "and we're going to play free association. I'm going to mention a name, and Yogi's just going to say the first thing that comes to mind. O.K., Yogi?"

"O.K."

"All right, here we go then. Mickey Mantle."

"What about him?" said Berra.

Self-control entails avoiding statements that cause unnecessary to-do. Berra is very careful about that. Ask him how he's going to differ from Martin as manager, and he says, "I don't get into that."

But self-control isn't the same as self-editing. Two years ago in Florida, Vernon played with Yogi in a scramble golf tournament (in which all players in a group tee off but thereafter play only the best of the balls). Berra hit a nice drive up the middle. Vernon followed with an almost identical shot. Vernon's drive was a bit better. But Berra lingered next to the ball he'd hit so well. "If I was playing alone," he said wistfully, "I'd play mine."

Most people would have stopped themselves before they said that. They would have had the same feeling, but they would have reflected, "I'm not playing alone, though, so. . . ." Then they would have sorted out all the contradictions in their feelings and said either nothing or something less memorable than what Berra said. Berra reacts more quickly and on two planes of possibility at once.

★   ★   ★   ★   ★

The posture must be steady and pleasant.
—YOGI PATANJALI

Berra thinks home plate is his room.
—CASEY STENGEL

★   ★   ★   ★   ★

Berra, who was awkward behind the plate at the beginning of his career, worked hard under the guidance of guru Bill Dickey—"Bill is learning me all his experiences"—and he became an extraordinarily heads-up catcher. Between pitches he was full of chatty hospitality, but while he was distracting the hitter, he wasn't missing a trick himself. Indeed, Berra is computer-fast at adding up gin scores. "He would be a brilliant nuclear physicist," says Garagiola, "if he enjoyed that kind of thing."

And when Berra saw a bunt or a steal of home coming, he would spring forward before the pitch had reached the batter. "If anybody'd swung," he says, "they'd've creamed me." But no one ever did. Berra was especially effective on squeeze bunts. Twice in his career he grabbed the bunt, tagged the batter before he could get away and then dived back to tag the runner coming in from third. That ties him with several other catchers for the lifetime record for unassisted double plays. "I just touched everybody I could," Berra explained after one of them.

On another occasion, Billy Hunter of the Orioles missed a two-strike squeeze bunt attempt on a pitch that was in the dirt. Berra trapped the ball, slapped a sweeping tag on Hunter, who was entitled to run because the third strike had hit the ground, and wheeled to put the ball on Clint Courtney sliding in. Alas, the umpire ruled that Berra had missed Hunter. Otherwise, Berra would hold the catcher's single-handed d.p. record singlehandedly. "Hunter was out, too," says Yogi today. "Out as the side of a barn."

The preceding Berraism is one that I just made up. I guess it won't do. It's Berraesque in that it entails a kind of refreshment of the concept of "out"—a soft-focus version of what E. E. Cummings called "precision which creates movement." (Cummings' own, not very pleasant, example of such precision came from vaudeville: "Would you hit a woman with a child?" "No, I'd hit her with a brick.")

But "out as the side of a barn" doesn't linger in the mind like Yogi's famous re-examination of two ordinary verbs: "You can observe a lot by watching." He actually did say that, except that it may have been "You observe by watching" in the original.

It's hard to make up a good Berraism.

★   ★   ★   ★   ★

> *One thing you cannot copy and that is*
> *the soul of another person or the spirit*
> *of another person.*
> —Yogi Bhajan

If you can't imitate him, don't copy him.
—YOGI BERRA

★　　★　　★　　★　　★

I was determined to make up a Berraism for this story. One that would pass for real and go down in lore alongside "How long have you known me, Jack? And you still don't know how to spell my name." (Which is what Berra said—really and truly—when announcer Jack Buck compensated him for appearing on a pregame show with a check made out to Bearer.)

Here is an ersatz Berraism that I worked on for weeks: "Probably what a pitcher misses the most when he doesn't get one is a good target. Unless it never gets there." Nope. It's too busy. A real Berraism is more mysterious, yet simpler. Stengel once asked Berra what he would do if he found a million dollars. Yogi said, "If the guy was real poor, I'd give it back to him."

To come up with a Berraism that rings true, you have to start with some real Berraistic raw material, which, in itself, may *not* ring true. Take the famous utterance, "It ain't over 'til it's over," which is so distinctively descriptive of a baseball game—a football or basketball game is often over with five minutes to go—and which we would like to think is even true of life.

Research through old sports-page clippings indicates that what Berra probably said was, in reference to the 1974 pennant race, "We're not out 'til we're out." That quickly became, "You're not out of it 'til you're out of it," which somehow evolved into "The game's never over 'til it's over," which eventually was streamlined into "It ain't over 'til it's over."

But I wouldn't call that a wholly manufactured product. Berra sprouted its seed. And he did so at a time when the expression "The game is never over till the last man is out" had become hackneyed, even if its meaning still held true. One thing Berra doesn't deal in is clichés. He doesn't remember them.

"Yogi gives short answers. And they're all mixed in with grunts," says Rizzuto, who adds, "but that doesn't mean he doesn't know as much as managers who'll talk forever." Usually these short statements aren't eloquent, and often they're more a matter of finger pointing, nudges, scowls, pats, shrugs and ingenuous grins than of words or grunts. And yet every time I talked to Berra this spring, he said something or other that I couldn't get out of my mind. For instance, giving me directions to the racquetball club he co-owns in Fairfield, N.J., he said, regarding how long I should stay on one stretch of road, "It's pretty far, but it doesn't seem like it."

As I drove to the club, I kept thinking that over. How could he know that a given distance wouldn't seem far to me? I thought it over so much that the distance went by even faster than I'd been prepared for, and I missed the turn. I should have remembered what Berra said about taking the subway to Brooklyn for the World Series: "I knew I was going to take the wrong train, so I left early."

★　　★　　★　　★　　★

> *There is a vital difference between an*
> *idiot or a lunatic on the one hand, and*
> *a yogi striving to achieve a state*
> *of mindlessness on the other.*
> —Yogi B.K.S. Iyengar

> *People say I'm dumb, but a lot of guys don't*
> *make this kind of money talking to cats.*
> —Yogi Berra
> on receiving a residual check from his
> Puss 'n Boots catfood commercial,
> in which the voice of the puss
> was played by Whitey Ford

★　　★　　★　　★　　★

In his boyhood, Berra was called Lawdie—a shortening of Lawrence. Had that name stuck, would there now be a cartoon character named Lawdie Bear? At any rate, there is one named Yogi Bear, an amiable, rotund figure who assures people he's "smarter than the average bear."

"They came out with that after Yogi won his third Most Valuable Player award," said Carmen. "And yet they claimed it had nothing to do with Yogi."

"Once somebody came up to me and asked, 'Which came first, you or the bear?' " says Yogi.

But how did Lawdie become Yogi? Historians agree it happened in his teens. At least five people, including Garagiola, have been credited for giving Yogi his name. Garagiola has said, "It was because he walked like a yogi." *The New York Times* once said it was because young Lawdie had taken up yoga-like exercises. According to other accounts, it was because nothing ever upset Berra, or because one day he was wrestling and spun out of his opponent's grasp, and someone said, "He spins like a yo-yo." Then someone else said, "You mean he spins like one of them yogis." The most established version is that Berra used to sit around serenely with his arms and legs crossed, and one of his American League teammates, having seen some yogis in a travelogue about India, said he sat like a yogi. Berra told me a few weeks ago that this last version was correct, except, "Nahhh. There wasn't any movie."

And yet this spring I also heard him telling reporters that he had no idea why he'd been dubbed Yogi. "I had a brother they called 'Garlic,' " Berra told one reporter who pressed him for possible explanations of his cognomen, "and his name was Mike." Berra did say that the original dubber was his American Legion teammate Bobby Hofman—one of the few people connected with youth baseball in St. Louis in the '40s who, according to my research, had never been credited before.

So there you are. Taped onto the Berras' refrigerator door in Montclair is a letter from a boy in San Francisco, which Yogi hasn't gotten around to answering:

> Dear Yogi Berra,
> My name is Yogi, and I am 9. I hate my name because kids at school joke about it a lot. All the time. You are the only other Yogi I ever heard of. Where did you get your name from? My teacher told me about you. I hope that is O.K. She said you just about invented baseball. How long did you play? Will you be my friend? I sure need one.
>
> > Your friend
> > Yogi Lisac
>
> P.S. What do your friends call you?
> Did you ever get so mad you wanted to punch somebody?

When Berra came into organized ball, he, too, was the butt of cruel kidding—people swinging from dugout roofs and calling him Ape was typical of this kind of humor—and he never fought back. He says it never bothered him, but that's hard to believe. Even some of the compliments he got would have upset most people. Cannon wrote that he and Berra were sitting in a restaurant when a woman stopped by the table.

"I don't think you're homely at all," the strange lady said.

"Thank you," replied Berra, sincerely.

In 1949, Cannon reported that some players had theorized that Berra swung at bad pitches because he was afraid of being ridiculed for taking a strike. "Notice how Yogi acts when he misses a ball?" one player was quoted as saying. "He shrinks and closes up. They kid him so much he's afraid of looking bad in the spotlight."

But if that was Berra's motivation for attacking every pitch he could reach, he turned that anxiety into a strength that caused opponents to consider him the Yankee they would lease like to face in the clutch. He was always at his best in the late innings. "You give 100 percent in the first half of the game," he's said to have said, "and if that isn't enough, in the second half you give what's left." And you don't look back to add things up.

"He doesn't dwell on mistakes," says Carmen. "When something happens, it's done. His wheels are immediately turning about what to do next. I guess it's a quality that successful men have. I read that about David Rockefeller when he made a bad loan."

★   ★   ★   ★   ★

> *Male and female make a union and this*
> *complete union is the greatest yoga.*
> —YOGI BHAJAN

> *She wasn't the first girl I had ever asked*
> *out, she was the third, but I could hardly*
> *believe my luck when it turned out that*
> *she liked me as much as I liked her.*
> —YOGI BERRA

★   ★   ★   ★   ★

It's clear, in her 50th or so year, that Carmen Berra will always be a great-looking woman. She and Yogi met in 1947 when he was a budding Yankee and she was a waitress at Stan and Biggie's in St. Louis. "He was honest. And simple," she says. "Wasn't a show-off. I was dating a lot of college boys at the time and I liked him in contrast."

Her name was Carmen Short. "My family came from England in the 17th century," she says.

"Yeah," says Yogi. "She's got more aunts and uncles!"

At the time, Carmen's family wondered why she wanted to marry a "foreigner" and Yogi's why he wanted to marry an "*Americano.*" But it has been a happy marriage, by all accounts, for 35 years.

When asked whether it's true that wise investments over the years have made him very comfortable financially, a near millionaire in fact, Yogi shrugs. "*I don't know,*" he says. "You'll have to ask Carm." But hasn't he been a remarkably successful businessman? "Well," he says, "I guess I've got a smart wife. She's a, whattayacallit, an inquirer. Where I'd say, 'Yeah, go ahead,' she'll say, 'Let's wait and look into it.' It's like with the furniture for the house. She's patient. She'll leave the room *bare* till she gets just the right thing."

Carmen serves on the board of a regional theater group, is on the committee that is working for the restoration of the Statue of Liberty and stays on Yogi's case. "Carmen said if you chew tobacco today, forget it. You don't have anyplace to come home to," says a young blonde employee at Berra's racquetball center. "She knows you chewed this morning, Yogs."

They have raised three solid sons: Larry Jr., 35, who caught in the minor leagues until he hurt his left knee and is now in the flooring business; Tim, 32, who played one season as a wide receiver for the Baltimore Colts in 1974 and now oversees the operation of the racquetball center; and Dale, 27, who makes $600,000 a year playing shortstop for the Pittsburgh Pirates. Dale, who has always lived with his parents in the off-season, is about to follow his older brothers' example by getting married and buying a house not far from the New Jersey homestead. What with grandchildren and in-laws, there are as many as 17 people around the Berra table at Thanksgiving. Yogi carves.

When his boys were kids, Yogi says, "They'd try to get me to play ball with them, and I'd say, 'Go ask your brothers. I *got* to play.'" Otherwise, they say, he was a warm, normal father. And now they regard him with evident affection. Because he was already in Florida for spring training, Yogi couldn't make Dale's engagement party this February, but he telephoned his best wishes. After he hung up, Yogi said, "And Dale, you know, he's good. He's good. He said: 'I miss you.'"

"He's masculine," says Carmen of Yogi. "Very strong. Physically and mentally, or should I say psychologically. I think he's very sexy."

Yogi smiles. He doesn't look surprised.

"But he's stubborn. Very stubborn. About everything. I don't even think he's Italian. I think he's German. He's Milanese, from the north of Italy. They're very clipped. Very strong. They have a lot of German in them."

Feldmarschall Steinbrenner, please note.

★　　★　　★　　★　　★

> *Man suffers for one reason: Man loses*
> *his innocence. When you lose your innocence,*
> *you end up with dispute. To regain innocence*
> *so that universal consciousness will serve*
> *and maintain you is the idea of this yoga.*
> —YOGI BHAJAN

How can you say this and that when
this and that hasn't happened yet?
—YOGI BERRA

★   ★   ★   ★   ★

Berra won't speculate as to how long he'll last as Yankee manager, except jok-ingly: "You better get this story out pretty soon." It should be remembered that in 1949 when the Yankees hired Stengel, who lasted as manager for 12 years and 10 pennants, some of the same things were said about him as are said about Berra now: that he was good for public relations, a funny guy, but not really a serious field leader. When Stengel was a player, they said the same thing about him that they said about Berra later: that he wasn't built like a ballplayer.

Stengel used to say of Yogi, "This is Mr. Berra, which is my assistant manager." He also said the Yankees would fall apart without Berra behind the plate, and that Berra was the best player he ever had, except for Joe DiMaggio. Such distinctly ungushy baseball men as Ted Williams, Jackie Robinson and Paul Richards all said Berra was an exceptionally smart player. His managing moves have been questioned in the past, but so have those of every other man-ager. No one accuses him of not knowing the game.

At the very least, Berra is a link with the old, proud Yankee days. The clubhouse today is full of players whom Steinbrenner acquired for big money after they became established and whom fans tend to think of more as former Reds, Padres and Twins than as Yankees. The team used to be a symbol of per-manence. Under Steinbrenner, Yankees have come and gone and been shifted from position to position. Now that the pinstripes are doubleknits, the team lacks real fabric.

Will Berra produce cohesion? "He knows players," says Smalley. "He's made it clear to each guy what's expected. A team takes on the personality of its manager. And Yogi is comfortable."

But not wholly laissez-faire. "Before, we had a Broadway clubhouse in here, all kinds of extraneous people," says Smalley. "Yogi says no visitors except family, and then only at certain times. I asked if I could bring in Bob James, the jazz pianist. Yogi said he'd go out and meet him, he'd give him a hat, but not in the clubhouse. I respected that."

"Everybody likes Yogi," said Steinbrenner when he announced Yogi's appointment, "and . . . respects him." The pause was just long enough to make the "respects" sound grudging. When I try to imagine how Berra and Stein-brenner will relate to one another, I can't shake the unpleasant image of a TV

commercial for a New York radio station that Steinbrenner and several uniformed Yankees appeared in a few years ago. When Yogi, who was then a coach,
began to say something in this commercial, Steinbrenner glared and snapped,
"Just sing, Yogi." Yogi smiled, sang and gave no indication that heavy conde-
scension bothered him. Self-control.

"To say that I don't have any worries or nerves is the opposite of the
truth," Berra said in his 1961 autobiography. *Yogi,* written with the aid of Ed
Fitzgerald. "I worry about getting old. I worry about not getting around on
the fastball. . . ."

Indeed, when Tony Cloninger struck him out three times on fastballs
one May day in 1965, Yogi immediately retired as a player. "I didn't go out
there to be embarrassed," he says.

"I worry," he went on in the book, "about keeping Carm happy so she
won't be sorry she married me, about the kids growing up good, and about
keeping out of trouble with God. I worry a lot."

He has always had trouble sleeping on the road. In his playing days his
insomnia exhausted many of his roommates, including Rizzuto, from whom
Berra often demanded bedtime stories. "Three Little Pigs, Three Bears, anything like that," Rizzuto says. "He said the sound of my voice put him to sleep.
I often thought of that when I started broadcasting."

"Relaxed?" says Carmen. "I don't know why people think he's so relaxed. He's a basket case!"

But it's a well-woven basket. "Some men are kind of hanging in the
balance," Carmen says. "It seems like they just might go off the deep end any
minute. I don't have to worry that Yogi is going to have a nervous breakdown.

"I look around at our friends. The men are heads of some of the
biggest corporations, they're members of the biggest law firms. And Yogi is the
envy of all of them. Since Day One, I saw that Yogi was the only man I knew
who loved his job."

That in itself, of course, doesn't make him a true yogi. "I am a yogi because it is in your mind," says the Yogi Bhajan. "The problem with man," the
Yogi Bhajan also says, "is that he is asked, 'Are you this or are you that?' But you
are not this nor that, you are as you are." Yogi Berra has said quite a few things
more thought-provoking than that.

The Thrill of the Grass

W. P. KINSELLA

I continue to find a warm spot in my heart for *Field of Dreams,* the movie version of W.P. Kinsella's *Shoeless Joe,* every time a residual check arrives in my mailbox. For reasons too absurd to go into, I am the player—billed in the credits as "Clean Shaven Centerfielder," and don't blink or you'll miss me—who catches the fly ball hit by the young Moonlight Graham character when he comes to the plate on that mystical Iowa cornfield.

The movie was great fun to be part of; all of us in uniform would gather an hour or so before our scheduled call to play for a while in an adjacent field (the *Dreams* field was off limits unless cameras were rolling). Whenever someone hit one out, we'd say he corned it. But hitting is hitting, no matter where you've come unstuck in time. The real challenge was trying to master our defensive positions with gloves that had neither webbing nor padding and weren't much bigger than winter mittens. The constant argument I had with mine gave me a pocket full of new respect for the old-timers and their talents.

The title story of Canadian-born Kinsella's 1984 collection of baseball tales, "The Thrill of the Grass," takes a thrilling stand against artificial turf. Kinsella's said its seed was planted when he had Jackson say in *Shoeless Joe* that he'd "wake up in the night with the smell of the ballpark in my nose and the cool of the grass on my feet. The thrill of the grass." The strike of 1981 would spread the fertilizer it would need to grow.

1981: the summer the baseball players went on strike. The dull weeks drag by, the summer deepens, the strike is nearly a month old. Outside the city the corn rustles and ripens in the sun. Summer without baseball: a disruption to the psyche. An unexplainable aimlessness engulfs me. I stay later and later each evening in the small office at the rear of my shop. Now, driving home after work, the worst of the rush hour traffic over, it is the time of evening I would normally be heading for the stadium.

I enjoy arriving an hour early, parking in a far corner of the lot, walking slowly toward the stadium, rays of sun dropping softly over my shoulders like tangerine ropes, my shadow gliding with me, black as an umbrella. I like to watch young families beside their campers, the mothers in shorts, grilling hamburgers, their men drinking beer. I enjoy seeing little boys dressed in the home team uniform, barely toddling, clutching hotdogs in upraised hands.

I am a failed shortstop. As a young man, I saw myself diving to my left, graceful as a toppling tree, fielding high grounders like a cat leaping for butterflies, bracing my right foot and tossing to first, the throw true as if a steel ribbon connected my hand and the first baseman's glove. I dreamed of leading the American League in hitting—being inducted into the Hall of Fame. I batted .217 in my senior year of high school and averaged 1.3 errors per nine innings.

I know the stadium will be deserted; nevertheless I wheel my car down off the freeway, park, and walk across the silent lot, my footsteps rasping and mournful. Strangle-grass and creeping charlie are already inching up through the gravel, surreptitious, surprised at their own ease. Faded bottle caps, rusted bits of chrome, an occasional paper clip, recede into the earth. I circle a ticket booth, sun-faded, empty, the door closed by an oversized padlock. I walk beside the tall, machinery-green, board fence. A half mile away a few cars hiss along the freeway; overhead a single-engine plane fizzes lazily. The whole place is silent as an empty classroom, like a house suddenly without children.

It is then that I spot the door-shape. I have to check twice to be sure it is there: a door cut in the deep green boards of the fence, more the promise of a door than the real thing, the kind of door, as children, we cut in the sides of cardboard boxes with our mother's paring knives. As I move closer, a golden circle of lock, like an acrimonious eye, establishes its certainty.

I stand, my nose so close to the door I can smell the faint odour of paint, the golden eye of a lock inches from my own eyes. My desire to be inside the ballpark is so great that for the first time in my life I commit a criminal act. I have been a locksmith for over forty years. I take the small tools from the pocket of my jacket, and in less time than it would take a speedy runner to circle the bases I am inside the stadium. Though the ballpark is open-air, it smells of abandonment; the walkways and seating areas are cold as basements. I breathe the odours of rancid popcorn and wilted cardboard.

The maintenance staff were laid off when the strike began. Synthetic grass does not need to be cut or watered. I stare down at the ball diamond, where just to the right of the pitcher's mound, a single weed, perhaps two inches high, stands defiant in the rain-pocked dirt.

The field sits breathless in the orangy glow of the evening sun. I stare at the potato-coloured earth of the infield, that wide, dun arc, surrounded by plastic grass. As I contemplate the prickly turf, which scorches the thighs and buttocks of a sliding player as if he were being seared by hot steel, it stares back in its uniform ugliness. The seams that send routinely hit ground balls veering at tortuous angles, are vivid, grey as scars.

I remember the ballfields of my childhood, the outfields full of soft hummocks and brown-eyed gopher holes.

I stride down from the stands and walk out to the middle of the field. I touch the stubble that is called grass, take off my shoes, but find it is like walking on a row of toothbrushes. It was an evil day when they stripped the sod from this ballpark, cut it into yard-wide swathes, rolled it, memories and all, into great green-and-black cinnamonroll shapes, trucked it away. Nature temporarily defeated. But Nature is patient.

Over the next few days an idea forms within me, ripening, swelling, pushing everything else into a corner. It is like knowing a new, wonderful joke and not being able to share. I need an accomplice.

I go to see a man I don't know personally, though I have seen his face peering at me from the financial pages of the local newspaper, and the *Wall Street Journal,* and I have been watching his profile at the baseball stadium, two boxes to the right of me, for several years. He is a fan. Really a fan. When the weather is intemperate, or the game not close, the people around us disappear like flowers closing at sunset, but we are always there until the last pitch. I know he is a man who attends because of the beauty and mystery of the game, a man who can sit during the last of the ninth with the game decided innings ago, and draw joy from watching the first baseman adjust the angle of his glove as the pitcher goes into his windup.

He, like me, is a first-base-side fan. I've always watched baseball from behind first base. The positions fans choose at sporting events are like politics, religion, or philosophy: a view of the world, a way of seeing the universe. They make no sense to anyone, have no basis in anything but stubbornness.

I brought up my daughters to watch baseball from the first-base side. One lives in Japan and sends me box scores from Japanese newspapers, and Japanese baseball magazines with pictures of superstars politely bowing to one another. She has a season ticket in Yokohama; on the first-base side.

"Tell him a baseball fan is here to see him," is all I will say to his secretary. His office is in a skyscraper, from which he can look out over the city to where the prairie rolls green as mountain water to the limits of the eye. I wait all afternoon in the artificially cool, glassy reception area with its yellow and mauve chairs, chrome and glass coffee tables. Finally, in the late afternoon, my message is passed along.

"I've seen you at the baseball stadium," I say, not introducing myself.

"Yes," he says. "I recognize you. Three rows back, about eight seats to my left. You have a red scorebook and you often bring your daughter . . ."

"Granddaughter. Yes, she goes to sleep in my lap in the late innings, but she knows how to calculate an ERA and she's only in Grade 2."

"One of my greatest regrets," says this tall man, whose moustache and carefully styled hair are polar-bear white, "is that my grandchildren all live over a thousand miles away. You're very lucky. Now, what can I do for you?"

"I have an idea," I say. "One that's been creeping toward me like a first baseman when the bunt sign is on. What do you think about artificial turf?"

"Hmmmf," he snorts, "that's what the strike should be about. Baseball is meant to be played on summer evenings and Sunday afternoons, on grass just cut by a horse-drawn mower," and we smile as our eyes meet.

"I've discovered the ballpark is open, to me anyway," I go on. "There's no one there while the strike is on. The wind blows through the high top of the grandstand, whining until the pigeons in the rafters flutter. It's lonely as a ghost town."

"And what is it you do there, alone with the pigeons?"

"I dream."

"And where do I come in?"

"You've always struck me as a man who dreams. I think we have things in common. I think you might like to come with me. I could show you what I dream, paint you pictures, suggest what might happen . . ."

He studies me carefully for a moment, like a pitcher trying to decide if he can trust the sign his catcher has just given him.

"Tonight?" he says. "Would tonight be too soon?"

"Park in the northwest corner of the lot about 1:00 a.m. There is a door about fifty yards to the right of the main gate. I'll open it when I hear you."

He nods.

I turn and leave.

The night is clear and cotton warm when he arrives. "Oh, my," he says, staring at the stadium turned chrome-blue by a full moon. "Oh, my," he says again, breathing in the faint odours of baseball, the reminder of fans and players not long gone.

"Let's go down to the field," I say. I am carrying a cardboard pizza box, holding it on the upturned palms of my hands, like an offering.

When we reach the field, he first stands on the mound, makes an awkward attempt at a windup, then does a little sprint from first to about halfway to second. "I think I know what you've brought," he says, gesturing toward the box, "but let me see anyway."

I open the box in which rests a square foot of sod, the grass smooth and pure, cool as a swatch of satin, fragile as baby's hair.

"Ohhh," the man says, reaching out a finger to test the moistness of it. "Oh, I see."

We walk across the field, the harsh, prickly turf making the bottoms of my feet tingle, to the left-field corner where, in the angle formed by the foul line and the warning track, I lay down the square foot of sod. "That's beautiful," my friend says, kneeling beside me, placing his hand, fingers spread wide, on the verdant square, leaving a print faint as a veronica.

I take from my belt a sickle-shaped blade, the kind used for cutting carpet. I measure along the edge of the sod, dig the point in and pull carefully toward me. There is a ripping sound, like tearing an old bed sheet. I hold up the square of artificial turf like something freshly killed, while all the time digging the sharp point into the packed earth I have exposed. I replace the sod lovingly, covering the newly bared surface.

"A protest," I say.

"But it could be more," the man replies.

"I hoped you'd say that. It could be. If you'd like to come back . . ."

314 . The Greatest Baseball Stories Ever Told

"Tomorrow night?"

"Tomorrow night would be fine. But there will be an admission charge . . ."

"A square of sod?"

"A square of sod two inches thick . . ."

"Of the same grass?"

"Of the same grass. But there's more."

"I suspected as much."

"You must have a friend . . ."

"Who would join us?"

"Yes."

"I have two. Would that be all right?"

"I trust your judgment."

"My father. He's over eighty," my friend says. "You might have seen him with me once or twice. He lives over fifty miles from here, but if I call him he'll come. And my friend . . ."

"If they pay their admission they'll be welcome . . ."

"And *they* may have friends . . ."

"Indeed they may. But what will we do with this?" I say, holding up the sticky-backed square of turf, which smells of glue and fabric.

"We could mail them anonymously to baseball executives, politicians, clergymen."

"Gentle reminders not to tamper with Nature."

We dance toward the exit, rampant with excitement.

"You will come back? You'll bring others?"

"Count on it," says my friend.

They do come, those trusted friends, and friends of friends, each making a live, green deposit. At first, a tiny row of sod squares begins to inch along toward left-centre field. The next night even more people arrive, the following night more again, and the night after there is positively a crowd. Those who come once seem always to return accompanied by friends, occasionally a son or young brother, but mostly men my age or older, for we are the ones who remember the grass.

Night after night the pilgrimage continues. The first night I stand inside the deep green door, listening. I hear a vehicle stop; hear a car door close with a snug thud. I open the door when the sound of soft soled shoes on gravel tells me it is time. The door swings silent as a snake. We nod curt greetings to each other. Two men pass me, each carrying a grasshopper-legged sprinkler.

Later, each sprinkler will sizzle like frying onions as it wheels, a silver sparkler in the moonlight.

During the nights that follow, I stand sentinel-like at the top of the grandstand, watching as my cohorts arrive. Old men walking across a parking lot in a row, in the dark, carrying coiled hoses, looking like the many wheels of a locomotive, old men who have slipped away from their homes, skulked down their sturdy sidewalks, breathing the cool, grassy, after-midnight air. They have left behind their sleeping, grey-haired women, their immaculate bungalows, their manicured lawns. They continue to walk across the parking lot, while occasionally a soft wheeze, a nibbling, breathy sound like an old horse might make, divulges their humanity. They move methodically toward the baseball stadium which hulks against the moon-blue sky like a small mountain. Beneath the tint of starlight, the tall light standards which rise above the fences and grandstand glow purple, necks bent forward, like sunflowers heavy with seed.

My other daughter lives in this city, is married to a fan, but one who watches baseball from behind third base. And like marrying outside the faith, she has been converted to the third-base side. They have their own season tickets, twelve rows up just to the outside side of third base. I love her, but I don't trust her enough to let her in on my secret.

I could trust my granddaughter, but she is too young. At her age she shouldn't have to face such responsibility. I remember my own daughter, the one who lives in Japan, remember her at nine, all knees, elbows and missing teeth—remember peering in her room, seeing her asleep, a shower of well-thumbed baseball cards scattered over her chest and pillow.

I haven't been able to tell my wife—it is like my compatriots and I are involved in a ritual for true believers only. Maggie, who knew me when I still dreamed of playing professionally myself—Maggie, after over half a lifetime together, comes and sits in my lap in the comfortable easy chair which has adjusted through the years to my thickening shape, just as she has. I love to hold the lightness of her, her tongue exploring my mouth, gently as a baby's finger.

"Where do you go?" she asks sleepily when I crawl into bed at dawn.

I mumble a reply. I know she doesn't sleep well when I'm gone. I can feel her body rhythms change as I slip out of bed after midnight.

"Aren't you too old to be having a change of life," she says, placing her toast-warm hand on my cold thigh.

I am not the only one with this problem.

"I'm developing a reputation," whispers an affable man at the ballpark. "I imagine any number of private investigators following any number of cars across the city. I imagine them creeping about the parking lot, shining pen-lights on licence plates, trying to guess what we're up to. Think of the reports they must prepare. I wonder if our wives are disappointed that we're not out discoing with frizzy-haired teenagers?"

Night after night, virtually no words are spoken. Each man seems to know his assignment. Not all bring sod. Some carry rakes, some hoes, some hoses, which, when joined together, snake across the infield and outfield, dispensing the blessing of water. Others, cradle in their arms bags of earth for building up the infield to meet the thick, living sod.

I often remain high in the stadium, looking down on the men moving over the earth, dark as ants, each sodding, cutting, watering, shaping. Occasionally the moon finds a knife blade as it trims the sod or slices away a chunk of artificial turf, and tosses the reflection skyward like a bright ball. My body tingles. There should be symphony music playing. Everyone should be humming "America the Beautiful."

Toward dawn, I watch the men walking away in groups, like small patrols of soldiers, carrying instead of arms, the tools and utensils which breathe life back into the arid ballfield.

Row by row, night by night, we lay the little squares of sod, moist as chocolate cake with green icing. Where did all the sod come from? I picture many men, in many parts of the city, surreptitiously cutting chunks out of their own lawns in the leafy midnight darkness, listening to the uncomprehending protests of their wives the next day—pretending to know nothing of it—pretending to have called the police to investigate.

When the strike is over I know we will all be here to watch the workouts, to hear the recalcitrant joints crackling like twigs after the forced inactivity. We will sit in our regular seats, scattered like popcorn throughout the stadium, and we'll nod as we pass on the way to the exits, exchange secret smiles, proud as new fathers.

For me, the best part of all will be the surprise. I feel like a magician who has gestured hypnotically and produced an elephant from thin air. I know I am not alone in my wonder. I know that rockets shoot off in half-a-hundred chests, the excitement of birthday mornings, Christmas eves, and home-town doubleheaders, boils within each of my conspirators. Our secret rites have been performed with love, like delivering a valentine to a sweetheart's door in that blue-steel span of morning just before dawn.

Players and management are meeting round the clock. A settlement is imminent. I have watched the stadium covered square foot by square foot until it looks like green graph paper. I have stood and felt the cool odours of the grass rise up and touch my face. I have studied the lines between each small square, watched those lines fade until they were visible to my eyes alone, then not even to them.

What will the players think, as they straggle into the stadium and find the miracle we have created? The old-timers will raise their heads like ponies, as far away as the parking lot, when the thrill of the grass reaches their nostrils. And, as they dress, they'll recall sprawling in the lush outfields of childhood, the grass as cool as a mother's hand on a forehead.

"Goodbye, goodbye," we sat at the gate, the smell of water, of sod, of sweat, small perfumes in the air. Our secrets are safe with each other. We go our separate ways.

Alone in the stadium in the last chill darkness before dawn, I drop to my hands and knees in the centre of the outfield. My palms are sodden. Water touches the skin between my spread fingers. I lower my face to the silvered grass, which, wonder of wonders, already has the ephemeral odours of baseball about it.

The Green Fields of the Mind

A. BARTLETT GIAMATTI

For a man who spent so much of his professional life studying the Renaissance, A. Bartlett Giamatti (1938–1989) was, not surprisingly, a Renaissance man himself. He was a scholar, a professor, the president of Yale, the president of the National League, and until his death just a few days after excommunicating Pete Rose from the game, the Commissioner of Baseball. He was also one of the game's most articulate and literate fans, a fan whose heart was broken a little every year when the Red Sox season ended—as it has annually since 1918—prematurely.

Giamatti's lovely, plaintive essay, "Green Fields of the Mind," was originally published in 1977 in the Yale Alumni Magazine, two years after Carlton Fisk hit the greatest home run in Red Sox history, and one before Yankee shortstop Bucky Dent would hit one of the worst, spoiling yet another October for Giamatti and his fellow suffering New Englanders.

I t breaks your heart. It is designed to break your heart. The game begins in the spring, when everything else begins again, and it blossoms in the summer, filling the afternoons and evenings, and then as soon as the chill rains come, it stops and leaves you to face the fall alone. You count on it, rely on it to buffer the passage of time, to keep the memory of sunshine and high skies alive, and then just when the days are all twilight, when you need it most, it stops. Today, October 2, a Sunday of rain and broken branches and leaf-clogged drains and slick streets, it stopped, and summer was gone.

319

Somehow, the summer seemed to slip by faster this time. Maybe it wasn't this summer, but all the summers that, in this my fortieth summer, slipped by so fast. There comes a time when every summer will have something of autumn about it. Whatever the reason, it seemed to me that I was investing more and more in baseball, making the game do more of the work that keeps time fat and slow and lazy. I was counting on the game's deep patterns, three strikes, three outs, three times three innings, and its deepest impulse, to go out and back, to leave and to return home, to set the order of the day and to organize the daylight. I wrote a few things this last summer, this summer that did not last, nothing grand but some things, and yet that work was just camouflage. The real activity was done with the radio—not the all-seeing, all-falsifying television—and was the playing of the game in the only place it will last, the enclosed green field of the mind. There, in that warm, bright place, what the old poet called Mutability does not so quickly come.

But out here, on Sunday, October 2, where it rains all day, Dame Mutability never loses. She was in the crowd at Fenway yesterday, a gray day full of bluster and contradiction, when the Red Sox came up in the last of the ninth trailing Baltimore 8–5, while the Yankees, rain-delayed against Detroit, only needing to win one or have Boston lose one to win it all, sat in New York washing down cold cuts with beer and watching the Boston game. Boston had won two, the Yankees had lost two, and suddenly it seemed as if the whole season might go to the last day, or beyond, except here was Boston losing 8–5, while New York sat in its family room and put its feet up. Lynn, both ankles hurting now as they had in July, hits a single down the right-field line. The crowd stirs. It is on its feet. Hobson, third baseman, former Bear Bryant quarterback, strong, quiet, over 100 RBIs, goes for three breaking balls and is out. The goddess smiles and encourages her agent, a canny journeyman named Nelson Briles.

Now comes a pinch hitter, Bernie Carbo, onetime Rookie of the Year, erratic, quick, a shade too handsome, so laid-back he is always, in his soul, stretched out in the tall grass, one arm under his head, watching the clouds and laughing; now he looks over some low stuff unworthy of him and then, uncoiling, sends one out, straight on a rising line, over the center-field wall, no cheap Fenway shot, but all of it, the physics as elegant as the arc the ball describes.

New England is on its feet, roaring. The summer will not pass. Roaring, they recall the evening, late and cold, in 1975, the sixth game of the World Series, perhaps the greatest baseball game played in the last fifty years, when Carbo, loose and easy, had uncoiled to tie the game that Fisk would win. It is

8–7, one out, and school will never start, rain will never come, sun will warm the back of your neck forever. Now Bailey, picked up from the National League recently, big arms, heavy gut, experienced, new to the league and the club; he fouls off two and then, checking, tentative, a big man off balance, he pops a soft liner to the first baseman. It is suddenly darker and later, and the announcer doing the game coast to coast, a New Yorker who works for a New York television station, sounds relieved. His little world, well-lit, hot-combed, split-second-timed, had no capacity to absorb this much gritty, grainy, contrary reality.

Cox swings a bat, stretches his long arms, bends his back, the rookie from Pawtucket who broke in two weeks earlier with a record six straight hits, the kid drafted ahead of Fred Lynn, rangy, smooth, cool. The count runs two and two, Briles is cagey, nothing too good, and Cox swings, the ball beginning toward the mound and then, in a jaunty, wayward dance, skipping past Briles, fainting to the right, skimming the last of the grass, finding the dirt, moving now like some small, purposeful marine creature negotiating the green deep, easily avoiding the jagged rock of second base, traveling steady and straight now out into the dark, silent recesses of center field.

The aisles are jammed, the place is on its feet, the wrappers, the programs, the Coke cups and peanut shells, the doctrines of an afternoon; the anxieties, the things that have to be done tomorrow, the regrets about yesterday, the accumulation of a summer: all forgotten, while hope, the anchor, bites and takes hold where a moment before it seemed we would be swept out with the tide. Rice is up. Rice whom Aaron had said was the only one he'd seen with the ability to break his records. Rice the best clutch hitter on the club, with the best slugging percentage in the league. Rice, so quick and strong he once checked his swing halfway through and snapped the bat in two. Rice the Hammer of God sent to scourge the Yankees, the sound was overwhelming, fathers pounded their sons on the back, cars pulled off the road, households froze, New England exulted in its blessedness, and roared its thanks for all good things, for Rice and for a summer stretching halfway through October. Briles threw, Rice swung, and it was over. One pitch, a fly to center, and it stopped. Summer died in New England and like rain sliding off a roof, the crowd slipped out of Fenway, quickly, with only a steady murmur of concern for the drive ahead remaining of the roar. Mutability had turned the seasons and translated hope to memory once again. And, once again, she had used baseball, our best invention to stay change, to bring change on. That is why it breaks my heart, that game—not because in New York they could win because Boston lost; in that, there is a rough justice, and a reminder to the Yankees of how slight and fragile are the circumstances that exalt one group of human beings over another. It breaks my heart because it was meant to, because it was meant to foster in me again the illusion that there was something abiding, some pattern and some impulse that could come together to make a reality that would resist the corrosion; and because, after it had fostered again that most hungered-for illusion, the game was meant to stop, and betray precisely what it promised.

Of course, there are those who learn after the first few times. They grow out of sports. And there are others who were born with the wisdom to know that nothing lasts. These are the truly tough among us, the ones who can live without illusion, or without even the hope of illusion. I am not that grown-up or up-to-date. I am a simpler creature, tied to more primitive patterns and cycles. I need to think something lasts forever, and it might as well be that state of being that is a game; it might as well be that, in a green field, in the sun.

About the Editor

Jeff Silverman, a former columnist for *The Los Angeles Herald Examiner*, has written for *The New York Times*, *The Los Angeles Times*, and several national magazines. The editor of *The First Chapbook for Foodies*, *The First Chapbook for Golfers*, and *The Greatest Golf Stories Ever Told*, he now lives with his family in Chadds Ford, Pennsylvania.

Permissions Acknowledgments